D0193156

Advance Praise for *Improving Your Measurement of Customer Satisfaction: A Guide To Creating, Conducting, Analyzing, and Reporting Customer Satisfaction Measurement*

"Few people have had the extensive first-hand experiences that Terry Vavra has had as a practitioner, consultant, and teacher in his field. To our benefit he has made much of it available to all of us in his latest book. This book is the definitive treatment of the subject of customer satisfaction measurement and management."

> Peter Garcia
> Director, Customer Satisfaction
> Xerox Corporation

"Improving Your Measurement of Customer Satisfaction is a powerful resource for anyone who is committed to effectively improving performance by understanding customer expectations and delivering customer delight. It serves as a real world handbook, detailing the processes and tools that lead to an effective customer satisfaction improvement system."

> Olga E. Striltschuk
> Director, Strategic Quality
> Motorola, Inc.
> Cellular Infrastructure Group

"Dr. Vavra's book is the new encyclopedia of customer satisfaction surveying and measurement. It provides everything you need to know about customer satisfaction measurement and surveying. This is an excellent reference guide for even the most experienced survey process owners. It shows all of the currently embraced choices in customer satisfaction measurement, reporting techniques, and survey design."

> Robert Dandrade, Senior Manager
> Customer Loyalty Program/Corporate Quality
> Digital Equipment Corporation

"Whether you are just beginning or have a well established customer service measurement process this book is a perfect reference guide."

> John McLaughlin
> National Customer Administration Manager
> Toyota Motor Sales USA

"Vavra has written a very complete text for customer satisfaction practitioners. He also offers an insightful, experience-based guide for anyone who wants to know more about how customer satisfaction measurement fits into achieving management's revenue and profit goals."

> Dick Fishburn
> Chief Information Officer
> Digital Equipment Corporation

"This is the most comprehensive book on customer satisfaction currently on the market."

> Professor Claes Fornell
> Director, CSI
> National Quality Research Center
> University of Michigan Business School

A valuable resource for those who are serious about improving customer satisfaction and loyalty. In fact, I would rename it, "Customer Satisfaction Management," because that is what it enables.

> Harvey Thompson
> Principal, Worldwide Customer Value Management
> IBM Global Services, Consulting Group

"I suspect that many future readers will use the exhibits as a manual. These features will make the book especially valuable as a text or training manual."

> Steven Andes, Ph.D., CPA
> Assistant Professor, Public Services Graduate Program
> DePaul University, Chicago, Illinois

Improving Your Measurement of Customer Satisfaction:
A Guide to Creating, Conducting, Analyzing, and Reporting Customer Satisfaction Measurement Programs

Also available from ASQ Quality Press

Measuring Customer Satisfaction: Survey Design, Use, & Statistical Analysis Methods, Second Edition
Bob E. Hayes

Mapping Work Processes
Dianne Galloway

Quality Quotes
Hélio Gomes

Understanding and Applying Value-Added Assessments: Eliminating Business Process Waste
William E. Trischler

Measuring and Managing Customer Satisfaction: Going For The Gold
Sheila Kessler

The Change Agents' Handbook: A Survival Guide for Quality Improvement Champions
David W. Hutton

Total Quality Service: A Simplified Approach To Using The Baldrige Award Criteria
Sheila Kessler

Creating A Customer-Centered Culture: Leadership In Quality, Innovation, and Speed
Robin L. Lawton

Customer Retention: An Integrated Process For Keeping Your Best Customers
Michael W. Lowenstein

LearnerFirst™ Process Management Software
with Tennessee Associates International

To request a complimentary catalog of ASQ Quality Press publications, call 800–248–1946.

Improving Your Measurement of Customer Satisfaction:
A Guide to Creating, Conducting, Analyzing, and Reporting Customer Satisfaction Measurement Programs

BY

Terry G. Vavra, Ph.D.
President, Marketing Metrics, Inc.—Paramus, New Jersey

and

Associate Professor of Marketing, Lubin School of Business,
Pace University—White Plains, New York

ASQ Quality Press
Milwaukee, Wisconsin

Improving Your Measurement of Customer Satisfaction: A Guide to Creating, Conducting, Analyzing, and Reporting Customer Satisfaction Measurement Programs
Terry G. Vavra, Ph.D.

Library of Congress Cataloging-in-Publication Data

Vavra, Terry G.
    Improving your measurement of customer satisfaction: a guide to
creating, conducting, analyzing, and reporting customer satisfaction
measurement programs / by Terry G. Vavra.
        p.   cm.
    Includes bibliographical references and index.
    ISBN 0-87389-405-7 (alk. paper)
    1. Consumer satisfaction—Evaluation. I. Title.
HF5415.335.V38   1997   97-11803
658.8'12—dc21   CIP

© 1997, Terry G. Vavra

10 9 8 7 6 5 4

ISBN 0-87389-405-7

Acquisitions Editor: Roger Holloway
Project Editor: Jeanne Bohn

ASQ Mission: To facilitate continuous improvement and increase customer
satisfaction by identifying, communicating, and promoting the use of quality
principles, concepts, and technologies; and thereby be recognized throughout
the world as the leading authority on, and champion for, quality.

Attention: Schools and Corporations
ASQ Quality Press books, audiotapes, videotapes, and software are available at
quantity discounts with bulk purchases for business, educational, or instructional
use. For information, please contact ASQ Quality Press at 800-248-1946, or
write to ASQ Quality Press, P.O. Box 3005, Milwaukee, WI 53201-3005.

For a free copy of the ASQ Quality Press Publications Catalog, including ASQ
membership information, call 800-248-1946.

Printed in the United States of America

 Printed on acid-free paper

American Society for Quality

Quality Press
611 East Wisconsin Avenue
P.O. Box 3005
Milwaukee, Wisconsin 53201-3005

DEDICATION

To those who strive to improve the quality of their organizations' products, services and customer servicing; may your success be considerable, your personal satisfaction substantial.

CONTENTS

Design: Creating an Effective Information Process   119

Delivery: Assessing Performance   187

Chapter 9

Monitoring Changes in Performance   367

Chapter 10

How to Achieve "Buy-In" of CSM Results   403

PREFACE

My admittedly ambitious goal in writing this book has been to assemble a book which can serve as *a definitive source of customer satisfaction measurement technology*. In doing so I've hoped to provide practitioners and students with a comprehensive text on every issue relevant to conducting, analyzing and reporting smart and effective customer satisfaction surveys. I'd like to think of my book as standing usefully proud next to Bob Hayes' excellent book, *Measuring Customer Satisfaction*. Having used Bob's book in my MBA seminars on customer satisfaction and in numerous professional seminars, I am indebted to his ground-breaking effort in writing *the* book on customer satisfaction measurement.

MY PERSPECTIVE

Personally, I have been involved in the measurement of customer satisfaction for the last 15 years. During this time, I have been fortunate to work with many well-respected, multi-national companies including Rolls-Royce, Motorola, Merrill Lynch, Ferrari and AT&T Wireless. So I believe I bring to this book a reasonably realistic perspective. During these years, my colleagues (at Marketing Metrics) and I have been asked to give talks and conduct workshops at various industry conferences in the US and abroad on how to improve customer satisfaction measurement.

These conferences have always been very well attended and our presentations well received. And, even though the number of these conferences proliferates, attendance at each continues to increase! The message seems clear; most major organizations today are committed to measuring the satisfaction of their customers and appear to want to do so in the most efficient, accurate manner possible. The majority of professionals engaged in this field seems to recognize the importance of improving their methodology and the accuracy of their surveys. Indeed, the reliance on customer satisfaction measurement is increasing. Not only are our surveys looked to for quality improvement information, but they are also being used to award incentive pay. And, the demand for proven linkages of satisfaction data with other criteria of success (namely corporate profitability) continues to increase. Despite these growing demands on customer satisfaction measurement, there are still relatively few books addressing the topic, and none as complete, I hope, as the book that follows in these pages.

THE BOOK'S ENVISIONED ROLE

I intend for this book to serve two, possibly three groups of customers. First, are the practitioners. I salute my colleagues in organizations around the world who daily convince their management that customer satisfaction is one of the most effective competitive tools in today's marketplace. Hopefully this book will not only provide them additional "logical ammunition," but will also serve them as a sourcebook answering whatever questions they might have and stimulating them with ideas for improving their methods and for managing survey content, analysis, and reporting.

The second customer group is students. Customer satisfaction is finding acceptance in the graduate and undergraduate curricula of many colleges and universities. This book is meant to be a useful text for such classes. Finally, the third group of customers; I hope this book might find value as a workbook to be employed in CSM training sessions and the many professional conferences on CSM that I have already described.

This book will provide the rationale, identify specific opportunities, and suggest specific programs to improve the measurement of customer satisfaction at a reader's organization. The message is appropriate for both consumer and business-to-business executives and transcends both the profit and not-for-profit sectors. Size of the organization is also irrelevant; all businesses can profit by showing their customers they wish to increase the satisfaction of their customers!

APPRECIATION EXTENDED

I am indebted to many individuals for helping instill in me the ideas I have described here. My many friends at Rolls-Royce helped direct me towards customer satisfaction measurement in the early 1980s. Thanks in particular to Howard Mosher, Ian McKay, Paul Beart, and Peter Lavers (all of Rolls-Royce Motor Cars). Guiseppe Greco of Ferrari North America, another strong advocate of customer satisfaction allowed me another avenue of experimentation. Olga Striltschuk (Motorola

Cellular Infrastructure Group) has perhaps been my strongest aid, because of her continual questioning of our ideas and suggestions as we have fashioned, with her, an award-winning multinational CSM program. Harvey Thompson of IBM Consulting has, over an association of half a decade shared with me his creative thinking on satisfaction and value management. He has stimulated my own thoughts and approaches.

My fine staff at Marketing Metrics has continually provided informational and moral support, led by my partner and wife, Linda Vavra. Doug Pruden, a devoted relationship marketer and respected colleague, has contributed numerous ideas and has read portions of the manuscript prior to its publication as has Dr. Satya Varagoor. Both Mary Zerbo, our Director of Secondary Research (at Marketing Metrics) and Kavir Fotedar (my graduate assistant at the Lubin School) have scoured vast databases in search of the article, "I thought I saw, once upon a time." They have worked wonders in tracking such vague recollections into actual photocopies for my reference. Rob Ebert has created many of the graphs and has assisted in the production of all computer runs. And Trice Gately, my administrative assistant, has coordinated much of the project for which I am extremely grateful.

Two organizations were very supportive of my initial efforts to develop this text, the publisher—the American Society for Quality Control and another related professional group, the Society of Consumer Affairs Professionals. I appreciate their encouragement, which validated the utility of my writing efforts; we all benefit from "a little help from our friends." Sue Westergaard, Jeanne Bohn and Roger Holloway of the ASQC were all a pleasure to work with. My thanks to three reviewers enlisted by the ASQC who provided very useful comments on earlier drafts of this book. They are: Steven Andes, Gary M. Hazard, and Antoinette Almeida. Steven Andes read the draft at two different stages and has made so many valuable comments, I have come to think of him as my co-author! Two of my students at Pace University also offered valuable critiques, thanks to Gita Bosch and Tim Andrews.

Perhaps one of my most satisfying experiences in writing this book has been the opportunity of working side-by-side with one of my three lovely daughters, Stacy Dallas Vavra, who has made her father very proud by her help as his editorial assistant. Thanks Stacy!

Finally, while writing the second half of this book, I was diagnosed with Hodgkin's disease (cancer of the lymph nodes). I owe my return to good health to the wonderful professionals at Sloan-Kettering Memorial Hospital, especially Dr. Carol Portlock, who guided me through the treatment to recovery!

THE BOOK'S ORGANIZATION

As to the organization of this book, a properly designed Customer Satisfaction Measurement project brings together five important areas:

- sampling/customer-participant selection
- questionnaire design
- interviewing/survey administration
- data analysis
- quality function deployment—building action plans

Each of these areas requires a special expertise, which I have attempted to describe and teach in this book. Hopefully it can serve the satisfaction professional as a single reference for each of these critical skills.

CONVENTIONS OBSERVED

Because I wish this book to have as broad an influence and application as possible, I will generally refrain from the use of "company," "brand," "service provider," "manufacturer," and so on. Instead I will use the term "organization" to imply *any* body that has an associated base of clients, customers, members, or donors whose satisfaction should be monitored.

Though I am not an advocate of the many acronyms our disciplines currently breed, I will resort to the use of a few in the realm of customer satisfaction, if only to save on type. *CSM* will be used to refer to the measurement of customer satisfaction. *CSP* will be used to reference a program for customer satisfaction. *CSI* will refer to any index or comparative customer satisfaction score.

More and more attention is being focused these days on customer value management. Indeed, satisfaction is one of the primary antecedents of perceived value. It appears that customer satisfaction data is most productive, if it is placed in the decisional context of managing better value for customers!

Terry G. Vavra
tvavra@marketingmetrics.com

A PROCESS MODEL

"Begin at the beginning, and go till you come to the end; then stop," was the Red King's advice to Alice. The Red King was obviously not tuned in/to processes, which purposefully lack a beginning and an end (we shall have more to say about this later). So, in a process how do you keep track of where you are, or better still where you want to be?

To assist the reader, the following model is offered as a "road map" of the process advocated by this book. Beyond the table of contents, the process model divides the author's comments into four areas of focus. We will use the process model to help remind us where we are from time to time.

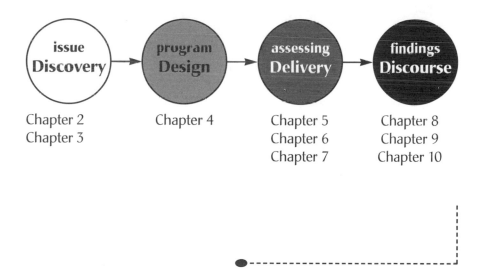

issue **Discovery**	program **Design**	assessing **Delivery**	findings **Discourse**
Chapter 2	Chapter 4	Chapter 5	Chapter 8
Chapter 3		Chapter 6	Chapter 9
		Chapter 7	Chapter 10

CHAPTER 1

The Philosophy of Customer Satisfaction

OVERVIEW

At the end of the 1990s most American businesses accord the measurement of customer satisfaction a high priority. This has been a result of numerous factors, not the least of which has been some rather remarkable corporate turnarounds based on strategic initiatives to understand customers' needs and then provide goods or services and the appropriate follow-up servicing to maximize customers' satisfaction.

A story told by Mr. Leonard Firestone, Jr., sets the basis for the measurement of customer satisfaction. Mr. Firestone, in describing what distinguishes success in some businesses and some people, told a homily of a downtrodden, yet hopeful individual philosophically explaining the nature of good fortune. *"Luck is how ya' treats people!"*, observed the individual alluding to the very real self-determining aspects of success.

Customer satisfaction measurement is a formalized, objective tool for assessing just exactly how *"ya treats people"* (both customers and employees)! Satisfied customers testify that an organization *is* quality oriented. Their satisfaction extends to both their lifetime and their lifetime value and their willingness to recommend an organization to others!

3

In this chapter, we will review the development of customer satisfaction measurement and the philosophy underlying the measurement.

A DEFINITION OF SATISFACTION

Customer satisfaction (according to a comprehensive review conducted by Yi (1993)) has been defined in two basic ways: as either an *outcome* or as a *process*. The outcome definitions characterize satisfaction as the end-state resulting from the consumption experience:

> the buyer's cognitive state of being adequately or inadequately rewarded for the sacrifices he has undergone (Howard and Sheth 1969, 145);
> an emotional response to the experiences provided by, associated with particular products or services purchased, retail outlets, or even molar patterns of behavior such as shopping and buyer behavior, as well as the overall marketplace (Westbrook and Reilly 1983, 256);
> an outcome of purchase and use resulting from the buyer's comparison of the rewards and the costs of the purchase in relation to the anticipated consequences (Churchill and Surprenant 1982, 493).

Alternatively, satisfaction has been considered as a process, emphasizing the perceptual, evaluative and psychological processes that contribute to satisfaction:

> an evaluation rendered that the experience was at least as good as it was supposed to be (Hunt 1977, 459);
> an evaluation that the chosen alternative is consistent with prior beliefs with respect to that alternative (Engel and Blackwell 1982, 501);
> the consumer's response to the evaluation of the perceived discrepancy between prior expectations and the actual performance of the product as perceived after its consumption (Tse and Wilton 1988, 204).

Yi observes that definitions have also varied with regard to their level of specificity. The various levels identified have included:

* satisfaction with a product
* satisfaction with a purchase decision experience
* satisfaction with a performance attribute
* satisfaction with a consumption experience
* satisfaction with a store or institution
* satisfaction with a pre-purchase experience

ROLE/IMPORTANCE OF CUSTOMER SATISFACTION IN CORPORATE AMERICA

A Developmental View

The age of mass distribution and mass marketing of products and services, so welcomed by most consumers and manufacturers, has had at least one negative consequence; it has distanced those who produce goods and services from those who consume them. In the artisan market preceding mass distribution, producers found out very quickly how satisfied or dissatisfied their customers were in the course of their frequent and necessary interaction with their customers. This face-to-face interaction reminded the producers daily of the sovereignty of their customers. The artisans readily accepted feedback from their customers and adopted the desired changes to help improve their products and to keep their customers. Customer satisfaction was a "daily phenomenon" (Eastman Kodak 1989).

Enter the era of mass distribution and the channels of distribution created to disseminate products and services. The system of mass distribution, a wonderfully productive process in so many ways, unfortunately distanced producers from their consumers by the distribution channel. This pipeline of products or services was maintained by intermediary "institutions" whose job it was to move the product or service from the manufacturer to the final consumer. Whether "captive dealers" or independent brokers, distributors or retailers, someone other than the producer was now "at the counter." A natural reaction was for the producers to give up or delegate responsibility for customer servicing, depending on the newly created intermediaries to look after customers' satisfaction. This seemed not only logical but economically sound. After all, the intermediaries were deriving profit from the sale of the products or services, why shouldn't they contribute in the form of providing after-sale service?

Delegating responsibility for customer satisfaction was a bad idea in two respects: first, it eliminated once and for all direct interaction with customers. Second, "out-of-sight, out-of-mind"; customers became a missing component in the producer's decision set. After all, if intermediaries continued to place orders, didn't that mean customers were continuing to buy? And if customers continued to buy, wasn't everything okay?

An Industry Perspective

The negative response to this question became a painful learning experience for many companies and industries. General Motors enjoyed a 52 percent share of the U.S. auto market in 1962 by apparently considering U.S. car buyers' needs and wants. However, it apparently lost sight of this key planning ingredient. During the 1960s and 1970s with a booming economy, increasing population and little foreign competition, the Detroit Big-3 found themselves able to sell just about all the cars they could produce. Management at GM and the other U.S. automakers shifted focus from customers' needs to production requirements, to cost-cutting practices and to the profit potential associated with acquisitions. With customers apparently satisfied, the automakers focused on expanding their share of market, not on continuing an interaction with their customers.

Professor Frederick Webster suggests that at this time, markets came to be defined as "aggregates of competitors" with the customer almost totally ignored (Philips, et al 1990). Japanese car manufacturers were the first to spot Detroit's shortsightedness and identify it as an opportunity for themselves. An example of their insight was Toyota's 1973 opening of a design center in Southern California to fine-tune its cars to American consumers' tastes.

Even though during the mid-1970s the quality of *all* automobiles was increasing, Japanese manufacturers' rate of improvement was much greater due to their orientation to consumers' definition of quality. Detroit failed to recognize the orientation to quality and customer focus that the Japanese were practicing until it was essentially too late. By 1980 Ford's market share had fallen from 23.5 percent (1978) to only 17.2 percent (Philips, et al 1990)!

The growth of the marketing research community during this same time period also served to undermine manufacturers' attentions to individual customers—seducing them with market or segment profiles. This aggregation of customers—often down to a single "average" customer for the organization, overshadowed the potential value of looking at data from smaller groups of customers with more specialized interests.

The U.S. Department of Agriculture was one of the first organizations to sponsor a survey of customer satisfaction. This study seems to be a singular turning point in orientation. The Department's Index of Consumer Satisfaction reported satisfaction information directly to business community policymakers (Pfaff 1973).

In the late 1970s, Xerox "awakened" to find its category almost dominated by its more customer-focused Japanese competitors. A corporatewide decision was made to institute customer satisfaction as Xerox's primary corporate goal. At about the same time, numerous other American firms began to understand that they too had disregarded their customers' needs as they pursued their own goals. It is clear a signal had been received; American businesses needed to get back into touch with their customers!

Evidence of Importance and Change

A 1994 survey conducted by the Juran Institute found that 90 percent of the top managers of more than 200 of America's largest companies agreed with the statement, "Maximizing customer satisfaction will maximize profitability and market share." And, about 90 percent of these companies evidenced their belief by funding some organized effort for systematically tracking and improving customer satisfaction scores (Fay 1994).

In a 1994 survey of 124 large U.S. companies, Mentzer and colleagues (1995) found 75 percent of the companies surveyed mentioned customer satisfaction in their mission statements. Though totally related, satisfaction preempted product/service quality, which was specifically mentioned in only 65 percent of the statements. Almost half of the mission statements addressed customer service (56 percent) and a customer orientation (49 percent).

Jack Honomichl, an observer of the U.S. marketing research industry has created an index of spending on customer satisfaction measurement. Honomichl tallies the gross revenues of 14 of the United States' largest marketing research vendors, which are attributable to customer satisfaction projects as well as similar revenue from 15 European firms representing the European Union. From 1990 to 1995, Honomichl's data shows a very impressive growth in the business of these firms related to customer satisfaction measurement (see Figure 1.1) (Honomichl 1996).

A survey conducted in both 1991 and 1994 by Marketing Metrics shows some dampening, however, of the ardor with which companies are committed to measuring satisfaction. Over this three-year period, the number of companies conducting a regular customer satisfaction assessment fell by about half (Marketing Metrics 1995)!

The hard realities of the intensive cost-cutting and "right sizing" of U.S. businesses during the 1990s may be, in part, responsible if commitment to customer satisfaction has, indeed, declined. Too often, lacking evidence of

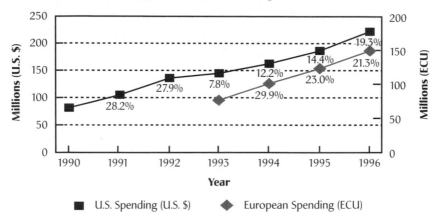

CSM Revenue in 15 U.S. and 15 European Firms Specializing in CSM
With Year-to-Year Change

Figure 1.1   Spending on Customer Satisfaction Measurement
Source: Inside Research (847) 526-0707, March 1997.

the direct contribution of satisfaction measurement to profitability, satisfaction measurement procedures have been viewed as cost centers and have become victims of economy drives.

However, in organizations familiar with TQM (for control of production and servicing quality), customer satisfaction has been "legitimized" by the Baldrige Award criteria. Customer satisfaction is the leading criterion for determining the quality actually delivered to customers through the product/service and by the accompanying servicing. Recently though, even the Baldrige has somewhat cooled on the importance of customer satisfaction. The reevaluated point allocation of 1995, reduced customer satisfaction from the singular most important concern, to one of the two highest weighted concerns. Joining satisfaction in 1995s scoring was business results—profitability.

MAXIMIZING THE SATISFACTION OF CUSTOMERS

A Win-Win Situation

Customer satisfaction has long-reaching impact on the current and perhaps future viability of an organization. Schlesinger and Heskitt (1991) demonstrate the relationship between satisfied customers and satisfied

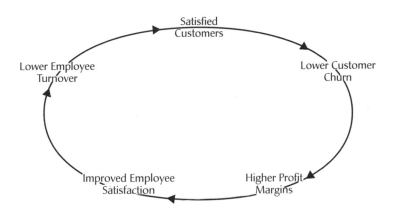

Figure 1.2   The Cycle of Good Service

Reprinted from "Breaking the Cycle of Failure in Services," by Schlesinger, L. A. and Heskitt, J. L., *Sloan Management Review*, Spring 1991, pp. 17–28, by permission of the publisher. Copyright 1991 by Sloan Management Review Association. All rights reserved.

employees with their Cycle of Good Service (see Figure 1.2). The cycle suggests that satisfied customers tolerate higher margins that can be used to better pay employees. This boosts employee morale, reducing employee turnover, which in turn helps produce more satisfied customers, and so on.

A good many U.S. companies and organizations have understood this process and have distinguished themselves by instituting exemplary customer satisfaction programs. *CIO Magazine* (1995) recognized ten such firms as "best in class" in customer satisfaction measurement in 1995. Table 1.1 lists the companies recognized.

Philosophically Pleasing

The orientation to customer satisfaction is no recent phenomenon. Many very successful businesspeople over the years have identified the importance of focusing on customer satisfaction. The British car manufacturer, Sir Henry Royce, whose name is synonymous with quality, laid down the primary principles of customer satisfaction in 1906 when he declared,

> "Our interest in the Rolls-Royce cars does not end at the moment when the owner pays for and takes delivery of the car. Our interest in the car never wanes. Our ambition is that every purchaser of a Rolls-Royce car shall continue to be more than satisfied" (Rolls-Royce).

Table 1.1   Firms Excelling in Customer Satisfaction Measurement

Company	Revenue	Employees	Business
L.L. Bean *Freeport, Maine*	$974M	3,500	Outdoor and casual clothing and equipment
Land's End *Dodgeville, Wis.*	$992M	7,500	Direct merchant
Lexus Div., Toyota Motor Sales USA *Torrance, Calif.*	N/A	325	Distributor of luxury automobiles
Motorola Cellular Infrastructure Group *Arlington Heights, Illinois*	N/A	7,000	Cellular equipment and services
Nordstrom *Seattle*	$ 3.9B	33,000	Fashion specialty retailer
Richfood *Richmond, Va.*	$ 1.3B	1,800	Wholesale food distribution
Ritz-Carlton Hotel Co., The *Atlanta*	N/A	14,000	Hotel management
Solectron Corp. *Milpitas, Calif.*	$ 1.5B	8,000	Electronic manufacturing services
Southwest Airlines *Dallas*	$ 6.2B	17,200	Commercial air travel
United Services Automobile Assn. (USAA) *San Antonio*	$ 6.2B	16,500	Insurance, financial services
Xerox Corp. *Stamford, Conn.*	$17.8B	86,300	Document-processing office equipment

Reprinted with permission from Hildebrand, Carol, "Service Stars," *CIO Magazine*, August 1995, pp. 90–96.

A similar appreciation (for customer satisfaction) is echoed by today's Toyota Motor Sales organization:

> Total customer satisfaction is the cornerstone of Toyota's business plan in the United States. It is our fundamental corporate philosophy and part of everything we do (Gieszl 1995).

Gordon Selfridge, an American and former associate of Marshall Field, journeyed to London in the late 1800s to create his own department store empire. His founding principle, was a philosophy possibly learned from Field. Selfridge's operating motto was, *"The customer is always right!"* (Cohen and Cohen 1980). Though often attributed to Field, this philosophy makes customer satisfaction the very heart of the business, the *raison d'être*.

The Connecticut dairystore magnate, Stew Leonard (showcased for American business by Tom Peters), has built on Selfridge's philosophy. He reminds retailers throughout the U.S. of the importance of customer satisfaction with the often quoted rules of his dairy superstores:

Rule #1: The customer is always right.
Rule #2: If the customer is ever wrong, reread Rule #1!

The Portland-based department store chain, Nordstrom, has built a reputation on its dedication to going to extreme lengths to create satisfied customers. This reputation alone, seems to have secured for it a beachhead in U.S. markets previously believed to be impenetrable because of the strong presence of incumbent stores like Bloomingdale's, Strawbridge and Clothier, Hecht's, and Neiman-Marcus. Nordstrom has redefined the nature of the department store business for these incumbents by giving customer satisfaction a top priority.

Mail cataloguer, L. L. Bean, has typified the trend of American businesses to recognize the importance of satisfying customers with its guarantee:

Our products are guaranteed to give 100 percent satisfaction in every way. Return anything purchased from us at any time if it proves otherwise. We will replace it, refund your purchase price or credit your credit card, as you wish. We do not want you to have anything from L. L. Bean that is not completely satisfactory.

The value of a focus on customer satisfaction is further evident in the practices of Baldrige Award winners, for example, as follows:

- Every six weeks, Xerox holds a Visitor Quality Day for customers at its Rochester, N.Y. headquarters.
- IBM Rochester designed its AS/400 minicomputer only after consulting with 250 customers.
- Solectron Corporation calls on each of its 120 customers every week to inquire about on-time delivery and satisfaction with its products.
- AT&T Transmission Systems Business Unit gathers information on customer needs through contact summaries, focus groups,

complaints, technical assistance requests, competitor evaluations, and customer surveys. At least once a year, major customers fill out detailed report cards to grade product and service areas (Nadkarni 1995).

A naive view of business might suggest that profit is the appropriate goal of an organization, but Ted Levitt (and others) have argued against this shortsighted view. Levitt says, from a practical viewpoint, the primary goal of an organization has to be customer retention (Levitt 1985). Only with a steady base of customers can an organization hope to make a profit. And only by first satisfying customers can a business ever hope to retain its current customers.

At Digital Equipment, CEO Robert Palmer has placed the highest attention on customer satisfaction, saying

> (to) ensure that the customer is the prime focus of everything we do . . .
> I pledge to focus on customer needs, beginning with listening to customer
> requirements. . . . Digital's strategy has one goal: rebuild shareholder
> value. That goal can be realized only by improving customer focus . . .
> nor will we alter our belief that customer satisfaction is the surest path to
> lasting shareholder value and sustained profits.

The Essence of Consumer-Oriented Marketing

The perspective of "consumer-oriented" marketing championed in the early 1960s by academics McCarthy (1960) and Kotler (1967), is based on determining what a target group of customers want, and then maximizing their satisfaction with the product or service. In this perspective satisfaction is at the very heart of the practice of marketing. Unfortunately, marketers in the 1990s seem to have developed a form of "satisfaction myopia" too often focusing on the physical characteristics of their product or service offerings rather than the benefit (or satisfaction) delivered to consumers. Whenever such a misorientation is present, customer satisfaction is likely not to be a top priority.

Professor Sandra Vandermerwe has reminded us of this shortsightedness of focusing on product characteristics rather than benefits. Vandermerwe (1994) utilizes Levitt's notion that the "core" of any product or service is its "want-satisfaction capabilities." If this is so, she reasons, the *true test of the appeal* (or value) of a product or service should not be *what goes in* (the quality of the product or service), but rather *the quality of the result* (what the product or service does for customers). Vandermerwe's perspective makes a strong argument for the importance of continuous customer satisfaction measurement.

Frequently businesses operate on the principle that if things go wrong, they'll hear about it from their customers. Countless investigations (many of them conducted by Technical Assistance Research Programs) document the fallacy of relying on customer complaints. In the first place, 50 percent of customers who experience a problem, *never complain to anyone!* Of the remaining half, most (45 percent) complain only to frontline personnel who either fail to escalate the problem up to management and/or mishandle solving the problem. Only 5 percent (one unhappy customer in 20) of all customers who have a problem actually voice it to management (Goodman and Ward, 1993). So, complaints are an inefficient method with which to monitor customer satisfaction.

ECONOMIC SUPPORT/REASONS

Competition with Quality-Focused Economies

During the post–World War II decades, Japanese companies were anxious to change their reputation in the United States where they had been perceived as a manufacturer of inferior quality merchandise. They evolved processes for measuring customer satisfaction and assessing the quality of competitive product offerings. Information gathered on customer preferences was then incorporated in company decision-making. Japanese business leaders studied and learned from American quality gurus, W. Edwards Deming and Joseph Juran (whose messages were largely being disregarded in the United States).

Even though the quality of U.S. goods was gradually improving year-after-year, the rate of improvement of the Japanese was much greater; they overtook U.S. manufacturers. It wasn't long before Japanese automobiles—once unsellable in the U.S.—were surpassing U.S. autos both in product quality and in sales. According to Juran, by 1975 though U.S. automakers didn't know it, the Japanese had already vastly surpassed them (this was true in other industries as well, most notably, consumer electronics). U.S. companies were "ambushed" for two reasons Juran claims,

> "The first had to do with their cultural bias. The American mindset saw the Japanese as copyists rather than innovators. The other reason U.S. companies failed to see the superior Japanese quality coming was that they

lacked the proper 'instruments' on their 'corporate dashboards.' The indicators they were watching didn't measure quality. The Japanese [indicators] did" (Juran 1993).

To compete with other quality-oriented economies today, it is absolutely necessary to collect the right data, to be attuned to the appropriate market indicators. Customer satisfaction in a world oriented to quality improvement is the appropriate indicator.

Improved Competitive Posture within One's Own Economy and Industry

Satisfaction is quickly becoming the key to competitive posture within a category or industry. Products or services initially secure life in the market by fulfilling a basic need. But only offering minimal functionality grants a product nothing more than commodity status. To ensure long-term market success, businesses have created brands. Brands allowed businesses to develop and sustain an image, differentiating one another's products in the eyes of consumers. Consider how Frank Perdue (entrepreneur, owner of Perdue Chicken, a northeast regional brand) was able to take a commodity—raw chicken—and elevate his brand far above the category, demanding more from the customer in exchange for his promise of better quality. Today most companies are leveraging branding to its maximum benefit. Product and service categories have become crowded with "parity brands," each with its own unique brand personality.

To further differentiate themselves, customer satisfaction is the next most likely strategy. Companies are recognizing that the brand that best satisfies its customers not only keeps them longer, but is also likely to benefit from positive word-of-mouth. There are ample success stories to illustrate this strategy. Motorola and Xerox are two companies that have focused on customer satisfaction as a competitive strategy. Motorola's commitment to quality and customer satisfaction has not only gained a Baldrige Award, but has allowed Motorola to maintain premium pricing in categories given to price competition. Xerox, also a Baldrige winner, successfully adopted customer satisfaction as a competitive tool to regain its dominant position in the photocopier category.

Improved Profitability

There is both an intuitive belief and mounting empirical evidence that improved customer satisfaction will increase organizational profitability.

Accounting Professor David Larcker of the Wharton Business School has determined that companies in the top quartile of customer satisfaction (according to the American Customer Satisfaction Index model) experience a higher appreciation in stock values than did the overall S&P 500 (5.3 percent in stock value against a much lower 2.7 percent). (Even more compelling, the top 10 food, personal care and tobacco companies on the ACSI model gained 15 percent in the same period—August 1994 to February 1995.) (Fierman 1995).

Fornell and Wernerfelt (1987, 1988) investigated the link between market share, servicing costs and satisfaction as they examined the efficacy of complaint handling on customer retention. They conclude there is a positive relationship between effective complaint management and retention (and therefore derived revenue). Buzzell and Gale's (1987) monumental analysis of the PIMS data provided evidence of the relationship between service quality and profitability. Those firms delivering the highest ROI's were those firms that also provided high quality service.

Reichheld and Sasser's (1990) frequently quoted data on the profit impact of reducing customer defection, clearly shows the value of retaining a greater proportion of customers in several service industries. Postulating a reduction in "churn" of just 5 percent, Reichheld and Sasser report impact on bottom-line profitability anywhere from +25 percent to +85 percent depending upon the specific service industry tracked.

Customer satisfaction is a "threshold requirement" for achieving customer retention though additional considerations help to improve retention.

Improved Customer Retention

Satisfaction extends customers' lifetimes and their lifetime values (the net value contributed through a customer's purchases). In addition, focusing on satisfaction helps eliminate the negative word-of-mouth potential of dissatisfied customers. It has been found that more than 90 percent of dissatisfied customers will not exert their own effort to contact a company to complain; they simply take their business to a competitor while voicing their dissatisfaction to other potential customers. Losing one dissatisfied customer may be more severe than it sounds; one dissatisfied customer may speak to as many as nine others, multiplying his/her dissatisfaction ninefold!

Most consumers, whether rational or simply hedonistic, are looking for manufacturers, suppliers, and retailers who maximize their satisfaction. If organizations take the time and effort to assess their current customers' satisfactions, they take a major step towards running a business that is customer-oriented, both for today's current customers and for future customers.

Improved Market Share

Traditionally market share has been identified as the result of conquest marketing activities (labeled "offensive marketing" strategies by Day (1977) and by Fornell and Wernerfelt (1987)). In this perspective market share is viewed as directly related to the level of advertising, sales promotion and other outreach marketing efforts. The only recognition in such models of satisfaction and customer retention, Rust and Zahorik point out, is through "adjustment terms" that incorporate the influence of loyalty or "buyer inertia."

Retention marketing activities ("defensive" strategies in Day's and Fornell's terms) posit that marketing dollars may be more efficiently directed at retaining current customers than at attempting to win new ones. Research conducted by TARP for the U.S. Consumer Affairs Office has given us the following:

> It is five times as costly to attract a new customer as to keep a current customer (TARP 1986).

Rust and Zahorik diagram the sources of business for a firm (see Figure 1.3). They identify four sources of customers in any one purchase cycle: retained customers, customers switching from competition, customers new to the category, and customers leaving the category. Different probabilities of success are associated with each of these four classes of customers. Because retained customers exhibit the highest probability for additional business, they deserve more attention and focus than they currently receive. On the other hand, new customers and customers switching over from competitors each have a much lower probability of occurrence; they deserve less attention.

HISTORY OF CUSTOMER SATISFACTION MEASUREMENT

Customer satisfaction measurement has its roots in the Total Quality Management movement, but was also explored early on from a social-psychological perspective by marketing theorists. While the TQM school focused on the more pragmatic application of satisfaction information to design and manufacture, the marketers explored

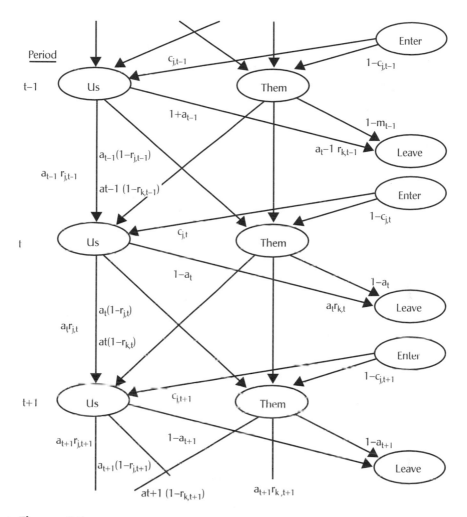

Figure 1.3   Sources of Business

Source: Rust, Roland, and Zahorik, Anthony J. "Customer Satisfaction, Customer Retention and Market Share," *Journal of Retailing*, Vol. 69, No. 2, Summer 1993, pp. 193–215.

the psychology of satisfaction—how it was formed and the nature of its impact on future purchase behavior.

The TQM Initiative

Background

As the quality management "gurus" (most notably W. E. Deming) sought to help manufacturers improve the quality of their products, they

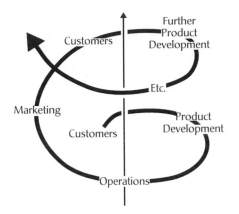

Figure 1.4   Juran's Spiral of Progress in Quality

Source: Juran, J. M., *Juran on Planning for Quality*, New York: The Free Press, 1988, p. 6.

recognized that internal metrics (for example, *conformance to specifications* or meeting *internally set objectives*) of quality were worthless. Unless quality was manifested in ways that were relevant and perceptible to the customer, improvement efforts were wasted. Deming's entire quality improvement process is rooted in customer information and feedback.

In describing his "Helix of Continuing Improvement," Deming says of customer research,

> The main use of consumer research [customer satisfaction measurement] should be to feed consumer reactions into the design of the product, so that management can anticipate changing demands and requirements and set economical production levels. Consumer research takes the pulse of the consumer's reactions and demands, and seeks explanations for the findings.
>
> Consumer research is a process of communication between the manufacturer and users and potential users of his product. . . . Through this process of communication the manufacturer discovers how his product performs in service, what people think of his product, why some people will buy it, why others will not, or will not buy it again, and he is able to redesign his product to make it better as measured by the quality and uniformity that are best suited to the end users of the product and to the price that the consumer can pay (Deming 1993, pg 177).

Deming's Helix of Continuing Improvement is mirrored in the "spiral of progress in quality" created by J. M. Juran, another TQM pioneer. Both quality-masters see customer input and feedback as the necessary input to direct product design and improvement (See Figure 1.4).

Deming further distinguishes three aspects of consumer research as follows:

1. research for discovery of problems, such as reasons for dissatisfaction;
2. research to obtain information on which to base prediction of the consumer's reaction to a change in the product;

3. research for quantitative estimates of numbers and proportions of households or of other users that have these problems (Deming 1986, 182).

He characterizes the first two as "analytic information"—necessary to improve the quality of the product or service offering. The third aspect of consumer research, Deming calls "enumerative information"— desirable information to adjust the manufacturer's production lots to the level of demand in the market. It is the analytic components to which CSM is oriented.

Juran adds that the three key questions of marketing research (CSM) to ask of consumers, should be the following:

1. What product features are of importance?
2. How does our product compare (on these features) to competitors' (products or services)?
3. What is the significance of quality differences (in these features) in terms of money demand or preference (Juran 1988, 47)?

Juran cautions the investigator to question the consumer's responses. Customers state their needs in their own language or terminology—frequently in the form of current product offerings, he says. But, what customers really desire are solutions to problems or experiencing benefits. It is necessary to ask customers, "Why are you buying the product? What service or benefit do you expect from it?"

While Deming and Juran focused on describing the type of information to collect, others in the TQM movement have concentrated more on how to act on the information collected in customer satisfaction surveys. Hauser and Clausing's (1988) work on operationalizing methods of Quality Function Deployment is typical of this movement. (See Chapter 10 for an extensive discussion of QFD methods.)

The Development of Satisfaction Theory

From marketing theorists and consumer researchers, two perspectives of studying satisfaction appear identifiable: approaching the study of satisfaction through *product performance,* and the study of satisfaction as its *own construct.*

Cardozo

Cardozo (1965) was one of the first marketing academics to investigate customer satisfaction. Cardozo's treatise borrowed heavily from social

psychology. To help understand the impact of satisfaction on future buying behavior, Cardozo suggested the rather novel joint application of
both Helson's "contrast effect"[1] as well as Festinger's cognitive dissonance
theory.[2]

Cardozo speculated that dissonance would prevail in purchases of
high involvement and substantial expended effort. This meant if customers had invested themselves in a product or service (either through
their involvement with the product or by expending considerable effort
to buy it or by paying a substantial price) they would actively work to reduce any difference between their actual experience with a product or
service and their prior expectations. This suggests a generally more favorable outcome for the manufacturer, since the customer would conceivably
increase her evaluations of experience or decrease her expectations (after
the fact) to reduce the experienced dissonance between high expectations
and low experience.

In purchases commanding little involvement, and requiring scant
expended effort, Cardozo posited that contrast theory would operate,
suggesting customers would be intolerant of much deviation of experienced satisfaction from their prior expectations. This situation is far less
forgiving for the manufacturer.

Howard and Sheth

The work of John Howard and Jagdish Sheth (1969) in their model of
consumer behavior laid important foundations for the process model of
satisfaction, which was developing in parallel with their work on consumers' prepurchase and postpurchase reconciliation of information and
feedback. Satisfaction was a variable included in their earliest models.

Oliver

Some of the most frequently cited, early satisfaction pieces are the work
of Richard Oliver (1977, 1980, 1981). Oliver initiated a focus on the antecedents of satisfaction, particularly the expectancy–disconfirmation

----

[1]The "contrast effect," as developed by Helson (1964) in his work on adaptation level theory,
suggests that people will tend to exaggerate the differences between stimuli or options that are
slightly different from their own, current opinions or stands.

[2]The theory of cognitive dissonance, developed by Leon Festinger (1957), concerns peoples' actions
when they are placed in a situation in which their actions or commitments are seen to be less than
ideal. Festinger described ways people attempt to reduce the "dissonance" of situation in which they
find themselves.

sequence. Oliver used Helson's adaption theory to suggest that expectations fix a standard of performance, providing a frame of reference for customers' evaluative judgments. Satisfaction was then viewed as a function of the baseline effect of expectations, modified by perceived disconfirmations.

Oliver established a process to describe how satisfaction is produced in this expectation–disconfirmation framework. Prior to purchase buyers form expectations of the product or service. Consumption of the product or service reveals a level of perceived quality (which can be influenced, itself, by expectations). The perceived quality either positively confirms expectations or negatively disconfirms them. Expectations serve, in Oliver's model, as an anchor or baseline for satisfaction, the positive confirmation or negative disconfirmation either increasing or decreasing the customer's resulting satisfaction.

Baldrige Focus

Background of the Award

In 1987 the U.S. Congress, alerted to the decline in quality of American-made products and services, decided to motivate companies to produce products and services of exceptional quality. Patterned after Japan's prestigious Deming Award (recognizing W. E. Deming's impact on quality in that country), the Malcolm Baldrige National Quality Award was instituted. The Award, named after a previous Secretary of Commerce, is privately funded and administered by the National Institute of Standards and Technology. Three application categories exist, manufacturing (SIC codes 01–39); service companies (SIC 40–89); and small business. The program has been established to recognize superior achievement in customer satisfaction and to serve as an educational tool as well. It is the intent of the application and review process to provide significant educational feedback to applicants as well as to showcase exemplary applicants for others to study and emulate.

Changes in the Criteria

The award is based on seven scoring categories. Prior to 1995, customer satisfaction was the most important of the categories. However, in 1995 business results was increased in importance to rank equally with customer satisfaction at 250 points (out of 1,000) each. (See Table 1.2 for a listing of 1997's criteria.) One unsettling thought, Baldrige examiners review applicants' processes for ascertaining customer satisfaction, but do not actually talk to or interview any applicants' customers themselves.

Table 1.2   1997 Baldrige Award Criteria

Categories/Items		Points
1.0	**Leadership**	**110**
	1.1 Leadership System	80
	1.2 Public Responsibility and Corporate Citizenship	30
2.0	**Strategic Planning**	**80**
	2.1 Strategy Development Process	40
	2.2 Company Strategy	40
3.0	**Customer and Market Focus**	**80**
	3.1 Customer and Market Knowledge	40
	3.2 Customer Satisfaction and Relationship Enhancement	40
4.0	**Information Analysis**	**80**
	4.1 Selection and Use of Information and Data	25
	4.2 Selection and Use of Comparative Information and Data	15
	4.3 Analysis and Review of Company Performance	40
5.0	**Human Resource Development and Management**	**100**
	5.1 Work Systems	40
	5.2 Employee Education, Training, and Development	30
	5.3 Employee Well-Being and Satisfaction	30
6.0	**Process Management**	**100**
	6.1 Management of Product and Service Processes	60
	6.2 Management of Support Processes	20
	6.3 Management of Supplier and Partnering Processes	20
7.0	**Business Results**	**450**
	7.1 Customer Satisfaction Results	130
	7.2 Financial and Market Results	130
	7.3 Human Resource Results	35
	7.4 Supplier and Partner Results	25
	7.5 Company-Specific Results	130
	TOTAL POINTS	**1000**

Source: National Institute of Standards and Technology, U.S. Department of Commerce, Technology Adminstration.

Economic Support

Beginning with the movement to adopt TQM methods in the late 1970s, and continuing throughout the 1980s, the linkage between customer satisfaction and profitability seems to have been accepted on faith. The logic seems sound. Quality products and servicing are likely to satisfy customers who will extend their purchasing lifetimes and increase their share of requirements allocated the company. Consequently (other things remaining equal) profitability should increase. Right? It now appears this is a fallacious assumption in that it fails to identify the costs of quality.

Several case studies bear out the incomplete logic. The Wallace Co., the 1990 small business winner of the Baldrige was bankrupt by January of 1992! IBM oriented itself to a "market-driven quality" campaign in 1990 winning the Baldrige in 1990 and NASA's George M. Low Trophy (for quality) in 1992. Yet, throughout 1992 IBM incurred losses totaling $5 billion, which increased to an additional $8 billion in 1993.

High quality and customer satisfaction are necessary, but do not guarantee profitability. Without a model linking quality programs to the bottom line, it is impossible to identify the action(s) most critical to improve the profit picture. (See Chapter 10 for an expanded discussion of satisfaction's link to profitability.)

Contemporary Advocates

Many consulting firms today, and especially those focusing on reengineering and transformation processes, have wholeheartedly embraced the logic of interviewing customers to learn their satisfactions and dissatisfactions with a product, service, or category.

The IBM Consulting Group utilizes a customer perspective and focus in defining its clients' problems. Gemini Consulting has regularly utilized "brown papers" (a flow-chart procedure somewhat similar to customer blueprinting) to better describe and then understand the amount and sequence of interactions with customers.

Syndicated Satisfaction Surveys

Early in the development of satisfaction surveys, one or two companies created syndicated or multiclient surveys. Sponsored by multiple firms in a category, such surveys provided a view of the category much the way Consumer Reports had done, except that the ratings were from actual customers. The surveys provided participating manufacturers with information not only about their own products, but their products in comparison with those of competitors. While most of the participating firms could easily have paid for their own surveys (and many do in concert with the syndicated surveys), these syndicated audits provided readings of competitors' success in a very cost-efficient manner.

The first industry targeted by the syndicated surveyors was the automotive industry—a good target because of Detroit's lagging quality in the presence of Japanese importer's preoccupation with competing on quality. Probably the most recognizable of the firms is J. D. Power. Beginning in the early 1990s, Power had expanded into other industries, including the personal computer, hotel and air travel industries.

While the syndicated surveys generate much useful information, one problem has been their attractiveness as advertising content. Seemingly in acknowledgment of the value of syndicated satisfaction ratings for advertising, J. D. Power has created a plethora of awards. Though the firm awards only two Customer Satisfaction Awards (one for cars and one for trucks), Power has created Quality Study Awards at 90 days, 1 year, and 5 years with 12 segments at each time period. This array of awards is enough to guarantee each of the Big-3 automakers more than one "customer satisfaction" award. The kicker is, while Oldsmobile may be the winner of the 90-day Initial Quality Award, it may not even appear among the One-year or Five-year Award contenders! This seems curious and causes one to question the validity of the criteria used for each Award. It seems undeniable that Power is trying to capitalize on the cachet of its awards for consumers.

THE AMERICAN SATISFACTION INDEX

Genesis

The American Customer Satisfaction Index roughly emulates a national measure conducted in Sweden, the Swedish Customer Satisfaction Barometer. The Swedish index was first reported in 1989.

Professor Claes Fornell of the University of Michigan and architect of the Swedish program developed the American index as a joint project between the National Quality Research Center of the University of Michigan School of Business and the American Society for Quality Control. Work was initiated in 1990 with a pilot project appraising 60 different approaches. Ultimately the survey procedure and the analytical process developed in Sweden were adopted to the American market.

Fornell's model expresses satisfaction as the result of three elements: perceived (experienced) quality; expectations; and perceived value (see Figure 1.5). Fornell further postulates that satisfaction subsequently influences complaining (or complementing) behavior; as well as customer loyalty. In the model he has operationally defined each construct. Furthermore, confirmatory factor analysis and linear equation modeling have been conducted to validate the relationships depicted in the model and the overall framework.

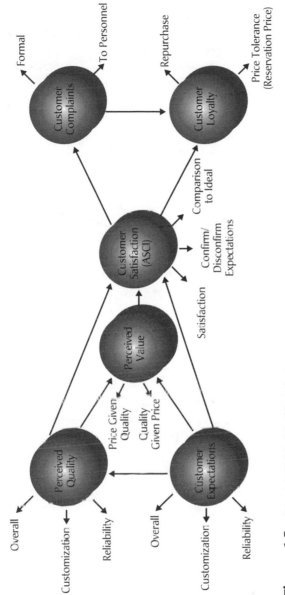

Figure 1.5 The ACSI Model of Satisfaction

Reprinted with permission, American Society for Quality Control and the National Quality Research Center, University of Michigan Business School, *The American Customer Satisfaction Index.*

The Survey

The ACSI survey gathers information on 203 specific companies (which account for 40 percent of all consumer expenditures) and seven governmental agencies, both serving consumer households. Numerous smaller companies are also included and aggregated with the 40 industries monitored, which collapse into seven economic productivity sectors.

Yearly results (reported quarterly) are based on interviews with approximately 30,000 consumers. Participants are "self-identified" purchasers of products from one or more of the 40 industries. Each consumer's satisfaction scores are allocated to the brand he/she identifies as having produced the last product purchased in the industry.

The survey's goal is to provide an understanding of the impact of quality to the GNP, national competitiveness and to the U.S. standard of living. Fornell argues that economic factors have heretofore been reacted to in isolation from consumers' reactions. For example, if prices increase, one is likely to blame inflation, rather than recognizing the production costs have simply increased to make a superior product. If consumers attribute the product with an increased cost added satisfaction, then economically the increase is justified. On the other hand, if productivity increases, but quality lessens, then this change in productivity will not likely be met with customer approval.

A Comparison of Industries

Based on the 1996, year-end results of the ASCI, the 31 industries can be arrayed according to their success in satisfying the American consumer. Table 1.3 presents these industry rankings. The soft drink, food processing, and personal care and cleaning industries topped the list, while restaurants, airlines and newspapers were the lowest rated industries. Comparing 1996 scores to those of 1995, personal property insurance, newspapers, and department stores exhibited the greatest decrease in scores. While 16 of the 31 industries tracked declined from 1995, only three showed improvement; restaurants, gas stations, and cigarettes (the remaining 12 industries lacked 1995 scores with which to form a change score).

Table 1.3   ACSI Scores by Industry

Product Category	1995 Score	1996 Score	% Change from '95
Soft Drinks	86	86	nc
Parcel Delivery—Express Mail	81	85	4.9
Food Processing	84	83	−1.2
Household Appliances	82	82	nc
Consumer Electronics—TV and VCR	81	81	nc
Communications: Long Distance Telephone Service	82	81	−1.2
Personal Care and Cleaning Products	84	80	−4.8
Beer	81	79	−2.5
Automobiles, Vans, and Light Trucks	80	79	−1.3
Apparel: Sportswear/Underwear	81	78	−3.7
Gas-Service Stations	80	77	−3.8
Communications: Local Telephone Services	78	77	−1.3
Cigarettes	82	77	−6.1
Athletic Shoes	79	77	−2.5
Solid Waste Disposal	77	76	−0.7
Utilities—Electric Service	74	75	1.4
Supermarkets	74	75	1.4
Insurance/Auto/Home/Personal Property	76	75	−1.3
Discount Stores/Department Stores	74	75	1.4
Motion Pictures	77	74	−3.9
U.S. Postal Service: Mail Delivery and Delivery Service	69	74	7.2
Life Insurance	75	74	−1.3
Commercial Banks	74	74	nc
Personal Computers	75	73	−2.7
Hotels	73	72	−1.4
Hospitals	74	71	−4.1
Restaurants—Fast Food—Pizza—Carry Out	70	70	nc
Broadcasting-TV (Network News)	76	70	−7.9
Newspapers	68	69	1.5
Airlines	69	69	nc
Local Police	63	61	−2.4
Internal Revenue Service	54	50	−7.4
National Average	**74**	**72.2**	**−2%**

nc = no change

The Multiple Roles of CSM

Information

The primary intention for measuring customer satisfaction is to collect information regarding either what customers report needs to be changed (in a product, service, or delivery system) or to assess how well an organization is currently delivering on its understanding of these needs. This is an *informational* role. As such, marketing research and psychological measurement have much relevance.

The disciplines of marketing research and psychological measurement have been most responsible for much of the progress in CSM made to date. But their perspective is also responsible for some shortcomings as well. Information collection is generally based on the cost-efficient methods of sampling the general base of customers. Findings from a statistically derived sample are then projected to the entire customerbase. The information collected is statistically representative, the technique is very cost efficient. It does, however, overlook the possible *marketing benefits* one might derive from a survey of a broader base of customers.

In general, the research procedures often required to structure and field appropriately designed CSM studies, may also serve as impediments to a survey that not only collects useful information, but also tells customers the organization cares and appreciates their advice.

Communication

It can be effectively argued that the very act of surveying customers conveys a very positive message; the organization is interested in its customers' well-being, needs, pleasures, and displeasures. While this is admittedly a "marketing message," there is nothing wrong, the author would suggest, in allowing a survey to serve both the *informational* and *communication* roles. The consequence of addressing the communication benefits is to require a substantially enlarged sample, maybe to conduct a census! For some organizations with customerbases exceeding one million customers, this will become exponentially more costly. But despite the increased expense, the hundreds of millions of dollars "gambled" in advertising each year dwarf the expense surveying the satisfaction of valued, current customers. To control costs, one could segment (stratify) one's customerbase to identify "heavy users" or one's most profitable customers. If not all customers are shown the respect of a satisfaction survey, hopefully at least the most valuable customers (the heavy users) would be included. The expense of measuring heavy users' satisfaction would be entirely justified by these users' higher than average purchase-volumes.

Is Satisfaction Enough to Keep Customers?

A Necessary But Not Sufficient Condition

Some authors have recently criticized the apparent overemphasis on customer satisfaction by repeating statistics such as the following.

> 60 percent of all defecting customers were either extremely or very satisfied according to CSM data

Several companies (Burke Customer Satisfaction Associates, Marketing Metrics, and so on) have spoken out on the value of measuring other issues besides just satisfaction. Loyalty and advocacy are two dimensions frequently suggested as necessary complements to satisfaction if an organization is to properly anticipate the dynamics of its customerbase.

A Hierarchy of Thresholds

American businesses have always used some element of their product offering as their basic competitive tool. This element has, all too frequently, been price. But when strategists were thinking, other elements have been instituted.

Branding and Quality

As branding first became prevalent, brands served to guarantee customers, who traditionally had experienced a range of quality in commodity products, of uniform quality. Thus Globe flour, one of the first branded packaged goods, guaranteed homemakers of a flour of uniform quality, package to package, shopping expedition to shopping expedition.

Satisfaction and Quality

As branding and brand imagery became the prevalent competitive tools, businesses began to adopt customer satisfaction as the new competitive tool. Demonstrating a focus on customer satisfaction to current customers, and talking satisfaction to potential customers offered a new way to prove the quality of their product or service offerings.

Loyalty: The Next Competitive Element

In the market of the late 1990s even satisfaction scores (in some industries) are reaching parity. It is believed loyalty will be the next competitive tool. But, to achieve loyalty, one must deliver at least *parity quality* (quality equal to that of competitors) and also offer at least as much satisfaction as one's competitors (parity satisfaction). Each of the previous stages are thresholds, once parity is achieved, the customer may seek out the organization, product or brand offering loyalty, the next highest element.

WHOSE RESPONSIBILITY IS CSM?

The Quandary

If there is today, a lack of a uniform effort directed towards satisfaction measurement and improvement, it is most likely because of the uncertainty (and lack of uniformity) of which department or which discipline within the organization is most responsible for customer satisfaction. At least three areas are today active in customer satisfaction measurement and improvement, the quality control school, the marketing school, and the customer service school.

The Quality Control School

This school early on was focused on internal metrics. Typical of this approach was the Bell System's approach to a definition of quality. The Bell System developed a rigorous set of measures defining telephone service quality from the perspective of the network switching engineer and the time and motion specialist. The metrics were continually measured. Unfortunately, the metrics may not have addressed customers' concerns and needs. They often were in direction juxtaposition to the customer's ideal—as in the measurement of the quality of directory assistance service only by how short the call could be made. Also, it is generally accepted that the later-established "TelSam" measurements, which were regularly presented to Public Utility Commissions, tended to be used in more of a defensive posture than out of any attempt to actually learn about customers' satisfactions with the quality of the service offering. Thus internal metrics and goals for these metrics came to represent quality.

But, Deming and his colleagues reminded the quality control school, that it was really the customer who should be defining quality and establishing priorities among the elements of quality—not the operating engineers.

The one shortcoming of this school is that, traditionally coming from an engineering or statistical background, these professionals have not been trained in surveying customers. Thus, when customer input has been desired, it has often been gathered in unscientific methods, or through methods lacking good social psychological guidance.

Even though the chief advocates for the quality control movement (Deming, Juran, and Feigenbaum) all taught the importance of input from customers, there are many instances where the zeal for internal measurements has predominated.

The Marketing School

The discipline of marketing began to understand the importance of satisfaction (in the work of Cardozo, Oliver, Day and Hunt, and others) in the late 1960s and mid-1970s. However, the marketing discipline has seemed more interested in applying its statistical modeling expertise to the prediction of sales and market share based on manipulations of the product, price, promotion, and distribution, than on understanding the impact of satisfaction on repeat purchase behavior, brand loyalty, or profitability. It appears that simply ascertaining satisfaction with a current product was looked down upon as far too trivial a pursuit to merit considerable attention.

Ralph Day of Indiana University and Keith Hunt of BYU became actively associated with the study of satisfaction in the mid-1970s, sponsoring a series of annual conferences on customer satisfaction, commencing in 1977. Although the conferences have been discontinued, a journal has been instituted in their place. The *Journal of Customer Satisfaction/ Dissatisfaction* is an annual publication presenting papers focusing on satisfaction phenomena (Hunt and Day 1988).

Similarly, neither the pioneering study of Cardozo nor Oliver triggered much subsequent research activity, but rather lay nearly dormant until recently. In the late 1980s, the American Marketing Association teamed with the American Society for Quality Control to host an annual conference on customer satisfaction. In the mid-1990s this is reportedly one of the most well-attended professional conferences. Yet, in other conferences of the American Marketing Association—especially the educator's conference, the topic of customer satisfaction is practically nonexistent.

The Marketing Sciences Institute has demonstrated an "on-again, off-again" flirtation with satisfaction having published some very seminal monographs—including an early one edited by Day and Hunt (1977).

But this institution has paradoxically avoided an ongoing commitment to the study of customer satisfaction.

The major opportunity, of course, is to assure that marketing professionals are trained with the appropriate skills to interact with customers and to discover customers' satisfactions and dissatisfactions. However, if marketing participates in the collection and utilization of this information, marketing must be brought closer together with the product-planning expertise of the Quality Control School to be fully integrated in the organization's product or service improvement processes.

The Customer Service School

All the time that Quality Control and Marketing have been separately developing their own perspectives towards customer satisfaction and quality, the rather separate discipline of customer service has been evolving. Starting first in customer service centers, and complaint departments, professionals in this field have probably had the greatest amount of interaction with dissatisfied customers. Unfortunately they have not had entrée into the strategic product or marketing planning areas of organizations. They have, instead, been relegated as tactical, support functions. Ironically, most of these areas are still looked upon as "cost centers" rather than being recognized for the very important work they do in recreating satisfaction and reinstilling loyalty.

There are notable exceptions. The GE AnswerCenter is an example of one corporation's understanding of the value of this function and its importance in nurturing customer satisfaction and loyalty. The motto of the AnswerCenter is, "If we leave a customer with questions or problems, some other manufacturer will answer them."

Professionals engaged in the customer service operation have a considerable potential to offer organizations. They have been trained to productively interact with customers, but often their goal is simply to placate and retain the customer. They must be brought into the movement of information collection so that their interactive skills can be harnessed to collect more complete and rich diagnostic information.

REFERENCES

Brookes, John. *The Telephone's First 100 Years*. New York: Harper & Row, 1976.

Buzzell, Robert D. and Bradley T. Gale. *The PIMS Principles*. New York: The Free Press, 1987.

Cardozo, Richard. "An Experimental Study of Consumer Effort, Expectations and Satisfaction." *Journal of Marketing Research.* 2, no. 3 (August 1965): 244–49.

Churchill, Gilbert A., and Carol Suprenant. "An Investigation into the Determinants of Customer Satisfaction." *Journal of Marketing Research.* 19 (November 1982): 491–504.

Cohen, M. J., and J. M. Cohen. *The Penguin Dictionary of Modern Quotations.* 2d ed. London: Penguin Books, 1980.

Deming, W. Edwards. *Out of the Crisis.* Cambridge, MA: Massachusetts Institute of Technology, Center for Advanced Engineering Study, 1986.

Day, Ralph L. "Toward a Process Model of Consumer Satisfaction." In *Conceptualization and Measurement of Consumer Satisfaction and Dissatisfaction.* Hunt, H. Keith, (ed.) Cambridge, MA: Marketing Science Institute, 1977.

Eastman Kodak Company. *Keeping the Customer Satisfied: A Guide to Field Service.* Milwaukee: ASQC Quality Press, 1989.

Engle, James F., and Roger D. Blackwell. *Consumer Behavior.* New York: Holt, Rinehart and Winston, 1982.

Fay, Christopher. "Royalties from Loyalties." *Journal of Business Strategy.* 15, no. 2 (March/April 1994): 47–51.

Fierman, Jaclyn. "Americans Can't Get No Satisfaction." *Fortune.* (December 11, 1995): 186–193.

Fornell, Claes, and Birger Wernerfelt. "Defensive Marketing Strategy by Customer Complaint Management: A Theoretical Analysis." *Journal of Marketing Research.* 24, no. 4 (November 1987): 337–46.

Gieszl, Yale. EVP Toyota Motor Sales, USA, Chairman of the Customer Satisfaction Committee.

Goodman, John A. and Dianne S. Ward. "The Importance of Customer Satisfaction." *Direct Marketing.* (December 1993): 23–26.

Hauser, John R. and Don Clausing. "The House of Quality." *Harvard Business Review.* (May–June 1988): 63–73.

Hildebrand, Carol. "Service Stars." *CIO Magazine.* (August 1995): 90–96.

Honomichl, Jack, private communication, 1996.

Howard, John and Jagdish Sheth. *The Theory of Buyer Behavior.* New York: John Wiley and Sons, Inc., 1969.

Hunt, Keith H. "CS/D—Overview and Future Research Direction." In *Conceptualization and Measurement of Consumer Satisfaction and Dissatisfaction.* Hunt, Keith H. (ed.) Cambridge, MA: Marketing Science Institute, 1977.

Hunt, H. Keith, and Ralph L. Day. (coeditors) *The Journal of Customer Satisfaction/Dissatisfaction.* Provo, UT: Consumer Satisfaction, Dissatisfaction and Complaining Behavior, Inc.

Juran , Joseph M. *Juran on Planning for Quality.* New York: The Free Press, 1988.

Juran, Joseph M. "Made in USA: A Renaissance of Quality." *Harvard Business Review.* (July/August 1993): 42–50.

Kotler, Philip. *Managerial Marketing, Planning, Analysis, and Control.* Englewood Cliffs, NJ: Prentice-Hall Inc., 1967.

Levitt, Ted. *The Marketing Imagination.* New York: The Free Press, 1985.

Marketing Metrics. "A Survey of Retention Marketing Use and Tactics." Paramus, New Jersey, 1995.

McCarthy, E. Jerome, and William D. Perreault. *Basic Marketing: A Managerial Approach.* Homewood, IL: Richard D. Irwin, 1960.

Mentzer, John T., Carol C. Bienstock, and Kenneth B. Kahn. "Benchmarking Satisfaction: Market Leaders Use Sophisticated Processes to Measure and Manage Their Customers' Perceptions." *Marketing Management.* 4, no. 1, (Summer 1995): 41–46.

Nadkarni, R. A. "A Not So Secret Recipe for Successful TQM. *Quality Progress.* (November 1995): 91–96.

Oliver, Richard L. "Measurement and Evaluation of Satisfaction Process in Retail Setting." *Journal of Retailing.* 57 (Fall 1981): 25–48.

Pfaff, Anita B. "An Index of Consumer Satisfaction." in *Proceedings of the Third Annual Conference.* Association for Consumer Research (November 1973): 713–37.

Philips, S., A. Dunkin, J. Treece, and K. Hammonds. "King Customer." *Businessweek.* (March 12, 1990): 88–94.

Reichheld, Frederick F. and W. Earl Jr. Sasser. "Zero Defections: Quality Comes to Service." *Harvard Business Review.* (September-October 1990): 105–111.

Rolls-Royce, Company records, Crewe, England, 1906.

Rust, Roland T., and Anthony J. Zahorik. "Customer Satisfaction, Customer Retention and Market Share." *Journal of Retailing.* 69, no. 2 (Summer 1993): 193–215.

Scheslinger, L. A., and J. L. Heskitt. "Breaking the Cycle of Failure in Services." *Sloan Management Review.* (Spring 1991): 17–28.

Technical Assistance Research Programs (TARP). *Consumer Complaint Handling in America: An Updated Study.* Washington, D.C.: The Office of the Special Adviser to the President for Consumer Affairs, 1986.

Tse, David K., and Peter C. Wilton. "Models of Consumer Satisfaction: An Extension." *Journal of Marketing Research.* 25, no. 2 (May 1988): 204–12.

Vandermerwe, Sandra. "Quality in Services: The 'Softer' Side is 'Harder' (and Smarter)." *Long Range Planning.* 27, no. 2 (April 1994): 45–56.

Westbrook, Robert A., and Michael D. Reilly. "Value-Percept Disparity: An Alternative to the Disconfirmation of Expectations Theory of Consumer Satisfaction." In *Advances in Consumer Research.* Richard P. Bagozzi, and Alice M. Tybout (eds.) Ann Arbor, MI: Association for Consumer Research, 1983, pp. 256–61.

Yi, Youjae. "A Critical Review of Consumer Satisfaction." in Zeithaml, Valerie (ed.) *Review of Marketing 1989.* Chicago: American Marketing Association, 1991.

APPENDIX TO CHAPTER 1:
A MODEL OF SATISFACTION

Satisfaction has been broadly defined as a satisfactory postpurchase *experience* with a product or service given an existing prepurchase *expectation*. To extend our understanding of the exact relationships preceding and following the formation of satisfaction, a model of satisfaction can be extremely helpful. Considering this value, it is surprising to find that few books on customer satisfaction actually present such a model! There is certainly no lack of models available for adoption; the theoretical literature offers a plentiful array. Perhaps other texts have been reluctant to present a satisfaction model that later may be supplanted by an improved version, or may fall into disfavor.

Despite the risk, the advantages of offering a model appear to outweigh the disadvantages. A model is an ideal way to identify key constructs of satisfaction and to speculate on the interrelationships of the constructs measured. Further, without a model, data collection can be incomplete, and analysis directed more by intuition than driven by hypothesized relationships. Consequently this book offers the satisfaction model depicted in Figure 1A.1. A majority of satisfaction models have Oliver's 1980 model as their primary influence (Oliver 1980). Our model also follows Oliver's. It utilizes the familiar "disconfirmation paradigm" established by Oliver (1980) and further advanced by Churchill and Suprenant (1982), which has become the core of so many later models.[3]

Our model is divided into three stages: antecedents, the satisfaction-formation process, and consequences. In both the antecedents and consequences stages certain mediators are also identified. While these may be implicit in other models, it is believed that explicitly recognizing them has special value for the practical assessment and interpretation of satisfaction scores. Specifically their existence should help to identify other measures or information, which should be collected during the measurement of satisfaction.

Antecedents

Prior experience is the most important antecedent of satisfaction. It serves as a "memory bank" of all of the previous experiences with a product or service. It is unlikely this experience is isolated from experiences with comparable products or services. On the contrary, it is probably highly comparative, most likely storing information on a relative basis.

It is reasonable to identify a number of factors that may temper or enhance **prior experience.** These influences, described in the box to the left of prior experience, are divided into *personal influencers* and *situational influencers.* The personal influencers have to do with characteristics of customers, most notably **demographics** (age, income, education, and so on) and with **personal expertise** or competency. (These suggest the value of segmenting customers at some time during the evaluation of ratings, since customers of similar demographics may be inclined to rate organizations in a similar fashion.) Reinforcement or contradiction from peers **(word of mouth)** is also advanced as a personal influencer, capable of modifying **prior experience.**

We often muse over differences for which personal influencers may be responsible. Rarely do we have substantial data to confirm our speculations.

----

[3]Oliver has further developed his original ideas in a 1997 book, *Satisfaction: A Behavioral Perspective on the Consumer.* This book provides an excellent resource for a complete understanding of the various components of the satisfaction model forwarded by Oliver and others.

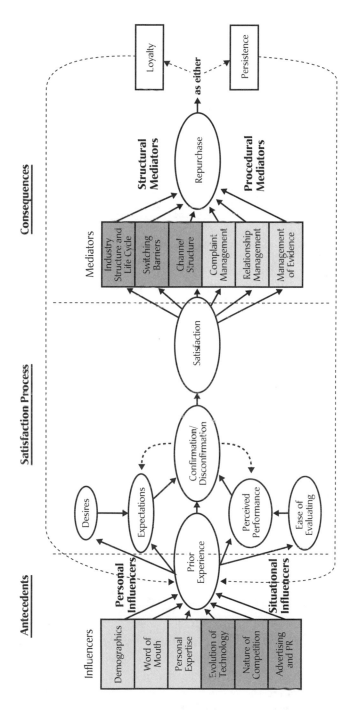

Figure 1A.1 A Model of Customer Satisfaction

Table 1A.1   Satisfaction Ratings by Age and Gender

	Gender	
Age Group	*Female*	*Male*
18–34	77	73
35–54	78	74
55 and over	84	80

Source: A special tabulation of ACSI data reported in Bryant, Barbara Everitt, and Cha, Jaesung, "Crossing the Threshold: Some Customers Are Harder to Please Than Others, So Analyze Satisfaction Scores Carefully," *Marketing Research,* (Winter 1996), 1996, pp. 21–28.

Table 1A.2   Satisfaction Ratings by Sector and Socioeconomic Status

	Socioeconomic Status		
Industrial Sector	*Lower*	*Middle*	*Higher*
ACSI–national average	83	78	75
Manufacturing–Nondurables	86	83	79
Manufacturing–Durables	84	81	80
Transportation/Communications/Utilities	83	77	72
Retail	79	74	69
Finance/Insurance	82	74	70
Services	80	76	74
Government/Public Administration	67	66	64

Source: A special tabulation of ACSI data reported in Bryant, Barbara Everitt, and Cha, Jaesung, "Crossing the Threshold: Some Customers Are Harder to Please Than Others, So Analyze Satisfaction Scores Carefully," *Marketing Research,* (Winter 1996), pp. 21–28.

A special tabulation of the ACSI database has just produced a fascinating insight into the existence of some of these demographic mediators and the size of their impact (Bryant and Cha 1996). Significant differences were documented for gender, age, socioeconomic status and area of residence (metro, nonmetro). Table 1A.1 shows how gender and age combine to produce even greater differences in satisfaction ratings than either one individually. Young men tend to be the most difficult to satisfy, while women over 55 years are the easiest. Socioeconomic status and industrial sector also interact dramatically. In Table 1A.2 it can be seen that while manufacturing nondurables achieves the highest overall satisfaction ratings, high socioeconomic customers are less satisfied, as they are across all sectors.

Situational influencers include the **evolution of technology** in the category, the intensity and **nature of competition** in the category and **advertising and public relations** activity. Each of these factors, it is believed, will similarly enhance or diminish a customer's **prior experience.**

The Satisfaction Process

As was suggested at the beginning of this section, the process of formulating satisfaction encapsulates a comparison of expectations with perceived performance.

Expectations

Olson and Dover (1979) defined expectations as

> beliefs about a product or service's attributes or preference at some time in the future.

Yi (1991) identifies two basic conceptualizations of expectations. One version, a more global perspective, has to do with an institutional perspective,

> Preconsumption beliefs about the overall performance of the product/service created by: previous experience; the organization's claims; product information; or word of mouth.

The other major view of **expectations** has more to do with a process internal to the customer, and is more "componential." Here, **expectations** are defined as the sum of beliefs about the levels of attributes possessed or offered by the product or service. Oliver and Bearden (1983) have observed, however, that there likely are two components of expectation: the *level* of performance expected, and the *certainty* of receiving that level of performance. Oliver and Bearden proposed operationalizing these components in a fashion similar to the "value-expectancy attitude model" of Fishbein (1975).[4]

Expectations are influenced by **prior experience.** It is believed that as **prior experience** becomes more and more satisfying, **expectations** for

----

[4]Fishbein's "value-expectancy" model of attitudes suggests weighting the importance (value) of each characteristic of an attitude object by the perceived likelihood of the object delivering each characteristic (Fishbein and Aijzen 1975).

future performance are adjusted ever higher. This is frequently referred to as "raising the hurdle" and is paradoxically why satisfying customers never becomes easier.

It is interesting to note how few satisfaction surveys actually avail themselves of a measure of **expectation.** Of forty customer satisfaction surveys collected and published by the Society of Consumer Affairs Professionals (1996) only *two* contain questions or tasks to assess expectations or link satisfaction appraisal to expectations.

Differences Between Expectations and Desires

Oliver's "componential definition" of expectations was described as:

> Expectations have two components: a probability of occurrence (for example the likelihood that a clerk will be available to wait on customers) and an evaluation of the occurrence (for example the degree to which the clerk's attention is desirable or undesirable, good or bad, and so on). Both are necessary because it is not at all clear that some attributes (attentive clerks, in our example) are desired by all shoppers (Oliver 1981, 33).

Spreng et al (1996) question the operational value of this definition observing that it can confound a customer's valuation of an event with his judgment of the likelihood of the event occurring. Thus, two customers of a store with identical judgments of the availability of sales clerks to assist shoppers, might produce different expectation scores, because one customer desired a salesclerk to approach him immediately upon entering the store, while the other customer preferred to be left alone until he requested help.

Spreng et al suggest decomposing the traditional expectations measure into two measures (1) **predictive expectations:** beliefs about the likelihood that attributes, benefits, or outcomes are associated with a product or service, and (2) **desires:** evaluations of the desirability of an attribute, benefit, or outcome, that is the extent to which the attribute, benefit, or outcome leads to the attainment of the customer's values.

In this view, expectations are future-oriented and are considered malleable. In contrast, **desires** are described as present-oriented and relatively stable. In a test of these constructs, Spreng et al found them to be empirically distinct. Secondly, they were found to have different effects on satisfaction; expectations had both positive and negative effects, while desires had only negative effects. In our model we adopt the concept of **desires,** as an influence on the formation of **expectations.**

Performance

The other component of the confirmation/disconfirmation comparison involves the **performance** of the product or service. There are two types of performance: objective and perceived. Objective performance, conformance to the specifications of design, is not easily operationalized because perceptions of performance undoubtedly vary across customers. **Perceived performance** on the other hand (the customer's recognition of performance) is the most easily measured.

Performance is also conditioned by prior experience. It may be that prior experience helps to make more salient certain aspects of a product's or service's performance. Impinging on judgments of performance is the **ease of evaluating** the actual performance of the product or service.

Ease of Evaluation

Anderson and Sullivan (1993) advance the ease of evaluating performance as a major influence in the determination of satisfaction. When performance of a product or service is more difficult for customers to evaluate, they suggest perceived performance will be assimilated *toward* expectations. In situations in which performance is more easily judged, they suggest perceived performance may be contrasted *against* expectations. More should be said about these hypotheses, but for the moment suffice the observation that not all products' and services' performances are evaluated with equal ease.[5]

Importance

One surprise to many satisfaction professionals should be the absence of any measure of importance in the formal satisfaction model. While importance is often an unchallenged component of many satisfaction surveys, it has no theoretical foundation for being included in the process.

The institution of importance undoubtedly has its roots in marketing research discipline. Characteristically marketing researchers would derive some prioritization of the performance attributes to identify which

----

[5]Customers' evaluation of the performance of a product or service is facilitated by the *management of evidence,* an activity few organizations engage in or conduct properly. Managing evidence means to supply customers with ample information about how the product or service has served them, and the many benefits delivered. Properly managing evidence relates to customers' use of the "value equation" and the benefits they understand a product or service has delivered versus its cost. The better evidence has been managed, the more benefits the customer is likely to perceive.

ones should be attended to first. As such the importance measure becomes a useful way of acting on the results of a satisfaction survey, but it does not substantively contribute to the formulation of satisfaction.

Confirmation/Affirmation/Disconfirmation

The heart of the satisfaction process is the comparison of what was expected with the product or service's performance. This process has traditionally been described as the **"confirmation/disconfirmation** process." Oliver (1980) was the first to suggest that expectations serve as a baseline or frame of reference against which customers' experiences are measured. Oliver described a three-step process. First, customers would form expectations prior to purchasing a product or service. Second, consumption of or experience with the product or service produces a level of perceived quality that is influenced by expectations. (If perceived performance is only slightly less than expected performance, assimilation will occur, perceived performance will be adjusted upward to equal expectations. If perceived performance lags expectations substantially, contrast will occur, and the shortfall in the perceived performance will be exaggerated.)

Perceived performance may either reinforce, exceed, or fall short of expectations. If expectations are in any way not met, rendered satisfaction decreases from the baseline level established by expectations. If, on the other hand, expectations are met or exceeded, satisfaction increases and expectations in future purchases/uses may be adjusted upward.

In describing the confirmation/disconfirmation process, "disconfirmation" has been used to describe both cases in which performance exceeds expectations as well as those in which performance falls short of expectations. This unfortunate use of the term "positive disconfirmation" to describe the situation in which experiences actually exceed expectations, seems, at best, confusing and may even create a misunderstanding of the workings of the model. We will adopt the logic of "affirmed" "confirmed," and "disconfirmed." The implicit logic is that satisfaction is related to the size and directionality of the "disconfirmation" of experience, that is:

- expectations will be considered as *confirmed* when perceived performance *meets* them;
- expectations will be considered *affirmed* (reinforced by positive disconfirmation) when perceived performance *exceeds* them;
- expectations will be considered *disconfirmed* (failed by negative disconfirmation) when perceived performance *falls short* of them.

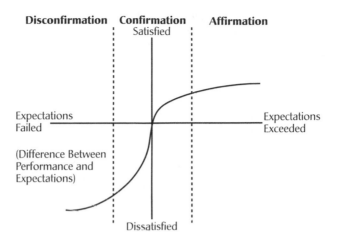

Figure 1A.2   The Satisfaction Function

Adapted from: Anderson, Eugene W., and Sullivan, Mary W., "The Antecedents and Consequences of CLustomer Satisfaction for Firms," *Marketing Science,* Spring 1993, p. 129.

The confirmation/disconfirmation process feeds back both to expectations and perceived performance (indicated by dashed lines in Figure 1A.1). The effect on expectation is to raise or lower future expectations. The effect on perceived performance may be qualitative. Affirmation or disconfirmation may selectively direct the customer's future performance judgments to focus on certain elements or aspects of the product or service in judging performance.

The Satisfaction Function

The behavior of satisfaction as a phenomena can be better understood if it is visualized as a function. Anderson and Sullivan (1993) plot satisfaction's response to the difference between perceived quality and expectation as a response function. Figure 1A.2 depicts the satisfaction function. As perceived performance exceeds expectations, satisfaction increases, but at a decreasing rate. As perceived performance falls short of expectations, Anderson and Sullivan utilize an asymmetric loss function to show that satisfaction will be more responsive to disconfirmation (negative disconfirmation) than to affirmation (positive disconfirmation).

The shape of the resulting satisfaction function is substantiated by much empirical evidence; for example the nature of word-of-mouth. Dissatisfaction produces far more negative word-of-mouth activity than satisfaction produces in positive word-of-mouth activity (TARP various).

The shape of the curve also makes clear the value to organizations in preventing dissatisfaction among their customers.

Consequences

Satisfaction is an intermediate construct perhaps instituted by the TQM community as a criterion measure of their desire to create, manufacture, and deliver those products and services which produce a maximum amount of satisfaction for target customers. But satisfaction is a temporal and imperfect measure. Organizations today are interested in maximizing customer retention and loyalty. But not all those who are satisfied, or those who repurchase will be loyal. The consequences of satisfaction are indeterminant. There is ample proof that satisfied customers are not always the most loyal customers (and vice versa). The behavioral consequence of customer retention is at best an intermediate sign that we have not immediately alienated a customer.

In our model, between satisfaction and repurchase we have identified an additional set of mediators, composed of *structural mediators* and *procedural mediators*. Structural mediators include the industry structure and life cycle, the switching barriers, and the channel structure. Each of these structural forces is posited to mediate the level of satisfaction. For example, a customer may be quite unhappy with a product or service experience, but if there are few or no competitors in the category, the customer is likely to be "retained" (that is, she will continue to conduct business with the organization until a reasonable alternate source of supply becomes available). Similarly a very satisfied customer will continue to buy even though the channel member supplying him is quite inefficient and unpleasant to do business with. Young industries, no doubt, are more effective at retaining even moderately dissatisfied customers simply because of the early dependence established between producers and customers in new categories. All of these situations are frequently referred to as the "customer as hostage" scenario.

Procedural mediators deal less with structure (hardware) and more with the "software" of industry business. A customer who is only moderately satisfied may repurchase in the short run because of a very talented marketing manager (or intermediary) who has established and continues to maintain a good relationship with the customer. Conversely, a satisfied customer may be dislodged because of a poor compliant management process.

Frequently Invoked Theories

As research into customer satisfaction has evolved, several different psychological theories have been applied to the relationship between expectation, perceived performance, confirmation/disconfirmation, and resulting satisfaction. Five theories from social psychology have been used most frequently. These theories' consequences for satisfaction are summarized in Table 1A.3.

Assimilation-Contrast Theory

In logic related to Sherif's Law of Social Judgment, there would supposedly exist "latitudes" (ranges) of acceptable performance, performance to which one might be "indifferent" and performance that would be rejected as unacceptable; all these ranges arrayed around the customer's actual level of expectation. (These latitudes vary in width depending upon the individual customer's involvement with the product and product category.) Assimilation-Contrast Theory suggests that if performance is within a customer's latitude (range) of acceptance, even though it may fall short of expectation, the discrepancy will be disregarded—assimilation will operate and the performance will be deemed as acceptable. If performance falls within the latitude of rejection (no matter how close to expectation), contrast will prevail and the difference will be exaggerated, the product deemed unacceptable.

Contrast Theory

This is a black or white view of the world. According to contrast theory, any discrepancy of experience from expectations will be exaggerated in the direction of the discrepancy. If a manufacturer raises expectations in his advertising for a product, and then a customer's experience is only slightly less than that promised, the product will be rejected as totally unsatisfactory. Conversely, underpromising in advertising and overdelivering will cause the positive disconfirmation also to be exaggerated.

Dissonance Theory

A decidedly different outcome is offered by applying Festinger's Theory of Cognitive Dissonance. Applying Festinger's ideas to affirmation and disconfirmation of expectation in satisfaction work, one concludes that customers might try to eliminate any dissonant experiences (situations in

Table 1A.3 Theories of Expectation-Disconfirmation in Customer Satisfaction

Theory	Product/Service Experience	Effect on Perceived Product Service Performance	Moderating Conditions	Effect
Contrast	positive confirmation negative disconfirmation	perceived performance enhanced perceived performance lowered		
Assimilation/ Contrast	small confirmation or disconfirmation	perceived performance assimilated toward expectations		
	large confirmation or disconfirmation	perceived performance contrasted against expectations	purchase is ego-involved	performance differences exaggerated
Dissonance	negative disconfirmation	perceived performance modified to fit with expectations	purchase made under conditions of ambiguity	less modification
Generalized Negativity	either confirmation or disconfirmation	perceived product performance lowered	purchase is ego involved, high commitment and interest	more modification
Hypothesis Testing	either confirmation or disconfirmation	perceived performance modified to fit expectations	purchase made under conditions of ambiguity	more modification

Adapted from: Yi, Youjae, "A Critical Review of Consumer Satisfaction," in Zeithaml, Valerie (ed). *Review of Marketing 1989*, Chicago: American Marketing Association, 1991.

which they have committed to an apparently inferior product or service) (Festinger 1957). Dissonance theory would predict that a customer experiencing lower performance than expected, if psychologically invested in the product or service, would mentally work to minimize the discrepancy. This may be done either by lowering expectations (after the fact) or, in the case of subjective disconfirmation, positively increasing the perception of performance.

Negativity Theory

This theory developed by Carlsmith and Aronson (1963) suggests that any discrepancy of performance from expectations will disrupt the individual, producing "negative energy." Affective feelings toward a product or service will be inversely related to the magnitude of the discrepancy.

Hypothesis Testing Theory

Deighton (1983) suggested a two-step model for satisfaction generation. First, Deighton hypothesizes, prepurchase information (largely advertising) plays a substantial role in creating expectations about the products customers will acquire and use. Customers use their experience with products (the product's performance) to *test* their expectations. Second, Deighton believes, customers will tend to *attempt to confirm* (rather than disconfirm) their expectations. This theory suggests customers are biased to positively confirm their product experiences. This is an admittedly optimistic view of customers, but it makes the *management of evidence* an extremely important marketing tool.[6]

REFERENCES

Anderson, Eugene W., and Mary W. Sullivan. "The Antecedents and Consequences of Customer Satisfaction for Firms." *Marketing Science.* (Spring 1993): 125–43.

Bryant, Barbara Everitt, and Jaesung Cha. "Crossing the Threshold: Some Customers Are Harder to Please Than Others, So Analyze

----

[6]See Vavra, Terry G., *Aftermarketing: How to Keep Customers for Life Through Relationship Marketing*, Burr Ridge, IL: Irwin Professional Publishing, 1995, for a complete description of the "management of evidence."

Satisfaction Scores Carefully." *Marketing Research.* (Winter 1996): 21–28.

Carlsmith, J. Merril, and Elliot Aronson. "Some Hedonic Consequences of the Confirmation and Disconfirmation of Expectancies." *Journal of Abnormal and Social Psychology.* (February 1989), 66: 151–56.

Churchill, Gilbert A., and Carol Suprenant. "An Investigation into the Determinants of Customer Satisfaction." *Journal of Marketing Research.* 19, (November 1982): 491–504.

Deighton, John. "The Interaction of Advertising and Evidence." *Journal of Consumer Research.* (December 1984), 11: 763–70.

Festinger, Leon. *A Theory of Cognitive Dissonance.* Stanford, CA: Stanford University Press, 1957.

Fishbein, Martin, and Icek Aijzen. *Belief, Attitude, Intention and Behavior.* Reading, MA: Addison-Wesley Publishing Company, 1975.

Helson, Harry. *Adaptation-level Theory.* New York: Harper & Row, 1964.

Oliver, Richard L. *Satisfaction: A Behavioral Perspective on the Consumer.* New York: The McGraw-Hill Companies, Inc., 1997.

Oliver, Richard L. "A Cognitive Model of the Antecedents and Consequences of Satisfaction Decisions," *Journal of Marketing Research.* 17, (November 1980): 460–69.

Olson, Jerry C. and Phillip Dover. "Disconfirmation of Consumer Expectation Through Product Trail." *Journal of Applied Psychology.* 64 (April 1979): 179–89.

Society of Consumer Affairs Professionals in Business. *Customer Satisfaction Survey Collection.* Bashem, M. Lauren, (ed.) Arlington, VA, SOCAP, 1996.

Spreng, Richard A., Scott B. MacKenzie, and Richard W. Olshavsky. "A Reexamination of the Determinants of Consumer Satisfaction." *Journal of Marketing.* 60, no. 3 (July 1996): 15–31.

TARP (Technical Assistance Research Programs), Alexandria, VA.

Yi, Youjae. "A Critical Review of Consumer Satisfaction." In Zeithaml, Valerie (ed.) *Review of Marketing 1989.* Chicago: American Marketing Association, 1991.

DISCOVERY: IDENTIFYING THE ISSUES TO BE MEASURED

One of the breakthrough insights in assessing customer satisfaction was the understanding that quality (as delivered in our products and services) *is not an objective thing* to be measured by conformance to engineering or design specifications. Rather, that quality (a primary determinant of satisfaction) is, frustrating as it may be to engineers and technicians, *a very subjective concept*, depending substantially on individually-derived cues and other soft data.

So the first learning for a satisfaction professional, is to never assume he or she knows eactly what the customer is looking for, or how the customer defines quality The customer's entire decision, purchase, use, and repurchase cycle ought to be investigated for every bit of insight it can give the professional concerning customers' concerns and requirements.

The Discovey phase is the time to listen to and investigate all sides of the company-customer interaction. Management's vision and assumptions should be explicated as well as competitors' apparent targets and goals.

issue Discovery

Chapter 2
Chapter 3

CHAPTER 2

Gaining Access to Customers

OVERVIEW

As an organization makes the decision to measure the satisfaction of its customers, there may be no serious thought given to the availability (or lack of availability) of anything so mundane as the identity of customers. If the topic comes up at all, it is probably assumed there is a usable customerbase. The incorrectness of this assumption commonly surprises everyone, from the chairperson or president to the managers and front-line staff. Sadly most organizations today lack a good description of who their customers are.

So, the unfortunate reality is that most organizations face considerable up-front work to *simply identify* who should be included in their measurement program! This identification process will take time, require resources and require the assistance of several internal departments. If it is not tackled, survey results collected only from those customers who are known will most certainly be biased, and quite possibly could be totally wrong.

In this chapter we will examine ways not only of identifying customers, but how to correctly organize the database (or customerbase) once customers are identified.

THE IMPORTANCE OF A CUSTOMERBASE

When the decision to measure customers' satisfaction is made, knowing exactly *who* an organization's customers are takes on very special significance. It may always have been assumed that someone, somewhere in the organization actually knew who all of the customers were. It is amazing to find how few companies really have a good fix on exactly who their customers are. From the local telephone company to the national appliance manufacturer to the neighborhood supermarket and the regional department store, few know their customers as well as they should. Some have embarrassingly little information. For example, a major telecommunications company did not even know the names of the telecommunications managers of its 100 most important accounts in a major metropolitan area! Or in another case, a computer manufacturer did not know the name of the Director of Computer Services at a major customer who had just ordered 1,000 of its PCs!

It is essential that all customers are known so that, if a sample is to be drawn, it can be as statistically random a sample as possible. Remember, for a sample to be considered random and not biased, every customer must stand an equal chance of being selected for participation. An equal chance of being selected requires that every customer's identity be known.

The determination to routinely measure customer satisfaction creates a new urgency for learning customers' identities, which probably should have been felt (or desired) all along. The poor condition or absence of a customer database places an added burden on the individual or department committed to measuring satisfaction. Now a second project must be established alongside the project of creating the satisfaction survey. An accurate customer database must be designed and built as well.

Creating a customer database requires a whole new set of skills. You will want to find a professional who is skilled in this special field. You will also want to spend some time considering exactly what information you will need or want to store. This includes both classificatory information about the customer (annual purchases, types of products/services purchased, special requirements/needs, and so on) as well as the opportunity to retain information collected in each wave of your future survey.

Where to Look for Customers' Names

Customers' names probably exist in several different areas within today's business organization. Oftentimes, the names are easily accessed through account or purchasing records. But other times, an extra effort will be needed to gain access to the names of the company's most valuable asset—current customers.

An Internal Customer Registration Process

There may be a customer registration process that is currently in place. When a manufacturer lacks the opportunity to interact directly with its customers, there may be a desire to identify as many end users as possible. Many consumer appliance and electronic components manufacturers have adopted the practice of packing CRFs (customer registration forms) with their products. This has become a relatively standard practice in the personal computer industry where there is the possibility of cross-selling another of the manufacturer's components.

If a CRF program exists, the names of those customers returning the registration forms may have been entered into a computer file. Unfortunately, it is just as likely nothing will have been done with returned forms and the information they contain. The author continues to find storage boxes filled with returned CRFs at many companies with whom he consults. It never ceases to amaze one how little attention is given to these forms. Though they may have been lovingly filled in by dutifully complying consumers, though they may contain praise or pleas for help, these forms are callously deposited in storage awaiting the day when someone in the organization directs some time, some attention, or some resources their way.

All too frequently a customer registration program is instituted without anyone having answered the question, "What will we do with the information once we collect it?" And seldom does anyone consider the costs of entering the data into computer files, or the costs of storing and maintaining it. It is simply collected because someone (rightfully) believes it *should* be collected.

Though registration forms have typically been returned by mail, recent technological innovations have offered several new methods for response. Consider those methods described in Table 2.1. If you are considering instituting some form of customer registration process, explore all of the opportunities available to you. Try to pick one that is most convenient for your customers and is the most reliable in returning data to you, with minimal errors and with quick turnaround.

Table 2.1   Methods for Customer Registration

Medium	Advantages	Disadvantages
Mail response form	• Low upfront investment • Accessible to all HHs and businesses	• Overused • Traditional lack of benefits to the customer now results in lower response rate • No confirmation—suspicion the card is not read or retained • Cost of manual data entry
Telephone keypad entry	• Accessible to 70% + of HHs and 100% of businesses • Sense of immediacy	• Lack of readout makes the quality of the data suspect • Customers will be unwilling to enter more than limited data
Telephone AVR	• Accessible to all HHs and businesses • Sense of immediacy	• Inflexible • Creates impersonal image for company • Fear that the organization may turn the contact into sales call
Fax	• Sense of immediacy • Low upfront investment	• (For consumer products) low penetration of fax machines • Cost of manual data entry
Mail back computer diskette	• Ability to modify questions and question sequence based upon information as it is provided	• Limited to customers with computers and who are computer literate
Computer by modem	• Sense of immediacy • (For computer software and hardware products) can be as simple as pressing a few keys for data and a single key to transmit	• (For consumer products) relatively low penetration and usage of computer modems
Computer through Internet	• Sense of immediacy • Relatively low long-term cost for marketer	• (For consumer products) relatively low penetration and usage of modems and internet. • (Though fairly insignificant) customer must pay for Internet access

As you review any registration processes already in place, you may wish to judge the adequacy of the methodology using the following suggested criteria:

1. speed with which the registration information can be received;
2. quality appearance of the process to the customer;
3. ability to generate cooperation (response);
4. cost efficiency;
5. ability to collect quality (error free) information;
6. ease of use, respect for customers' time;
7. applicability across cultures; doesn't violate cultural sensitivities;
8. protects volunteered information, respecting customers' privacy.

The Accounting Department

The accounting department's accounts receivable file probably has a fairly accurate collection of current customers who pay by credit. But consider the possible contents of the *name field* in this file. If the database is a business-to-business database the name field probably simply reads "Accounts Payable." If there is an actual name, chances are it is someone in the customer's accounting department, *not* the decision maker. For consumer-oriented businesses a name probably exists in the database name field, but is the name the household *decision maker* or simply the household *bill-payer?* On the consumer side, there is probably one or at most two decision makers per household, but on the industrial, business side there can be many decision makers and influencers. All of these individuals should be identified and be given consideration as participants in any customer satisfaction survey.

It is also questionable how long customers' names remain on Accounting's list. If this list will be a major input for your customer database, it is desirable to find out exactly how long past or lapsed customers' names remain on the list. When are names deleted? Are past customers' names transferred to another database? If so, both databases (current and lapsed) should be merged (and purged to eliminate duplicates) to create the customerbase from which your customer satisfaction survey will be conducted.

Customer Service

Customer service departments are quite busy these days responding to customers' communications, predominantly phone calls, but some by mail and a few from the Internet as well. These departments have the opportunity to record the identities of customers who contact the organization. Occasionally, but certainly not routinely, the customer's name, address, and phone number will be captured. Sometimes customer service departments will store this information, but sometimes—for reasons as pragmatic as cost or as shortsighted as a lack of appreciation of the value of the information—they will discard the identities of the customers who have contacted the organization.

Ideally, customer service centers should maintain databases of all those customers contacting the firm. The issue the customer voiced an opinion about, and the nature of this opinion (complaint or compliment) should also be recorded. These names, addresses, and issues can later be appended to or merged with the main customerbase. If the information is merged, the source of the names (customer service) should always be noted. These customers may represent the "vocal minority" of the organization's customer franchise. As such they probably deserve to be treated somewhat differently.

Sales Promotion Area

As organizations utilize sales promotions, they will often collect the names and addresses of customers responding to a premium offer or participating in a contest or redeeming a coupon. While the sales promotion area will normally not budget for data entry of this information, it becomes a possible source for some additional customer names and addresses. If such information exists, it should be considered as another source of customers' names. It would, naturally, need to be merged and purged against other sources of names. Among other consumer packaged goods manufacturers pursuing this opportunity, Seagram maintains a worldwide database of customers who have responded to offers or events (Curtis 1996).

Branch Offices

Frequently branch offices, because of their proximity to customers, or because salespeople working out of these locations actually call on customers, will have small files of customer information for their local customers. This information is usually very rich in the details that may be known about the customer, however, two problems exist. The data may be informally collected and stored, and therefore costly to add to the main database. Also, there may be some question of ownership. Quite often salespeople believe customers to be *their* property. Consider the customer databases of any high-end cosmetics company. The names and addresses of customers are always routinely collected and stored by the commissioned salespeople at department store counters. Unfortunately when the salespeople leave to change jobs, they often take the files with them! Though the manufacturer's product is clearly why the customer came to a store and purchased a product, these employees have been allowed to maintain a stranglehold over this very valuable information!

Where no formal customerbase exists, it may be tempting to ask salespeople to submit the names of their customers. This method, however, is fraught with problems. The sample generated can not help but be biased. Undoubtedly salespeople will in some way screen the names of those customers they offer up. It is unlikely they will submit the names of any customer whom they know to be less than totally satisfied.

Point of Contact

Sometimes customers are asked to identify themselves by filling out forms available in offices, showrooms, on planes, in hotel rooms, and so on. These programs are also likely to produce biased samples since they rely on customers' own personal interests to submit their names. These programs generally attract only the attention of "motivated" customers—those who are exceptionally satisfied or dissatisfied.

External Firms/Suppliers

One process for establishing a customer database that is often accepted, concerns an outside database vendor. There are several nationally syndicated companies in the business of building customer databases for manufacturers. These vendors have offered manufacturers a virtually free data entry service. Customer registration forms (CRFs) packed with manufacturers' products are directed to one of these vendors by carrying their address. The vendor offers to upload the customer data to a computer file, free of charge! This means a manufacturer can begin to build a customer database without any major investment. It seems very attractive, but several unfortunate consequences accompany this method.

1. These syndicated services have relied on a standard questionnaire format, which requests much more information than just the customer's name. Because they are intended for a broad base of customers, many of these questions may be irrelevant to the product and the product category of any one manufacturer and, as such, may aggravate the manufacturer's customers. (The battery of questions is an activities and interests profile, including questions such as, Do you sew? Do you read the Bible?, and so on. Although the manufacturer can specify some questions to be asked specific to its product, it must also allow the vendor's set of questions to be asked as well. The total number of questions, 30 or more also will serve, by their sheer quantity, to reduce response rates.

2. While the syndicated service will not charge the manufacturer for data-entering the names and other information, the service reserves the right to tally penetration statistics of product ownership within postal zip codes. From this data, and the data from competitors' customers, the service will produce product-usage reports detailing product usage by zip codes. These reports are offered for sale to anyone, including the manufacturer's competitors. Though the service will never sell one manufacturer's customers' names and addresses to its competitors, simply disclosing zip codes of high product usage areas gives up valuable information.

3. The service's CRF forms require customers to affix *their own postage*, reducing response rates, possibly biasing the sample, and indirectly implying the manufacturer to be too cheap to offer business reply mail privileges to its customers. The service also will make no effort to acknowledge receiving customers' cards with a return "thank you." This means that customers can perceive the manufacturer as unappreciative of their efforts in registering their purchase.

4. Finally, if the manufacturer should wish access to its own customers' names and addresses, it must pay a service fee to receive the information in magnetic form or on labels or lists. This places the manufacturer at arm's length from its own customers. And, needless to say, over repeated requests for reports and address labels, the service fees can mount up.

Now a new syndicated customer registration process is becoming available. Working primarily with computer hardware and software, companies like Pipeline Communications, Inc. are offering software toolkits that allow manufacturers to build their own customized questionnaire and embed it in their software or RAM hardware to be administered to a customer as she first turns on the hardware or installs the software. The software administers the registration CRF and then provides several options for the return of the information: by modem, email, printed for return by fax, or postal service.

For such services, manufacturers pay the vendor for each customer who registers. And, the information the customer submits goes only to the sponsoring manufacturer, eliminating many of the problems of the older syndicated registration process. Claimed participation rates are impressive—from 40 percent to 80 percent (Businesswire 1995)!

Government Agencies

Some consumer products (in particular automobiles, handguns, and so on) require registration with the local, state, or national government. When such registration is required, and the data is publicly available, it may usually be purchased. (Exceptions do occur. The Motor Vehicle Departments of several states—most notably New York—have sometimes decided not to offer their data for sale.) Purchasing customer lists this way provides not only the names of your own customers, but those of competitors as well. This makes this source particularly attractive, except for the fact the data is equally available to competitors as well!

Which Source to Use?

With so many opportunities the satisfaction professional may feel overwhelmed. Actually, any one program will probably only have a few of all of these methods available. And, necessity will probably dictate using more than one of the methods to maximize the number of customers' names identified.

A RESEARCH ORIENTATION VERSUS A CUSTOMER ORIENTATION

Deming's mandate, "Find out what customers want," has sanctioned the field of customer satisfaction measurement. For better or worse, customer satisfaction measurement has generally employed the survey techniques developed in marketing research. Over the years, marketing research has established reasonably strict survey guidelines borrowed from the discipline of survey research and public opinion measurement. These protocols are oriented to the ethical conduct of surveys among the broad populations, the protocols were not created in response to monitoring *customers'* opinions. A manufacturer's customerbase as a survey population requires some very special considerations. While some may disagree, customer satisfaction research can be considered to represent a very special survey situation, much different from traditional marketing research or public opinion measurement. These differences supersede some of the prohibitions established to monitor conduct in public opinion situations. Table 2.2 lists many of these differences.

Table 2.2   The Difference Between Marketing Research and Customer Satisfaction Measurement

The Issue	Marketing Research	CSM
Who to survey	A sample—a statistically representative sampling	A census—all customers should be given the opportunity to participate
Participants' identities	Kept confidential—participants' answers are never read individually, only when combined with other participants' answers in averages, distributions, etc.	May require feedback—individual's ratings should be examined, searching for individuals with specific problems requiring solutions.
Acknowledgment of Participation	Not essential—establishing goodwill with sample is irrelevant, it is unlikely they will ever be sampled again	Essential—their participation in future surveys is desired, it is also desirable to establish goodwill so they will continue to buy our products/services
Repeated measurements?	No, participants will become "sensitized" to the issues, making their responses less valid	Essential, we need to track the growth or decline in individuals' satisfactions
When to survey	A single "wave" may be sufficient	Continuous surveying is best, it is less likely to reflect one specific contact event and more likely to reflect the cumulative experience with the organization
The purpose	To collect information	To collect information, to solve specific customers' problems, and to communicate to all customers their opinions are desired

Perhaps the most critical difference between a survey research mentality and a customer satisfaction mentality is the research community's insistence of respondent anonymity. Customers don't necessarily want to remain anonymous! Consider the following:

- Customers *may expect to hear back* from the survey group. Their answers to survey questions may also be requests for help. Many believe there exists an implied contract between an organization conducting a CSM and its customerbase.

- Customers are a special case of a "panel." Customers, by definition, already have an ongoing relationship with the company. Repeated CS measurements become an additional component of that relationship.

The two outlooks clash in both overt and subtle ways. Invariably the customer loses if the research perspective is slavishly adhered to.

The Etiquette of Caring for Customers

Regardless of the department or area responsible for conducting a customer satisfaction survey, it must be understood (and agreed) that the survey itself is a very important communication to customers. It makes certain implied (and perhaps explicit) promises about the organization's interest in and responsiveness to its customers. It is imperative that a CSM be executed with more concern and follow-through than the typical "one-shot" marketing research survey!

Customer satisfaction work needs to draw on the strengths of marketing research practice, while establishing its own set of practices. Satisfaction measurement projects need to add a sensitivity to the management of customer relationships, which may be missing in current marketing and survey research methods. It must be recognized that satisfaction survey respondents, who have taken the time to comply with a request to furnish information, are more than survey participants, they are cherished customers of an organization. Their relationship with the organization should be strengthened as a result of the survey, not taxed. Survey researchers routinely deal with infinite populations. They exploit each member of the population who will talk to them, hoping to collect the information they have been retained to collect. While ethical survey companies would never offend survey participants, they are likely to view respondents as a replenishable commodity. Customers, as survey participants, expect and deserve far greater sensitivity to their value. In the conduct of satisfaction interviewing, the customer's feelings should be tantamount—equal to concerns for the quality of the information!

Acknowledging Customers' Participation

It is imperative that responding customers' cooperation be acknowledged. In the U.S. today all of us are bombarded with requests to tell suppliers how satisfied they are making us. While many of us have dutifully completed numerous such surveys, we are becoming skeptical of the whole process. Not only does our response go unacknowledged, but—to make matters worse—we fail to see any improvement in the product or service we have just critiqued. In these situations, it seems evident that the satisfaction survey has been more lip service than part of any well thought-out improvement process. Otherwise, our suggestions would be acknowledged, perhaps an intended solution might even be relayed back to us.

Each customer participating in a satisfaction survey must be sent an acknowledgment of his returned questionnaire. He must be thanked for taking the time to help the organization serve him better by providing his feedback. This is also the perfect time to reinforce the organization's dedication to listening to its customers.

Responding to Individual Customer's Stated Dissatisfactions

What should we do when an individual customer reports a malfunction or complete dissatisfaction with our product or service? Traditional marketing research would forbid follow-up to that individual, saying that his or her anonymity was promised and that follow-up betrays this promise. Yet what is the end result when a customer's report of dissatisfaction goes unanswered? Chances are the customer becomes frustrated, and assumes the company or organization is uninterested in him or her. Satisfaction measurement is not only a survey process, but the invitation to correspond with the sponsoring organization on matters pertaining to satisfaction. Correspondence (or dialoguing) requires the necessity of responding to each participating customer. It may serve both camps to conclude all satisfaction surveys with either a permission question or a negative option statement:

> Please check below to indicate your willingness to have your answers reviewed by our customer care staff. This means you may be contacted about specific issues you raise. Unless you do not wish your name disclosed with your ratings, check the box below.

The Difference Between a Sample and a Census

It is also necessary to decide on the degree of a CSM program's *coverage*. Here, again, the marketing research and customer satisfaction perspectives differ. There are two roles a CSM can play: an *informational* role—collecting information to help it improve its products/services and processes, and a *communicational role*—demonstrating to customers the organization's desire to correspond with each customer to serve her better and to learn more of her expectations and needs.

If a program is to be instituted only for the informational component, a sample is adequate. The company need only draw a random sample of customers for each survey period and field the study.

The problem with conducting a satisfaction measurement program as a sample is its minimal coverage of the total customer base. CSM programs convey a very special message, "we care about our customers' opinions, suggestions and level of satisfaction." The communication role of CSM cannot be properly satisfied by only a sample (unless major portions of the customerbase are "sampled" with sufficient frequency that all customers receive the message of concern from the organization).

When is it appropriate that only a sample of customers hear this message? Part of the answer is in the economics of the situation. CSM is expensive. The size of some customerbases will make a census very costly—especially for low-margin products and services. But customers' commitment to an organization is what keeps the organization in business. Investing in measuring all customers' satisfaction is probably a good investment in the future of the business. It certainly improves the probability that customers will remain loyal to the company. The decision is a strategic one, which must be considered with care.

WHICH CUSTOMERS SHOULD BE INTERVIEWED?

The question, "Which customers should be interviewed?" may catch some off guard. The question reminds us all that there are numerous customer groups that should be considered for inclusion (See Figure 2.1). The choice of which of these customer groups should be included in any customer satisfaction survey is not nearly as easily answered as it might seem on its face. The best response to this question probably is "It depends upon the specific objectives identified for the customer satisfaction survey." Admittedly there generally may be multiple objectives. Try to

---

Current Customers
   High Value Customers
   Special Interest Customers
   Vocal/Conspicuous Customers
Past Customers
Potential Customers
Competitors' Customers

Figure 2.1   Customer Groups Which Are Appropriate for Interviewing

focus on the primary objective. (If multiple customer groups are to be included, the survey's analytical plan will necessarily have to address how the groups' results are to be reported and possibly combined.)

Current Customers

Certainly the feelings of *current customers* will be a prevailing informational need. But sometimes (in a situation of shrinking business volume or brand share) it will be entirely appropriate to include *past customers* and/or *competitors' customers*. Current customers should not be thought of as a homogeneous group. It will generally be advisable to have classificatory information about customers available for the sampling and analytical stages. This is why it is so important to drive the survey with information from the customerbase.

Because all customers are *not* created equal, the decision must be made of which current customers to interview, and how many of them to include in the satisfaction measurement process. In fact, simply identifying what is meant by a *current* customer may be more of a challenge than one might imagine. You will have to create a profile of the behaviors you associate with currency. Almost always, you will want to be able to identify your most important customers (important by dollar volume, their position, reputation or "visibility," or length of association with your firm). To "read" the responses of important customers with statistical confidence, you will need to include an adequate number of them in your total sample.

This discussion is not meant to imply that all customers are *outside* the organization. More and more frequently customer satisfaction surveys are being conducted among *internal* customers. These surveys audit how well one department or unit serves other departments or units within the same organization.

Past Customers

Past customers represent a rich source of information about product or transactional failures. When customers have to contact you to terminate their relationship, you will want to consider instituting a standard "exit interview." This interview, conducted when the customer notifies your organization she will no longer be purchasing your products or services, attempts to determine exactly why the customer is terminating her relationship. Obviously many manufacturers or service providers, distanced from customers by a distribution network or channel, can not determine when a particular customer stops buying their services or products.

Without this knowledge, it is impossible to conduct an exit interview. Without information from exit interviews, past or lapsed customers become an important subsample in a customer satisfaction process. Naturally, a somewhat different introduction will need to be used. But otherwise the questionnaire, in issues and questions, should remain as similar to the current customer survey as possible.

Potential Customers

Considering *potential customers* brings with it all of the danger of catering to individuals who may never, ever be converted into actual customers of a company or a category. Beware of efforts to expand categories. All too often these efforts are pipe dreams. Except in very new categories or industries, or in the case of new, highly innovative products, those for whom the product is relevant will generally already have self-selected product or category usage. New-to-the-category users are very expensive to develop. And, their needs may be much different than current customers', and especially different from high-value customers. Modifying the product offering in the hope of attracting more users, tempting as it may be, is generally impractical.

Consider an example from the pet food industry. How feasible is it to attract new customers to the dog food category? One would first have to buy dogs for all of those consumers he hoped to attract! While not as obvious in other product and service categories, usage is generally very self-selective. Winning new customers over just is not that easy! The main lesson is to focus on current customers because they "drive" the category.

Competitors' Customers

Why spend money and effort interviewing competitors' customers? Well, they happen to represent one of the best sources of benchmark data available, though finding them and interviewing them pose special considerations, some of them ethical. However, if available, their responses can prove to be an invaluable aid in interpreting the ratings of current customers. Competitors' customers may be dealt with as one group (Customers of Competitors), disregarding their specific supplier, or you may sample customers of each of your major competitors (Company A's Customers). Your analytical plan will assist you in making this decision.

Your interest in competitors' customers is in how they rate the competitor. These ratings levels provide you an invaluable benchmark with which to interpret ratings given to your product and service by your customers. There have been some suggestions, however, that competitors' customers could be asked to rate the product and service quality they expect they would have received from your company (Hauser, Simester, and Wernerfelt 1994). This seems, however, more perception than actual experience; generally satisfaction surveys are oriented to measuring actual (as opposed to imagined) experience.

Measurement Requirements

Whether the satisfaction measurement program is to be fielded as a *sample* or as a *census,* a complete listing of all customers (the "population") is necessary. Unfortunately, this apparently simple requirement may prove to be one of the more difficult demands of the entire measurement survey. If you encounter severe problems in identification, try to determine if any bias will be introduced into your survey by interviewing only those customers whose identities you currently have. For example, are all missing customers: (1) from one region, (2) purchasers of one specific product, or (3) serviced by a particular distribution channel? If you were to find such a systematic explanation for absence from your customer listing, it is quite possible that proceeding without the unlisted customers would produce a picture of satisfaction that would be *biased.* That is, the resulting satisfaction scores would not have included the ratings of a particular class of customers. This group might have very different opinions from those who have been included in the survey.

Existing Databases

Where a customer database currently exists it will be wise to subject the list to some scrutiny. You must satisfy yourself as to the completeness, accuracy, and thoroughness of the list before instituting it as the backbone of your satisfaction assessment process.

In the purchase of all products and services, one or more individuals will have made the purchase decision and they deserve consideration for having their satisfaction measured. The situation is most complex in the case of business-to-business (industrial) satisfaction measurement programs. Here, there may be an extensive cohort of individuals, from the purchasing agent whose name is the most likely to have been captured. Other important individuals include the decision maker(s), users, and maintenance parties. Not only should these individuals be identified, but their relative importance in future acquisitions should also be ascertained. This information may be used to combine ratings and possibly weight the ratings by relative influence.

In consumer products the number of individuals involved in the purchase will be fewer, but mapping the relative influence will be no less difficult. The household bill payer will not necessarily be the decision maker and primary user. Again, the billing database is indifferent to these issues.

Creating a Database

It is recommended that once a customerbase of adequate representation is identified, a separate "satisfaction tracking database" be established. This will be a copy of the customerbase, with special modifications. A separate database is desirable for several reasons:

1. It should be accessible at all times to the satisfaction measurement team. "Piggybacking" the satisfaction database on an existing company-wide file may result in competition from other departments for access to the file.
2. To properly sample and analyze the returned data, certain information about customers will be useful. This information may have to be appended to the file, extending the size of the current file.
3. The satisfaction tracking file will require linking to other relational databases to enable storing satisfaction scores from many years' worth of surveys. This linking will generally not be welcomed to an existing (accounting) file.

Depending upon the overall size of the customer database, a micro- or a minicomputer should be appropriated on which to install the database. Established software should be utilized. Rarely will a database warrant customized programming. In most applications, an off-the-shelf database program will suffice. As you establish your file, you may want to consider the software programs listed in Table 2.3.

Selecting Survey Participants

The Sampling Frame

Classical sampling theory requires a listing of individuals—the sample frame—be aggregated containing the identities of those in the population we wish to sample, in this case our customers. A department store using its database of charge customers as a sampling frame would not represent all of its shoppers, only those who paid for their purchases with the store's charge card.

Table 2.3   Database Software Programs

Program	Vendor	Platforms Supported	Special Capabilities
User Databases (easy to use)			
Delphi	Borland	Windows	
Approach	Lotus	Windows	
Access Microsoft	Windows		
Programmer Databases (higher functionality, more difficult to use, programming skills required)			
FoxPro	Microsoft	DOS, Windows	
dBase	Borland	DOS, Windows	
Clipper	Computer Associates	DOS, Windows	
Information Systems (close to mainframe capabilities, programming knowledge required)			
Oracle	Oracle	Various	
SQL Server	Microsoft	Windows NT	SQL–Structured Query Language is also supported by most of the other programs in this section
Pick	Pick Systems	Pick OS	

From the sampling frame of sufficient size a sample must be drawn to yield an "in-tab" sample statistically large enough to accommodate the information we wish to derive from it. Notice that response rates mediate between the number of customers drawn from our sampling frame and the number of completed interviews we finish with, according to the following relationship:

$$\text{initial sample} = \frac{\text{completed (in-tab sample)}}{\text{anticipated response rate}} \tag{2.1}$$

Unfortunately response rates in the U.S. today are decreasing dramatically. They may generally be anticipated as falling somewhere between 15 percent and 60 percent depending upon the fielding method used, and of course the population being surveyed. (Industrial, business-to-business customers can be either more or less cooperative depending upon the way the survey is presented to them and their perception of self-value in the survey.) Response (or cooperation rates) are a result of several factors, including:

- our inability to reach customers drawn to be included in our sample (because they have moved or because we have incomplete information on them);
- customers' innate willingness to cooperate with our requests for information;
- (in industrial situations) companies' policies preventing employees from responding to surveys;
- inability to reach the customer because of her activity level (excessive travel, exceptional activity, and so on);
- intrusiveness of the interview process or perceived length of the interview/questionnaire.

There are three characteristics of a sample frame that ought to be understood.

Comprehensiveness.   A sample only represents the sample frame from which it has been drawn. If the sample frame omits groups of customers, the sample will be biased against those customers excluded (for example the non-charge customers of the department store described above).

Probability of selection.   Is it possible to determine how often or how many times an individual customer may be included in the sample frame? For instance, if a listing of transactions is used as the sample frame, frequent buyers will be represented several times. If each customer's frequency of purchases is also recorded in the sample frame, then the probability of each customer being selected can be derived.

Efficiency.   In some cases, sample frames consist of more units than those to be sampled. For example, a customer listing may contain both present and past customers. A decision may have been reached to interview only current customers. The presence of past customers in the list can likely be controlled for by a screening question asking each potential survey respondent when she last purchased. But notice, the more nonrelevant sampling units are included in the sample frame the *less efficient* the frame is for cost efficient interviewing.

Types of Samples
The process used for drawing the sample affects the quality of survey estimates in several ways:

1. if the sample frame excludes some types of customers, survey estimates will be biased to the extent the missing customers' differ from those included;
2. if the sampling process is not probabilistic, the sample will likely not represent the population from which it is drawn; the probability of selection must be known for each customer;
3. the size and design of a probability sample, together with the extremity of what is being measured determine the sampling errors, and/or the appropriate size of the sample.

There are four main sampling techniques that are applicable to customer satisfaction measurement: random, stratified, cluster, and quota. We will discuss each of these methods.

Random (Probabilistic) Sampling

Using the sample frame, the exhaustive listing of all customers, we can establish an unbiased selection procedure offering each customer an equal (or known) chance (or likelihood) of being selected. Two procedures are widely used to select the specific customers who will be interviewed:

The "nth" Customer.   In this procedure, the number of customers in the customerbase is divided by the required initial sample size. The resulting number is the "nth" interval. Now, within the first nth names in the list, a random number is drawn from a table of random numbers. (Most statistics textbooks contain random number tables. Simply open the book to the table and without controlling your selection, place your finger or pencil on a starting number. At this point read the digits in order until you accumulate enough digits to form a number within the interval 0-to-the-nth number.) The selected customer name is the first customer and also the starting point, from that customer on, every "n-th" additional customer is selected.

Let's assume you have 15,000 customers. You have decided to interview 1,500. Dividing 15,000 by 1,500 yields 10. In other words you will interview every 10th customer, starting at a random customer 1–10 from the beginning of the list. Looking at a table of random numbers, you might place your finger on 3. You would then select the customer who's third on the list and every 10 customers thereafter. This means customers 3, 13, 23, 33, and so on will be selected for your initial sample.

Random Number Generator.   Though somewhat more involving, you can repetitively use a random numbers table to select all of your respondents. Generate as many random numbers as customers you need to interview using a computer program or computer spreadsheet. Then use those random numbers to pull from your customerbase, the identities of those customers to be interviewed. For example, using the above parameters, you would generate 1,500 random numbers—all between the range of 1–15,000. (Numbers outside this range are simply discarded.) Once you have generated the 1,500 random numbers, you use these to identify the customers you will interview. Let's say the first three random numbers you have generated are 830, 12,341, and 92. You would enter your customer list and select the 830th, 12,341st, and 92nd customers in your customer list. You would proceed until you had identified all 1,500 customer names. While this appears laborious, most database programs can easily generate a random sample.

Stratified Random Sampling

A random sample will probably represent all of the customer types in your customer list, but some special circumstances need to be addressed. Let's stay with the customerbase of the previous example. What if the 15,000 customers contained 3,000 very important customers. With random samples, a random number customer selection procedure should provide about 300 of these customers. But random samples are truly random. In any *one* selection, you might draw only 150 of these customers or you might draw 450 or more!

The fact of the matter is that if these 3,000 customers (20 percent of the customerbase) accounted for 65 percent of your total sales, you may wish to read their satisfaction levels with considerably higher precision than the satisfaction of the remaining 80 percent of your customers who aggregately account for only 35 percent of sales. Without stratifying your customers, a sample based on the 15,000 customers would produce a more precise measurement than is needed of your low-value customers and would offer less precision among your high-value customers.

Consider another scenario. What if half of your 15,000 customers had been with you for five years or longer. Chances are their opinions about your products and servicing might have a lower variance than the remaining, 7,500 newer customers. Treating your customers as a homogeneous group, your variance estimate for your 15,000 customers would be an average of the lower-variance long-term customers and the higher-variance newer customers. In fact, the total population variance would understate the variance of new customers and overstate the variance of long-time customers. The ramification? Because a single sample would have been drawn based on the average variance across two very different groups, you would end up sampling more current customers than necessary and fewer new customers than preferred.

Stratified sampling is the smart sampling choice when either of these two scenarios prevail, subgroups whose satisfaction ratings have different distributions, and subgroups who represent different levels of importance to your strategic planning. You can save yourself money and increase the precision of your findings by stratifying your population.

To implement a stratified sampling plan, you need to include strata membership (high-value, low-value, for example) within your sample frame. You will then estimate variance within each stratum and draw the appropriate number of customers. Essentially, you will decide how many customers of each stratum to interview, and then you may use either of the above mechanisms for drawing the particular respondents in each stratum.

Cluster Sampling

In most companies today, customers are widely distributed geographically, and as more and more companies become global, their customer-bases not only cover an ever expanding geography, but also bring new languages into consideration as well. In such circumstances, cluster sampling may make sense.

Because both stratified and cluster sampling involve dividing the total population into subgroups, they seem similar. The difference is in the composition of the subgroup and the role the subgroup performs.

- **In stratified sampling** subgroups are formed of similar customers, maximizing within subgroup homogeneity, then a sample of *customers* is randomly drawn from *each* strata.
- **In cluster sampling** subgroups are formed of different customers (maximizing within group heterogeneity), who happen to live, work, or otherwise be mutually available, then a sample of *subgroups* is randomly drawn, with a specified number of customers within each subgroup interviewed.

Quota Sampling

Although quota sampling is sometimes viewed as an asciential procedure, it really is not. The primary reason a quota sample might be used is that while customer segments are known to exist, the sample frame might not contain the classificatory information to properly assign potential survey participants to the appropriate strata (or segments) prior to their being interviewed. In quota sampling, each interviewer is assigned a quota—a number of customers to interview within each segment or stratum. Using a few qualifying questions at the beginning of the interview, the interviewer will attempt to determine to which segment each new customer contacted belongs. Once a customer's stratum or segment is known, the interviewer will continue with the interview if his quota for that stratum is yet unfilled. Otherwise, he will thank the customer and terminate the interview.

Determining the Appropriate Sample Size

Sample sizes are usually determined by one or more of the following criteria:

1. **Judgment or historical precedent** Many samples are sized by judgment alone. Convention within a company (or industry) can also influence how many customers are interviewed. Oftentimes *prima facie* validity will be used to determine sample size.
2. **Analytical considerations** When survey results need to be interpreted and acted upon at a regional or operating level, a minimum sample size must be allocated at this level. The total sample is then a simple summation of the subsamples at the regional or operating levels.
3. **Budget** Quite frequently samples are constrained by the number of customers we can afford to interview. (Interviewing costs are normally supplied by field services on a CPI (cost per interview) basis. Once you have received competitive bids for interviewing you will have some idea about how many customers your budget will allow you to interview.)
4. **Specification of a desired level of statistical precision** The most scientific method for determining sample size is to base it on the level of statistical precision (or projectability) desired for your survey results.

If you are choosing the statistical precision method for assessing sample size, there are three constructs you will need to familiarize yourself with. They are:

- the *standard error of the estimate* (SE)
- the *confidence interval* you will accept,
- the *confidence level* you require

These constructs are almost totally interdependent, which makes affixing them, individually, somewhat difficult.

The Standard Error of the Estimate

Determining how many customers will constitute an adequate sample requires one to have knowledge of the actual population including the population's *standard deviation (normally approximated by the sample's standard error [SE])* for the phenomenon you are measuring. Paradoxically, the standard error (or an estimate of it) is one of the findings you will ultimately discover through your survey! In this way such statistical phenomena are circular; though the survey is the only way to quantify them, you require an estimate of them to determine among how many of your customers your survey ought to be conducted!

There are several ways around this apparent conundrum.

1. The question can be answered with historical data. For instance, it may be that some surveys have been conducted among your customers in the past. If so, an analysis of the results of these surveys can be used to produce estimates of the likely standard error associated with each of the previous rating scales. One can then simply average over the standard errors to calculate an average survey standard error. It is not inappropriate to use historical data. It has been claimed that variance (the source of SE) changes more slowly over time than do means (the actual levels of outcomes). Thus, even though we are conducting a new study to see how means may have changed, it is probably safe to assume the population variance underlying the means has not changed significantly.
2. Because rating scales have both an absolute beginning and an end, the mean and variance of such scales are interrelated. Taking a 7-point scale, if a mean of 5.5 is observed, then there must, necessarily be a large number of ratings of "7" and "6" creating a relatively tight distribution of scores, hence a smaller variance. If a mean is closer to the scale's midpoint, say 3.5, conceivably the spread of observed scores could be much broader, creating a larger variance. Using this logic, estimates have been made of variance associated with rating scales of different lengths. See Table 2.4.
3. Guesstimates can be used to create a likely SE. Recognizing that in normally distributed data 99.5 percent of all sample means will fall within ±3 standard deviations of the population mean (6 standard deviations in total), one can estimate the standard deviation

Table 2.4   Estimates of SE Associated with Response Scales of Different Lengths

Number of Scale Points	Typical Range of Variances
4	0.7–1.3
5	1.2–2
6	2–3
7	2.5–4
10	3–7

Source: *Research on Research*, No. 37, Chicago: Market Facts, Inc., undated

$[\sqrt{variance}]$ by taking an assumed range of likely answers and dividing the range by six. For example, on a 10-point scale, if we assume that all answers (for a particular variable, say overall satisfaction) will fall between 3 and 10, then the standard deviation would be 8/6 = 1.33 and the variance would be (1.33) = 1.77.

The Confidence Interval (The Degree of Precision)

A confidence interval describes a range of scores about an observed sample outcome (a mean or a proportion) which identify scores we must accept as all representing the same underlying population mean or proportion. If a sample's observed mean on a 10-point satisfaction scale is 7.5, the confidence interval places a numeric range (for example, ±.5) about that observed mean within which we would expect the majority of means from an indefinite number of additional samples to fall. The width of the confidence interval depends both on the magnitude of the observed mean, and on the satisfaction professional's required degree of precision. The degree of precision describes our toleration for an imprecise estimate (our acceptance of a wide confidence interval) or our desire for a highly precise estimate (our requirement for a very narrow confidence interval).

The width of the confidence interval is totally up to the survey professional to specify. Here is one way to assign it. Suppose your last CSM showed overall satisfaction with your organization was 7.5 (on a 10-point scale). Your management assumes (hopes) overall satisfaction has subsequently been improved. Management's goal is an average of 8.0. Your objective would be to establish a narrow enough confidence interval about the old mean of 7.5 such that a new observed mean of 8.0 could not be interpreted as a sample mean from a population whose mean was still

7.5, but rather represented a sample mean from a *new* population whose true mean was now 8.0—a true significant increase. To make this statement, the confidence interval you would place around 7.5 must be smaller than ±.5. (Notice that .5 is the difference between the new target level for satisfaction, 8.0 and the former measured value, 7.5.) Let's choose an interval of 7.5 ± .45.

Assume you will read the results at a 95 percent level of confidence. This means that 8.0 must lie beyond the range of 7.5 plus .45 or 7.95. With this confidence interval, you can rest assured that 95 percent of all observed means from a population whose mean is still 7.5 will lie in the range 7.5 − .45 to 7.5 + .45 or 7.05 to 7.95. A new observed mean of 8.0 would indicate it did not come from the same distribution of satisfaction scores. One could safely conclude, in this case, that satisfaction had increased!

The Confidence Level (The Degree of Confidence)

The level of statistical confidence one may ascribe to a survey's findings is again, totally at the discretion of the satisfaction professional. The "default level" in social research is 95 percent. It is ironic that most social surveys are subjected to so precise an outcome when many medical experiments (with considerably higher stakes riding on them) may lack such demanding confidence. The 95 percent confidence level is probably used too automatically in many satisfaction surveys. Many satisfaction professionals may not know they have the liberty to choose the level, or they may not understand the ramifications of changing it. In many cases a confidence level of 90 percent, 85 percent or even 80 percent may be sufficient. The reason to adopt a lower confidence interval is the substantial impact the confidence level has on sample size. Decreasing the confidence level from 95 percent to 90 percent can relax the number of customers who must be interviewed—lowering the survey's cost dramatically. Lower levels of confidence may be especially defensible in "caretaker situations" where no substantial change (either improvement or deterioration) is suspected.

Essentially the confidence level you choose denotes your willingness to be wrong (that is, to say satisfaction has increased when it's actually remained constant). At the conventional 95 percent level, you are insisting that 95 times out of 100 you wish to be correct. That is, you will tolerate only 5 errors in 100 tries. Stated this way, the reader may see why we've questioned the blind observance of a 95 percent level. For many business decisions, a 9 out of 10 record (that is, a 90 percent confidence level) would be quite satisfactory, maybe even 8½ or 8 times out of 10!

Table 2.5   Values of the Standard Normal Deviate

Desired Level of Confidence	Area Under the Normal Curve
60%	0.84
70%	1.04
75%	1.15
80%	1.28
85%	1.44
90%	1.64
95%	1.96
99.5%	2.81

By all means consider how severe are the consequences of your actions that will be based on the CSM outcome. Also consider your likely starting points. If your overall satisfaction is likely to be low initially, as long as you see improvement at a lower level of confidence (80 percent to 85 percent) that may be sufficient. On the other hand, if you must determine which operating region is satisfying its customers best, then you will probably want to invoke a more stringent confidence level.

The level of confidence you select influences the Z-score or normal deviate used in the calculation of sample size. For a 95 percent level of confidence, the Z-score is 1.96 (2 is an acceptable substitution and makes calculation easier). Other values of Z may be read directly from a table of normal deviates. The most commonly used values are shown in Table 2.5.

Calculating the Appropriate Sample Size with Metric Data (means)

Using these constructs, you can determine how many cusotmers you should interview according to one of several formulae. If you are measuring metric data (overall satisfaction on a 10-point scale), the appropriate sample size is given by the relationship in Equation 2.2.

$$sample\ size\ (n) = \frac{Z^2}{\left(\dfrac{confidence\ interval}{2}\right)^2} \sigma_{\bar{x}}^{\,2} \qquad (2.2)$$

Where:

$$Z \; = \; \text{the standard normal deviate (Z-score)}$$
appropriate for your level of precision (2 for a
95% level of confidence)

confidence interval = the range about the sample mean you are willing
to tolerate (for example ±.5 = 1.0)

$\sigma_{\bar{x}}$ = standard error of the estimate

Calculating the Appropriate Sample Size with Nominal Data (proportions)

If your primary criterion variable is a proportion, then you can use Equation 2.3 to determine your appropriate sample size. Notice that in Equation 2.3 the standard error of the estimate (for a proportional answer) is approximated by the term (pro (1-pro)).

$$sample\ size\ (n) = \frac{Z^2}{\left(\dfrac{confidence\ interval}{2}\right)^2}\ (pro(1-pro))^2 \quad (2.3)$$

Where:

$$Z \; = \; \text{the standard normal deviate (Z-score)}$$
appropriate for your level of precision (2 for a
95% level of confidence)

confidence interval = the range about the sample mean proportion you
are willing to tolerate (for example ±3% = 6%)

pro = the expected sample proportion (that is, 80%
saying "extremely satisfied")

Some Misconceptions about Sample Size

There are three common misconceptions about sample size.

1. The adequacy of a sample depends upon the fraction of the total
   population surveyed. This is based on the naive understanding of
   statistics that representation of some minimal proportion, say at least
   5 percent, of a total population will make a sample accurate.
   However, sampling error is independent of the fraction of the
   population included in a sample. Conversely, the size of the
   population has virtually no impact on how well a sample can describe
   the population.

2. Standard opinion industry sample sizes are best. It is commonly believed that a good national sample consists of 1,500 respondents. (This is a frequently cited number in public opinion polls.) While this sample size may be reasonable given the particular characteristics of a national opinion issue, each phenomenon has its own statistical properties and samples should be decided based on the specific properties of the phenomenon being estimated.

3. Sample sizes can easily be calculated from the level of acceptable error or the precision of the results desired. Some warn it is unreasonable to base a sample size decision on a single variable since most surveys contain numerous variables and estimates. It is also probably unrealistic to specify an acceptable margin of error from only sampling since error is introduced from many other sources in addition to sampling.

The appropriate way to determine sample size is first to identify an analytical plan. The key component of any analytical plan is usually not an estimate of confidence intervals, but rather an identification of the analytical groups within the population for which separate estimates are required (that is, *high value* customers, *long-term* customers, *first-time* customers, and so on). The appropriate question is how many customers within each of these analytical groups should be interviewed; the total sample then becomes an aggregate of the minimum acceptable number to be interviewed within each of the analytical groups.

Central Limit Theory tells us that regardless of the distribution of the underlying population, as samples exceed 30 customers in size, the distribution of sample means will be normally distributed. We will suggest 50 customers as the minimum number of customers advisable in an analytical grouping, but 100 customers is probably a safer number. (Safer in the sense you will receive fewer questions about statistics based on subsamples of 100 than you would with subsamples of only 50.)

How to Store Customers' Names and Information

"Flat files" Versus Relational Databases

The organization (specification) of a customer database is critical to its utility for a good customer satisfaction process. In the early days of data processing, information such as customer lists was stored in "flat files."

————————— **In flat files, the organization of data records is sequential.** —————————

Data on Magnetic Tape

Adams, Adele	Adams, Bosley	Adams, Charles	Adams, Cynthia	Adams, David	Adams, Harriet	Adams, Joann

Access is necessarily sequential; to retrieve David Adams' record, the preceding four records must be passed.

————————— **In relational files, organization is by random access.** —————————

Data on a Disk

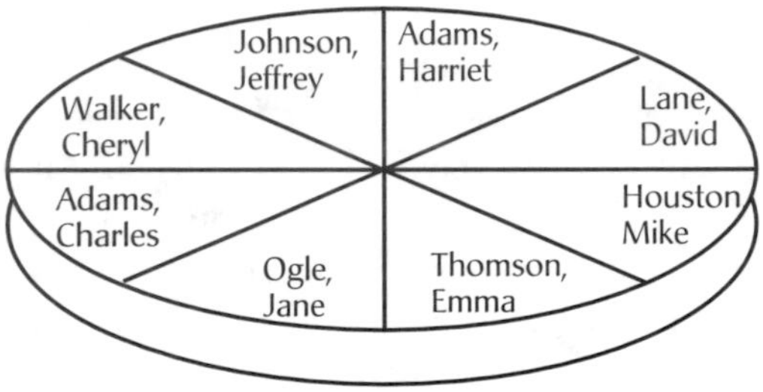

Index

Customer	File Location
Adams, Adele	221350
Adams, Bosley	553351
Adams, Charles	010789
Adams, Cynthia	870023
Adams, David	312004
Adams, Harriet	010792
Adams, Joann	230009
•	
•	
Johnson, Jeffrey	010791
Johnson, Leonard	334100
•	
•	
Walker, Barry	600034
Walker, Cheryl	010790

Access is direct, the index table identifies the location of each customer's record.

Figure 2.2   The Difference Between Flat Files and Relational Database Files

These files had fields for each information bite to be collected on customers. Spaces were held for the information, whether or not it was actually known. Once the fields had been specified in a "flat file," adding a new bit of information meant reorganizing the entire file—or placing the new information at the very end of the information string, a less than ideal location. And, the file was sequential. To access a particular customer, the computer had to start at the beginning of the file or tape and read sequentially through the entire "datastring" to the desired name or information. For each subsequent name to be located, the process was essentially reinitiated, from the first name on the list. The advent of relational databases changed this perspective (See Figure 2.2).

The revolutionary file structure of relational databases essentially changed the entire way customer information can be stored. A relational database allows an indefinite number of additional database files to be indexed or keyed to the primary database. One or more "keys" are used as unique identifiers with which to link the records between related databases. A key is any number that uniquely identifies each customer. In the automotive industry a convenient key is the Vehicle Identification Number (the VIN is an industrywide totally unique number), though for a manufacturer whose owners might possess more than one of the manufacturer's vehicles, the VIN is less than ideal.

A relational database means a satisfaction professional can start with a rather meager, maybe even generic customerbase file. This file would contain the primary identifying information about the customer. This database, call it the primary file, can be quickly assembled from information in-house or with the sales force. Then, bit-by-bit satisfaction, repurchase, and loyalty information can all be added to this primary file, through additional, physically separate databases. But the information will all be available jointly, because each new database will also contain the unique key or customer identifier, by which all information known about a customer can be *related*. Relational databases clearly were a magnum leap for the maintenance and longitudinal tracking of customer satisfaction data!

Regardless of the format of the datafile, there are still some overriding housekeeping concerns you'll want to observe as you complete the design of your database. Your database will only be as useable as it is complete in its *coverage, accuracy,* and *thoroughness*. Table 2.6 elaborates on these basics of database construction.

Batch Mode

The *batch mode* is the oldest perspective of satisfaction data storage. It evolved from the way tab-houses and computer centers processed survey results in the past. Data from one survey wave would be viewed as a *stand alone* file. The analysis of this file would be completed and then the data would be stored as boxes of cards or on magnetic tape as a flat file. Little or no regard would be given to how or if the data might be compared with future survey waves (except in the very static comparison of summary statistics in a written report covering a subsequent survey period).

Because computer storage has, until only recently, been very expensive there has been an aversion towards keeping data from previous

Table 2.6   Review of a Customer Database

Characteristic	Explanation
Coverage	What percent of all "buying units" (customers, companies, households, etc.) are represented in the database? Ideally the proportion should be as close to 100% as possible.
Accuracy	How accurate is the data? For example, Spelling, Titles, Currency of addresses, Proper gender identification (where desirable), Years doing business with our organization, Goods or services typically purchased.
Thoroughness	How well the data describes the individual customer. For example, in household data are the purchase decision process known? For industrial customers, are the Purchasing Agent, Primary Decision Maker and Primary User identified?

surveys active and accessible to current analyses. Even though data storage costs have now dramatically decreased, many in-house computer centers and some research companies still operate in this outdated mode.

Improvements—Combining Across Dimensions Of Importance

Old habits are hard to break, especially when they are formed as the result of another (the computer) department's standard operating procedure. What's tearing down such short-term thinking is the availability of desktop PCs with massive storage and analytic capacities—literally rivaling the mainframes of yesterday. In such a context, satisfaction data from many different survey waves may be kept "alive" and used in several, new ways. Consider each of the following ways in which a satisfaction database could be organized.

Issue Mode

This is an isolated view. It focuses on an issue and its growth or decay over time as the key information to be learned. In this view the customer associated with the view is incidental. The goal is only to form a profile of the issue over time.

A major disadvantage of this method is that there is no diagnostic information to be related to the occurrence of the issue. With the data collapsed over customers, it is impossible to ever relate certain ideological perspectives with particular customer types.

Segment Mode

Here, the aggregate customerbase is broken down into segments. The most logical segment to examine separately is high value customers. Other segments of interest might be "benefit segments" (customers who are oriented to a particular feature or attribute clustered together); demographic segments or geographic segments. This view at least allows viewing the data through different sets of customer eyes. But again, typically at only one occasion. So this perspective does not allow a longitudinal analysis.

Longitudinal Mode

In this perspective the survey data from each measurement period is stored in the raw—by each individual customer. In general, so long as storage space is not an insurmountable problem, all of the data for each successive wave of the survey will be retained and stored.

Prerecruiting for Participation

Response Rates are Declining

Response rates to survey research are declining in general; for all industries among all customer types, for all companies. The terrifyingly high refusal rates (58 percent in 1995) are shown in Figure 2.3. While this data is not specific to satisfaction surveys, it is unlikely that satisfaction survey cooperation rates will be substantially higher. A number of factors are responsible for the rise in refusal rates.

- Previous participation has not been acknowledged. As sad as it is, most customer satisfaction surveys are undertaken on limited budgets, and with a research mentality. The simple courtesy of acknowledging a customer's participation may not be understood. However, since many satisfaction studies are conducted among only samples of the customerbase, the likelihood of recontacting the same customer ever again, within the near future is small. Hence, the importance of reinforcing the customer's participation is downplayed.
- Limited budgets also constrain the amount of communication that may be undertaken in any one measurement wave. Hence the costs of a follow-up acknowledgment discourage the activity.
- The presentation and packaging of most customer satisfaction surveys is shoddy. There often seems to be inadequate funding to execute the survey in a truly stylish manner. Appearance can

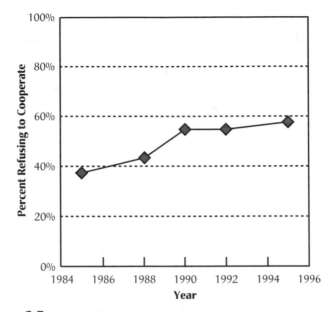

Figure 2.3   Survey Research Refusal Rates
Sources: 1985 and 1988—Your Opinion Counts survey research industry survey
            1990 and 1992—Walker Research, Industry Image Survey
            1995—Council for Marketing and Opinion Research

influence response rates; a cheap appearance can suggest evidence of the organization's low commitment to the CSM process.

These perspectives must be overcome. The research mentality must be replaced with a customer-relationship mentality. In such a perspective, reinforcing the customer's participation is essential. Relationship marketing stresses the value of dialoguing with customers. So customer response must be rewarded, to be encouraged in the future. And, satisfaction projects must be funded with sufficient resources so that they can be conducted in a style and manner befitting their extreme value to the organization.

Prerecruitment

To increase the response rate in a survey, it is a good idea to prerecruit customers before contacting them with a questionnaire. The prerecruitment can do several things. First, it legitimizes the survey. The customer will not be alarmed that someone knows he owns a product and is being asked about its performance. Second, prerecruiting collects information about when is the most convenient time for the customer to be contacted. When the survey is administered during a convenient time, it is more likely the customer will participate

To prerecruit, the survey sample is contacted, generally by telephone (letter is also acceptable) and told they have been selected to participate in a customer satisfaction survey. They may be alerted to watch for a questionnaire in the mail, on the Internet, or a telephone call or visit from a personal interviewer. They are always given the opportunity to tell when it would be most convenient for them to be contacted, minimizing the intrusiveness of the survey on their personal schedule.

INCENTIVES?

Participating in a CSM (from the customer's perspective) is time and labor intensive. It is appropriate and reasonable to give our customer, the potential survey respondent, some incentive for her labors. Often in an industrial setting, the simple hope of having the product better customized to the customer's needs or seeing an improvement in servicing or delivery will be a sufficient incentive. Self interest through high involvement is a strong motivator. Always leverage the direct benefits to your customer through survey participation as much as possible. This is the strongest motivation. In some industrial settings any additional incentive, especially a monetary incentive, may be inappropriate or even against the customer's organization's policy. (Governmental agencies will often forbid employees from receiving any monetary payment from a supplier's organization. Even though well-meant, an incentive offered in this situation could lose a contract!)

When some additional incentive is either necessary (because the product or category is *not* highly involving) or desirable (to insure a minimum response rate), there are two options: "preincentivating" or "postincentivating."

When to Incentivate

Preincentives

Preincentivating means delivering some reward prior to the potential respondent having completed the satisfaction interview.

Preincentivating plays on both the attention value of the incentive delivered with the request for survey participation as well as the guilt created by the potential respondent having received something of value.

Merchandise or money included with a mail questionnaire heightens the attention the mailing receives. It also probably minimizes the likelihood of the mailing being immediately discarded.

Having received something of value hopefully creates guilt stimulating the potential respondent to complete the interview. Unfortunately not all customers who are preincentivated will faithfully complete the interview. Some incentives are therefore wasted.

Postincentives

Postincentivating means promising a reward to the potential respondent in return for him having completed the interview.

Postincentives generally must be greater than preincentives. But, since some preincentives will be wasted, this is usually quite feasible. The rationale here is, why not provide a nice incentive for those customers who actually complete the survey as opposed to giving all customers something, regardless of them having completed the survey.

Positioning the Incentive

The way the incentive is positioned is important. Most customers' time and labor will be very important and costly. An incentive should never be presented as fair compensation for the time, labor, or value of the information. Most satisfaction professionals will present the incentive as a *token of appreciation*. In this way it is made clear that in no way is the incentive seen as a fair compensation for the responding customer's efforts. The incentive is simply a way of saying "thank you."

Types of Incentives

Informational

The most all-round effective and acceptable incentive is an informational incentive—offering survey participants a summary report of the data collected. Not only does this intrigue potential respondents, but it is believed it adds a level of authentication to the survey if the sponsor is willing to share some of the findings. Of course not all of the information can (or should) be reported. But usually there are some classificatory questions (types of uses the product is put to, positions, interests of survey respondents, and so on) that may be interesting to potential respondents. In offering an informational incentive, it should always be made clear that only some of the results will be reported, to prevent hard feelings when not all of the information is received. Information as an incentive also escapes problems of sending money to customers—a practice that may be prohibited by industrial customers' employers or may cause private customers to question why the company can be so free with money as an incentive. The informational incentive is particularly appealing among certain customer groups among which money would be considered tawdry.

Monetary

Having touted the benefits of information as an incentive, it must quickly be added that "money speaks louder than words." Money is certainly the most effective incentive among consumers where there may be fewer prohibitions constraining our activities. One caveat, don't ever position—or even *imply* that the money is sufficient, quid pro quo remuneration for the customer's time in completing the survey. Always offer the money as *a token of appreciation.* Some customers get offended when small amounts of money are offered seemingly to offset the expense of their time, or to compensate them for the value of their input or opinions.

Merchandise

Sometimes merchandise can be an effective incentive. This is especially the case when the survey sponsor can acquire an item that has considerably greater perceived value than its cost to the survey sponsor. Cameras might be such an example. One might acquire a large number of inexpensive SLR 35mm cameras for $5–15, which might have the perceived value of $25–50 to customers.

Affinity merchandise featuring the logo of the survey sponsor is also something to be considered. A corporate logo appears to increase the value of items for many Americans. Merchandise has the added advantage of permanence, constantly reminding customers that their opinion was sought and rewarded.

Additional Products/Services

Occasionally it will be possible for a survey sponsor to offer additional units or amounts of the actual product (or service) in exchange for survey participation. For example, for completing a survey at a movie theater, a moviegoer might be offered a half-price or full-price ticket for future admission as an incentive for submitting to a survey about the theater.

Table 2.7 Comparison of Methods of Incenting Customers to Respond

Business Customer Survey	Consumer Customer Survey
1. Promised Service/Product Improvement	1. Cash
2. "Sanitized" Survey Results	2. Additional Products/Service
3. Cash	3. Affinity Merchandise
4. Affinity Merchandise	4. Donation to a National Charity
5. Donation to a National Charity	

Table 2.7 identifies the most common incentives and compares their relative efficiencies in both industrial and consumer populations.

REFERENCES

Businesswire. "Pipeline Communications Expands Global Capabilities to More than 90 Countries." December 26, 1995.

Curtis, James. "Special Report: Database Marketing." *Precision Marketing.* (February 5, 1996): 17–19.

Hauser, John R., Duncan I. Simester, and Birger Wernerfelt. "Customer Satisfaction Incentives." *Marketing Science.* 13, no. 4 (Fall 1994): 327–50.

CHAPTER 3

Satisfaction and the Key Measurement Issues

OVERVIEW

Setting out on a mission to measure customer satisfaction is fraught with traps and pitfalls. One of the most subtle is the assumption that the organization knows what to ask customers in order to measure their satisfaction. Most internal department heads will have a ready list of things they would like to know from customers. But all too often these lists pertain more to increasing internal efficiencies than to increasing external satisfactions.

The secret to formulating an effective customer satisfaction survey is to balance internal, operational issues originating with departmental operations with external issues more focused on customer needs. Therefore, a customer satisfaction survey should always be initiated with a "discovery process" conducted both among customers and among employees. This investigation, made even better if conducted among a diverse groups of customers and employees, will help establish laundry lists of requirements and expectations.

Do not assume you (or your management) already know the issues. What you know as issues may have changed in importance or may have been superseded by new issues. The success of your satisfaction survey depends on your identifying the *current* key issues by which to gauge your organization's satisfaction performance.

The value of an Exploratory Investigation

Internal Models (Inside Looking Out)

Some of the poorest corporate decisions are made in 50th floor board-rooms without any insightful information about customers' expectations, needs or satisfactions. *Assuming* customers' key issues and problems are known and understood has put many a company out of business. While many salespeople have a unique insight into customers' desires, totally re-lying on salespeople's understanding is similarly dangerous. Assuming you know all the answers about your product and category is an isolation-ist view of the marketplace and is often labeled "inside looking out." That is, the view is the corporate view (however right or wrong) projected out to the marketplace.

The consequences of the internal view predominating any satisfac-tion measurement, may be a focus on measuring *efficiency* rather than *ef-fectiveness*. Numerous marketing authors including Drucker (1996) and Levitt (1983) have established the problems of focusing on efficiency. Ef-ficiency, a reasonably easy concept to measure, is simply measuring how well we are doing that which we are already doing. The efficiency point of view can be typified by past New York mayor, Ed Koch's frequent question, "How am I doing?" Efficiency is an *internal perspective* oriented towards maximizing returns on current effort and resource allocation.

Effectiveness is an entirely different issue. If Ed Koch had been in-terested in measuring his *effectiveness,* he would have asked, "What *should I* be doing (that I'm *not doing* already)?" Effectiveness has to do with doing the right things rather than doing things the right way. Effective-ness is a more difficult issue for internal employees to confront. It re-quires them to question all their processes, maybe even the existence of their department! Customers' external perspective is invaluable in provid-ing suggestions to improve the effectiveness of organizations.

When you know some things are right, questions directed at effi-ciency are not all bad. Just make sure you also include some questions about effectiveness! This issue has also recently been represented in the "lit-tle q, big Q" paradigm. Juran (1992, 11–13) characterizes little q issues as those dealing more with quality in a narrow sense—the definition of qual-ity as conformance to internal specifications. While big Q defines quality in a more global sense, addressing the satisfaction of customer needs.

For an Understanding of Customers, Ask Customers

Too often the most obvious solution to the question, "What do customers *really* want?" is to simply gather some customers together and ask them! This is the perspective of stepping outside the organization, and "looking in," seeing your products and activities as your customers see them. Dialogues with customers can range from very informal conversations to structured in-depth interviews or Customer Listening Groups[sm]. Unlike focused discussion groups, wherein there is a product or a service to be evaluated, in Customer Listening Groups, the goal is to allow customers to talk about what they like, what they need, and how they assess the adequacy of products and services. (We discuss Customer Listening Groups in greater detail on page 97 of this chapter.)

Customer listening groups are almost always revealing. Having videotaped some of these groups for a major service company, company executives watching the tapes were overheard to comment, "They look like *kids*!", "Our customers can't be *that* young!", "Why do they judge service quality *that* way?"

Gap Models of Expectations

In their work building the SERVQUAL model, Zeithaml (1990) and her colleagues identified six planning gaps that could arise between an organization and its customerbase if the appropriate information were not collected (See Table 3.1).This model shows in how many different ways (six altogether) there may be misalignment between what customers are ideally looking for and what factories produce and service providers offer.

Table 3.1   Planning Gaps Existing Between Management's Vision and Customers' Needs

What Customers Desire - ▸ *Needs/Expectations*	Gap 2
What Customers Think Will Happen - - - - - - - - - - - ▸ *Modified Expectations*	Gap 3
What Customers Perceived Happened - - - - - - ▸ *Perception of Performance*	
	Gap 6
	Gap 1
What the Factory/Delivery Point Produced - - - - - - - - - - - - - - - - - - ▸ *Reality*	
Management's Goals for Product Quality/	Gap 4
Service Performance - ▸ *Management's Goals*	
Management's Perceptions of Customers Desires - ▸ *Management's Vision*	Gap5

Adapted from: Zeithaml, Valerie, Parsu Parasuraman, and Leonard Berry, *Delivering Quality Services*, New York: The Free Press, 1992.

The authors advocate closing the information gaps by conducting ascertainment projects like satisfaction studies, in which not only current satisfactions are measured, but expectations are elicited as well. It is the explication of these expectations that will better help management close some of its gaps concerning customers' *actual* desires.

Recurring Reexamination

Many readers will think of exploration as a onetime process. It shouldn't be. Some CSM practitioners are passionate about calling their entire activity chain a "process." They disdain the terms "program", "project", or "study" because these terms imply temporality. All have beginnings and endings. But *processes* can be truly circular. So it is with the exploration phase of the CSM process. You should revisit exploration on a regular basis. You will almost always learn from it. It will never cease to amaze you how much things have changed, and how much more understanding there is to be gained.

Customers' Requirements and Needs

A Definition of Customer Requirements

Hayes (1992) defines customer requirements as "those characteristics of the product or service which represent important dimensions." Hayes encourages working these "dimensions" into specific examples or performance-related statements for administration in a survey.

Juran (1989, 39) is more precise. Consumer needs, Juran believes, can be represented in a hierarchical structure, a "pyramid" of needs. He envisions customer requirements in a three-component hierarchy composed of primary, secondary, and tertiary needs. He suggests that consumers will respond to questions about their desire for a product or service in one of three levels:

- to satisfy primary needs (their "requirements" from the good or category)
- to satisfy secondary needs (essentially the consequences of the requirement)
- to satisfy tertiary needs (the end benefits of the requirements or needs)

Juran's supposition sets up the following possibility. One of a consumer's stated needs (or requirements) for an automobile might be "styling." Probing the value of this requirement to the consumer, the secondary need of "recognition by one's peers" might be disclosed. Finally, a resulting tertiary need (or end benefit) might be providing the customer "status." The only element missing from Juran's discussion is a clear understanding of what determines into which level a specific need would fall.

The Structure of Customer Requirements

Consider the following interpretation. The highest level of customer needs, the most pervasive, should be considered *purchase motives*. These motives represent global needs, which dictate whether or not a product or service is considered at all relevant to a consumer's situation. They are the driving motivations directing a consumer in a particular need state to consider a specific product or service as likely to satisfy that need state.

The second level of needs, it is proposed, should be considered as *customer requirements*. Requirements decompose the more generic purchase motives into more pragmatic and less conceptual areas. Finally the third level of needs can be interpreted as *performance measures or attributes*. These are the most basic (and common) means for evaluating the satisfactoriness of the product or service. They are, to borrow Juran's (1992, 109) terminology the "language of things" (See Figure 3.1). It is at this level we generally question our customers about the performance of our product or service.

Using Laddering to Achieve a Complete Picture

Jonathan Gutman and Thomas Reynolds (1988), have developed a process for harnessing "means-end" chaining, which can be possibly useful in elaborating on customers' requirements. Building on earlier theories characterizing personal values as either "terminal" or "instrumental," laddering assumes customers choose between organizations in a product or service category based on the organization perceived as most instrumental in helping achieve their desired consequences.[1] Laddering uses a series of directed, probing questions to elicit perceived linkages by customers between attributes, consequences and values. In the present case it is believed that laddering could become a useful procedure for identifying the linkages between customers' *motives, requirements,* and *attributes.*

----
[1]Milton Rokeach (1979) is generally credited with proposing a model of personal values including values that represent desired end-states (*terminal values*) and behaviors and actions required to achieve these end-states, the *instrumental values.*

PERSONAL BANKING

Purchase motives	Customer requirements	Performance measures
Portfolio management	Secure transactions	Insured accounts Access to account information
	Accessibility	Flexible hours ATM/Credit card access Numerous branches Telephone inquiries after hours
	Advice/Consultation	Good research reports Makes frequent recommendations
Increase wealth	Cost benefit	Competitive interest rates Low maintenance fees Low balance requirements

Provide financial security

LUXURY AUTOMOBILE

Purchase motives	Customer requirements	Performance measures
Good investment	Financial stability	Good resale value A car others desire to own
	Economical to operate and maintain	Fuel efficient Reasonable repair bills
Status conferred	Car's/manufacturer's reputation	A luxurious car A respected manufacturer
	A recognized car	Limited production High-priced
Safety	Prevent physical harm	Good braking Safe in crashes Airbag system
Motoring enjoyment	Performance	Road-holding Acceleration Interior comfort/amenities
	Appearance	Exterior appearance

Figure 3.1   The Structure of Customer Requirements

Laddering, which melds both qualitative interviewing with quantitative analysis, is accomplished in the following sequence.

- Utilize a "discovery procedure" (repertory grid, preference ordering, or difference by occasions) to help customers identify performance attributes they associate with your category (Gutman and Reynolds find the typical participant is generally capable of generating only 10–12 different distinctions within a product category.)
- Select the most important attributes to carry forward (you may use judgment to select these attributes based on previous knowledge, or it's fair to ask participants to rank order the attributes, in which case you only proceed with the top six or so);
- Advance the selected performance attributes into the laddering exercise. This phase presents the customer with one performance attribute at a time. For each attribute the customer is asked a series of importance probes:

1. Why is it important to you that a product have/offer (performance attribute)?
2. Why is that (reason from [1.]) important to you?
3. And why or in what way is that (reason from [2.]) important to you?

- Code the attributes, requirements and motives generated in the above steps and tabulate the relationships forming common attribute-requirement-motive chains.
- Create a final, hierarchical value grid displaying the overall linkage of performance attributes, requirements, and motives.[2]

Gutman and Reynolds suggest several different discovery procedures to help identify the different product attributes customers institute to structure a product category. These methods include:

The Repertory Grid (Kelly 1955) Customers are presented with several triads of products or brands within an industry. For each (randomly assembled) triad, the customer is asked: "Of these three products, which two are most similar? How are those two similar? How are those two different from the third product?"

----

[2]The interested reader is referred to Gutman's and Reynold's article, "Laddering Theory, Method, Analysis, and Interpretation," (1988) for a more complete description of this admittedly complex data collection and analytical procedure.

Preference Ordering   Brands of a product or service are presented to customers who are asked to sort the brands according to the customer's preferences for the brands. Once a preference order is established, the customer is asked, "Why do you prefer the most preferred brand? In what ways is it different from the second most preferred brand? The third most preferred brand?, What makes the least preferred brand last?"

Occasion Differences   Customers, it is believed, offer the most useful information when they are in a personally relevant and meaningful context towards a product or service. Sometimes, mentally placing customers in a product/service use-occasion can help them describe some very useful distinctions between product alternatives or reasons for preferring particular products or services. Within the laddering step, a typical sequence would be as follows:

Category: personal computers—Product attribute: affordable

Interviewer's probe	*Customer's response*
Why is it important to you that a personal computer be *affordable?*	Because I have to stay within my department's *budget.*
Why is it important to you that you stay within your *department's budget?*	Because if I overspend, I'll be *criticized.*
And why is it important to you that you not be *criticized?*	Criticism will hurt my short- and long-term *career growth.*

The ascent up the ladder from the attribute "affordable" to the requirement "avoid criticism" to the motive *career growth* forms an interesting chain. With 10–15 customers, each volunteering 10–12 attributes and laddering 6–8, one can amass 60 to 120 different ladders, which may then be consolidated.

TYPES OF REQUIREMENT EXPLORATIONS

The purpose of exploring issues with customers is to escape the parochialness or myopia of blindly projecting management's preconceived notions to the customerbase and therefore using management's definitions of issues to compose the satisfaction survey. The way in which customers' input is solicited may include any number of proven methods. The important element is opening the consideration of issues beyond those already known (and seemingly understood by management). We will describe three techniques in this chapter. Later, in Chapter 5, we will evaluate when it is best to use different techniques.

Customer Listening Groups^{sm}

Logistics

Customer Listening Groups assemble a group or groups of customers together to help you identify their requirements, needs, and expectations. Because 8–12 customers can be gathered together in a discussion room at one time, listening groups represent an efficient method for soliciting customer input. By conducting two to four groups, usually at least two groups per major region of your operating territory, you can collect a variety of issues by tapping a geographically disperse and therefore potentially diverse collection of your customers.

To conduct customer listening groups, you will need a fair understanding of the composition of your customers to help identify possible segments of your customerbase that ought to be represented. For example, if there is a small cadre of very important customers, which will almost always be the case, at least one group should be conducted among these high-value customers. It will be more difficult to assemble them. They may be geographically dispersed. Their time may be more precious. While you may be sensitive to minimizing your demands on them, their input is critical to your investigation. And, to proceed without hearing from them would be a terrible mistake.

Groups should be conducted with representatives of each major segment or grouping of customers. This will ensure that voices of all types of customers are heard. Frequently the voices will all form a consensus. In this happy situation, you face identical needs across all customer groups. Generally though, your customer groups will *not* form a consensus. In this situation, you'll be challenged to reconcile or at least understand the differences you have discovered.

You will need to recruit customers' participation either in person or by telephone. Once you have recruited your group-members, follow up with a reminder letter to tell them how much you value their input and how important their ideas can be for your satisfaction program. The day before the group, it is a good idea to reconfirm customers' attendance by telephone.

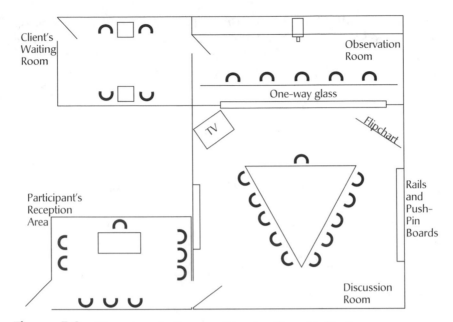

Figure 3.2   Illustration of a Customer Listening Group Facility Layout

Also, it is generally beneficial to invite your management to observe the listening groups. By observing they will better accept the recommendations from the groups, without questioning why issues are or are not present in the final survey instrument.

Conduct

A Customer Listening Group may be conducted in any conference room, though "neutral territory" is preferable. Inviting customers to your offices or to your factory may unconsciously influence the information they provide. Often consumer research facilities offering discussion rooms with adjoining observation rooms are a preferable alternative. Discussion rooms in such facilities feature a wall of one-way glass allowing your colleagues and management to observe the conduct of the session. These facilities will also have audio- and videotape recording capabilities to allow you to easily record the sessions (If you will be doing so, you should inform your customers and ask their permission.) (See Figure 3.2).

If you do not have access to a consumer research facility or if you prefer a more informal setting, you may use a hotel conference room almost as well. While a hotel room will lack an observation room, you can still arrange for the listening group to be videotaped, by placing a unpersoned camera with a wide-angle lens in the room. Participating customers, who will initially be aware of the camera, will soon lose their concern, and will generally engage in reasonably candid conversations.

You may also use a conference room at one of your customers' offices, but this may be an uncomfortable location for others of your customers to come to. Also, you will be less able to control the environment, arrange for refreshments, videotaping, and so on.

Always provide ample refreshments (a light meal, snacks, soft drinks, and so on) for both your customers and your observers. The productivity of such groups (and the satisfaction of your observers) is always influenced by their creature comforts. If you show appreciation to them with a nice meal and ample beverages, they will generally be far more talkative and participative than if you leave them hungry and thirsty.

You will need to select a moderator for your session. You should ideally select someone familiar with your products/services and your customers, yet not directly known by them. Trained moderators are easily located and hired. Several listings of practicing moderators are published annually (AMA 1996; Quirk's Marketing Research Review 1996; Marketing Tools 1996). On the other hand, you may decide against a professional moderator in favor of someone on your staff or on your program team. The group discussions will benefit from having someone intimately familiar with your company, your category and your product/service conducting the groups. You, a colleague or perhaps if you are working with a CSM consultant, someone from the firm's staff, should be able to moderate with this "inside knowledge."

In preparation for the group, you should formulate a moderator's guide (see Table 3.2). This is a list of the issues you anticipate discussing, in an order you consider optimal. It is generally best to start with fairly general issues, finally narrowing down to very specific issues. This sequence not only minimizes imposing your preconceived notions on the groups, it also allows the group to become fairly vocal in influencing the topics discussed and their specific order. You will want to use a variety of techniques in the groups to coax out answers and points of view. Try using some of the techniques described in Table 3.3.

While talking to customers in groups can be useful in "pulling some customers out of their shells," you must also consider the negative effects of group dynamics. There will be situations in which one customer may try to dominate the discussion, or assert herself through expertise. Or a customer may come prepared to discuss a particularly troublesome problem he is

Table 3.2   Sample Moderator's Guide for a Customer Listening Group

MODERATOR'S GUIDE
VIP Cellular Subscribers
Thursday, November 3, 1994

Elapsed Time	Topic	Data Method
0:00	**I. Introduction**	
	A. Listen to the participants speak out about what is important to them.	
	B. Discussion will be recorded and observed.	
	C. Share opinions, but respect others' opinions; register your point of view.	
	D. Moderator's role, make sure all opinions are heard; divide time between topics.	
	E. Members introduce themselves.	
	1. Where do you use your cellular phone?	
	2. Craziest, most exotic place you have ever called from.	
	3. How far from home have you used your cellular phone?	
0:10	**II. What service companies have provided you with truly exceptional service?**	*Private List*
	A. Specific examples.	
	B. What makes a service company great?	*Easel List*
	C. What are the key components of quality service?	
	III. What service companies do you expect to still be a customer of in five years?	*Discussion*
	IV. What service companies do the best job of making you feel well-serviced?	
	A. Who are they?	*Easel List*
	B. What do they do for you to make you feel this way?	*Easel List*
	IV. What service companies do the poorest job of making you feel well-serviced?	
	A. Who are they?	*Easel List*
	B. What do (or don't) they do for you to make you feel this way?	*Easel List*
0:25	**VI. What about providers of cellular service?**	
	A. What level of servicing do they provide?	*Discussion*
	B. How do they compare with your best and poorest companies?	

Table 3.3   Techniques to be Used in a Customer Listening Group

Technique	Explanation
Projective Techniques	
Personality Associations	Participants equate companies or brands with well-known personalities (from radio, tv, movies). These personalities can be real or fictional. When the meaning of the association is not immediately obvious, group members can be asked to guess why one of the group has offered the association. Later the group member can confirm or disconfirm the group's explanation.
Sentence Completions	The moderator starts a provocative sentence, group members must complete it. This is generally done by asking group members to privately record their responses first (on supplied tablets), and then sharing them, later.
Expressive Drawing	Group members can be asked to draw a picture of a typical service representative, salesperson, customer, etc.
Anthropomorphization	Participants are asked to represent companys or brands with objects, animals, fabrics, gems, etc. With the characterizations established, group members are asked to explain why the representations are appropriate.
Table-Top Mapping	The group is presented with flags or signs representing all of the competitors (or brands) in a category and are asked to arrange them in some order on the conference table. As a configuration appears, the moderator may ask group members to explain the groupings and to guess what the rationale might have been for the grouping.
Probing Techniques	
Straightforward Probe	The moderator asks group members to expand on their answers by using direct questions such as, "Why do you say that?," "Why do you feel that way?" or "Could you explain that a bit more?"
Third Party Probe	A participant is asked to explain or comment on a statement or explanation made by another group member.
Silent Probe	After hearing a group member's answer, the moderator purposefully pauses for serveral seconds prompting additional comments from the group member or discussion from other group members.
Parrot Probe	The moderator repeats or paraphrases the participant's response to confirm what was said, and possibly gain an elaboration.
Usage Probe	The moderator asks group members to describe the circumstances surrounding the last time they used a particular service or service provider.
"What if" Probe	The moderator creates a hypothetical situation concerning a product or service and asks group members to comment/elaborate.

having. This customer may solicit the group's support. The well-trained moderator can handle such situations, hopefully without excessively aggravating the customer involved. The "dominator" must be politely reminded there are other participants whose opinions are equally important. Concerning the "expertiser" the group must be reminded his or her point of view is no more valid to you than theirs.

It is important to create an open and supportive climate in your listening groups. You want an environment that maximizes the likelihood of hearing from each and every customer. Often asking for a private vote on personal notepads will assure that you sample the diversity of opinions that exist in a room even if some customers are reluctant to verbally assert their personal points of view. The role of the moderator is to make the discussion table safe for diversity and difference of opinion. One way this can be done, is for the moderator to offer the following analogy:

> "If I were to ask what was the color of the sky, we'd have some concurrence of opinion that it was a shade of blue. But, if I asked you each to describe the taste of a cola soft drink, we'd have 10 very different descriptions. Each description would be equally valid, no matter how different from the others it might be."

You will also want an easel pad in the conference room to allow the moderator to make lists of issues and to prioritize issues as they are volunteered. Such easel pad lists are a great way to achieve group consensus on priorities, the most important key issues, and so on.

If you do invite observers, give some thought to managing them. Warn them against overreacting to the groups. The last thing you want is an observer seizing on one obscure opinion or issue and taking that back to the workplace with her as an "important finding." Remind your observers that the groups are not projectable; that you're simply amassing lists of possible issues to subsequently be quantified. After each group it is a good idea to "debrief" your observers. Invite each of them to describe one or more insights they picked up during the group. Listening to each other's relatively different observations will reinstate for each observer how subjective reactions to a group discussion can truly be.

Reporting

The findings from customer listening groups are generally reported using both written reports and videotapes or edited videotape summaries. The most important output from such groups will be, of course, a listing of requirements and needs, with some exploration of levels of performance (expectations). So, unlike focus groups, the report from a listening group need not be as comprehensive. On the other hand, if interesting insights are learned in the course of the groups, it will be to the benefit of the customer satisfaction program, if a thorough report is issued. Of course, the standard "qualitative research caveats" apply. The groups may provide interesting explanations and anecdotes, but their results should not be generalized to the larger population of customers—that is the job of the satisfaction survey! As a reminder of the exploratory nature of customer listening groups, preface your group report with a qualification similar to the following:

> Customer Listening Groups (like the groups described in this report) seek to develop insights into customers' needs and reactions to the dimensions of satisfaction; they cannot provide quantitatively precise evaluations.

> By reason of the small size of the groups, the special recruiting techniques employed and the study objectives themselves, it should be clearly agreed that the work is exploratory in nature. The "findings" from such groups should be considered, therefore, only as hypotheses for future and more sophisticated quantitative study. The opinions of the groups are not (nor were they intended to be) projectable to any larger population. The primary purpose for conducting the groups is to stimulate thinking.

> We recommend, therefore, that this report be read and reviewed in a "qualitative" rather than a "quantitative" frame of mind.

> Terry G. Vavra, Ph.D.
> Moderator
> March 1996

To illustrate why you are contemplating carrying certain issues forward into your quantitative survey, you can edit the real time videotape into some specific "video bites," which capture your customers articulating certain of their concerns. Editing the videotape of your customer listening groups provides you with an excellent tool to use to demonstrate the different points of view held by some customers. Make sure you request a "time code" be added to your videotape as your group is recorded. This time code makes editing much easier. You will also need to observe the discussion (on a real time basis) to identify the most pertinent comments. Having noted the clock time of these comments (or the on-screen time from a clock display) will allow you to find the representative comments much more quickly in a editing session.

Sometimes in the absence of such "evidence" (from customer listening groups), operating areas or departments reviewing the issues you plan to assess may dismiss the relevance or importance of certain issues. Their intuitive belief may be, "We do not have to ask about our documentation, *it is not an issue!*" If you have videotape of customers complaining about documentation, you will have less trouble keeping documentation among the issues you measure for satisfaction.

On-site Visits

Logistics

Customer on-site visits are exactly what the name implies—visiting a number of customers at their workplaces, homes, or wherever they use your product or service. Ideally, your visit will be scheduled for a time when they will be actively involved in your product or service, so that their reactions to your quality and servicing will be entirely fresh. If this is not practical, at least visiting them in their own environs increases the likelihood they will furnish you insights relevant to their consumption of your products or services.

To arrange some on-site visits, you will again have to be familiar with different classes or segments of your customers. You will want to schedule visits to members of each of the segments you so identify. Obviously, the on-site visit is somewhat more practical in industrial, business-to-business categories (where individual customers account for much larger single purchases) than in consumer categories, but the on-site is not totally out of the question in consumer goods.

You will need to recruit customers' participation (in person or by telephone), then follow up with a reminder letter. The day before the visit, it is a good idea to reconfirm the customer's willingness to participate by telephone, especially if you are going to be traveling long distances to meet with the customer.

On-site visits are the least burdensome method for your customers to help you gather the input you need, since *you go to them!*

Conduct

You will need to contact and recruit your customers for your visit a few weeks in advance of your planned visit. It is a good idea to follow your telephone conversation with a letter confirming the appointment and your purpose for meeting with your customer. Generally you should provide a brief outline of the questions (or at least issues) you would like their advice on. You will also be able to show them how you expect to progress from one topic to another in your discussion.

Prior to visiting your customers, you will want to write a discussion guide. This guide will be very similar to the moderator's guide for the Customer Listening Sessions, but can allow for more interaction with your customer, and more directioning from your customer. Because you will be talking "one-on-one" you do not have to worry about group dynamics as in the Listening Sessions.

Generally it will be a good idea to ask if you can tape-record the session. This will allow you to be a better listener, relieving you of the burden of taking notes (This is exactly how you should explain your desire to record the session.) If your customer seems uneasy about the tape recorder, do not push it. Sometimes customers will ask you to turn off the recorder as they make a certain statement. This is all fine, encourage as much candor as possible.

Reporting

Reports from on-site visits will be somewhat more laborsome to develop. While you may wish to prepare a written report of your customer listening sessions, you will almost certainly need to do so for any on-sites you conduct. The reason for this is there will be no video recording as you might have in the listening groups. And, while you will have an audio recording, it is still more useful to have a written report.

Make sure to include ample verbatim comments. Your points will carry greater weight when communicated in the words of customers. Try to synthesize similar ideas across the interviews you have conducted, rather than reporting on each interview separately.

Customer Communications, Letters, and Telephone Calls

Logistics

The mail, phone calls and today, even the e-mail, your organization receives are all a well-spring of information about customers' requirements and needs. Unfortunately, this is probably the most difficult information to capture and summarize even though it is free and it already exists. Different departments may handle each type of customer communication. And, rarely if ever, will the departments record the conversations or tabulate the issues as they come in. Instead, customer service representatives work each customer contact (call or letter) as a separate "case" striving to resolve it. When they do, they move on to the next challenge, without documenting the nature of the contact, nor the type of resolution.

If letters are retained, you will probably have to reread them and code the nature of each complaint (or compliment). Telephone conversations, due to their nature, will most likely have been lost in the wires, their information and customers' identities will probably all have been lost.

Conduct

The traditional means for summarizing the content of "mailbags" has been to assign numeric codes to each new issue identified. Then each letter is assigned one or more codes to represent the issue or issues included. These codes are tallied on separate score sheets, or in an accompanying computer tabulation. Additional codes can be instituted to represent the strength of the position advocated, and so on. In more sophisticated systems, content analysis may be employed to assign greater quantitative information to the correspondence.

More recently computers have become involved in the manipulation and summary of customer mail. Most often the correspondence is entered into computer files, and then some form of content analysis is applied. Common procedures include:

> *Searching for Keywords*   Each response containing a keyword is listed with the keyword underlined in the context in which the customer used it.
> *Sorting Responses by Customer Characteristics*   Responses of customers conforming to the search characteristics are listed along with descriptive information identifying the particular customer.
> *Frequency counting* A simple tally can be maintained of issues.[3] This is ideal for constructing *Pareto charts* (to be discussed in Chapter 6). Pareto charts allow an organization to analyze the complaints associated with dissatisfaction with a product/service and then to direct remedial actions.

Reporting

If you institute a relatively quantitative analysis of your customer communications, then reporting the substance of this information will be easier.

----

[3]For more information on these procedures see *Verbatim Analyzer: Response Processing Software,* Marketing Metrics, 1988.

Your report should identify the key issues, their concentration among any particular groups of customers, and some severity judgments. You will be able to communicate much of this in summary, frequency tables.

Where a quantitative analysis does not exist, you will need to be more careful of your interpretation. You are quite likely to focus on comments which reinforce or agree with perceptions you have. Try to keep as objective a point of analysis as possible. You will nevertheless need to summarize the more frequent and more important comments, gleaned primarily from your reading of the communications.

Executive Soundings^{sm}

Logistics

Your organization's personnel is a good repository of information about customers' requirements and needs. Both executives and customer contact representatives can provide useful insights. All employees, however, are likely to "put their own spin" on issues, selectively reinforcing their own biases. Nevertheless, it is still a good idea to meet with employees at different levels and in different departments throughout your organization to tally their perspectives of customers' requirements and needs.

Within these interviews you will meet with the heads of various departments who will be "customers" of your customer satisfaction survey. It is vital you hear their concerns and questions. And, it is vital that you establish their involvement in (and "ownership" of) the project. Without this sort of upfront "buy-in" your survey results may not be as constructively received. The best CSM project is one that all affected departments thoroughly support.

Conduct

You should identify key executives in your company's organization, both those who have maximum contact with external customers or very little.

Arrange an appointment to speak with each executive you identify. It is a good idea to precede your meeting by sending a list of the topics or issues about which you seek the executive's viewpoint. Your purpose is to identify the most important attributes for inclusion in the future (or ongoing) customer satisfaction measurement program.

Reporting

Reporting findings from executive soundings is really true two-way communication. You will not only be reporting what you have discovered but also reinforcing issues you already have identified. In other words, you can use this report to both show and achieve greater consensus. Though the practice is open to debate, some satisfaction professionals actually conduct executive soundings using their satisfaction survey. They ask executives to answer the survey as they believe the organization's customers will. The purpose of this exercise is to later show executives how wrong they were in their understanding of customers' desires and needs. The discrepancy becomes obvious as executives' ratings or feelings are compared to those collected from customers.

Moments of Truth

Logistics

As managers of customer interactions, we have become aware that our customers' satisfaction will often depend on how they are treated in a specific situation. The customer may make a special request, or may find a product does not work as they had expected, or an employee may initiate an action towards the customer. Each of these situations can become, what Jan Carlzon (1987), former president of Scandinavian Airline Systems, called a "moment of truth."

Borrowed from the "moment de veridad" of the Spanish bullring when the matador and bull size each other up, a customer's moment of truth is every bit as dramatic. It is in moments of truth, Carlzon said, that organizations are either "created" (their image shored up in a customer's mind) by living up to the customer's expectations, or organizations are "destroyed" by failing a customer's expectations.

Inventorying moments of truth is becoming a routine tool for improving the quality of services (Vavra 1995). For example, the IBM Consulting Group in its Customer Value Management℠ dissects customer interactions into moments of truth to help its clients better manage the delivery of quality services or quality processes.

A moment of truth analysis will often start with a blueprint or brown paper of an interaction with a customer. A *blueprint* or *brown paper* is nothing more than a diagrammatic representation of an organization's interaction with a customer. The name "brown paper" is derived from the fact that many such analyses are drawn on brown, butcher shop, or kraft wrapping paper. They were first suggested for the management of service quality by Lynn Shostack (1977). The resulting diagram should show every bit of interaction, written, verbal in person, verbal on the phone, and so on. Evidence of such interactions is actually attached to the diagram (which can often cover the wall or walls of a standard conference room).

Not all moments of truth are equally important. Some are so important the customer's ultimate satisfaction depends on them. These moments of truth have been distinguished as "critical incidents." Patterned after psychologist Flanagan's (1954) critical incident methodology, critical incidents have been popularized in marketing by Bitner, Booms, and Tretault (1990). Bitner, Booms, and Tretault found that so-called critical incidents could be identified through a four-question sequence. The questions suggested are:

Consider a time when you had a particularly satisfying or dissatisfying experience with (Brand or Firm Name):

1. When did the incident happen?
2. What specific circumstances led up to this situation?
3. Exactly what did (brand or firm) or its employees say or do?
4. What resulted that made you feel particularly satisfied or dissatisfied?

A result of this questioning will be a list of "critical incidents"—events that are so important that satisfaction or dissatisfaction with them flavors the customer's satisfaction of the *entire interaction* with your organization.

As incidents are volunteered by a sample of customers, they will have to be processed. You can establish your own coding categories or you can conduct a Pareto analysis on the incidents. Bitner, Booms, and Tretault found three categories (regarding the actions of the organization) collapsed the critical incidents they collected. The categories were:

- an employee initiating an encounter at his/her own volition;
- an employee responding to a product or service failure;
- an employee answering a customer's special request.

Conduct

The value of the moments of truth analysis follows Juran's mandate to "be the customer." Similarly the American Indian challenged others to "walk a mile in my moccasins [shoes]" to better understand the situation one found himself in. In moments of truth excursions, the analyst essentially becomes the customer and examines the situation and the evidence (or lack of it) supplied by the organization. It is always eye-opening, it is usually highly productive, and it can foster "breakthrough" insights that help organizations "turn themselves around."

Reporting

Reports from critical incident methods are generally frequency tables identifying those incidents most associated with satisfaction and those most associated with dissatisfaction. In some cases the identification of the incident itself may carry some learning or discovery value.

Summary/Comparison

Each of these methods for creating a list of performance attributes has its own strengths. Consider your situation carefully before selecting the method or methods you will use. Once you select the methods, make sure to leverage each technique to maximize the value of the information you collect.

A REALITY CHECK

Validating Against Existing Models

The previous section has described several methods for empirically identifying attributes your customers and your management describe as defining quality in the product or service you sell. It is a good idea to reflect on how exhaustive the attributes (and their underlying "dimensions") are in describing the category. Fortunately, some external lists exist to serve as useful "checklists" with which to compare your listings. This cross-check can provide a "reality check" to determine how many different dimensions your list taps, and if—for whatever reason—you have missed a dimension.

Author David Garvin (1988), in his book *Managing Quality*, provides a comprehensive list of the eight dimensions he believes summarize customers' judgment of the quality of products. These dimensions are:

- **Performance**—the satisfactoriness of the primary operating characteristics of the product;

    The acceleration of my Honda is excellent.

- **Features**—the secondary characteristics that supplement the product's basic functioning;

    The brightness control on the monitor is very useful.

- **Reliability**—the likelihood of the product failing or malfunctioning within a specified time period;

    The printer has performed reliably without breakdowns since I purchased it.

- **Conformance**—how closely the product's design and operation match pre-established specifications or users' expectations;
  The sharpness of the picture is exactly as the literature described it.

- **Durability**—the amount of use one gets from a product before it physically deteriorates or becomes obsolete;
  The printer lasted as long as I expected.

- **Serviceability**—the speed, courtesy, competence, and ease of repair of a product;
  When needed, it was easy to have my vehicle serviced.

- **Aesthetics**—subjective elements of personal judgment regarding how the product looks;
  The external appearance of the monitor is very attractive.

- **Reputation**—the general image and reputation of the company.
  Motorola has an excellent reputation for computer chips.

In a companion work by authors Valerie Zeithaml, Parsu Parasuraman, and Leonard Berry (1990), *Delivering Quality Services,* the authors offer a similar listing of dimensions that they propose define customers' judgment of quality in services:

- **Reliability**—the ability to perform the service dependably and accurately;
  When CNA Insurance promises to do something by a certain date, they do it!

- **Responsiveness**—willingness to help customers and provide prompt servicing;
  Employees of Fleet Financial Services are never too busy to respond to my requests promptly.

- **Assurance**
  - **Competency**—possessing the required skills and knowledge;
    MicroSoft customer service reps are always able to identify and help fix problems.

  - **Courtesy**—politeness, respect, considerationn and friendliness of service personnel;
    Employees of United Airlines are always polite and courteous.

  - **Credibility**—trustworthiness, believability, and honesty of the service provider;
    Allstate Insurance agents can be trusted completely.

- **Security**—freedom from danger, risk or doubt;
  AARP works hard to keep my insurance coverage adequate to my needs.

- **Empathy**
  - **Accessibility**—approachability and ease of contacting;
    You never have to wait to get an appointment to see someone at Prudential.
  - **Communication Skills**—keeping customers informed in language they can understand, and listening to their response and questions;
    AAA of New Jersey reps can explain the many issues of automobile insurance understandably.

  - **Understanding the customer**—Taking the effort to getting to know customers and their particular needs;
    Employees of the Ritz-Carlton always see I get all the special requests I've made on previous stays.

- **Tangibles**—the condition of the "physical evidence" surrounding the delivery of the service.
  The branch offices of Prudential are very professional looking.

If your listing of performance attributes fails to include one or more attributes to represent each of these dimensions, you may want to rethink the comprehensiveness of your list. It should be easy to create your own attribute to represent the missing dimension(s). On the other hand, you can always go back to customers and probe the meaning and/or relevance of the dimension(s) in your category for them.

BALANCING MANAGEMENT'S NEEDS WITH CUSTOMERS' INTERESTS

The ideal survey will contain attributes that are meaningful to customers and management alike. Some of management's proposed attributes may relate directly to performance goals ("internal metrics") they have established for themselves. The relevance of some of these to end-use customers is sometimes questionable, however, if you have space in your survey, include as many as you can. You will be pleased to see how compelling will be your customers' likely indifference to these attributes. As you model the importance of the attributes (or measure it directly) you will have direct evidence about the importance (or lack of importance) of each of the attributes. This will be information that is generally incontestable to management.

Recognizing that your survey will not be capable of assessing all issues, your major objective should be to balance some of management's key information needs with the issues that customers have told you what matters the most to them. By this balance, you will not turn off management, they will see your measurement program as meeting many of their informational needs. You will also remain true to your objectives by including issues that customers have volunteered as important. As you collect data, you will have information with which to compare both sources of issues; customers and management. This will generally be a learning experience for management as they see some of their "pet issues" superseded by customers' issues.

Customer satisfaction surveys usually tap three relatively distinct areas of customer-organization interaction:

- **transaction performance**—transactions are defined as any interaction with the organization or its intermediaries: the selling effort, the servicing effort, responsiveness to customer questions, and so on;
- **functional performance**—this is a measure of how well the product or service performed in satisfying the customer need for which it was intended;
- **reliability performance**—this is a measure of performance over time, how maintenance-free the product was, how long-lasting was the result of the service, and so on.

While it is possible to assess all three aspects in one survey, this is normally not a good idea.

Many companies, Xerox for example, have restructured their satisfaction measurement process to compliment the comprehensive annual satisfaction survey with a survey of customer's satisfaction with transactions, the survey being conducted within a few days of the actual transaction. Most automobile companies (Toyota and Rolls-Royce among others) measure their owners' satisfaction at several points in the relationship. Typically an initial satisfaction survey is conducted within a week or two of delivery (this survey will focus on the sales and delivery experience—a transaction-orientation). After the owner has had sufficient time to fully experience the performance of the car (say 3 to 6 months) a more detailed performance satisfaction survey is conducted (a measure of functional performance). Finally, some time out in the ownership experience (18 to 24 months) a third survey will be conducted. This survey will focus on the reliability performance and the quality of the "relationship" with the manufacturer.

REDUCING THE LIST

If the mechanisms described above (for eliciting issues) have been at all successful, you will arrive at this stage with too many issues to investigate! So the challenge now is to simplify for your customers' benefit. The list of issues must be reduced to minimize any redundancy which may have crept in and to retain the most important issues. There are two basic ways of simplifying the list: judgment and statistics.

Judgmental Procedures

Judgment is probably the least satisfactory way of reducing the number of performance items to be carried forward. Because customers have been included in the discovery process to avoid internal biases, it seems self-defeating to end the process with an internal, judgment-driven reduction. Why won't the same biases that operated at the outset now cancel out customer-volunteered issues because they are devalued or disbelieved? One possible defense may be the very nature of learning. Managers may be so impressed with the discrepancy between their list of supposed customer priorities that they totally rethink their view of the customer. If this happens, then reduction of items through judgment may not be as biased as might have been initially expected. It is realistic to add, however, that not all managers are as open-minded. If judgment is to play a role in your reduction of issues, several different managers should be asked to review the list. For each item they suggest be excluded, they should be asked to explain their reasons for excluding the item.

Judgment will, no doubt, have to be used to some extent; either as a substitute for a statistical reduction procedure or to conclude such a procedure.

Statistical Procedures

Several different statistical procedures can be meaningfully used to help reduce the number of issues to be carried forward to your CSM. Almost all will require some intermediate data to be collected from customers.

Reducing Issues with Factor Analysis

Factor analysis is a statistical technique that identifies correlations among lists of issues or items (SPSS, SYSTAT, SAS). The way it does this is by establishing "factors" or evaluative dimensions for each of the major pieces of information conveyed in a group of issues or items. Then each individual item's correlation with the construct factor or dimension is represented by a correlation coefficient. (We discuss the technique of factor analysis in Chapter 8, in this chapter we will simply review its application to the reduction of performance items.)

Figure 3.3 shows a typical output from a factor analysis. Although the output will look somewhat confusing, it is actually fairly easy to interpret. The final step of the analysis is called a "rotated loadings matrix." This matrix is akin to a table of correlation coefficients between each of your performance items and a construct variable called a "factor." When two or more performance items each correlate highly with the same factor, this is evidence the performance items are each measuring essentially the same construct. In such a case, it is safe to eliminate one or more of the performance items without losing any information from respondents.

To conduct a factor analysis you will need some actual ratings (generally taken from a pre-test of your satisfaction questionnaire). You will need to survey a sample of more customers than you have trial performance items. For example, if you are considering 30 different items for

Rotated Factor Loading Matrix (Attributes sorted by Factor)

Performance Attribute	Factor I	Factor II	Factor III
Courteous front desk	**0.85003**	0.45632	0.33205
Courteous reservation clerks	**0.79665**	0.32567	0.19194
Reservation accuracy	**0.65005**	0.12906	0.33509
Helpful front desk	**0.55442**	0.34011	0.29004
Helpful reservation clerk	**0.50531**	0.02387	0.33459
Room rate per night	0.40045	**0.79003**	0.04567
Room condition	0.33564	**0.72044**	0.11299
Types of rooms	0.20114	**0.68867**	0.40005
Cleanliness of room	0.15009	**0.60289**	0.22955
Accessible location	0.23567	0.39981	**0.88411**
Shuttle bus frequency	0.28901	0.35922	**0.70789**
Expedient check–out	0.11345	0.45119	**0.66701**
Expedient check–in	0.04789	0.11288	**0.65099**

Factor I Interpreted as Courtesy
Factor II Interpreted as Room Value
Factor III Interpreted as Accessibility

Figure 3.3   Sample Factor Analysis Output to Reduce the Number of Items

inclusion in your survey, you should attempt to get evaluations of your service/product on the 30 items by at least 30 customers if possible. Ratings from fewer than 30 customers can be used, however, the resulting analysis is simply less definitive.

Reducing Issues with Cluster Analysis

Cluster analysis is a technique related to factor analysis. Some cluster analysis procedures are actually factor analysis applications. But an additional set of cluster analysis procedures—the hierarchical procedures—approach similarity in a somewhat different perspective. Using clustering analysis to check for redundancy in your pre-test questionnaire, offers a somewhat different insight from that achieved by factor analysis. In factor analysis each performance attribute is looked upon as a component of another variable, the factor. In cluster analysis, your performance attributes are treated more as distinct entities, and their similarity or dissimilarity to other attributes is the driving force of the analysis.

Hierarchical clustering programs produce dendograms or tree diagrams that depict the relationship of your attributes. In Figure 3.4, 13 potential attributes for a hotel satisfaction survey have been clustered. The sooner two attributes are linked (on the left-most portion of the horizontal axis) the more similar they are. Figure 3.4 shows the most similar attributes are "courteous front desk" and "helpful front desk." Removing one or the other of these attributes will not substantially effect the amount of information you collect from your survey. You should retain the one with more meaning, more actionability, or the attribute with the lower non-response rate. You should avoid the temptation to combine them into one question. Merging issues will confuse your customers, and will make your interpretation of results more difficult.

The next cluster of similar attributes contains "helpful reservation clerks" and "courteous reservation clerks." Again, one of these items should be deleted. The first and second clusters combine next, suggesting you may wish to retain the two "helpful" items. Moving from left to right, there is a gap before the next cluster of attributes combine, suggesting more uniqueness in these attributes. A final result, might be only reducing the 13 to 11 attributes by simplifying the first two clusters. A more aggressive approach would be to reduce the 13 attributes to 6, with an attribute representing each of the major clusters. One version of a six-attribute questionnaire would include: reservation accuracy, room rate per night, cleanliness of room, expedient check-in, shuttle bus frequency, and

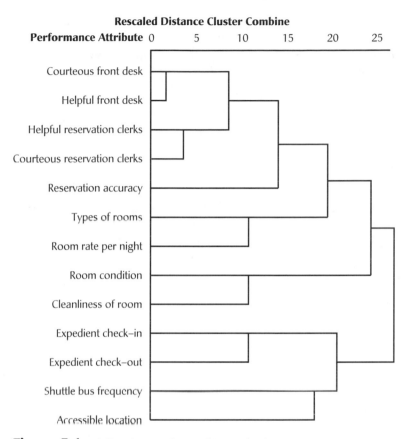

Figure 3.4   A Dendogram from a Cluster Analysis

Source: Douglas, Vicki, "Questionnaire Too Long? Try Variable Clustering," *Marketing News*, February 27, 1995, p. 38.

accessible location. The last two attributes are the last to join in the dendogram, indicating they bring more unique information to the questionnaire than any of the other 11 attributes. They should be retained in future questionnaires.

REFERENCES

American Marketing Association, New York Chapter. *The Green Book.* New York City, 1996.

Bitner, Mary Jo, Bernard C. Booms and Mary Stanfield Tretault. "The Service Encounter: Diagnosing Favorable and Unfavorable Incidents." *Journal of Marketing.* 54, no. 1 (January 1990): 71–84.

Carlzon, Jan. *Moments of Truth.* Cambridge, MA: Ballinger Publishing Co., 1987

Drucker, Peter F. *The Executive in Action.* New York: Harper Business, 1996.

Flanagan, John C. "The Critical Incident Technique." *Psychological Bulletin.* 51, (July 1954): 327–357.

Garvin, David. *Managing Quality.* New York: The Free Press, 1988.

Hayes, Bob E. *Measuring Customer Satisfaction: Development and Use of Questionnaires.* Milwaukee: ASQC Quality Press, 1992.

Juran, J. M. *Juran on Quality by Design: The New Steps for Planning Quality into Goods and Services.* New York: The Free Press, 1992.

Kelly, George, A. *The Psychology of Personal Constructs.* New York: W. W. Norton and Co., Inc., 1955.

Levitt, Theodore. *The Marketing Imagination.* New York: The Free Press, 1983.

Marketing Metrics. *Verbatim Analyzer: Response Processing Software.* Paramus, NJ, 1988.

Quirk's Marketing Research Review. "A Guide to Focus Group Moderators." April 1996.

Reynolds, Thomas J., and Jonathan Gutman. "Laddering Theory, Method, Analysis, and Interpretation." *Journal of Advertising Research.* (February-March 1988): 11–31.

Rokeach, Milton. *Understanding Human Values.* New York: The Free Press, 1979.

Shostack, G. Lynn. "Breaking Free From Product Marketing." *Journal of Marketing.* 41, no. 2 (April 1977): 73–80.

SAS, SAS Institute, Cary, NC, (919) 677–8000.

SPSS, SPSS Inc., 444 N. Michigan Avenue, Chicago, IL, (312) 329–2400.

Vavra, Terry G. *Aftermarketing: How to Keep Your Customers for Life Through Relationship Marketing.* Burr Ridge, IL: Irwin Professional Publishing, 1995.

Zeithaml, Valerie, Parsu Parasuraman, and Leonard Berry. *Delivering Quality Services.* New York: The Free Press, 1990.

DESIGN:
CREATING AN EFFECTIVE
INFORMATION PROCESS

With the informational elements identified in the Discovery phase, it is necessary to create a viable survey program that will collect the most important elements of information, while maximizing customer participation and satisfaction. (Do not create a satisfaction measurement program that ends up frustrating and thereby dissatisfying customers!)

The goals of this phase are to understand which pieces of information are most important to collect and then to decide how to collect the information from customers using the most efficient and palatable collection method. It is also necessary to specify exactly which customers are to be included in the survey process and what you expect to learn from each type.

program
Design

Chapter 4

CHAPTER 4

Designing the Questionnaire

OVERVIEW

Most of us, through many experiences in answering other companies' questionnaires, somehow feel we too can be adept at writing a questionnaire. But writing an *effective* questionnaire is a highly developed skill requiring special training. Writing an effective questionnaire means accomplishing a complex task with numerous levels of decisions. For example, the overall sequencing or flow of the questionnaire is very important and can influence answers given in subsequent questions. Yet all too frequently, designers fail to examine the "macro-structure" of the questionnaire (that is, the flow and design of the interview itself). Instead, the designers focus on the particular wording of individual questions, comprising the "micro-structure."

At the micro-level, the number of decisions to be made in writing an individual question is staggering. For example, there is the decision of whether to ask a question in an "open-ended" or "closed-ended" format. Several additional decisions accompany the selection of closed-ended questions. For example, what type of response scale should be used?

121

Should the scale be "verbal" or "numerical"? And, how many response options should be provided, a large number or a small number? Also, should an even or odd number of response categories be provided?

These are just a few of the considerations to be made in composing a satisfaction survey questionnaire. This chapter will examine each of these major issues in detail.

MACRO CONSIDERATIONS OF QUESTIONNAIRE DESIGN

Interview Flow and Sequence

The Logic of the Question Sequence

You will usually have some logical flow in mind related to the questions you wish to ask a customer. This flow usually will start with very global issues and will ultimately zero in on some very specific, precise issues. It is generally appropriate to ask the global questions first, getting the customer in the "product/service usage" frame of mind. Then you can narrow in or funnel to the more specific questions. With this sequence, questions about more specific issues will seem logical and expected to the customer. You will also have stimulated your customer's thinking about the totality of your product and its purchase and use context prior to asking the detailed questions.

You may find it useful to outline the flow of your interview. Most word processors have outline processors that allow one to expand and contract text from listing only section headings of an interview to a complete listing of all questions (see Figure 4.1). By reminding you of the overall structure of your interview, as you enter additional questions, the outline processors allow you to keep track of the flow of your interview, without fixating too narrowly on particular questions.

In section A of Figure 4.1, an entire page of the questionnaire is shown (produced by the outline processor). In section B the outline processor has diminished the outline by one level, showing now only the questions (without responses). In section C, the outline has been further diminished, now showing only the major sections of the questionnaire. By toggling between views (the entire questionnaire to only questions or only sections) the survey professional can maintain a good grasp of the questionnaire's flow.

Section A: The Entire Questionnaire
  I. *About Your Rolls-Royce Motor Car*
    1. In which name is your Rolls-Royce motor car registered?
          Self
          Company
          Leasing Company
          Other (please specify)
    2. Did you part exchange (trade in) a car for this Rolls-Royce?
          Yes
          No
  II. *Your Attitude About Our Dealers*
    3. How would you rate the Rolls-Royce dealership on the following?
        3A. About the Dealership
              Convenience of location
              Ease of access (parking . . .)
              Exterior appearance of the showroom
              Interior appearance and layout of the showroom
              Quality of sales personnel
              Availability of literature and information
              Convenience of opening hours
        3B. About Your Salesperson
              Level of product knowledge/ability to answer questions
              Demonstration of the motor car, its features and contents
              Professionalism of the negotiation and sale
              Explanation of aftersale service and warranty
              Tour of service facilities
        3C. Condition of Your Rolls-Royce at Time of Delivery
              Cleanliness of interior
              Cleanliness of exterior
              Vehicle's mechanical condition
              Delivery on time
    4. Why did you select this dealer to purchase this Rolls-Royce?
    5. Would you recommend this dealer?
          Yes
          No
          Please comment
    6. Please give us your overall ratings.
          Overall Satisfaction
          With your selling dealer
          With your Rolls-Royce motor car
  III. *About Yourself*
    7. What is your date of birth?
          Month/Date/Year

Figure 4.1   Using an Outline Processor to Build an Interview

8. Would you confirm the industry you are in and the products or services you deliver (e.g., property developer). If convenient, please attach a business card.
9. And your position in the business.
10. Are you self-employed?

    Yes

    No
11. Who is the principal driver, and who else may drive the motor car?

Section B: Collapsed to Question Level

I. About Your Rolls-Royce Motor Car
1. In which name is your Rolls-Royce motor car registered?
2. Did you part exchange (trade in) a car for this Rolls-Royce?

II. Your Attitude About Our Dealers
3. How would you rate the Rolls-Royce dealership on the following?
4. How did you select this dealer to purchase this Rolls-Royce?
5. Would you recommend this dealer?
6. Please give us your overall ratings.

III. About Yourself
7. What is your date of birth?
8. Would you confirm the industry you are in and the products or services you deliver (e.g. property developer). If convenient, please attach a business card.
9. And your position in the business.
10. Are you self-employed?
11. Who is the principal driver, and who else may drive the motor car?

Section C: Collapsed to Section Level

I. About Your Rolls-Royce Motor Car
II. Your Attitude About Our Dealers
III. About Yourself

Figure 4.1—*Continued*

Order Effects

Some questions can provide information, answers, or suggestions influencing how your customers might respond to other questions later in the survey. The order between such suggestive questions and other survey questions is critical to prevent biasing responses to the subsequently placed questions. Order effects manifest themselves both in terms of *consistency* and *saliency*. Consistency order effects cause customers to try to make subsequent answers and information consistent with their answers to previous questions. Saliency order effects occur when earlier questions make an experience or issue more salient or available than it otherwise would have been, thus influencing a subsequent answer. To guard against order effects, try to step back and review the question sequence within your questionnaire, paying particular attention to possible sequence problems between questions. Problems are most common after questions that must explain an issue or situation. Questions about the issue ought to precede the explanatory question.

As your interview progresses from one informational goal to another, it is always a good idea to tell your customer-respondents you are shifting questioning-gears. The more you help a customer understand what information you are after, the better the quality of the information you collect will be. And, when you change your questioning, let your customers know, they will appreciate the lead, and will provide you more relevant information.

The Sponsorship Issue

There are two schools of thought in the philosophy of asking questions. Some would suggest telling respondents *as little as possible* about the reason for asking the questions and how the information collected will be used. Exemplifying this perspective is current marketing research methodology in which the intent or interest of studies is traditionally disguised. The goal is to reduce respondent bias. By telling the respondent as little as possible about who is sponsoring the study, what the informational objectives are and how the information will be used, it is presumed the respondent will have less chance to consciously influence the survey results in the direction she would like to see the sponsor act.

The alternative school of thought on sponsorship suggests being candid with customers and providing an honest description of the survey's goals. This position is based on the realistic assumption that respondents will invariably try to guess the reasons for conducting the survey. It is human nature to be inquisitive, especially when we are being asked to spend time and provide information. If respondents guess wrongly, they may bias the results in the wrong direction. And so, this position argues, one might as well level with the respondent, hoping that this frankness will create a more positive attitude toward the survey and hence more honest responses. This means not only telling the customer the purpose of the survey, but providing indications throughout the interview when informational objectives shift to other areas.

Candidness hardly eliminates respondent bias, however. There will still be those advocates of the organization who will use the survey to "congratulate" it for doing a good job. There may be a like number of disgruntled customers who use the survey to vent on a particular issue.

The author believes in confiding with customers by identifying the organization as sponsor of the survey. Coincidentally, from a purely practical point, most customer satisfaction surveys are more efficiently conducted if they openly identify the sponsor's brand and sponsorship. If questions are to be asked about very specific products and services, it would be impossible (and unwise) to attempt to disguise or shield the true intent of the survey or keep the sponsor's identity secret.

In the special case of surveying your competitors' customers for competitive benchmarking, you will have to modify this suggestion. It would be unethical to represent yourself (or your interviewers) as your competitor—in approaching competitors' customers. Instead, you will want to identify a third-party research firm to conduct such a benchmarking subsample. Normally these interviews are described to potential respondents as an *industry survey*.

There is, in addition, the goodwill benefit of telling your customers that your survey is being sponsored by your organization. This conveys interest in customers' satisfaction and a desire to hear their ideas for product/service improvements. The only way an organization can derive this credit is by identifying itself. Being open and forthright with customers achieves this goodwill.

It is also more likely that customers will take their time to complete an interview if they know its purpose and how their answers will be used. In essence, you rely on your organizational goodwill with customers to urge their cooperation. In this sense, the cooperation rate itself becomes a possible criterion of satisfaction (the higher the cooperation, the greater the evoked loyalty and apparent satisfaction).

Interview "Appearance"

Too many customer satisfaction surveys seem to have been composed without the slightest thought being given to what their language and appearance will convey to customers. A satisfaction survey is a communication from the corporation just like any letter, magazine, or advertisement. The interview and the survey process both communicate information about the sponsoring organization. When an understanding of these communication values is absent, design and production of the questionnaire will likely be dismissed as unimportant. This is again often the mindset of marketing research. While improved layout and presentation of a customer satisfaction survey adds cost to the project, the failure to properly attend to these aspects may antagonize or frustrate current customers and thereby deteriorate the very element the survey is intended to measure—satisfaction. If the organizational area charged with measuring satisfaction is unprepared to improve the communication aspects of a survey, help should be sought from within the organization, generally from corporate communications, advertising, or customer relations. These departments should have a wealth of ideas for making the survey sound or look professional and caring.

The Oral Interview

What is the "appearance" of a telephone interview? An oral interview is, after all, intangible. Yet the interview will have a very definite "appearance" in your customers' minds. The appearance is influenced by your introductory script: the way you greet your customer, how you explain your motives for seeking customers' assistance. Further, the appearance is defined by the brevity or length of the interview, and how easy or difficult it is for your customers to supply the information you are gathering. The appearance is also influenced by the training and by the professionalism of the interviewers conducting your survey. (One of the difficulties with telephone interviewing is that such interviews are almost always subcontracted to large telephone interviewing or telemarketing operations. The management of these businesses is dedicated to professionalism and will generally strive to hire quality people. However, individual moments of truth still will occur in which customers can be treated rudely, in which the interview script appears to disregard a point of view the customer may have already communicated or the interview is so long or tedious as to frustrate a time-conscious customer.)

The Printed Questionnaire

It is much easier to envision the appearance of a printed questionnaire. Anything tangible has an appearance. It seems ironic that so few organizations stop to consider the importance of the appearance of their surveys. In a focus group conducted by the author, a customer characterized a majority of the customer satisfaction surveys he had received by saying, "And take a look at the paper they're [the surveys] printed on—it's like toilet paper and they look like a student wrote them! What does that tell me about the importance these companies attach to these surveys?"

We all spend endless hours discussing the contents of our surveys, yet all too often when it comes to laying them out and printing them, we may leave the task to a clerical person who lacks the proper training and an understanding of the questionnaire's importance to really do a great

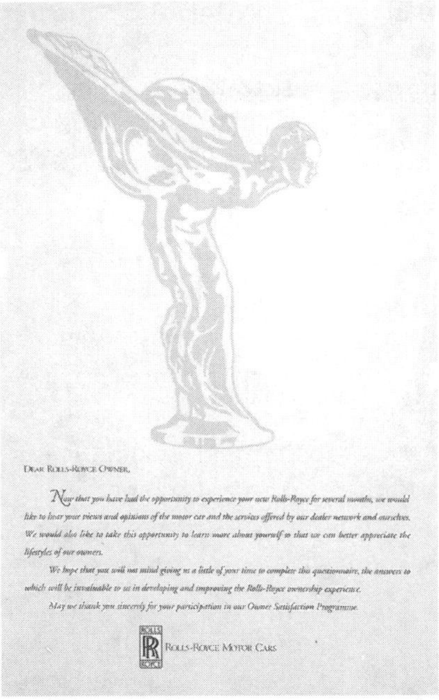

Figure 4.2   Formatting Questionnaires

job composing it. And, then when it comes to printing the survey, in the interests of the budget, corners may be cut again. Budgetary concerns may even dictate that customers affix their own postage! Obviously, all of these compromises ultimately communicate an unfortunate message to our customerbase.

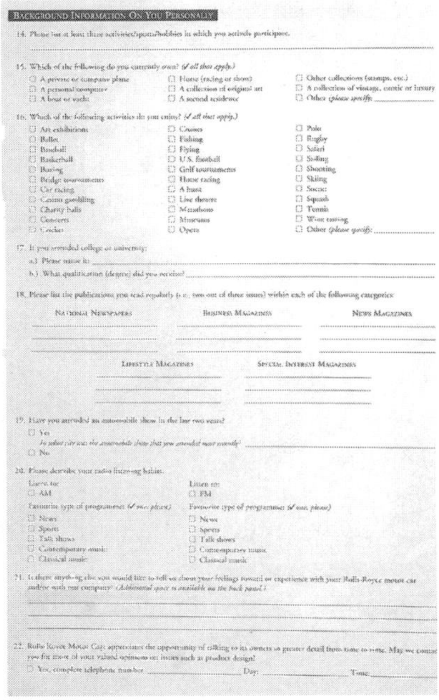

The printed layout should contain plenty of white space—allowing it to "breathe." Such a layout will be more inviting to potential respondents than a questionnaire that looks like an IRS 1040. The layout should be as visually interesting as possible, to encourage the respondent's participation. Use more than *one* typeface for visual variety, but use no more than three different fonts. Color can also jazz up the appearance of a printed questionnaire, but again be conservative, two colors is a good rule of thumb. Graphics also make a questionnaire more visually stimulating. Logos, borders and shading all help the organization and the appearance. Use arrows and guidelines to assist with skip patterns and branches. Shading can help keep respondents on the right line in a complicated response grid and can also highlight instructions or brand names. Notice how some of these rules are applied in the sample questionnaire (see Figure 4.2).

Electronic Surveys

The technology we employ in our surveys may also give a message about our organization to our customers. In general, customers would prefer to have us use those technologies that:

- minimally intrude on their personal or corporate lives
- make responding easy for them
- provide assurance of speedy and certain return of the information
- are fun, not tedious

Customer satisfaction researchers, like their marketing research counterparts, seem reluctant to try new media. While the stakes of failure are high, we should nevertheless experiment with some of the newer survey methods that are made possible by the evolution in communication technologies. Fixating on a method that was once efficient for the possible purpose of maintaining wave-to-wave comparability, overlooks the possible advantages of newer technologies.

There are several new administration and response technologies that all of us should be evaluating. These new methods are largely focused on incorporating the computer into our measurement systems.

Computer/Diskette Administered.
Ways to involve customers' computers in administering surveys have been discussed for some time (Maher and Vavra 1989, Atherton and Vavra 1989). Administering an interview on a computer diskette is a very convenient method to use in certain situations. The diskette may be used to pre-load an interview into PCs at a shopping mall research facility, a dealer's showroom, or some other central facility where your customers may be accessible. Alternatively, the diskette may be delivered via the mail, requesting customers to start the diskette interview on their computers. This later method requires your customers to have access to a computer, either at home or at work. While this requirement may still be a stretch for many consumer products, if you are involved in a high tech area, computers may be allied to the product or be a part of your customers' lives. Obviously, business populations are more easily interviewed by computer. (The flexibility and low intrusiveness of the diskette-administered interview make it a very convenient way for business customers to cooperate with a survey.)

The Internet has recently become the focus of much attention as an efficient customer surveying tool. As companies and other organizations develop special pages for their current customers, this may prove to be an ideal forum within which to accumulate satisfaction measurements.

Interview Flow and Sequence

Questionnaires can be thought of as having three parts: an introduction, a main body, and a conclusion. The introduction initiates the information task. It identifies the survey's sponsor (generally your organization) and the interviewer (if interviewer-administered). It offers a reason for the survey, may tell how the collected information will be used, and starts collecting information—usually with a fairly easy, nonthreatening question answered with an easy to use response scale.

The main body of the questionnaire continues to gather information—perhaps of a more demanding nature. It should be organized into sections each focused on a different aspect of the product or service. To organize the flow of the interview, it is a good idea to group questions into sections. Each section serves to direct the customer's attention to a new central issue. By organizing the larger number of questions into a smaller number of sections, it will make the interview task appear simpler and easier for respondents. Grouping generally increases the efficiency of a questionnaire.

Finally, the third part of the survey, is the conclusion section. In this section it is customary to collect information about the survey respondent and his or her purchasing unit (household or organization). Particularly sensitive or delicate questions (like household annual income, annual sales, personal share of influence in selecting suppliers, and so on) are generally placed last where they will minimally disrupt the collection of information. By this time in the interview, the customer may have become comfortable enough with the interview to answer sensitive questions, which at the outset would have been a turn-off. Some customers may be reluctant to provide the information. Some may actually terminate the interview when asked these questions. However, the majority of their opinions have already been collected, making their information, up to this point, usable.

Questionnaire Sections

Generally, the major areas of a company's product or service can become useful sections of the questionnaire (for example, sales, product performance, after-sale support, and so on). Each section can be preceded by a descriptive statement alerting the respondent to the new topic, "Now we are interested in your evaluation of our *parts and service operation*." The only disadvantage to this form of organization is the potential of setting up a global response set, either the familiar halo effect or a pitchfork and horns effect. Response sets occur when your customer either enjoys your product/service immensely or has a basic problem with your product/ service. In either case, the overall positive or negative attitude tends to color the ratings given to other aspects of your product or service. Because of the overall positive or negative tendency, your opportunity to ferret out aspects of superiority or inferiority is minimized.

Similarly, sections of the questionnaire can be organized around a specific measurement. Often we concentrate on performance ratings in one section and on the measurement of importance in a separate section. Within each of these sections it is ideal to utilize only one or two measurement tasks or response scales. Such a focus lends a coherency to the flow of your questionnaire.

Branching and Flow

It will generally be necessary to direct customers through the questionnaire, sometimes advancing them past sections irrelevant to them or to their experience with your organization. Flow through a questionnaire is effected by *branching instructions*. It is a good idea to map out your intended sequence or flow of your questionnaire. You can use a tree diagram (like the one in Figure 4.3) to show branching conditions at each critical question.

Several different branching patterns can be considered:

Implied branching—follow-up questions

Have you shipped by our overnight service?   [ ] yes [ ] no
   (If yes) How many times?   _____ (times)

Explicit branching—continuation and skip

   20.   Have you visited our factory?
         [ ] No (Skip to question 30)
         [ ] Yes (Continue with question 21)
   21.   When did you last visit our factory?
         [ ] within the last 3 months (Skip to Q 25)
         [ ] 4 to 6 months (Skip to Q 25)
         [ ] 7 to 12 months (Continue with Q22)
         [ ] longer than 12 months ago (Continue with Q22)

Branching must be affected more carefully for self-administered questionnaires than for interviewer-administered ones. Of course, computer assisted interviews automate all branching, avoiding many of the mistakes caused by respondents or/and interviewers failing to correctly follow branching instructions.

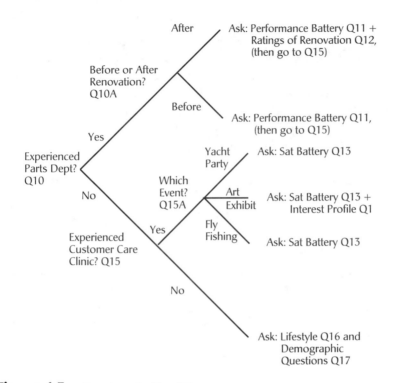

Figure 4.3   *Questionnaire Tree Diagram*

Overall Satisfaction

One of the most important questions of order has to do with the place-ment of the overall satisfaction question. Even though satisfaction with a product or service will be rated on a number of performance attributes, it is still very desirable to ask customers' *overall satisfaction* with our service or product. This rating becomes a very useful analytic tool as well as a highly meaningful criterion on its own right.

There are two logical locations for the overall satisfaction question, either *preceding* the performance attributes inventory or *following* the in-ventory. The rationale that accompanies each location is:

- **Preceding**   By asking overall satisfaction first, one is more likely to get an unbiased measure of customers' actual satisfaction. Placement first on the questionnaire will prompt the customer to mentally review his or her actual state of mind at that particular time, regarding the organization, product, or service. It is sometimes claimed that placing the overall satisfaction first generates lower satisfaction ratings, that negative information about the company is somehow more salient in most customers' minds. The advantage to placing the overall satisfaction question first, is that the assessment is made on the customers' *own terms.* When placed at the end of the listing of performance attributes, the surveyor has, to some extent, defined the domain in which satisfaction is to be judged.

- **Following**   Asking overall satisfaction last may seem somewhat more logical to some respondents since they will have mentally reevaluated the organization as they have rated it on each of the performance attributes. This tends to make the customer's rating more studied or "informed." It is reasonable to assume that modeling overall satisfaction as a function of performance ratings will produce a cleaner model when overall satisfaction is asked at the end of the performance attributes. On the other hand, asking overall satisfaction first and then modeling it on performance attributes may provide an interesting estimate of the completeness of the issues covered by the performance attributes. If the predictability of the model is low, then it may be assumed that there are additional aspects of performance which should be discovered and included in the attribute inventory.

Instructions

Any interview will require some instructions, whether interviewer-administered or self-administered by customers. Unfortunately the rule seems to be to offer scant instructions. We seem to compose our questionnaires with the belief that customers are as familiar with question types and response scales as we are. Obviously they are not. You should always provide instructions that include:

- an introduction to the interview itself, including why the information is being collected and how it will be used;
- a description of the general flow or organization of the interview;
- intermediate instructions preceding a group of questions to be answered in a similar way;
- an instruction regarding skip or branching patterns;
- clear directions on how to return the completed questionnaire or survey.

Obviously the simpler the questionnaire structure and the clearer the instructions, the better will be the quality of the data collected.

Administered

We'd like to know how important each of several characteristics are to you in selecting a company/supplier in the (*ABC Industry*). For each characteristic I read, please give me a rating from 1 to 10 where "one" means "not at all important" and "ten" means "extremely important." (READ ALL CHARACTERISTICS, A THROUGH K, BEGINNING AT PRE-X'D. CIRCLE IMPORTANCE RATING RESPONDENT GIVES FOR EACH CHARACTERISTIC IN **COLUMN A** BELOW.) How important would you say . . . (READ FIRST CHARACTERISTIC) . . . is? (CONTINUE THROUGH ALL CHARACTERISTICS)

Now, I'll read the same characteristics again and ask you this time to rate the performance of XYZ Company on each characteristic according to how well you believe XYZ performs or delivers the characteristic. Again we'll use a scale from 1 to 10, but this time "one" will mean "poor performance" and "ten" will mean "excellent performance." (READ ALL CHARACTERISTICS, A THROUGH K BEGINNING AT PRE-X'D. CIRCLE PERFORMANCE RATING RESPONDENT GIVES FOR EACH IN **COLUMN B** BELOW.) How would you rate XYZ Company's performance on . . . (READ FIRST CHARACTERISTIC) (CONTINUE THROUGH ALL CHARACTERISTICS)

Self-Administered

Below, in the center box, we've listed a number of characteristics (a through k) you might consider in selecting a company/supplier in the (*ABC Industry*). We'd like to know how important each of these characteristics are to you in selecting a company/supplier. Please rate their importance by circling a number from 1 to 10 in **Column A** on the left side of the page. Notice that "1" represents "not at all important" and "10" represents "extremely important." Please give us an importance rating for all characteristics.

Now, please re-read the list of characteristics (a through k). This time please rate XYZ Company according to how well you believe XYZ performs or delivers on each characteristic by circling a number from 1 to 10 in **Column B** on the right side of the page. This time notice that "1" represents "poor performance" while "10" represents "excellent performance." Please make sure to rate XYZ's performance on all characteristics.

Figure 4.4 Illustrations of Interviewer Instructions and Self-Administered Instructions

Conventions exist in marketing research for the appearance of interviewer instructions. These instructions are generally typed in all capital letters and placed inside parentheses (see Figure 4.4). This is a fine practice to adopt for customer satisfaction surveys, but do not allow a survey vendor to unthinkingly use this same format on customer self-administered question-naires. The capital letters can be distracting and draw attention away from the questions among customers not accustomed to seeing

Table 4.1   Importance of Question Instructions

Q3. Please rate the following:

    not at all important   extremely important

  1   2   3   4   5

  _____ Acceleration
  _____ Miles per gallon
  _____ Braking
  _____ Road-holding
  _____ Positive steering response

rev Q3 How important are each of the following attributes of automobiles (a through e)? Please use a scale ranging from 1 (not at all important) to 5 (extremely important). You may use any number from 1 to 5. Please rate each attribute by placing a rating on the line to the left of each attribute.

  _____ (a) Acceleration
  _____ (b) Miles per gallon
  _____ (c) Braking
  _____ (d) Road-holding
  _____ (e) Positive steering response

instructions communicated in this way. Try using italics or a smaller typeface to differentiate instructions from questions in self-administered formats.

Alreck and Settle (1995) list four issues that instructions for a particular question can address:

- what item or issue is to be evaluated;
- what criterion or standard should be used in the evaluation;
- how to use the response scale provided;
- exactly how and where to report or record responses.

The importance of adequate instructions, unfortunately, is often only understood after seeing how customers may have misunderstood our intentions. For example, consider Question 3 in Table 4.1. Because there happens to be five attributes and a five-point rating scale, some customers might use the numbers from 1 to 5 to indicate a *ranking* rather than a rating. The revised Question 3 attempts to better guide customers in answering.

Avoid two-part instructions. When you have a grid requiring two judgments (for example, importance and performance) it will be awkward to list the attributes twice in a self-administered survey. You can solve

Table 4.2   How to Handle Two-Part Instructions

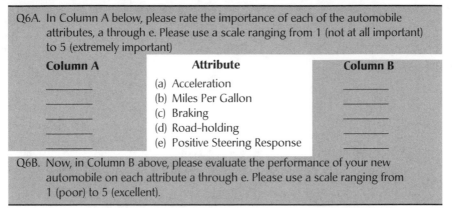

Q6A. In Column A below, please rate the importance of each of the automobile attributes, a through e. Please use a scale ranging from 1 (not at all important) to 5 (extremely important)

Column A	Attribute	Column B
_____	(a) Acceleration	_____
_____	(b) Miles Per Gallon	_____
_____	(c) Braking	_____
_____	(d) Road-holding	_____
_____	(e) Positive Steering Response	_____

Q6B. Now, in Column B above, please evaluate the performance of your new automobile on each attribute a through e. Please use a scale ranging from 1 (poor) to 5 (excellent).

this possible confusion by listing the attributes only once, but providing spaces for both judgments. Just make sure your instructions are divided and in sequence (see Table 4.2).

MICRO CONSIDERATIONS OF QUESTIONNAIRE DESIGN

Before discussing specific issues, let us review some basic objectives for writing successful questions. First of all, be parsimonious in conceiving your questions. Make sure each question you construct is absolutely necessary for your survey. Also keep in mind exactly how you will be able to use the answers you receive. Secondly, control yourself from asking information which you should already have in your customerbase, but if not already in your customerbase, then perhaps available in your organization's billing database. For example, though it might fit in the flow of your interview, you probably should not have to ask how long each customer has been your customer. That information should be known.

In an opposite vein, make sure you ask enough questions to discover the information you need; sometimes one question will be insufficient to gather the specific information you require. There will be times where you will need to ask more than one question. For example:

Q7. Why do you use our products?

One customer might answer this question, "Because of their high quality," while another customer might mention, "A business associate recommended you." In this case you probably need to ask two questions:

Q7A. Why did you first start using our products?

Q7B. What is your primary reason for continuing to use our products?

Question Types

As you begin to write specific questions there are a wide range of issues you will need to consider. In this section we discuss many of the most important.

What's Being Measured?

Questions Collecting Factual Information.

These are questions that can generally be answered in short responses; yes, no; trier, repeat buyer; and so on. They are generally easy for respondents to complete. As such, one should consider using one or more of this type of question at the beginning of a questionnaire, to get potential respondents involved in the questionnaire with a minimum exertion of effort.

The goal of factual questions is to obtain accurate information. Because of their apparent objectivity, it is likely survey professionals assert considerable trust in the responses to this type of question. There is considerable literature showing that responses to factual questions are often fairly accurate, however, the answers can become more subjective than might be imagined. For example, one company learned that its delivery of a complex piece of electronic equipment to their customers was inter preted by most to mean the delivery of an assembled and running piece of equipment, not just a box ready for hours of assembly by themselves. Accuracy in factual questions, therefore, depends both on what is asked and how it is asked. There are four explanations for inaccurate reporting to factual questions:

- Customers do not understand the question, or the event or behavior described; the question may lack meaning for customers;
- Customers do not know the answer (either the wrong person has been selected in the sample unit to answer the question, or no one in the sample unit knows the answer);
- Although customers know the answer, they cannot recall it;
- Customers are reluctant, for some reason, to report an answer in the context of a survey.

Questions Measuring Attitudes.

As the character Lucy has often remarked to Charlie Brown of the Peanuts comic strip regarding school exams, "I most like [test] questions where the answers are more a matter of opinion." Both survey professionals and customers alike, enjoy questions in which they can give opinions. Attitudinal questions go even a step further than opinions. They require evaluation—an expression of one's degree of liking or disliking something. As such they are highly subjective; in direct contrast to the objectivity of factual questions.

Questions Predicting Behavior.   So-called "behavioral" questions certainly are not behavioral measures. The only way to collect truly behavioral data would be to wait and observe a customer increasing her purchases, referring someone, and so on. Certain issues (likelihood to repurchase, likelihood to recommend) have traditionally been asked in a statement describing an intended behavior. Our hope is to get as close to intended behavior as possible by asking customers to express personal willingness to engage in the behavior ("I will *definitely rebuy*," "I will *probably recommend* this brand to my friends"). It is believed that behaviorally worded questions evoke some additional personal involvement from respondents. We tend to rely on such intention statements as predictive of ultimate behavior.

Questions to Collect Demographics.   Many customer satisfaction surveys do not take advantage of the data-collection opportunity to learn more about their customers from a demographic and possibly "pyschographic" standpoint. Although questionnaire length must be watched, it is true that once a customer starts to answer a survey, you have a very good chance they will answer all sorts of questions—product-related and those of a more personal nature.

   If your customer satisfaction survey represents one of the few (or perhaps only) times you dialogue with customers, it makes sense to strategically collect descriptive information about them. This gives you the chance to fill in the gaps of your customerbase—a little at a time (on successive waves of your survey). Because of the likely personal nature of these questions, they are often best marked "OPTIONAL." We usually place them at the end of the questionnaire, after the customer has already gotten involved in answering questions. The answering momentum, we assume, will urge them through this group of questions as well. It is also a good practice to tell customers why you want the information and how it will be used. By all means, assure your customers the demographic information will be kept confidential and will not be shared with other companies. Too many consumers these days are savvy to the business practice of selling or exchanging mailing lists.

Open-Ended Versus Closed-Ended Questions

There are three basic types of questions that may be used in a satisfaction survey:

- open-ended or "verbatim" questions
- closed-ended questions where response options are not read
- closed-ended questions where response options are read

Open-ended questions are unstructured questions that allow customers to answer in their own words, and mention any issue they choose (no matter how seemingly insignificant it may seem). The issue can be objectively described, treated as an anecdote, or passed along as word-of-mouth. The important element is the issue of non-constraint. The subject of the response, the terminology used and the description of satisfaction are all totally up to the customer to select. In this way open-ended questions are directed at *exploration* of an issue, helping surveys:

- identify salient issues (which may or may not be part of the current questionnaire);
- sample the relevant terms used by customers to describe the issue; and
- define the appropriate evaluative spectrum that customers use to judge performance.

Their use is appropriate when not enough is known about an issue or concept to formulate reasonably inclusive response categories (for a closed-ended format), and when the subject of a question is a sensitive issue.

Open-ended questions are also generally the most enjoyable for customers to answer since they are in complete control. It is a good idea to always ask at least two open-ended questions in a satisfaction survey. One of those open-ended questions should probably be used to probe, and therefore better understand, the overall satisfaction rating a customer offers. ("Why did you rate your overall satisfaction with us at this level?") The other open-end question should probably come at the end of the survey and ask the simple question, "Is there anything else you would like to communicate to us?"

Because of their potential value in helping explain anticipated or especially unanticipated survey outcomes, some experts recommend distributing open-end follow-ups throughout interviews with certain groups of customers, for example those found to be overall less satisfied (this presumes the overall satisfaction is to be asked early in the interview).

Alternatively, open-ended questions as probes might be randomly distributed throughout *all* customers' interviews, being attached to a random set of questions in each interview. This means that the burden or imposition on any one customer is still slight, yet probing follow-up information is made available on virtually every question in the questionnaire. Such randomized follow-ups would necessarily employ generalized language:

> Could you tell me a little more about what you mean?
> Could you say more about what you have in mind?
> I see—could you give me an example?

Despite their immense potential value, open-end questions pose substantial challenges in analysis and reporting. Among these problems are: (1) they fail to indicate a specific response dimension, thus respondents are free to answer in any way or quantity they desire; (2) they produce data (results) that are difficult to compare and collapse for analysis; (3) they require extensive time and effort to accurately record; (4) they impose a more formidable response task on respondents; and (5) they may generate inappropriate reasons/irrelevant information. In Chapter 6 we will discuss these difficulties and offer some specific suggestions.

Closed-ended questions offer the customer, the interviewer, or both a list of possible responses for the question. These response categories are created to cover almost all responses anticipated. Because closed-ended questions pre-list the most important response options, as a question type they are clearly aimed at *quantification;* being an efficient way to assess the popularity or priority of known or existing issues. Though an occasional response may not have been anticipated, such a response will not substantially affect the major findings of the survey. Closed-ended questions are efficient then, because they help control the length of the interview and therefore increase the number of customers one will be able to interview. These questions use knowledge about the customerbase to simplify information gathering. Because responses are generally pre-listed or read aloud, closed-ended questions are more likely to unambiguously communicate to customers an appropriate answering frame of reference. Finally, they are very easy to report on, requiring at the very least only frequency counts.

Closed-ended questions generally require some form of scalar response. Even in the form of an adjective or attribute checklist, frequency is the criterion of measurement.

Scale Types

Our motive for conducting a customer satisfaction survey is to ascribe *order* to issues and *magnitude* to levels of satisfaction. These two goals require scalar questions as opposed to open-ended questions. Responses to satisfaction questions can best be represented by a choice of position along some continuous response spectrum. A response scale is simply a verbal representation of that response spectrum. If scales are used to collect data then results can be represented as distributions—counts of the frequency with which each scale response was chosen by customers as the response most representative of their feelings. Scales can be described as an efficient and practical means for collecting information from customers.

The Language of Scales

In general, for a scale to perform in a unidimensional way, it should—to the extent it is possible—rely on only *one word* or *quality*. The scale:

> extremely satisfied
> somewhat satisfied
> neither satisfied nor dissatisfied
> somewhat dissatisfied
> extremely dissatisfied

conforms with this requirement. It is clearly measuring *satisfaction*. It appears to convey both order and offers interval properties such that the distances between each scale response are approximately of equal semantic intensity or increment.

A newer scale being investigated,

> outstanding
> very good
> satisfactory
> somewhat lacking
> poor

is less obviously unidimensional. (It very well may communicate a single continuum to respondents, but the different qualities used in each scale position make unidimensionality less likely and open the possibility of additional dimensions.)

The frequently used scale,

excellent
very good
good
fair
poor

seems (by virtue of its widespread use) to have convinced many satisfaction professionals of its unidimensionality and interval properties. However, because different words (and therefore possibly different qualities) are used, its appropriateness must be questioned. Though it is possible a critic might recognize the scale as not truly unidimensional, this scale is nevertheless one of the most frequently used verbal response scales.

The Specificity of Scales

Because scales are used to obtain information from a customerbase, we must be able to compare one customer's response to another's. All customers must utilize a similar scale within the survey to make answers comparable. In some questions the response scale may be implied,

How old are you?

In this question, most customers would identify years as the related response scale. In other cases it may be more efficient to supply a suggested response scale, since customers could conceivably choose different response scales;

How long have you owned a Professional Frisbee™?

Some could answer in months, some in years, some abstractly, "a while." An adequate solution is to explicitly state the response scale within the question:

For *how many years* have you owned a Professional Frisbee™?
_____ Years

In many cases as we measure satisfaction, the particular scale we wish customers to use, will be impractical to mention within the question. (That is, we may have a seven-point verbal scale we wish used, which if fully articulated would confuse the question related to it.) Such a response scale ideally should be described outside of the question. Generally, the response scale is described before or after (possibly both) the question is asked.

Using a scale from 10 to 1 where 10 represents 'excellent' and 1 represents 'poor,' please rate our company on each of the following issues.

Identifying the appropriate responses before the question is read, helps the respondent consider the responses along with each rating issue (attribute). Ponder the satisfaction continuum you have established and where (along its length) your customers' particular satisfaction may lie.

The Metric Properties of Scales

Despite the metric of the questions we ask, our format will often be of the type: multiple-choice, single-response. There are important exceptions as in the case of the adjective checklist question, but generally our questions will offer a range of responses asking customers to choose the *single* response that best describes his feelings. There are four categories of response scales, formed on the basis of the metric underlying them. In this section we will describe each, show examples and discuss the type of analysis each supports.

Nominal Scales.   The most basic form of a response scale is the nominal scale, so named because the information it provides is truly "nominal." Nominal scales are classificatory by nature, nothing more. There is no implication of superiority of one nominal scale response over another, though familiarity often leads us to associate ranks with some nominal classifications (that is, quarterback versus defensive guard, young versus mature, and yes versus no). The prevailing rule in assembling a nominal scale is to fashion the categories so they will be mutually exclusive, and of enough numbers so as to exhaust the range of the phenomenon to be nominally described.

The most prevalent use for nominal scales in satisfaction measurement questionnaires is in collecting classification information; for example "operating regions" (east, central, south, west); "position at a company" (technician, sales rep, r&d staff, manager); and SIC codes.

To quantify nominally scaled data, we assign the responses number-codes, for example: *new customer–1; existing customer–2.* In this application, however, the numbers 1 and 2 carry *no magnitude value* whatsoever, they convey only *identity value.* They stand as easily tallied markers for the nominal categories. Therefore, it is inappropriate to think that *existing customers* having been assigned a numerical code of 2 are better than new customers, or that there are twice as many of them. For analysis, nominal scaled data supports only frequency counts, nothing more. It is not permissible in a sample of 70 existing customers and 30 new customers to say the average customer is 1.7 [(.70*2+.30*1)/1.0]. We can only conclude that 70 percent of our sample were of the class "existing customers" and 30 percent could be classified as "new customers." The mode is the only measure of central tendency that can be calculated from a nominal scale.

Nominal scales are by far the easiest type of scale for respondents to answer. But the tradeoff for this simplicity, is that the data collected supports the least powerful analyses. Because data collected by nominal scales are not normally distributed, nominal data is considered "nonparametric."[1]

Ordinal Scales.   The next most rigorous response scale is the ordinal scale. Ordinal scales measure and convey order or dominance. As attributes or customer needs are responded to using an ordinal scale, we will be able to conclude that the attribute at the top of the list is more important or more desired than the second, third, and remaining items. If a customer indicates *price* is the most important attribute we code it a "1." If *durability* were the second most important attribute, we would assign it the code "2," "3" to *appearance,* the third most important attribute, and so on. The numeric order of the assigned codes (1,2,3) represents the *order* of importance, indicating that price is considered more important than either durability or appearance, and that durability supersedes appearance. It is important to note that using the number system—1,2,3 . . . —is done only to indicate order. Perhaps it would be more appropriate to use the alphabetic system a,b,c . . . since a common mistake made is to conduct numerical analyses on the codes. They are there only to indicate order. They can not tell us how much more important price is over durability, only that it is *more important.*

Contrary to the conventional practice of reporting average ranks, ordinal data really only supports calculation of *frequencies,* the *median,* and the *mode.* (We will have more to say about the median and mode in Chapter 6.) Given the following survey data:

----
[1]Data is frequently described as either "parametric" or "nonparametric." Parametric data is normally distributed, while nonparametric data does not follow a normal distribution. These classifications tell the analyst which of two different series of statistical tests to use for statistical significance. A "t test" is one of the most common tests for parametric (normally distributed data) while a "chi-square test" is a similarly well known test for nonparametric data.

Order of Importance	Customer D	Customer J	Customer M	Customer V
First Importance	Price	Price	Price	Price
Second Importance	Durability	Durability	Durability	Durability
Third Importance	Service	Appearance	Appearance	Appearance
Fourth Importance	Appearance	Service	Service	Service

Order of Importance	Customer S	Customer H	Customer Q
First Importance	Appearance	Appearance	Price
Second Importance	Price	Service	Appearance
Third Importance	Durability	Durability	Service
Fourth Importance	Service	Price	Durability

Considering this survey data, the appropriate report would be

	Median Rank	Mode Rank
Price	2	1
Durability	3	2
Appearance	3	3
Service	3	4

Because data collected by ordinal scales are not normally distributed, like nominal scale data, ordinal scale data is also considered nonparametric.

Interval Scales.   Interval scales add a third property to response scales—that of meaningful intervals between the responses. This means differences can be compared. The difference between 2 and 3 is therefore understood to be equal to the difference between 4 and 5. What interval scales lack is an absolute zero point. In practice, the zero point is set arbitrarily.

A traditionally used example of an interval scale is the temperature scale. With temperature we can say that 90°F is warmer than 60°F, and we can say that an increase from 60°F to 70°F is the same as an increase from 80°F to 90°F. Similarly we can say that the *difference* between 70°F and 90°F (20 degrees) is twice the difference between 60°F and 70°F (10 degrees). Although we can say 90°F is warmer than 60°F, we cannot say it is 50 percent warmer! (To prove this to yourself, convert 90°F and 60°F to Celsius values and see how incorrect such an interpretation would be.)

Interval scales support the most common calculations of mean, as well as frequencies, median, and mode. Data collected with interval scales is assumed to conform to normal distributions; the scale produces parametric data.

Ratio Scales.   Ratio scales are the most powerful type of response scale because they possess a true zero point. Many of the most common measurements in our lives are ratio scales: length, volume, weight, and speed. While ratio scales support the most robust mathematical analyses, they seldom apply to the subjective concepts measured among customers. For example, it is difficult to arrive at a common understanding of zero satisfaction, since this concept would be very much subjective; one customer to another.

Ratio scales support all types of numerical analysis and produce parametric data. See Table 4.3 for a comparison of the analyses supported by each of the four response scales.

Structural Issues

There are a number of issues that deal with the structure of the questions you assemble in your survey. In this section we will discuss a number of them.

Uniformity.   An important consideration is that once you establish a policy regarding each of these issues, strive for the uniform application of the issue throughout your survey. Try to keep the length of most of your scales the same. Do not vary the number of response positions you provide simply for variety. Customers responding to a satisfaction survey will attempt to simplify the task as much as possible. They would like to acclimate themselves to your scale structure as quickly as possible to make

Table 4.3 Statistical Methods Appropriate to Scales of Measurement

Scale	Basic Comparisons	Examples	Appropriate Statistical Measures of			
			Central Tendency	Dispersion	Association or Correlation	Significance
Nominal	Identity	Customer-Noncustomer Marketing region SIC code	Mode	Information	Contingency correlation coefficients	Chi square
Ordinal	Order	Preference for brands Social class Street addresses	Median	Percentiles	Rank-order correlation Spearman r_n Kendall's Tau Kendall's W	Sign test Run Rest Mann-Whitney U-Test
Interval	Comparison of intervals	Attitude towards brand Purchase likelihood Performance ratings of product, service	Arithmetic mean	Standard deviation Average deviation	Product-moment correlation Correlation ratio	t test F test
Ratio	Comparison of absolute magnitudes	Units purchased Dollars spent Probability of purchase, repurchase	Geometric mean Harmonic mean	Percent variation Coefficient of variation		

Adapted from: Hughes, G. David, Attitude Measurement for Marketing Strategies, Scott Foresman and Co, Glenview, IL, 1971, pg. 121, and Churchill, Gilbert A. Jr, Marketing Research: Methodological Foundations, 5th Edition, Chicago, The Dryden Press, 1991, p. 415.

Table 4.4   Ganged or Matrixed Question Grids

Below please rate the importance of each of the ten motor car attributes (a through j) in COL A, using a 1 to 10 scale; where "1" represents "not at all important" and "10" represents "extremely important." Then in COL B, please rate your current satisfaction with your motor car on each of the ten attributes (a through j) using a scale of 1 to 10; where "1" represents "not at all satisfied" and "10" represents "extremely satisfied."

		Column A *Importance Rating*	Column B *Satisfaction Rating*
(a)	Reliability		
(b)	Driving comfort		
(c)	Acceleration		
(d)	Braking		
(e)	Road-holding		
(f)	Fuel efficiency		
(g)	Comfort of ride		
(h)	Steering		
(i)	In-car entertainment		
(j)	Vision from the driver's seat		

their task of responding easy. If you capriciously change the scale length or number of response categories from question to question, you increase the work your customers have to do just to track response mechanisms; the quality of the information you collect as well as your response rate will suffer.

Ganged or Matrixed Questions.   When a similar rating, like performance or delivery is to be asked over a number of attributes, the attributes should be assembled in a grid or matrix to simplify the task for customers and interviewers alike. However, be aware that two important sources of bias are present in such grids (see Table 4.4).

The order of the attributes may set up a response condition. Ideally the order of the attributes should be rotated (if "customized interviews" [see p. 167] or computer administration are being used this can easily be accomplished). In interviewer-administered surveys, the questioning should begin at a randomly selected attribute for each new customer.

To increase the accuracy of data recording, consider using shading or drawing lines between pairs of attributes to guide customers or interviewers from each attribute to the associated response section.

Also consider "split-sampling" your customers or interviews by reversing the order (polarity) of your response scales. Placing your most positive response on the left for the entire sample will bias results to some extent. (This is especially true in verbal interviews when interviewers will read the responses.) So half of your interviews should be collected with an *excellent to poor* scale and half with a *poor to excellent* scale. But the important thing to remember, for the sake of uniformity, do not change the order within any interview! Change the order only from one customer to the next. Require each customer to use only *one* progression throughout his or her entire interview.

Totally Anchored Versus End-Point Anchored.   To elicit feelings from our customers on each of the performance or quality issues we have in mind, it is necessary for us to envisage a continuum of response favorability. Hopefully, the continuum we imagine will be very similar to that existing in the minds of our customers. The continuum should range from the most negative of attitudes to the most positive. To make a scale usable for customers to report their satisfaction, we have to define the intensities we have in mind. To do this it is common practice to place labels on the continuum to define *directionality* and *increments of intensity*. We then ask our customers to consider their own opinions and attitudes and indicate where they stand on the continuum.

There will, of course, be differences in the semantic meaning customers attach to any label we link to a scale position. Our intended meaning may be different from their understood meaning. Notwithstanding these differences, the labeled continuum is still useful so long as customers who place themselves on the favorable end, in general, feel more positive than those customers who place themselves on the unfavorable end. To the extent customers differ in their exact understanding of each scale point, any continuum could be accused of lacking *construct validity*. Even so with low construct validity a response continuum would still have value in helping us separate our favorable customers from our unfavorable customers.

There is a decision to be made concerning labels. This has to do with how many labels will be used. Because we have admitted some semantic variation is inevitable, it is generally preferable to minimize this by only labeling the end-points of your scaling continuum. If intermediate points are also labeled, there is the opportunity for further variation and for the possibility of the scale becoming multidimensional (see Figure 4.5).

Many Points Versus Few Points.   This concern includes a trade-off. The more response points you offer, say 10, the better the metric of

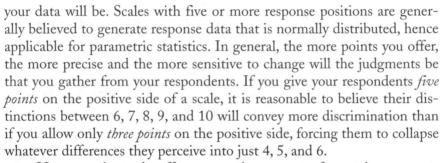

Figure 4.5   Response Scale

your data will be. Scales with five or more response positions are generally believed to generate response data that is normally distributed, hence applicable for parametric statistics. In general, the more points you offer, the more precise and the more sensitive to change will the judgments be that you gather from your respondents. If you give your respondents *five points* on the positive side of a scale, it is reasonable to believe their distinctions between 6, 7, 8, 9, and 10 will convey more discrimination than if you allow only *three points* on the positive side, forcing them to collapse whatever differences they perceive into just 4, 5, and 6.

However, the trade-off concerns the amount of mental energy you are asking respondents to exert as they respond to your questions. A ten-point scale, by allowing more precise discrimination, requires more mental work from your respondents. The more work you ask them for, the more tedious your questionnaire will be for your customers and the lower their cooperation rate.

Odd Versus Even Number of Points.   The issue of an odd versus an even number of scale response points has almost everything to do with whether or not you view *neutrality* as an acceptable answer in a survey question. However, be warned, for in addition to providing a neutral response alternative, a mid-point response has unfortunate consequences. It will invariably be used by respondents who prefer to remain indifferent or neutral on certain issues. Seven-point scales, followed by five-point scales currently appear most popular. If you prefer to discourage fence-sitting you should avoid odd-numbered scales.

In situations in which you desire to force a perspective, an even number of scale positions will accomplish this for you. Generally ten-point or six-point scales appear to be preferred. The author favors a ten-point scale.

The Do Not Know/No Experience Option.   Attitudes about offering a "do not know" response option vary widely. Some believe the "do not know" response offers respondents an easy way out, alleviating them from mentally working a question to reach a real point of view. Those holding this position would argue, that as a customer, one must have *some* impression, no matter how vague, of an organization's performance on all elements of its operation and products. These satisfaction professionals would favor forcing the respondent to form an opinion. (It is possible, of course, that some customers who actually lack an opinion will tire of this assumption and sooner or later terminate the interview either out of frustration or out of concern for giving meaningless attitudes.) The author believes that in most satisfaction surveys it is fair to force the issue, encouraging customers to search their souls for an attitude about your organization.

Many other satisfaction professionals think it is appropriate to offer a "do not know" option. These professionals would admit the possibility that an aspect of the product or the organization was somehow perhaps irrelevant or unimportant to certain customers.

Everyone can probably agree that it is futile and wrong to ask for a rating when a customer simply has not experienced a specific element of the organization, product, or service. For these situations allowing customers to check an allied "No Experience/Not Applicable" box is probably desirable.

Please describe your satisfaction with our dealers' trade-in program

poor   excellent

[ ]1   [ ]2   [ ]3   [ ]4   [ ]5   [ ]6   [ ]7   [ ]8   [ ]9   [ ]10

❏ no experience, not applicable

Measuring Overall Satisfaction

Obtaining a measure of your customers' overall satisfaction, as an independent judgment is vital. Some satisfaction professionals overlook this opportunity deciding instead to simply aggregate the ratings they were given on individual performance measures. This is unwise for a number of reasons. First, in such a case one would lack a suitable variable to use for any statistical modeling. Second, this position makes the assumption that all of the appropriate performance measures have been asked. If either insignificant measures are included, or significant measures are excluded, the summation of these performance measures will be biased and will provide an inaccurate estimate of actual overall satisfaction.

The format with which you assess your customers' overall satisfaction with your company must be established. It can take any number of forms, from a recognized format used by many other organizations to your own customized format, which may reinforce your organization's culture or image. Stew Leonard in his Connecticut diary superstores asks simply, "How'm I doing"? In contrast, CNA Insurance would probably decide to ask its commercial accounts' satisfaction in a more formal manner. On the other hand, customers of the Cracker Barrel restaurant chain would probably think it out of character if Uncle Herschel (one of their company icons and, apparently, a real person) asked, "Please rate your overall satisfaction with our stores." They would be expecting a folksier, more neighborly question. The bottom line is, do not necessarily be a slave to convention. As long as you do not need to compare your satisfaction scores to any outside your company, using your own, personalized format is fine.

To expand your options, Table 4A.1 in the appendix to this chapter shows over 40 different scales Hausknecht (1990) has accumulated from the literature.

The Scale.   In general, it has usually been assumed that for analytical purposes, it is ideal if the measurement of overall satisfaction and each of the performance variables all utilize the same response scale. The author favors a 10-point numeric scale, verbally anchored only at the end-points. This scale would then be used to measure overall satisfaction as well as to assess performance on each of the performance attributes. As mentioned previously, Wittink and Bayer (1994) have proposed a hybrid design in which overall satisfaction is measured on a 10-point scale while individual performance attributes are more simply measured on a binary (yes-no) scale:

> Have you experienced a problem with our product related to [*performance attribute*]?
> [ ] Yes
> [ ] No

Wittink and Bayer report "superior results" and greater statistical efficiency using this 10-point scale–binary scale combination.

The Best Measure of Overall Satisfaction.   While many surveys are fielded with a single measure of overall satisfaction, other criterion questions may also be asked, like intention to repurchase and likelihood of referring the company or brand. Usually the summary quality question will be asked as:

> In general, how would you rate our overall quality?

Recently Ryan and his co-authors (1995) have studied the value of a "composite measure of overall satisfaction." They recommend assessing overall satisfaction with three questions, which they suggest increases the reliability of the measure and taps more aspects of a possibly multidimensional phenomenon. Their three questions are:

1. In general, how satisfied are you with *COMPANY* on a scale ranging from "completely dissatisfied" to "completely satisfied"?
2. How well did *COMPANY* meet your expectations? On a scale from "did not meet my expectations" to "exceeded my expectations"?
3. When thinking of your ideal company, how well does *COMPANY* compare on a scale from "very far away" to "very close to my ideal"?

Regardless of the specific format you use, always assess overall satisfaction somewhere in your survey, and do so with a scale of similar metric to your performance measure.

Hauser (1991) in an ambitious project has compared various measures of overall satisfaction. To compare the consequences of satisfaction measures, Hauser imagines a "salesperson's dilemma." Consider a very demanding customer who will buy the salesperson's product because the customer perceives it as best on the market, but who is unlikely to be fully satisfied with any product. If the salesperson is rewarded only on sales, he will seek the sale. But if the salesperson is rewarded only on satisfaction, he will likely forego this sale. On an aggregate basis, Hauser poses the issue of a company either attracting one million "extremely satisfied" customers or one million "extremely satisfied" customers and 1 million "mildly satisfied" customers. While the second scenario is the more profitable, it would produce only moderate average satisfaction ratings, the first scenario results in the highest company satisfaction rating.

Hauser considers the conventional assessment of overall satisfaction (as we have described it) "monadic" in nature, only the measured company is considered. To offer some remedy for the paradox described in his "salesperson's dilemma," Hauser identifies two other potential measures of overall satisfaction:

- **relative satisfaction measurement:** The customer is asked to rate satisfaction with a brand compared to other brands. The set of comparative brands is either: the customer's evoked set (those brands seriously considered for purchase) or the aware set (those brands of which the customer is aware).

- **share-weighted satisfaction:** Because of the salesperson's dilemma (described above) if all customers' satisfaction scores are added, rather than averaged, the less satisfied customers impact the calculated satisfaction scores less. In a sampling context, average satisfaction (across competitiors) can be weighted by each brand's market share.

While Hauser lacks data for the share-weighted measure, he is able to correlate two forms of the relative satisfaction measure (aware brands, evoked brands) and the traditional "monadic" measure to market share data. His analysis shows the highest correlation exists between market share and the relative rating of aware brands method.

Bradley Gale (1994) has similarly campaigned for the use of comparative measures.

Magnitude Estimation

Magnitude estimation (Lodge 1981) is a scaling technique that attempts to adapt the kinds of ratio scales developed in psychophysical measurement to attitude scaling. Those attracted to this relatively new technique are likely frustrated by one or more of the following:

- the substantial limits imposed by the ordinal quality of much survey response data;
- the information lost from offering response categories that often constrain the range of opinion; and
- the loss of precision resulting from analyzing ordinal-data as if it were of higher, interval quality.

An example of magnitude estimation in satisfaction measurement research, would be as follows:

> We are interested in your overall satisfaction with our brand. To answer this question, consider our best competitor. We'll assign a score of 100 to this company. Now, please use this score to rate your satisfaction with our brand. For example, if you think our brand is three times as good, you'd assign us a score of 300 compared to the 100 for our competitor. Or, if you think our brand is only half as good as our best competitor, you'd assign us a score of 50. Now, compared to our best competitor at a score of 100, overall how satisfied are you with our brand?

Performance Assessment

Beyond measuring overall satisfaction, you will almost certainly wish to assess specific performance issues. Without additional measures beyond overall satisfaction, improvement plans would be difficult, if not impossible, to properly implement. Consequently, most customer satisfaction surveys also include inventories of performance measures to be similarly rated by customers. The first choice to be made is the response scale: verbal or numeric. Numeric response scales will use only a pair of words, usually an adjective (*friendly*) and its antonym (*unfriendly*) with numeric responses in between:

Unfriendly [ ]1 [ ]2 [ ]3 [ ]4 [ ]5 [ ]6 [ ]7 [ ]8 [ ]9 [ ]10 Friendly

Verbal response scales will often make a statement about performance and then provide "Likert-type" statements of agreement or disagreement with the performance described.[2]

The dealership is a friendly place at which to have my car serviced

[ ] strongly agree
[ ] somewhat agree
[ ] neither agree nor disagree
[ ] somewhat disagree
[ ] strongly disagree

Performance statements can be written from a number of different perspectives. There is no right or wrong perspective. Part of your decision will simply be what "feels right" for the relationship you have with your customers.

Descriptive Phrasing

Performance ratings written in a descriptive statement usually make a positive statement and then ask for agreement/disagreement:

My automobile accelerates very well

[ ] Strongly agree
[ ] Somewhat agree
[ ] Neither agree nor disagree
[ ] Somewhat disagree
[ ] Strongly disagree

----
[2]The psychologist, Rensis Likert (1932) created this now familiar set of responses as the rating format for a battery of questions directed toward an attitude object. Using proscribed weights (5,4,3,2, and 1) for each response position, a total (summated) score was formed for each subject, representing the subject's attitude toward the object. Today, the term "Likert scale" is most frequently used to simply describe the five-position scale offering varying degrees of agreement.

Qualitative Phrasing

Qualitative questions pose a question about the product's/service's performance and ask for a response that rates the performance:

How would you rate the acceleration of your automobile?

[ ] Excellent
[ ] Very good
[ ] Good
[ ] Only fair
[ ] Poor

Comparative Phrasing

Performance ratings can be framed against expectations—either absolute or against competition:

The acceleration of my automobile is . . .

[ ] Much better than I had expected
[ ] Better than I had expected
[ ] As I had expected
[ ] Somewhat less than I had expected
[ ] Much less than I had expected

The acceleration of my automobile is . . .

[ ] One of the best of all automobiles
[ ] Better than many automobiles
[ ] About the same as most automobiles
[ ] Worse than many automobiles
[ ] One of the worst of all automobiles

Binary Performance

Performance can be rated in a binary way, indicating simply whether or not a performance area has been the source of any problems or dissatisfaction (Wittink and Bayer, 1994).

Have you experienced any problems with the acceleration of your automobile?

[ ] Yes
[ ] No

Response Scales

Response scales can be verbal, numeric, or pictorial. Each scale type seems to have its fans and its detractors.

Verbal Scales.   Those who favor verbal scales reason that they are the most colloquial way of assessing a respondent's state of mind. Such scales provide a continuum of verbal responses in a graduated order:

How satisfied are you, personally, with the acceleration of your automobile?

[ ] Completely Satisfied
[ ] Somewhat Satisfied
[ ] Neither Satisfied nor Dissatisfied
[ ] Somewhat Dissatisfied
[ ] Completely Dissatisfied

Verbal response scales are patterned after sentence completion tasks allowing the customer to finish a statement:

The acceleration of my automobile is . . .

[ ] Excellent
[ ] Very Good
[ ] Good
[ ] Fair
[ ] Poor

Some people worry about the extent to which verbal response scales convey a uniform or shared meaning (see p. 141). It is also difficult to find words with a uniform difference in intensity, such that it can be claimed the scale positions have *equal intervals* between them. For example, is the difference between "excellent" and "very good" the same as the difference between "very good" and "good"? Some would argue the difference between excellent and very good is greater.

There is also the worry that verbally anchored responses stay entirely unidimensional, that is that they rely on only one semantic continuum (that is, "good" to "bad"). If the labels introduce more than one continuum, the scale fails to stay unidimensional (that is, "good" to "lacks caring").

Numeric Scales

Numeric scales, when anchored only on their end-points, are more likely to escape the problem of multidimensionality. It is much easier to consider them unidimensional.

Please describe your automobile's acceleration:

poor   excellent
[ ]1 [ ]2 [ ]3 [ ]4 [ ]5 [ ]6 [ ]7 [ ]8 [ ]9 [ ]10

However, many worry about the level of abstraction customers have to use to select a number between the anchored end-points to represent their state of mind. Certainly such abstraction requires an adult customerbase and one that is reasonably intelligent or self-assured.

The one problem with numeric scales is the possible mixed meaning of the end-points. We all strive to be "number one" suggesting "1" might be the more favorable number. Yet members of each gender look for a member of the opposite gender who's a "perfect 10." Specifying the most favorable end-point on a numeric scale will always be difficult. The most important practice is to provide ample reminders throughout the interview of the meaning of the "1" or of the "10." We will advocate a scale increasing in favor from "1" equaling "poor" to "10" equaling "excellent."

School Grading Scales

Some recently have favored using a "school grading system" as a response scale. The main benefit of such a scale is the near universal (at least within the United States) understanding of the end-points (grade *A* representing "excellent" and grade *F* representing "failing") as well as a fairly good shared understanding of the points in between.

Please grade your automobile's acceleration:
[ ] A   [ ] B   [ ]C   [ ]D   [ ]F

There is much in favor of a scale with such a universal understanding.

Pictorial Scales

Pictorial scales are especially good for measuring the satisfaction of children and for introducing an air of informality and humanness to a questionnaire.

How do you feel about your automobile's acceleration?

But if pictorial scales appear too cutesy they may backfire. So use them thoughtfully and parsimoniously.

Semantic Differential Response Scale

The semantic differential response scale format may be considered a variation on pictorial scales. In this scale, a number of intervals separate two "bipolar adjectives" (adjectives of opposite meaning). Customers check the interval which indicates both which adjective best represents their feelings and by how much.

> Describe your automobile's acceleration:
> powerful   [ ]   [ ]   [ ]   [ ]   [ ]   [ ]   [ ]   sluggish

Alternatively, geometric figures of diminishing size may be used to indicate different shadings of opinion.

> Describe your automobile's acceleration:
>
> powerful   O   o   .   o   O   sluggish

Question Wording

KIS[3]

The rule of thumb for successful question writing is to "keep it short, simple, and single-minded." You can remember this using "KIS" cubed (to the third power). Most questionnaires today include questions that are far too complex, use unnecessarily confusing industry jargon, and often involve more than one issue or incorporate more than one question. Stanley Payne (1951), in an excellent book on question wording, wrote in 1951:

> If all the problems of question wording could be traced to a single source, their common origin would probably prove to be in taking too much for granted. We questioners assume that people know what we are talking about. We assume that they have some basis for testimony. We assume that they understand our questions. We assume that their answers are in the frame of reference we intend[ed].

Obviously, Payne's view is as relevant today as it was when he made his observations. Table 4.5 summarizes five rules to keep question wording understandable.

Table 4.5   Considerations in Choosing Appropriate Wording for Survey Questions

Goal	Discussion
Focus	Every question should have a single, specific issue or topic. Avoid questions that confuse customers by introducing multiple issues.
Brevity	Questions should be kept as short as possible. As questions get longer, it is more difficult for the customer to forget earlier components of the question. Also, long questions are more likely to lack focus and clarity. Some enforce a "25 words or less" discipline.
Clarity	The meaning of a question should be completely clear to all respondents. Virtually all customers should interpret the question in exactly the same way.
Appropriate vocabulary	Words and terms used in survey questions should come from customers' everyday vocabulary. Do not try for a sophisticated sounding question; settle for one that communicates.
Correct grammar	The most effective questions are one written as simple sentences; avoid complex or compound sentence structures.

Adapted from Alreck, Pamela L., and Robert B. Settle, *The Survey Research Handbook, Second Edition.* Burr Ridge, IL: Richard D. Irwin, 1995.

Shared Definition

Receiving useful information from a satisfaction survey requires that both the company and the customer have equal meanings in mind in the wording and response to a question. In writing a specific question, the satisfaction professional will attempt to establish a common frame of reference. This is especially important for terms on which answers to questions will be heavily dependent. For example, in the question:

> When using Tide, please rate your satisfaction with the sudsiness of Tide

the manufacturer undoubtedly has clothes washing in mind (the primary use for which a laundry detergent is intended). But what if a particular customer mainly uses Tide for washing woodwork? She might answer the question differently than those who use Tide for washing clothes. In this case "using" is surprisingly vague. Instead, the question would be far less ambiguous if worded:

> When washing clothes with Tide, please rate your satisfaction with the sudsiness of Tide

Recall of the Past

Far too often satisfaction professionals ask questions as generalities. Customers rarely have the memory of, nor interest in, events surrounding the use of our product or service that are specific enough to satisfy our thirst for information. The recall of events (like changing the type of product used) may be particularly problematic if:

- the decision was made mindlessly in the first place;
- the event was relatively trivial to the customer;
- the event happened in the distant past;
- the event was comprised of a sequence of events or precipitating events.

Saliency of the event is the determining factor and even though some major events may seem likely to be salient, it is still useful to provide customers with cues to bring the event into greater focus. Converse and Presser (1986, 20–21) recommend four techniques to facilitate the accuracy of historical information:

- bounded recall
- narrowing the reference period
- averaging
- the use of landmarks
- cueing

There is evidence that even when a specific time frame is offered, "In the last six months . . .", customers are often guilty of "forward telescoping." This tendency results in customers elongating the time period in search of relevant events—causing overreporting. *Bounding* requested recall institutes a benchmark or baseline study, and then tracks behavior with continuous updates. In this way customers are questioned about events occurring since the last interview.

It is certainly worthwhile to *narrow the reference period* of a survey. We appear all too convinced that customers keep excruciatingly detailed memories of their interactions with our organizations and our services and products. Obviously they do not. The best practice is to reduce the time period to the shortest, most recent time period of value.

As a rule, asking about *specific events* is preferable to asking about generalities. When auditing usage one should identify a specific time frame:

How much of our solvent did your factory require in the last 24 hours?

Even though some heavy users will be undercounted due to extenuating circumstances (the production line was shut down for retooling yesterday), this form of questioning will provide more accurate data over your entire customerbase. Some researchers have found that following a time-specific question with an average question, helps to correct for circumstance variability on an individual customer basis. Consider this sequence:

> How much of our solvent did your factory require in the last 24 hours?
> Is that amount of solvent typical of the amount you used on a daily basis over the past 10 operating days?
>
> [ ] Yes
> [ ] No
>
> (If no) How much solvent does your factory typically use on a 24-hour basis?

Landmark events can be offered as another way of sharpening customers' recall of events or usage of the past. Major events can help to anchor the timing of other events, for example,

> Since the start of Daylight Savings time this spring, how many times have you shopped for hardware?

Offering cues can further help to increase the accuracy of recall of past events. Cues stimulate recall by drawing on associations. Because humans' memory tends to use a great variety of coding schemes to store information, something that is "forgotten" may be made accessible if the correct storage file is opened.

Hypothetical Questions

It is generally best to avoid "What if . . ." or "Imagine that . . ." sorts of questions. Because your customers will invariably have had direct experience with your services and products, hypothetical questions may be easy to avoid. On the other hand, hypothetical reasoning is at the very heart of trade-off questioning—especially the cost/benefit type. It is best to use such questions sparingly and to recognize the burden they place on your customers to answer them. Refer to Table 4.6 for a general listing of these and other, common question wording problems.

Table 4.6   Actions to Avoid in Writing Survey Questions

Practice	Explanation
Unstated Criteria	The judgment criteria respondents are expected to use must be completely obvious, or stated in the question.
Inapplicable Questions	Questions asked in a survey must be applicable to all respondents who will be asked to answer them.
Example Containment	Examples offered in questions may inadvertently introduce bias. Any examples used should be as all-inclusive to the category (or class of actions) as possible.
Overdemanding Recall	Be realistic in expectations of how long (or how much) respondents can reasonably be expected to remember.
Overgeneralizations	Generally survey questions should probe for specific quantities, events or behaviors. Generalizations may be appropriate as responses to global questions, when seeking orientations, habitual actions or policies. Otherwise, a question should not allow a generalization as a response.
Overspecificity	Avoid asking respondents for a precise response that the respondent is unlikely to know—and one which may be more precise than that required for a reasonable interpretation or analysis.
Overemphasis	Avoid using words that overstate or exaggerate conditions or responses. When it's necessary to describe a condition understating is probably desirable to using words that are overly dramatic or constitute drawing a conclusion.
Ambiguous Wording	All words used in questions should have the greatest common meaning possible. Industry slang or terminology should be avoided unless it is the only way to communicate an issue.
Double-barreled Questions	Often we inadvertently ask two questions at once, as in asking whether or not an action has been taken and then why. Such compound questions should be separated into two questions, perhaps with the second conditional on responses to the first.
Leading Questions	Questions that suggest or lead to a particular response must be avoided at all costs. Sometimes satisfaction surveys are unconsciously biased to rate "how well we're doing".
Loaded Questions	Questions that include value laden examples or explanations are "loaded" in the sense that the word or phrase used subtly affects responses.
Inadequate Wording	Questions must be fully explained, avoid the use of any shorthand or incomplete sentences.

Adapted, in part, from Alreck, Pamela L., and Robert B. Settle, *The Survey Research Handbook, Second Edition*. Burr Ridge, IL: Richard D. Irwin, 1995.

RELIABILITY AND VALIDITY

Reliability and validity are concepts of measurement that are frequently discussed, yet often misunderstood. Both are necessary qualities to strive for in the composition of a satisfaction survey process. To place them in perspective, consider the measurement of satisfaction represented by the following:

> measured = true satisfaction + systematic error (bias) + random error
> satisfaction

In this relationship, the quest for validity is the attempt to eliminate (or minimize) systematic error and the quest for reliability is the elimination (or minimization) of random error. Diagrammatically validity and reliability can be described in terms of rifle patterns on a target. In Figure 4.6, the target in the upper left-hand corner shows a compact pattern of shots all on the bullseye. The rifle (satisfaction instrument) in this case has hit its mark and does so time after time. This target demonstrates the effect of a survey that is both valid and reliable. There is no target in the lower left. Theorists suggest that without reliability, a question or questionnaire cannot possess validity. The upper right target shows an instrument that is reliable, yet fails to measure what it aims for. Finally the lower right shows a lack of both validity and reliability.

Of the two concepts, reliability is more objectively and more easily assessed than validity.

Validity

A question (or survey) is valid to the extent it measures what it is supposed to (thought to) measure, and only that! To be valid the measure must be free of systematic influences that move responses in another direction. When a systematic influence is allowed, the measure is said to be *biased*. Bias is the enemy of validity. Bias can be introduced through:

- poor sampling—speaking to a sample of predominantly happy or unhappy customers;
- faulty wording—wording that leads or evokes a particular response;
- sloppy administration of interviewing—interviewers are able to bias customers' responses;
- inaccurate data editing and recording—decisions in editing or entry introduce higher or lower scores than customers intended;
- inappropriate interpretation of the results—the satisfaction professional asserts his perspective into the interpretation of survey results.

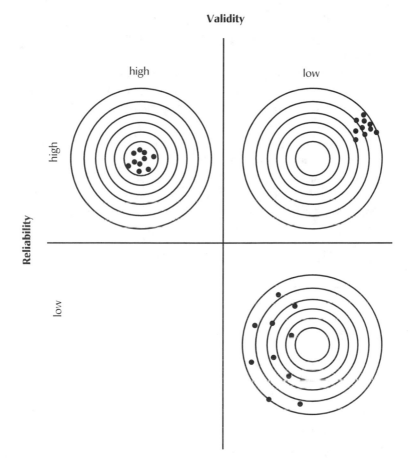

Figure 4.6   Demonstrating Validity and Reliability

There are no direct statistical tests for the validity of a question or of the data it produces. Here are four different forms of validity and the way they are generally ascertained:

- **Content (face) validity**   Content validity is determined by how logically it appears that a question or questionnaire appears to measure that which was intended to be measured. Content validity concerns not only the appropriateness of the questions asked, but also how inclusive the questions are to the measured construct.
- **Construct validity**   Construct validity is determined by the extent to which a question represents an underlying construct (like customer

loyalty) and the extent to which the question relates to other associated constructs (repeat purchase intention, satisfaction, and so on) in an expected way.

- **Predictive (pragmatic) validity**   Predictive validity is the most practical of all forms of validity. It is ascertained by the extent to which a question accurately predicts an anticipated action or response to other related measures.
- **Convergent validity**   A question is said to possess convergent validity if it displays scores similar to other questions measuring the same underlying construct. Convergent validity is related to concurrent validity, which tracks how accurately a question reflects real concurrent differences or is correlated with known values of the underlying constuct.

Reliability

Reliability means freedom from random error—if a measure repeatedly produces the same response, it can be considered reliable. As random error decreases, reliability increases. How is error introduced? Through a variety of sources:

- questions with ambiguous or uncommon terms—to which customers respond with guesses;
- sloppy data recording by interviewers—causing random errors in the data;
- sloppy data entry—introducing random errors;
- poor sampling procedures—drawing unkowledgeable customers or those inexperienced in a particular product or service encounter.

Several tests or testing procedures exist with which to test for reliability. One series of tests labeled tests for *internal consistency* are applicable to assessing the reliability of "homogeneous" tests. Homogeneous tests, like our satisfaction survey, are instruments in which all measures or questions attempt to lead to or measure the same underlying construct, satisfaction. The reliability of tests or surveys attempting to measure multiple constructs (satisfaction, loyalty, company image, and demographics) is better assessed with test-retest schemes, these test for *instrument stability*.

The predominant test for internal consistency reliability is *Cronbach's coefficient alpha*. This is a test of how well related each of the items or questions in the questionnaire are. A commonsense approach to assessing internal consistency would be to form a total score for each customer and then calculate a Pearson correlation coefficient for each question with the overall score over all customers. Those questions that displayed a below average correlation with the total score could be interpreted as having little in common with the remainder of the questions. Cronbach's alpha α performs a similar test in an easier way.

$$\alpha = \frac{n}{n-1}\left[1 - \frac{\Sigma V(y_i)}{\Sigma V(y_i) + 2\Sigma\Sigma C(y_i, y_j)}\right] \tag{4.1}$$

Where n = number of questions in the questionnaire
$\quad$ V = variance of each question
$\quad$ C = covariance of each question with every other question

Bohrnstedt (1983) points out that if the questions can all be assumed to have equal variance (which is likely if your response scales are uniform throughout your questionnaire) that formula 4.1 simplifies to formula 4.2:

$$\alpha = \frac{n\bar{p}_{ij}}{1 + (n-1)\bar{p}_{ij}} \tag{4.2}$$

Where n = number of questions
$\quad$ p = average correlation among all n questions

CUSTOMIZED SURVEYS

With advances in technology has come the ability to customize individual interviews to each of our customers in ways far easier and more efficient than in the past. By driving your selection of who to distribute your questionnaire to with your customerbase, you have the opportunity to draw on information stored with each of your selected customers' names. This historical information will allow you to prepare questionnaires that are much more personalized and indicate to your customers you know how they have rated you in the past.

The most embarrassing question in a customer satisfaction survey, it seems to the author, is the proverbial, first-question, *Which model(s)/product(s)/service(s) of ours do/did you use/buy?*

Surely if the CSM is intended as a component of a customer retention or loyalty program, such a question aborts the very nature of the sought relationship. One of the first items of information to link to a customer's name (whether obtained through internal records or from the customer's voluntary registration) is the identity of the products and services she buys from your organization. Once you have this information, it should control all of your correspondence and satisfaction measurement information.

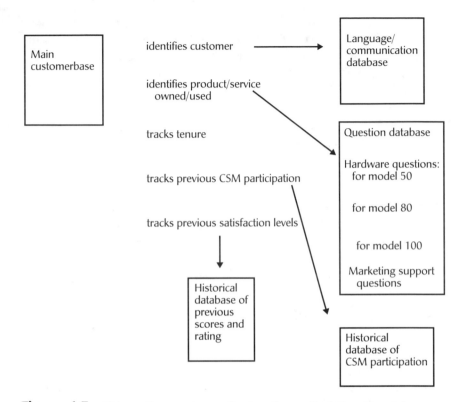

Figure 4.7   Using a Customerbase to Produce Personalized Questionnaires

In one industrial product for which the author has designed a CSM program, the customer interview is completely assembled "on-the-fly"; driven by the product ownership information contained in the main customerbase using merge-fields in the base document. This means that not only is the customer not troubled with mundane questions about product/service usage, but additionally, there will be no product-driven skip patterns in the interview, because only those questions and only those response scales relevant to the equipment the customer owns are ever asked! The customerbase information produces a totally personalized interview, appropriate to that customer's equipment, use, and tenure. (See Figure 4.7 for an illustration of how the customerbase can help assemble a personalized interview.)

PRETESTING THE SURVEY

Types of Pretests

Pretesting, the most important "insurance" a surveyor can acquire for the success of a customer satisfaction project, is unfortunately all too infrequently practiced, and when practiced may not be fully utilized. Pretesting can be conducted both among representative customers and representative interviewers (if the survey is to be interviewer-administered). Three general types of pretests can be identified:

- a customer "participating" pretest
- a customer "undeclared" pretest
- an interviewer "debriefing" pretest

Different forms of pretesting should be considered based on the final field method to be used in distributing the questionnaire; interviewer-administered or self-administered. Pretesting can also be extended to include an examination of the presentation materials accompanying the interview (a cover letter, the interviewer's introduction, and so on) as well as the return or data collection procedure. Ideally, the pretest should be carried as far as testing the proposed analytical plan with some of the collected data.

Customer Participating Pretest

In this case, the participating customer is told the survey is in a pretest phase. He is asked detailed questions about each phase of the interview as it is administered. While asking detailed probes about every question in the questionnaire would be impractical, either the most important questions can be probed, or probing for questions can be rotated throughout the pretest sample. In this way some customer comments would be received for each and every question. Generally one or more of three follow-up probes can be asked:

> What do you think this question is trying to measure?
> Is there a better way we could have asked you this question?
> Was any part of the question difficult to understand or confusing?

Sometimes a format called a "protocol session" will be used, in which the customer will be asked to "think out loud" as she ponders each question. While this format seems reasonable, tests have shown participants are unlikely to criticize any but the most blatant of poor questions. (Hunt, et al 1982) So assert your own judgment even though customers may not appear troubled by a particular issue.

Customer Undeclared Pretest

In the undeclared pretest format, the customer is not alerted to the fact that she is participating in a pretest. The interview is simply administered as it would ultimately be administered. Responses will be recorded, tabulated, and examined to see if adequate distributions are being generated by each question. This type of pretest can be combined with the Interviewer Debriefing Pretest for even more diagnostic insight.

Interviewer Debriefing Pretest

In this version of a pretest (applicable only to interviewer administered interviews), the interviewers conducting the pretest are asked to take notes on how they perceive each question to work, particular problems they may have had with questionnaire instructions, with the wording of particular questions, or in explaining a response scale to responding customers. The interview can be audio (or video) tape-recorded to provide an objective record of the interview as well.

Special Considerations for Interviewer-Administered

As interviewers administer a pretest, notes and their observations can be reviewed in a debriefing focus group after the surveying is completed. Their experiences can also be audio (or video) tape-recorded to provide an objective record of the pretest interview. Such recordings can be submitted to a form of content analysis in which coders assign specific event-codes to each event or question response, such as:

1. Whether or not the interviewer read the question as it is worded;
2. Whether or not the participating customer asks for clarification;
3. Whether or not the participating customer initially gives an inadequate answer that requires the interviewer to probe.

In an assessment of pretesting techniques, Fowler (1993) reports that if one or more of these problems occurs in more than 15 percent of the responses to a particular question, that question is likely to produce distorted data or to be highly susceptible to interviewer bias.

Special Considerations for Self-Administered Surveys

Self-administered questionnaires probably deserve the most amount of pretesting. In an interviewer-administered survey faulty procedures and other problems can be modified as the study is conducted. In a self-administered survey there is no such similar reprieve from problems discovered after the survey has been distributed. Self-administered questionnaires can be pretested by either the *undeclared* or *participating* methods. In an *undeclared* pretest, the survey would simply be distributed to a small sample of customers and later reviewed for internal consistency and tabulated to judge the coherency of the findings.

If pretesting is to be done as a *participating pretest,* the customer might be given a second questionnaire for her comments on the satisfaction survey. Alternatively, she might be interviewed by telephone immediately after completing the questionnaire (a request accompanying the pretest questionnaire could ask the customer to call an 800 telephone number for a follow-up interview). Another way of pretesting a self-administered questionnaire, is to have an interviewer (or someone on the CSM project team) deliver the questionnaire to a customer and ask him to complete it while the interviewer waits. Afterwards, the interviewer could ask several diagnostic questions:

1. Were the instructions clear?
2. Were the questions worded clearly?
3. Did you experience any problems understanding the type of responses that were expected?

The Focus of Pretesting

The objective of the pretest is to examine the interview process both from the perspective of individual questions as well as the questionnaire and interview in its totality. Specific issues are relevant at each level.

At the Question Level

There are three issues to be assessed of individual questions.

Variation/Sensitivity.   It is important to determine if a question produces a reasonable distribution of responses during the pretest. If the responses to a question are heavily skewed to one end or the other of the response continuum, it may be that there are not enough response categories, or that the continuum represented in the responses must be skewed to the more frequently used endpoint to allow greater definition of answers at this end point. For example, consider the initial distribution discovered in a pretest below. Then, look at the distribution after the scale was shifted to the positive end point.

Pretest			Revision		
Scale 1		Responses	Scale 2		Responses
"Poor"	5	0			
	4	0			
	3	10%	"Fair"	5	5%
	2	25%		4	10%
"Good"	1	65%		3	25%
				2	40%
			"Excellent"	1	20%

Meaning.   The success of questions to communicate is heavily dependent upon the terminology and phrasing they employ. Often the meaning investigators intend is not the meaning customers comprehend. Either customers do not hear the question as it was written, or they fail to understand one or more of the words used. Despite their misunderstanding, customers will invariably answer all but the most obtusely worded questions without raising the question they have or the clarification they might require. They do so not in an attempt to hide their "ignorance" but because their expectation of a satisfaction survey is sensibility. They will "translate" obscure questions into questions that seem "reasonable" from their perspective as they strain for meaning.

Task Difficulty.   We should endeavor to ask questions that our customers are able to answer, as opposed to questions we want to know. Information that we seek sometimes is not as important or as salient to our customers as it is to us. It is important to avoid asking overly demanding questions or questions that are overly precise—requiring a response metric that may be totally outside customers' experience.

At the Questionnaire Level

Other issues to be assessed in the pretest have more to do with the structure and flow of the questionnaire or the interview in its *entirety*.

Flow/Sequence of the Questionnaire.   This is an admittedly subjective appraisal. And, simply reading through one's questionnaire is generally not enough. Listening to how the questionnaire sounds as it is read aloud can help you spot awkward transitions and areas of deadly monotonous attribute ratings. How well the chosen language communicates is another consideration. For interviewer-administered surveys how the questionnaire *sounds* is the key. Make sure your questions are concisely worded with the direct objective stated clearly in the first few words. Also, listen for the coherency of your introductory transitions from section to section. Do they shift the customer's mind to the appropriate new subject matter? If not, how can they be improved?

Order of the Questions.   We have previously discussed "funneling" in the flow of the interview starting with more global questions, then progressing to the more specific. Suffice it here to remind yourself the value not only of starting the interview with questions that by their nature are more interesting, but also questions that directly relate to the announced subject of the survey—quality in your products or services. Review your questionnaire to see that it establishes a prima facie validity in the first few questions.

For telephone interviews, one researcher (Frey 1983) has suggested placing an open-ended question early in the survey to allow the participating customer to find his "telephone voice." This establishes the interview as a dialogue, and builds customer involvement early on. Otherwise, the customer finds himself listening to a seemingly endless list of closed-ended questions, which may not allow him to volunteer that one precious insight that only his words will convey.

Sprinkling factual (even demographic) questions throughout the interview (rather than clumping them all at the end) may offer the customer some relief from the intensity of evaluation and scalar rating questions.

Skip Pattern Performance.   This is a check for logic sequences in your draft questionnaire. With a schematic that identifies the particular conditions to be taken into account, you can have colleagues role-play these conditions to see if they are properly routed through your questionnaire.

Also examine your questionnaire's flow as if it were a road map. Can you use your instructions to get from the start to the finish easily? Have you provided adequate road signs along the way?

Time/Length—Interest/Attention.   Though less obvious than the three previous considerations, monitoring the fatigue of customers through the questionnaire can be a very useful finding from a pretest. Most of our customer satisfaction questionnaires are too long, ask far too many questions and are less interesting than they could be. In interviewer-administered surveys customer disinterest and fatigue will be observable during the pretest as uneasiness, hostile body language and verbal expressions of impatience. The survey research industry has traditionally condoned personal interviews of up to one-hour in length, though the Government's Office of Management and the Budget has suggested surveys be limited to $\frac{1}{2}$-hour or less. However, in today's channel surfing, commercial zapping, world of instant gratification, 60 minutes can seem an eternity. The author recommends personal interviews last 30–45 minutes, no longer. Telephone interviews should be limited to 20 minutes. The permissible length for self-administered interviews is probably dictated more by the number of pages or weight of the questionnaire than by the actual time required to complete the instrument.

Length, of course, is highly subjective. It is both a function of our informational goals and the perspective we adopt within our interview. It is necessary for us to optimize the number of issues we investigate, but perspective is also important. Too many questions hold the customer "hostage," without really involving him in the interview. That is because the questionnaire is written from the company's perspective, not the customer's. Dale Carnegie said the sweetest word in the English language is "me." If an interview is structured to allow the customer to participate in the topics selected for probing, if it provides ample opportunity for the customer to elaborate (when she desires) on ratings and evaluations, then 20 minutes will seem too short a time!

The best rule is to keep your questionnaire as short as possible and to encourage as much active participation from responding customers as possible.

Especially important are customers' reactions to "ganged" questions, in which the same question format is repeatedly used across a number of issues, for example, performance or importance ratings across attributes. Do such sections of the questionnaire sustain the customer's interest or cause her to lose interest? Maintaining a uniform response scale has been advocated throughout our discussion of questions. This section is not meant to challenge that recommendation. We are simply suggesting a sensitivity to the reaction customers may have to a frequently and repeatedly used response format. If the response grid can be interspersed with other questions it will at least provide some variety.

REFERENCES

Alreck, Pamela L., and Robert B. Settle. *The Survey Research Handbook.* 2nd ed. Burr Ridge, IL: Richard D. Irwin, Inc., 1995.

Atherton, Carolyn, and Terry G. Vavra. "Pretesting New Information Products Using Electronic Self-Administered Surveys." *Conference Proceedings Technology in Marketing Conference.* Sponsored by the American Marketing Association Conference, Chicago, June 25–28, 1989.

Bohrnstedt, George W. "Measurement." in Rossi, Peter H., James D. Wright, and Andy B. Anderson (eds.), *Handbook of Survey Research.* New York: Academic Press, 1983.

Churchill, Gilbert A. Jr. *Marketing Research: Methodological Foundations.* 5th ed. Hinsdale, IL: The Dryden Press, 1991.

Converse, Jean M. and Stanley Presser. *Survey Questions: Handcrafting the Standardized Questionnaire.* Newbury Park, CA: Sage Publications, 1986.

Fowler, Floyd J., Jr. *Survey Research Methods.* Newbury Park, CA: Sage Publications, 1993.

Frey, J. H. *Survey Research by Telephone.* Newbury Park, CA: Sage Publications, 1983.

Gale, Bradley T. *Managing Customer Value.* New York, NY: The Free Press, 1994.

Hauser, John R. "Comparison of Importance Measurement Methodologies and Their Relationship to Consumer Satisfaction." MIT Marketing Center Working Paper, no. 91–1, 1991.

Hausknecht, Douglas. "Measurement Sales in Customer Satisfaction/Dissatisfaction." *Consumer Satisfaction/Dissatisfaction and Complaint Behavior.* 3, 1990: 1–11.

Hunt, Shelby, Richard D. Sparkman, and James B. Wilcox. "The Pretest in Survey Research: Issues and Preliminary Findings." *The Journal of Marketing Research.* 19, no. 2 (May 1982): 269–73.

Likert, Rensis. "A Technique for the Measurement of Attitudes." *Archives of Psychology.* no. 140, 1932.

Lodge, Milton. *Magnitude Scaling: Quantitative Measurement of Opinions.* Beverly Hills, CA: Sage Publications, 1981.

Maher, Bill, and Terry G. Vavra. "The PC Versus the Pencil."
    Pharmaceutical Executive. (June 1987).
Payne, Stanley L. *The Art of Asking Questions.* Princeton, NJ: Princeton
    University Press, 1951.
Ryan, Michael, Thomas Buzas, and Venkatram Ramaswamy. "Making
    CSM a Power Tool." *Marketing Research.* 7, no. 3: 11–16.
Wittink, Dick, and Leonard Bayer. "The Measurement Imperative."
    Marketing Research. 6, no. 2 (Fall 1994): 14–22.

ADDITIONAL RESOURCES

Fowler, Floyd J., Jr. *Improving Survey Questions.* Thousand Oaks, CA:
    Sage Publications, 1995.
Schuman, Howard, and Stanley Presser. *Questions and Answers in
    Attitude Surveys: Experiments on Question Form, Wording and
    Context.* Thousand Oaks, CA: Sage Publications, 1996.
Sudman, Seymour, and Norman Bradburn. *Asking Questions.* San
    Francisco: Jossey-Bass, 1982.

APPENDIX TO CHAPTER 4:
MEASURES OF SATISFACTION

Because there appeared to be a lack of continuity in the utilization of various scales in customer satisfaction measurement, one researcher, Douglas Hausknecht (1993) collected a database of over 40 different question formats that had been described, used or suggested in the satisfaction research literature. He suggests the scales are represented in two continuua: cognitive to affective and verbal to graphic.

Table 4A.1 reproduces all of the scales Hausknecht identified.

Table 4A.1   Measures Used in Consumer Satisfaction Research

(a) Evaluative/Cognitive Measures in Consumer Satisfaction

Verbal

Disconfirmation measures _____

1. My expectations were:

Too high: It was poorer than I thought	Accurate: It was just as I thought	Too low: It was better than I thought

   :____ :____ :____ :____ :____ :____ :____   (Oliver 1997)[a]

2. _____ was much better(worse)[b] than I expected.

Very Strong Yes	Strong Yes	Yes	?	No	Strong No	Very Strong No

   (Swan, Trawick and Carroll 1981)

3.

Much more than I expected 1	Somewhat more than I expected 2	About what I expected 3	Somewhat less than I expected 4	Much less than I expected 5

   (Aiello, Czepiel, and Rosenberg 1997)

4. Derived measure for attribute levels

   (Level currently provided) – (Level ideally desired) – Disconfirmation

   (Westbrook and Oliver 1981)

Degree of satisfaction measures_____

5. Overall, how satisfied have you been with this _____ ?

100%	90	80	70	60	50	40	30	20	10	0%
Completely Satisfied					(Half & Half)					Not at all Satisfied

   (Moore & Shuptrine 1984; Oliver & Bearden 1983;
Oliver & Westbrook 1982; Westbrook 1980b; Westbrook 1981)

Table 4A.1–*Continued*

6. ____ was very satisfactory (unsatisfactory)

Very Strong Yes	Stong Yes	Yes	?	No	Strong No	Very Strong No
____	____	____	____	____	____	____

(Swan, Trawick and Carroll 1981)

7. How satisfied were you with ____ :

Very Dissatisfied	Somewhat Dissatisfied	Slightly Dissatisfied	Neither	Slightly Satisfied	Somewhat Satisfied	Very Satisfied
____	____	____	____	____	____	____

(Oliver and Bearden 1983; Oliver and Linda 1981)

8. Were you satisfied/dissatisfied? (Choose one.)   (Gronhaug and Arndt 1980)

9.

I am always or almost always satisfied with . . .	I am sometimes satisfied with . . .	I am sometimes dissatisfied with . . .	I am always or almost always dissatisfied with . . .
____	____	____	____

(Day and Bodur 1978; 1979)

10.

I am quite satisfied with . . .	I am somewhat satisfied with . . .	I am somewhat dissatisfied with . . .	I am quite dissatisfied with . . .
____	____	____	____

(Day and Bodur 1979)

11.

Completely Satisfied (Dissatisfied) 1	Very Satisfied (Dissatisfied) 2	Satisfied (Dissatisfied) 3	Somewhat Satisfied (Dissatisfied) 4	Not Satisfied (Dissatisfied) 5
____	____	____	____	____

(Aiello & Czepiel 1979; Aiello, Czepiel and Rosenberg 1977)

12.

Very Satisfied 1	Somewhat Satisfied 2	Neither Satisfied Nor Dissatisfied 3	Somewhat Dissatisfied 4	Very Dissatisfied 5
____	____	____	____	____

(Aiello, Czepiel and Rosenberg 1977; Mowen and Grove 1983)

Table 4A.1–*Continued*

13. Now that you've actually used the product, how satisfied with it are you?

Dissatisfied   Satisfied

—   —   —   —   —   —   —   —   —   —

(Bahr 1982)

14. Completely   Fairly   Not too
Satisfied   Satisfied   Satisfied

——   ——   ——

(Hughes 1977)

15. I am satisfied with _____ ,

Agree ____: ____: ____: ____: ____: ____: ____: ____: ____: Disagree

Other evaluations _____ (Oliver and Bearden 1983)

16. To what extent does this ____ meet your needs at this time?

Extremely   Extremely
Well   ____: ____: ____: ____: ____: ____: ____: ____: ____: Poorly

(Oliver and Westbrook 1982: Westbrook 1980b)

17. Summed semantic differential scales of satisfaction.

(Oliver and Bearden 1983; Oliver and Westbrook 1982; Westbrook and Oliver 1981)

18. Likert Scales   (Oliver 1980a)

19. Satisfactory or Dissatisfactory occasions/products as judged by respondent.

(Day and Bodhur 1978; Locker and Dunt 1978, Richins 1983a)

Graphic

20. Imagine that the following circles represent the satisfaction of different people
with _____ . Circle 0 has all minuses in it, to represent a person who is
completely dissatisfied with _____ . Circle 8 has all pluses in it, to represent a
person who is completely satisfied with _____ . Other circles are in between.

Which circle do you think comes closest to matching your satisfaction with
_____ ?

Write the circle number here: ____

(Oliver and Bearden 1983; Oliver and Westbrook 1982; Westbrook 1983; Westbrook and Oliver 1981)

Table 4A.1–*Continued*

---

21. Here is a picture of a ladder. At the bottom of the ladder is the worst _____
you might reasonably expect to have. At the top is the best _____ you might
expect to have. On which rung would you put _____ ?

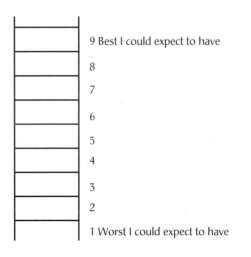

9 Best I could expect to have

8

7

6

5

4

3

2

1 Worst I could expect to have

(Andrews and Withey 1976)

(b) Emotional Affective Measures in Consumer Satisfaction

Verbal

22. Likert scales
   a. I am satisfied with _____ .
   b. If I had it to do over again, I would _____ .
   c. My choice to _____ was a good one.
   d. I feel bad about my decision concerning _____ .
   e. I think that I did the right thing when I decided _____ .
   f. I am not happy that I did what I did about _____ .
   Agree . . . (9) . . . (7) . . . (5) . . . Disagree
   Strongly Agree . . . . Strongly Disagree

(Moore & Shuptrine 1984; Oliver 1980a; Oliver and Bearden 1983;
Oliver and Westbrook 1982; Westbrook and Oliver 1981)

Table 4A.1–*Continued*

23. Mark on one of the nine blanks below the position which most closely reflects your satisfaction with _____ .

Delighted	Pleased	Mostly Satisfied	Mixed	Mostly Dissatisfied	Unhappy	Terrible	Neutral	Never Thought About It
____	____	____	____	____	____	____	____	____

(Jordan and Leigh 1984) {7 items};[c] Moore and Shuptrine 1984;
Oliver and Bearden 1983; Oliver and Westbrook 1982; Westbrook and Oliver 1981)

24. Content analysis of subject-provided protocols with scoring for satisfaction or emotional statements.

(Locker and Dunt 1978; Westbrook 1980b)

25. Scales measuring separate emotions.
Please indicate the extent to which each word describes the way you feel with respect to _____ .

1	2	3	4	5
Very Slightly or not at all	Slightly	Moderately	Considerably	Very Strongly

Adjectives "loading" on each of the ten emotional dimensions[d]

1) Interest–Excitement, 2) Enjoyment–Joy, 3) Surprise–Startle, 4) Sadness–Anguish, 5) Anger–Rage, 6) Disgusted–Revulsion, 7) Contempt–Scorn, 8) Fear–Terror, 9) Shame–Shyness and 10) Guilt Remorse

(Westbrook 1987; Westbrook and Oliver 1984)

Graphic

26. How do you feel about _____ ?
I feel:

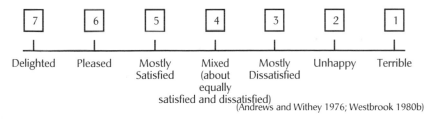

Delighted	Pleased	Mostly Satisfied	Mixed (about equally satisfied and dissatisfied)	Mostly Dissatisfied	Unhappy	Terrible

(Andrews and Withey 1976; Westbrook 1980b)

A   Neutral (neither satisfied nor dissatisfied)
B   I never thought about it.

Table 4A.1–*Continued*

---

27. "Feeling" Thermometer
    Where would you put ____ on the feeling thermometer?

    WARM 100°–Very warm or favorable feeling
    |
    | 85°–Good warm or favorable feeling
    | 70°–Fairly warm or favorable feeling
    | 60°–A bit more warm or favorable than cold feeling
    |
    ————— 50°–No feeling at all
    |
    | 40°–A bit more cold or unfavorable feeling
    | 30°–Fairly cold or unfavorable feeling
    | 15°–Quite cold or unfavorable feeling
    |
    COLD   0°–Very cold or unfavorable feeling

    (Andrews and Withey 1976; Oliver and Westbrook 1982; Westbrook and Oliver 1981)

28. Faces scale
    Here are some faces expressing various feelings. Below each is a letter.

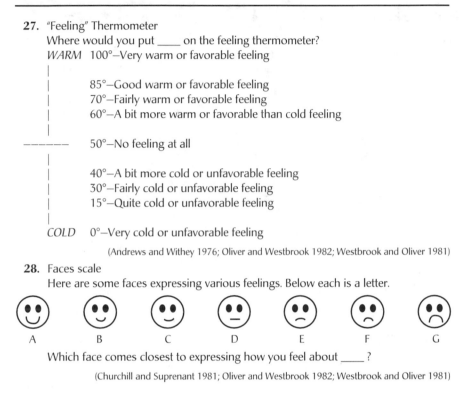

    A   B   C   D   E   F   G

    Which face comes closest to expressing how you feel about ____ ?

    (Churchill and Suprenant 1981; Oliver and Westbrook 1982; Westbrook and Oliver 1981)

(c) Behavioral/Conative Measures in Consumer Satisfaction

Verbal

Behavioral intentions _____

29. Because of ____ I would come (shop) here again.

Very Strong Yes	Strong Yes	Yes	?	No	Strong No	Very Strong No
____	____	____	____	____	____	____

    (Swan, Trawick and Carroll 1981)

30. How likely are you to play with (use) ____ in the future?

Very Unlikely	Unlikely	Likely	Very Likely
–2	–1	+1	+2
____	____	____	____

    (Jordan and Leigh 1984)

Table 4A.1–*Continued*

31. Knowing what you know now, what are the chances in ten (10) that you would choose to use the _____ again?

| 0 | 1 | 2 | 3 | 4 | 5 | 6 | 7 | 8 | 9 | 10 |

No Chance   Certain

(Oliver and Bearden 1983; Westbrook and Oliver 1981)

Graphic (Observational)

32. Measures of time and extent of use.

(Bjorklund and Bjorklund 1979)

33. Filing complaint as sign of dissatisfaction

(TARP 1979)

34. Loyalty, repurchase as sign of satisfaction.

(LaBarbera and Mazursky 1983)

Notes to accompany table

[a]Citations provided are meant to serve as examples of scale use, not to provide an exhaustive bibliography.

[b]Some parenthesized modifications of what was essentially the same scale are presented for the sake of simplicity.

[c]In this case, the scale was compressed by omitting the neutral responses.

[d]Again, for the sake of simplicity, all of the adjectives which were used are not presented in this figure.

Source: From *Journal of Consumer Satisfaction, Dissatisfaction & Complaining Behavior,* Vol. 3 (1990). Reprinted with permission.

REFERENCES

Aiello, Albert Jr. and John A. Czepiel. "Customer Satisfaction in a Catalog Type Retail Outlet: Exploring the Effect of Product, Price and Attributes." in *New Dimensions of Consumer Satisfaction and Complaining Behavior.* eds. Ralph L. Day and H. Keith Hunt. Bloomington, IN: Indiana University, 1979, pp. 129–135.

Aiello, Albert Jr., John A. Czepiel, and Larry J. Rosenberg. "Scaling the Heights of Consumer Satisfaction: An Evaluation of Alternative Measures." in *Consumer Satisfaction, Dissatisfaction and Complaining Behavior.* ed. Ralph L. Day. Bloomington, IN: Indiana University, 1977, 43–50.

Andrews, Frank M., and Stephen B. Withey. *Social Indicators of Well-Being.* New York, NY: Plenum Press, 1976.

Bahr, William J. "Consumer Dissatisfaction or Disappointment: The Critical Difference." in *New Findings on Consumer Satisfaction and Complaining.* eds. Ralph L. Day and H. Keith Hunt. Bloomington, IN: Indiana University, 1982, pp. 33–39.

Bjorklund, Gail, and Richard Bjorklund. "An Exploratory Study of Toddler's Satisfaction With Their Toy Environments." in *Advances in Consumer Research.* Vol. 6, ed. Wilkie, William L., Ann Arbor, MI: Association for Consumer Research, 1979, pp. 400–406.

Churchill, Gilbert A. Jr. and Carol Surprenant. "An Investigation into the Determinants of Customer Satisfaction." *Journal of Marketing Research.* 19 (November 1982): 491–504.

Day, Ralph L., and Muzaffer Bodur. "Analysis of Average Satisfaction Scores of Individuals Over Product Categories." in *New Dimensions of Consumer Satisfaction and Complaining Behavior.* eds. Ralph L. Day and H. Keith Hunt. Bloomington, IN: Indiana University, 1979, pp. 184–189.

————. "Consumer Response to Dissatisfaction With Services and Intangibles." in *Advances in Consumer Research.* Vol. 5, ed. H. Keith Hunt. Ann Arbor, MI: Association for Consumer Research, 1978, pp. 263–272.

Gronhaug, Kjell, and Johan Arndt. "Consumer Dissatisfaction and Complaining Behavior as Feedback: A Comparative Analysis of Public and Private Delivery Systems." *Advances in Consumer Research.* Vol. 7, ed. Jerry C. Olson. Ann Arbor, MI: Association for Consumer Research, 1980, pp. 324–328.

Hausknecht, Douglas, "Measurement Scales in Consumer Satisfaction/Dissatisfaction." *Consumer Satisfaction/Dissatisfaction and Complaint Behavior.* 3, 1990, pp. 1–11.

Hughes, Donald A. "An Investigation of the Relation of Selected Factors to Consumer Satisfaction." in *Conceptualization and Measurement of Consumer Satisfaction and Dissatisfaction.* ed. H. Keith Hunt. Cambridge, MA: Marketing Science Institute, 1977, pp. 300–332.

Jordan, Kathi A., and James H. Leigh. "Race and Sex Differences of Children in Satisfaction and Other Factors Associated with Video Games." in *Advances in Consumer Research.* Vol. 11, ed. Thomas Kinnear. Ann Arbor, MI: Association for Consumer Research, 1984, pp. 94–99.

LaBarbera, Priscilla A. and David Mazursky, "A Longitudinal Assessment of Consumer Satisfaction/Dissatisfaction: The Dynamic Aspect of the Cognitive Process." *Journal of Marketing Research.* 20 (November 1983): 393–404.

Locker, David and David Dunt. "Theoretical and Methodological Issues in Sociological Studies of Consumer Satisfaction with Medical Care." *Social Science and Medicine.* 12 (July 1978): 283–292.

Moore, Ellen M. and F. Kelly Shuptrine. "Disconfirmation Effects on Consumer Satisfaction and Decision Making Processes." *Advances in Consumer Research.* Vol. 11, ed. Thomas C. Kinnear. Provo, UT: Association for Consumer Research, 1984, pp. 299–304.

Mowen, John C. and Stephen J. Grove. "Search Behavior, Price Paid, and the 'Comparison Other': An Equity Theory Analysis of Post Purchase Satisfaction." in *International Fare in Consumer Satisfaction and Complaining Behavior.* eds. Ralph L. Day and H. Keith Hunt. Bloomington, IN: Indiana University, 1983, pp. 57–63.

Oliver, Richard L. "Measurement and Evaluation of Satisfaction Processes in Retail Settings." *Journal of Retailing.* 57 (Fall 1981): 25–48.

_____. "A Cognitive Model of the Antecedents and Consequences of Satisfaction Decisions." *Journal of Marketing Research.* 17 (November 1980a): 460–469.

_____. "Effect of Expectation and Disconfirmation on Postexposure Product Evaluations: An Alternative Interpretation." *Journal of Applied Psychology.* Vol. 62, no. 4 (1977): 480–486.

Oliver, Richard L., and William O. Bearden. "The Role of Involvement in Satisfaction Processes." *Advances in Consumer Research.* Vol, 10. eds. Richard P. Bagozzi and Alice M. Tybout. Ann Arbor, MI: Association for Consumer Research, 1983, pp. 250–255.

Oliver, Richard L., and Gerald Linda. "Effect of Satisfaction and Its Antecedents on Consumer Preference and Intention." *Advances in Consumer Research.* vol. 8, ed. Kent B. Monroe. Ann Arbor, MI: Association for Consumer Research, 1981, pp. 88–93.

Oliver, Richard L., and Robert A. Westbrook. "The Factor Structure of Satisfaction and Related Postpurchase Behavior." in *New Findings on Consumer Satisfaction and Complaining.* eds. Ralph L. Day and H. Keith Hunt. Bloomington, IN: Indiana University, 1982, pp. 11–14.

Richins, Marsha L. "Negative Word-of-Mouth by Dissatisfied Consumers: A Pilot Study." *Journal of Marketing*. 47 (Winter 1983a): 63–78.

Swan, John E., I. Frederick Trawick, and Maxwell G. Carroll. "Effect of Participation in Marketing Research on Consumer Attitudes Toward Research and Satisfaction with a Service." *Journal of Marketing Research*. 18 (August 1981): 356–363.

Technical Assistance Research Programs (TARP), Alexandria, VA, 1979.

Westbrook, Robert A. "Consumer Satisfaction and the Phenomenology of Emotions During Automobile Ownership Experiences." in *International Fare in Consumer Satisfaction and Complaining Behavior*. eds. Ralph L. Day and H. Keith Hunt. Bloomington, IN: Indiana University, 1983, pp. 2–9.

_____. "Sources of Consumer Satisfaction With Retail Outlets." *Journal of Retailing*. 57 (Fall 1981): 68–85.

_____. "A Rating Scale for Measuring Product/Service Satisfaction." *Journal of Marketing*. 44 (Fall 1980b): 68–72.

Westbrook, Robert A., and Richard L. Oliver. "Emotion and Consumer Satisfaction in Product Ownership/Usage." unpublished manuscript, 1984.

_____. "Developing Better Measures of Consumer Satisfaction: Some Preliminary Results." in *Advances in Consumer Research*. Vol. 8, ed. Kent B. Monroe. Ann Arbor, MI: Association for Consumer Research, 1981, pp. 94–99.

DELIVERY: ASSESSING PERFORMANCE

With the survey process designed, your goal is to assess your organization's actual performance, in terms of its products or services, its ability to conduct customer transactions and the longer term, after-sale reliability of the product or service and dependability of the organization's after-sale accessibility and support.

In this phase we are essentially measuring how well your product or service meets the expectations and needs of your defined customer group.

assessing
Delivery

CHAPTER 5

The Logistics of Satisfaction Data Collection

OVERVIEW

While in the mid-1980s a questionnaire asking a customer's satisfaction was something of a novelty, in the mid-1990s virtually every organization, it seems, is administering satisfaction questionnaires. Wherever one goes, there is an innocuous form asking our opinion of the products or services we have committed to and the servicing we have received. As a result of this ubiquity, the American business community and public (and, increasingly global customers as well) are becoming "desensitized" to the measurement of satisfaction.

The decrease in the novelty of satisfaction assessment offers challenges to both the professional who has an existing program in place and wants to maintain or increase participation as well as the initiate professional who may just be creating a CSM program. While the subjects of the last three chapters (customer identification, measurement issues, and questionnaire design) are important, your CSM project will live or die by the quality of your fieldwork! Quality in the field process includes: the professionalism of the interviewing staff (or the appropriate structure of the questionnaire packet); controls for bias introduced by interviewers, the quality of the questionnaire instructions and the validity of the questions.

The satisfaction professional of today faces considerable challenges in conceiving new approaches to the customerbase to stimulate customers' active participation. New technologies are evolving that promise to make survey participation easier, but CSM professionals will still bear a sizable burden in encouraging their participation. In this chapter we will examine the consequences of the field methodology. And, we will provide rules of thumb for when each of several different field procedures are best.

A Comparison of Field Procedures

How Your Survey Will Be Administered

The way your survey will be administered, usually called the "field procedure," is a difficult decision to make. There are three common field methods: Personal interviews, Telephone interviews, and Mail interviews. But these three commonly discussed methods overshadow several other techniques and make the task of method selection seem overly simplistic. In choosing a field method you cannot avoid making considerable trade-offs. For example, although interviewers create attention value for your survey and contribute substantial "energy" to the project (by completing interviews on schedule and by minimizing the number of customers who terminate during an interview), they also increase your field costs and introduce their own biases, which may contaminate your survey results. If you choose to avoid the costs of hiring personal interviewers by using a mail-delivered survey (requesting your customers to self-administer the survey), you will suffer lower response rates and often receive incomplete data. There is no perfect answer. The satisfaction professional must choose between field procedures by maximizing her outcomes.

In the past there have been two major field procedure alternatives available to surveyors. These were interviewer-administered and self-administered methods. Today, technology has introduced a third category of newer methods we will refer to as "machine administered."

Even though we have identified three field methods, the basic distinction is still, "Do *you* wish to administer your survey to your customers (by interviewer or by machine) or do you want *your customers* to administer your questionnaire to themselves?"

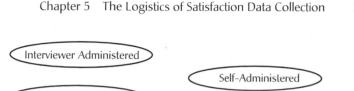

Figure 5.1   The Three Possible Fielding Methods

Table 5.1 establishes eleven criteria for comparing the three field methods. In this section we will further examine the most frequently used field procedures. We will specify the advantages and disadvantages of each method, as well as provide guidelines for when one or another should clearly be your preferred field method.

Interviewer–Administered Interviews

Method Overview

- most expensive
- access to a geographically dispersed customer base varies by specific method
- high impact–highest response rates
- demanding (inflexible) on customers' schedules
- interviewer can probe customers for insights and can check for completeness of each answer
- a reasonably complex interview can be administered
- order effects can be controlled and minimized

Interviewer-administered surveys, if not the oldest field method/procedure are certainly the method most frequently discussed for collecting customer research information. For some the format is synonymous with survey research.

Personal Interviews

Personal interviews as a customer satisfaction data collection format, take the form of in-home or "on-site" interviews, exit or in-service interviews, or any other method in which interviewers will confront your customers directly. If your customers are not clustered in specific areas, the personal interview format will be very expensive and very difficult to coordinate. (In such cases, a telephone-administered survey will be your better choice.)

Table 5.1 Comparison of Basic Fielding Methods

Characteristic	Interviewer-Administered	Machine-Administered	Self-Administered
Degree of Control Maintained How much control over the customer's use of the questionnaire is maintained?	Substantial	Substantial	Little
Obtrusiveness/Impact How much attention does the method command? How intrusive is it on the customer's activities/schedule?	Substantial	Moderate	Little
Cooperation Rate How much cooperation does the method evoke?	High	Moderate to High	Low
Cost How costly is the field method?	$$$	$$	$
Complexity of Questions Accommodated What level of question complexity does the method accommodate?	High Complexity	High Complexity	Low Complexity
Allows Interruptions Can customers start and stop answering the questionnaire to attend to other obligations?	No	Yes	Yes
Allows Collection of Observational Data Can observations about the customer be collected during the interview?	Yes	Some	No
Minimizes Order Effects Does the method allow for the control of order effects or is the customer prevented from seeing the entire interview by looking ahead?	Yes	Yes	No
Allows Complex Skip Patterns How complex can skip patterns be?	Moderately Complex	High Complexity	Low Complexity
Ability to Embed Customer's Language/Terms When the customer uses specific terminology in answering one question, can this be captured and used in subsequent questions to maximize the customer's understanding?	Somewhat	Yes	Not Easily
Minimizes Interviewer Bias Does the method control interview bias?	No	Yes	Yes

The personal interview format is logistically the most complex field method. There are numerous steps to be undertaken. Many of these steps will be taken care of for you, if you have hired a research vendor/partner to help conduct your CSM. If you are conducting your CSM internally, you can still avoid some of the steps, by hiring an interviewing field service. (See this chapter's Appendix for a discussion of how and where to find interviewing field services.)

You will need to perform each of the following steps to conduct your survey by personal interview:

1. recruit interviewers (or hire an interviewing service);
2. train the interviewers familiarizing them with your project and your questionnaire;
3. establish quality controls for the conduct of your interview and for recording your data;
4. supervise your interviewers;
5. establish a "standardized interview."

Using internal staff to conduct your interviewing is generally not a good idea. Sometimes it seems reasonable to use your organization's field or sales force to conduct the personal interviews. After all, they are in the field and as dispersed as your customers. And, your customers know them and are accustomed to talking to them. The problem is, they may be part of your organization's problem. If so, it is unlikely customers will tell them that to their faces. In conclusion, it is better to overlook the seeming benefits of using your own staff in favor of finding an unbiased interviewing staff.

Computer Administered Personal Interviewing

Less frequently used (than its telephone counterpart), but no less powerful, Computer Administered Personal Interviewing (CAPI) involves an interviewer reading an interview from a computer (generally a portable or laptop) in a personal meeting with a customer. Perhaps the customer has been recruited in the lobby of a bank or in an airline's departure lounge. The interviewer administers the interview from the computer and enters the respondent's answers directly into the computer. Again, the computer can administer skip patterns and embed terminology on a real time basis, simplifying the interviewer's job and making the interview more personalized for each respondent.

Telephone Interviews

Telephone interviews are probably one of the most frequently used formats by which to collect customer satisfaction data. Their relatively high cooperation rates, the generally thorough nature of the data, and their capability to accommodate reasonably complex interviews with intricate skip and branching patterns explains their popularity. Unfortunately, their major drawback is the general lack of customers' telephone numbers in organizational customerbases! A secondary drawback is the method's inability to show participating customers questionnaire materials (show cards, attribute lists, and so on) and the resulting need for customers to visualize all questions and response scales.

Today telephone survey companies exist that are able to field very large surveys using banks of 100–400 telephone lines. Any one of these firms will be delighted to provide you a cost estimate for conducting your survey.

Central facility telephone interviewing operations attempt to train their interviewers in the basics of good interviewing principles. The trouble is, these companies face extremely high employee turnover rates, so new, relatively inexperienced interviewers are constantly handling calls. The companies monitor a proportion of all of the interviews their employees conduct. However, it is obviously impossible for them to monitor *all* of the interviews, so the supervisory staff faces a demanding role in maintaining quality. Generally, the largest of these facilities will be handling several different surveys at the same time. This further minimizes the attention each individual client's survey receives.

It is always a good idea to visit the facility you have retained to either observe the interviewer-briefing and/or interviewing sessions for your survey. If you attend the briefing you may wish to conduct some or all of this important instructional meeting. It sets the tone for how well your survey will be conducted. It is always a good idea to specify that you wish the same interviewers to work on your survey day after day, instead of having the facility's entire workforce rotated through your survey. (If it is impossible to retain the same interviewers, intermediate briefing sessions may have to be specified until virtually all of the interviewers working at a facility have received a formal introduction to your survey, its goals and special instructions that accompany any specific questions you may have created.)

You may also monitor telephone interviews off-site in your office or home. Virtually all telephone facilities offer this feature. You will have to consider, however, the ethics of monitoring. A third party, especially someone from your company, eavesdropping on the interview may stretch the ethics of confidentiality a bit. One way to overcome this is for your interviewers to read an increasingly familiar disclaimer at the beginning of the interview,

> "In order to maintain quality control, some or all of this interview may be monitored. If you do not wish our conversation to be monitored you may state your desire for a private interview."

Computer Administered Telephone Interviewing

Computer Administered Telephone Interviewing (CATI) is fast becoming the most preferred if not the most common type of telephone interview. In this format, interviewers sit at CRTs or PC workstations. A central computer relays the survey to each interviewer's workstation. Frequently "predictive dialing" is also incorporated into a CATI operation. Predictive dialing relies on the central computer to dial customers' telephone numbers. As a customer answers the computer's call, the call and an appropriate version of the questionnaire are "hot-transferred" to an interviewer's computer workstation and telephone headset. At the workstation, the interviewer reads the questionnaire from her CRT and keys in responses as the customer volunteers them.

CATI interviewing systems automatically administer all skip patterns. The responding customers' volunteered terminology from answers to previous questions may be captured and embedded in subsequent questions. For example in critical incident surveys, once the respondent has described the incident all future questions in the survey referring to the incident may describe it using the respondent's own terminology, "when the shower went '*on the fritz.*'"

Maintaining Productivity Records from Telephone Interviewing

Because telephone interviewing is so costly, it will behoove you to closely monitor the effort your telephone interviewing facility is placing behind your survey and the productivity of the customerbase you have provided to generate completed interviews. The two most common forms are the Survey Call Report and the Call Record Sheet. The Survey Call Report is a summary report of all of the calling activity the telephone interviewers have invested in your survey. It shows the total number of dialings,

Response	Cooperators	Contacts	Calls	Percentage
Total Dialings			1050	100.0%
Answering Machine			150	14.3%
No Answer (after 3 attempts)			78	7.4%
Busy			34	3.2%
Disconnected Number			15	1.4%
Number Change			21	2.0%
Duplicated Number			3	0.3%
Other Phone Problems			3	0.3%
Total Contacts		100.0%	746	71.0%
Call Back		16.8%	125	11.9%
Refusal		4.2%	31	3.0%
Business/Government		0.0%	0	0.0%
Language Barrier		1.6%	12	1.1%
Breakoff (respondents terminated during call)		0.9%	7	0.7%
Deceased		0.3%	2	0.2%
Other Phone				
Total Cooperators	100.0%	76.3%	569	54.2%
Terminate–Q1a No Longer Use Our Product	3.2%	2.4%	18	1.7%
Terminate–Q1b Not Used Product in Last 6 Months	4.2%	3.2%	24	2.3%
Terminate–Q2 Not the Decision-Maker	0.4%	0.3%	2	0.2%
Terminate–Over Quota by Product Type	4.2%	3.2%	24	2.3%
Terminate–Security Risk Dealer, Retailer	0.2%	0.1%	1	0.1%
Total Completes	87.9%	67.0%	500	47.6%

Figure 5.2   Survey Call Report

the total number of contacts, and the total number of completed interviews. In Figure 5.2, one can see that to complete telephone interviews
with 500 customers, it was necessary to make 1,050 dialings. From these
dialings: 746 (71 percent) resulted in contact with a person; 569 (54 percent) agreed to cooperate; and 500 were completed as interviews. Even
though all 1050 names and numbers were from our customerbase, we
were not able to complete interviews with each one. The completion proportions are what your field costs will be based on (in Figure 5.2 that is
48 percent), so it is a good idea to make sure you understand how calls
are tracked by telephone survey units.

The call record sheet tracks the events occurring in attempting to reach just one customer. Such information, whether in paper and pencil format, or in easily updated "counters" in a computer are a must for accurately understanding how the names pulled from your customerbase are being pursued by the interviewing service. For example, it is common industry practice that each number be tried at least three times (always on different days and at different times).

Machine Interviews

An increasingly popular and powerful way of administering all forms of surveys is by electronic means. In general, satisfaction measurement surveys seem to have lagged behind in the transition to these important new ways of collecting data. Ironically, customer satisfaction should probably have led the transition; satisfaction professionals have answers for the major problems inhibiting the growth of electronic surveying. They know their customers' accessibility to computers or their literacy; and satisfaction professionals can provide privileged access to satisfaction survey pages on their Internet sites protected by the customer's account number and other private information. Both of these issues have retarded the general growth of electronic interviewing.

Electronic interviews interestingly enough, satisfy many of the problems with the more traditionally administered surveys. They are relatively cheap; they allow customers to answer at their own convenience; and the complexity and length of the interview are concealed from the customers' direct scrutiny.

Planning an electronic survey is somewhat different from writing a traditional paper and ink questionnaire. It is a good idea to first think through the major areas of the interview. Then you can visualize the interview in a storyboard format, looking at the interview from a screen-by-screen perspective. This will help you plan transition screens, and how and when you may wish to present any visuals.

The "Appearance" of Administered Surveys

Every interview has an "appearance." While it may seem easier to consider the appearance of a printed questionnaire, the sound of a telephone interviewer on the telephone, or the appearance of a personal interviewer, each serve as cues to your customers about your concern for them and your commitment to a professional assessment of their satisfaction. No doubt, many customers have been turned off by these cues, when an organization decides to cut corners and economize in the administration of

Customer Name: _____

Customer Tele. No. _____

Questionnaire No. _____

Interviewer Initials _____

| CALLS | | No Answer | | Answered | | | | CALL BACKS | | ELIGIBLES | |
| | | | | | | | | | | | |
Date	Time	Busy	No answer	Discon-nected	Not Available	Eligible, Refused	Not Qualified	Date	Time	Terminated	Completed
1)											
2)											
3)											
4)											
5)											
6)											
7)											
8)											
9)											
10)											

DISPOSITION

Figure 5.3 Call Record Report

a satisfaction survey. For example, a major U.S. insurance company adopted a uniformly inexpensive format of a mail questionnaire for its entire base of commercial policyholders. Even though 1/20th represented 80 percent of its revenues, the satisfaction professionals decided not to spend more money to survey these 10,000 policyholders with a more stylized and customized questionnaire.

If one thinks the situation through, it becomes very clear how important it is to make a professional impression on customers when contacting them in a satisfaction survey. Do consider each of your measurements of customer satisfaction as an important communication to show customers your organization's regard for them and the importance you place on customer satisfaction.

Self-Administered Interviews

Method Overview

- least expensive
- wide geographic (even global) coverage is easy
- low to moderate impact, require initiation by customer—cooperation rates will be lower
- the interview can include exhibits, pictures, and so on
- interview structure and individual questions must remain reasonably simple
- customers' responses will never be quite as complete or detailed as desired

Self-administered surveys must necessarily perform several tasks. They must:

- encourage participation by their expressed purpose or objective and by their physical appearance;
- capture the required information as accurately as possible;
- convey the information back to the company.

Accomplishing all of these is no small task so view any customer-administered survey as a special challenge.

Mail Surveys

In these days of stuffed global mailboxes, a mail delivered customer satisfaction survey faces very strong challenges. That is not to say you should not consider using mail. It simply means you will have more of a challenge completing your survey if you should happen to choose mail as your preferred field method. The problem is not just the volume of mail individuals and businesses receive, but the fact that so much of this mail masquerades as a survey or other highly important information. As a result, the public (and businesspeople as well) have become desensitized to some of the language and claims you may wish to use to attract their attention to your mail-delivered survey. Also, not beyond question is the quality of the postal delivery services of many of the developed nations of the world. And, the lack of a trustful service in other nations.

Having issued all of these caveats, the mail is a very cost efficient fielding method. Further, mail-delivered surveys, if they catch your customer's attention, are a very polite, sensitive way to gather information at a time when the customer is ready to provide the information. The trick is gaining attention for your mail packet and then incenting your customer to complete your questionnaire and return it as quickly as possible.

To gain impact (and in some cases to assure prompt delivery) some satisfaction professionals are using high impact delivery mechanisms. These include *dimensionalizing* the satisfaction questionnaire by perhaps mailing it in a box or very large envelope. Also, using any of the overnight, international courier services to distribute your questionnaire will convey urgency and added importance. Unfortunately, you will pay considerably more than you would pay the national postal service.

Customers often worry about the return of questionnaires through the mail. An outer envelope should always be supplied. While "one-piece, self-mailers" may seem an attractive format, they seldom offer customers the sort of confidentiality they might want for their very private evaluations and their reports of product usage. It is generally an appreciated gesture (and a pragmatically wise decision) to provide a postage paid, addressed return envelope. Again, you will convey more urgency by using a courier service. But, national postal services may also suffice, especially if they have a "Priority Mail" service.

The primary advantage of the customer-administered survey is the minimal interference on your customer's life. The mail-delivered questionnaire can be answered whenever your customer has some free time and is psychologically ready to critique your organization. You will generally receive some well thought-out responses. Unfortunately the mail questionnaire's politeness and consideration, is also its undoing. By being so nonintrusive, and so permissory, mail questionnaires often get set aside and misplaced. Response rates are notoriously low. Reminder mailings, or follow-up telephone calls may boost response rates somewhat, but except for unique situations, rarely above 30 percent. (One mail survey the author has designed regularly receives a 70 percent response rate, but this is sadly the exception, rather than the rule!)

You will necessarily have to discipline yourself to keep a self-administered satisfaction survey short and simple. Complicated skip patterns and questions will not get followed or answered. Also, build in extra time in your schedule for responses. The majority of responses to a mailing will be returned within 12–18 days. But you will receive some three months—even one year later. Obviously you cannot wait for three months, but try to be realistic as well.

If your survey requires any visuals or exhibits, you can try including them with the mailing. It is generally a good idea to enclose such exhibits in their own separate envelopes within the mailing envelope. Envelopes containing exhibits should be plainly labeled:

> "Envelope A—Open only after completing Question 8 of the enclosed Satisfaction Survey", etc. . . .

You may even wish to try using different colors. And, even though you may wish respondents not to look at everything at once, chances are some customers will open everything at once, reading your directions only later.

The Cosmetics of Self-Administered Surveys

The cosmetics of self-administered surveys are much more important than with any other form of interviewing. In a self-administered satisfaction survey there are several elements to consider:

- The size of the questionnaire and the quality of the paper it is printed on. A questionnaire that's letter size paper (8½ in. × 11 in.), matches well with a cover letter. Consider using 11 in. × 17 in. paper, which is then folded into an 8½ in. × 11 in. booklet.
- A booklet format can appear more professional, and is definitely preferable to several pages stapled together. If more than four sides (panels) are required, two sheets of 11 in. × 17 in. paper may be used and saddle stitched (down the long fold) to form a booklet.
- Always use at least 20 lb. paper.
- The color of the questionnaire should probably be white or ivory. Avoid bright colors (rather than attract attention as is sometimes thought, they will more likely give your mailing a tacky, unprofessional appearance).

- Use your company letterhead for the cover letter, unless you have decided to conduct your survey blind. (*Blind* refers to a questionnaire mailed without identifying your organization as sponsor.) Then you will require a third party's letterhead. Black or blue ink is preferable, especially printed on white or ivory paper, it will give your questionnaire a professional appearance.
- Printing your packet in two colors will also increase its professional appearance, but resist using more than two colors!
- An 8½ in. × 11 in. questionnaire or an 11 in. × 17 in. booklet can each be three-way folded to fit in a #10 business envelope.
- For responding, a #9 envelope will fit inside the #10 outer envelope and yet will still contain the completed questionnaire for return mailing.

Postage—Questionnaires should always be mailed first-class, but with large mailings a postal code presort will help reduce mailing costs. (Computer programs for the PC exist that will order your customerbase according to zip code and SCF zones for maximum USPS savings.) Mailings where postage is paid by affixed stamps traditionally have produced the highest response rates. When postage is paid by a bulk rate, preprinted indicia the lowest response rates have been noticed. This is apparently because of the public's association of bulk rate indicias with junk mail mailings. In general, providing a business reply return envelope will also stimulate the highest response rate since customers will not have to look for stamps. In industrial surveys where outgoing mail goes through the mailroom for posting, prepaid return postage may be less a factor in encouraging responses. However, in customer satisfaction work when asking *any* consumer for his/her time to answer a questionnaire, providing return postage is always a nice courtesy.

Recently, some organizations have experimented with "high impact" delivery systems. Courier systems (Federal Express, DHL, UPS) give the outbound questionnaire a sense of importance and urgency. Questionnaires delivered by such courier systems are more likely to get to their intended addressees (gatekeepers—like secretaries—will be less likely to hold back such seemingly important documents).

Cover letter—With a customerbase established to drive a CSM project, you will want your cover letter to be completely personalized, recognizing your customers by name. You may even want to indicate the number of years each customer has participated in your satisfaction assessment process. Such recognition clearly shows your customers you are listening to them and will give recognition to their consistent input.

Surveys Distributed during Service

One generally gets a better read on the quality of its products and services if the customer has had the opportunity to "gestate" the service experience. The Marriott hotel chain abandoned in-room surveys in place of telephone surveys placed to a guest's home or office a few days after the stay. Reportedly, the chain found the quality of the information collected at a later time was better (in-room forms were apparently completed in a hurry as the guest departed, providing only minimal information). The cooperation rate with the later telephone interview was also higher.

Notwithstanding the disadvantages of in-service interviewing, there are times when the sheer convenience of having customers assembled will suggest the survey be conducted during the service-delivery or in the facility. For example, conducting a survey during an airplane flight. The passengers can be so much more efficiently surveyed while they are in the plane than at a later date. (In the airline situation, cooperation rates will probably be higher during the service than if administered later because of passenger's desires for in-flight activities.)

When customers physically are available to you (as in their visit to a bank, their participation in a conference, and so on) it may again be overwhelmingly more efficient to distribute and collect your satisfaction survey at your facility. But try to be realistic in how much information you request from customers involved in a service or when visiting a facility, their time and attention will be limited.

Machine Administered Interviews

Method Overview

- moderate cost
- require a computer literate customerbase with computers or access to computers
- offer the richest data (both volunteered as well as observed data are possible)
- respectful of customers' time, schedule, and preferences for when to answer such a survey

Machine-administered surveys are the newest form of interviewing available to the satisfaction professional. As such they represent both tremendous opportunities, but also the need to learn more about their capabilities, special requirements and limitations. They offer the control of the interviewer-administered survey, along with the economy of the self-administered methods. Most importantly, they can personalize an interview in far more subtle ways than the personal interviewer is generally capable of. It is generally believed that customers will more freely and openly respond to a computer than to a person, or even perhaps to a self-administered form.

The primary limitation of machine-administered surveys is their requirement that all customers are computer literate and have access to a computer.

One of the unique aspects of a computer-administered interview is the ability to "observe" the customer as she completes the questionnaire. For example, how long did the total interview take? How much (or how little) time did the customer spend on each question? All of these questions can be answered as the computer "watches" the customer complete the interview.

Other possibilities for machine-administered interviews include showing the customer how he rated the company previously before asking for a current rating. (Or, perhaps the alternative format, collecting current data, then showing previous data, and asking the customer to explain the major changes.)

In computer interviews the author has created, an incentive is promised at the beginning of the interview. When the customer reaches the end of the survey, he is given the opportunity to play a game of chance or skill to possibly increase his incentive.

The main "overhead" to be paid in this survey format, is the development of a real time questioning software. Programs like Visual Basic™ can be used to create a custom interview. Also, marketed software exists including Ci3™ software, and InterviewDisk™ (Sawtooth Software, Marketing Metrics).

Diskette in the Mail

One of the earliest versions of machine-administered interviews involved programming a satisfaction survey on a computer diskette and then distributing the diskette by mail to a sample of customers. After the customers completed the interview (on their own computer or one at their workplace) they returned the diskette by mail to the organization. Each returned diskette contained all of the customers' answers to be uploaded into a host computer for tabulation and analysis.

This method was found to encourage sizable response rates (as high as 95 percent) due to its novelty, its high impact, and its respect for customers' time schedules. Unfortunately, as the threat of computer viruses has increased, customers are becoming somewhat less willing to load a strange diskette into their computer, though your organization's sponsorship may assuage such fears. (You could also include a virus scan program, or invite your customer to scan your diskette before loading it.)

On a Bulletin Board, on the Internet

If routines have been developed for general computerized interviewing, chances are these can also be made available on the Internet. Consider offering a special page in the organization's Internet site, requiring customers to identify themselves as bona fide customers before they are allowed entry. Within this site, customers could be invited to complete a customer satisfaction survey relative to their current purchases or transactions. While not all customers would have access to this questioning format, chances are the information that would be collected would be very rich in content and insight.

By Kiosks in Malls and Service Facilities

Another way to use computerized interviews is to make them available to customers through computer terminals placed in locations of high contact with customers. Some companies have created attractive stands or kiosks within which a computer and other peripherals may be placed with access for customers. A customer satisfaction survey could be preloaded in a computer in such a stand. This would be particularly convenient for air travelers, hotel guests, auto dealership service departments, casinos, anywhere customers come to a central location.

The problem, of course, is the self-selection by customers of who will answer the questionnaire. Also, it would be difficult to keep a single customer from answering multiple times—especially if he or she had a particular issue they wished management to attend to.

The method suffers from all of the other problems discussed earlier relating to surveying at the location at which the service or product is sold or distributed. (Refer to p. 203) Yet, its immediacy, and high impact make it an attractive field method to consider.

Hybrid Interviewing Administration Designs

"Hybrid designs" can be conceived by combining two or more of the above techniques to take advantage of the special benefits of each technique. Some common combinations include:

Phone–Mail–Mail

In this design, a telephone call is used to identify the correct person (or unit) to interview. For instance, a company may not have the name of the primary decision maker in its billing database. Rather than send a questionnaire to "Accounts Payable" or the Accounting Department with a request that the questionnaire be forwarded, the preceding telephone call would help to identify the individual (or individuals) most responsible for the purchase of the product or service. Then, the questionnaires could be mailed to the specific persons identified.

Phone–Mail–Phone

The above design can be further enhanced when data collection is either required in a hurry, or may include some tasks needing to be administered to the customer. To collect the responses, an appointment can be made for the callback interview in the first phone call, or the customer can be given a toll-free number to call when he completes his portion of the questionnaire. When he calls the telephone number, an interviewer can collect his current answers and then administer the additional portion of the interview.

Phone–Computer/Internet

Customers could be recruited by telephone to dial into an organization's computer bulletin board to complete a computerized survey, receive a diskette in the mail, or visit an organization's Internet site to answer a CS questionnaire. The advantage here would be controlling who would complete the survey. By providing selected customers an identification number, their identity could be verified, and multiple responses could be prevented.

Other Administration Technologies

Automatic Voice Recognition (AVR)

Some groups are already using AVR and other telephone technologies to either conduct a complete "outbound interview" or to simply collect information from customers calling into a toll-free telephone number (an "inbound interview"). Most such technologies are very cost efficient, administer reasonably good interviews (since they are computer driven) and free the professional from having to deal with interviewers, and worrying about bias introduced by them. The unfortunate downside of most of these methods, is the possible message of uncaring they communicate to customers due to their impersonal tone and nature.

The Red Lobster restaurant chain uses an AVR-administered survey (applied to a statistically random sample of its diners, identified as they pay for their meal). The survey is a reasonably pleasant seven-minute interview. Unfortunately, as the author was participating, the equipment froze. There was no easy recovery.

If you are willing to experiment with new technology, try to provide disaster check options in case of malfunctions!

The Internet

As has already been established, of all the new opportunities on the horizon, none promise as much potential as the Internet. An organization's home page would seem to be an ideal place at which to collect satisfaction information. (A major qualification is, of course, the extent to which your customers are computer literate and have access to computers.) Requesting customers to identify themselves and provide some password or other security device, they could be allowed entrance into a special, customer area. Part of this area could be the administration of a computerized satisfaction interview.

Obviously, Internet visitations will be highly self-selecting among your customers. It is probably not a good idea to rely on an Internet-administered survey for your general CSM, but it seems fine for conducting special, transaction specific surveys, where you can invite customers to log into your Web-site. The Internet offers a very convenient, and for the present, a very inexpensive dialoguing medium.

Fax Surveys

The facsimile machine seems to offer promise for the conduct of short, quick turnaround CS studies. A questionnaire distributed by facsimile is almost certain to attract some attention as it is received. And, if return is allowed by fax as well, there is both an implied urgency to the return and a certainty that the surveying company will not only receive the completed questionnaire (for those distrusting the mail services) but also the inviting idea that the response will be logged immediately. The author has had considerable success with fax-back surveys. While this format would seem to be primarily limited to studies within a country, there are international fax mailboxes. (AT&T's 1-800USADirect phone service allows for the receipt of faxes internationally.) These mailboxes can generally be accessed on a worldwide, toll-free basis. Once a reply is faxed to the mailbox, it is either automatically passed along to the company, or it stays in the mailbox until it is retrieved.

Computer Bulletin Boards

With the universality of the Internet, and the ease of logging onto a homepage, computer bulletin boards are probably already an "early relic" of the computer era. However, for those of your customers who are accustomed to using bulletin boards to place orders or to dialogue with other customers, the bulletin board may offer an efficient way to collect some quick responses to some relatively well-defined issues. (It would be difficult to utilize all of the tools for which computerized interviews excel in a bulletin board environment—unless a programmed questionnaire was downloaded to the customer's computer.)

E-Mail Surveys

E-mail is fast becoming the preferred method of intracompany correspondence. Businesspeople appear to dedicate a certain amount of time each day simply reading and responding to their e-mail. (It is likely this attention surpasses their attention to regular, surface mail.) Is e-mail an ideal medium within which to conduct customer surveys? A poll of executives within a major U.S. firm were given three options for how they would like to be surveyed (in an internal customer satisfaction survey). E-mail was their first choice, followed by surface mail, with telephone the least preferred medium.

Yet, an executive in another major firm observed that e-mail surveys would not work in his opinion, since e-mail lent itself to quick answers on matters of scheduling or decision-making. This executive's opinion was that this response-mindset would impede e-mail surveys from collecting well thought-out, reasoned responses; it is too "instantaneous" in its character. The best answer is to survey your customers' attitudes about e-mail surveys and then pilot your use of e-mail, comparing it to other survey field methods in cooperation rate, response time, quality of the information collected, and percentages of no answers.

Interactive TV

If and when interactive TV arrives, it may afford yet an additional medium for interviewing customers, especially private consumers in their homes. The potential advantage of the interactive television interview will be its better distribution (throughout the population) as well as its more simplistic operation. The interactive system utilized will have to be two-way and fully addressable to make it useful for the satisfaction measurement industry.

Table 5.2   Comparison of Field Procedures

	Mail	Telephone	In Person	Computer
Cost	Low	Moderate	High	Low
Turnaround time	Slow	Fast	Moderate	Moderate
Cooperation rate	Low	Moderate	High	High
Geographic coverage	Excellent	Excellent	Difficult	Excellent
Interviewer bias	None	Moderate	Substantial	None
Interviewer supervision	None Required	Excellent	Poor	Excellent
Quality of response	Poor	Better	Best	Better
Permissible questionnaire structure	Simple	Complex	Complex	Complex
Who's in control?	Respondent	Interviewer	Interviewer	Computer
Obtrusiveness	Low	High	High	Low
Ability to cope with interruptions	Easy	Difficult	Difficult	Easy
Length of interview	Short	Medium	Long	Long

A Comparison of Techniques

To summarize the advantages and disadvantages discussed in this section, Table 5.2 identifies the primary characteristics of four specific field methods.

WHOM TO INTERVIEW

Too many times we may rush to the conclusion that we know *exactly who* are the customers for our products and services. Evolving discussions suggest that studying exactly *who* a customer is for one's products or services is well worth the effort. Consider the situation depicted in Figure 5.4. Supplier I produces machinery to be used by its customers (among them, Companies A, B, and C). A, B, and C, in turn, use Supplier I's machinery to produce a product for their customers (Customers 1–9). Supplier I recognizes the importance of customer satisfaction, and decides to conduct a CS measurement process. Who should it interview and what are the important issues?

Supplier I's executives are in daily contact with executives from Companies A, B, and C. Feeling they understand the category fairly well, Supplier I's executives have suggested a list of performance attributes that

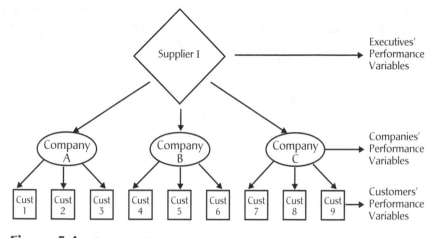

Figure 5.4   Suppliers, Companies and Customers

they believe will measure the satisfactoriness of the machinery they sell in a survey of their immediate customers, Companies A, B, and C. The identified attributes will be, no doubt, a result of Supplier I's:

- internal culture;
- the focus of its management;
- the pressures and requests its sales, marketing, and services people hear from their customers, Companies A, B, and C.

What if prior to conducting its survey, Supplier I pre-interviews some executives of all three companies in an effort to "sidestep" some of their own biases, in creating the list of performance attributes. They are likely to discover a somewhat different list of attributes that define satisfaction. This list will obviously be influenced by the internal culture, the focus of management, and the pressures and requests the sales, marketing and services employees of the three companies hear from their customers, Customers 1–9.

Should Supplier I use the two lists generated and interview only executives in Companies A, B, and C to ascertain customer satisfaction? While this is the way most customer satisfaction surveys are currently constructed and administered, there is probably a better way. The reason is that both the Companies A, B, and C and Supplier I ultimately succeed *only if* the products the three companies produce meet the needs of the ultimate customers in the category, Customers 1–9. If Supplier I and the three Companies go to their end-use customers, they are likely to generate yet another list of performance attributes. This list is probably more valid. Influenced by the Customers' internal cultures, Customers' focus on issues, and the needs the Customers have from the category and from products produced by the category, this list will probably be a more valid indicator of the satisfaction Supplier I actually delivers.

Conventional wisdom often sends an organization like Supplier I only as far along the channel as its immediate customer. Yet Supplier I and Companies A, B, and C only succeed to the extent that the three Companies' customers (the end-use customers) are totally satisfied. And of course, the criteria the end-use customers bring to the evaluation of satisfaction are likely to be much different from the way *either* I or A, B, and C anticipate satisfaction will be defined.

Current Customers

Current customers are a necessary and the most obvious target for a satisfaction survey. Just make sure at what level(s) in your distribution channel you want to interview. With today's complex distribution channels, there are generally multiple intermediaries. Each of these intermediates can be considered "customers." Selecting several of them may be appropriate.

It is becoming increasingly common to hear of the "channel as customer." This perspective recognizes that these important intermediaries have special needs, which if attended to, help them function more effectively. Suppliers who acknowledge and service these special needs will probably encourage stronger loyalty than suppliers who either fail to recognize the needs, or decide not to satisfy them.

As intermediaries are acknowledged, it is also important not to omit the end-use customer, as was established at the beginning of this section.

Competitors' Customers

Competitors' customers are an important customer segment to pay attention to. Many of them will have made a conscious choice against your organization (by selecting a competitor). Others will actually be past (and lost) customers of yours. In either case, their perceptions of quality and their special needs and requirements are an important informational component for future strategic planning.

Customers of competitors become an important customer group to benchmark against. Gaining access to them is, however, far more difficult than interviewing your own customers. There are several ways you might find them:

- randomly placed interviews hoping to encounter (by natural incidence) as many of them as possible. (This works best for competitors who have substantial shares of your market. It is an inefficient way to interview customers of new or niche companies.);
- industry lists or association databases which may identify individuals or companies by source of supply;
- your own customers who may also buy from your competitors;
- a wide screening of your market using some other survey device or organization to identify customers of each competitor in your category.

Past (Lost) Customers

Lost customers are, generally, a competitor's current customer. However, they may be interviewed for their satisfaction with the previous organization as a way of identifying major problems the organization has. They will be accessible only if their names have been maintained on the customerbase, or if their names have been transferred over to a special, lost customer database. They will sometimes be slightly less cooperative than current customers, especially if the previous organization's identity is made known. Still, they are generally impressed that the company cares enough to contact and to ask them questions.

Internal Customers

Juran's perspective, NOAC ("next operation as customer") reminds us that we *all* have customers; the term "customer" is not an outside phenomenon, it applies *inside* organizations as well. With this in mind, many organizations have initiated internal customer satisfaction surveys. Even though there is little need to impress internal customers, the study should still be conducted in a formal, and a professional manner. Often having the internal study conducted by an external vendor will add further credibility to the effort. An outside vendor may also promise individual employees their identities will be protected boosting cooperation rates and the quality of information gathered.

Executives and Employees

Surveys of your own executives and employees may also be undertaken. The simplest way to do this is to ask your employees to complete your *customer* satisfaction survey. You can ask them to complete the survey in the same way they think your organization's actual customers will answer. You will then compare your executive's scores (as a total group) to the survey results from your actual customers. Generally such a comparison will open some eyes. Without putting anyone on the spot, you will be able to reinforce the importance of auditing customers' needs by showing how your employees misunderstand them.

Stakeholders

Those who have a vested interest in an organization's success are stakeholders. Be they members of your corporate board, stockholders or citizens in the communities where factories or other facilities are located, all have interest in the operation and success of your organization. Their requirements and satisfactions with your performance ought to be assessed on a regular basis. Increasingly stakeholders are being included as a standard subsample for CSM surveys.

WHEN TO INTERVIEW

Interviewing at Regular Intervals

There are those individuals and those industries that prefer conducting their customer satisfaction measurement at certain times of the year. There are two general explanations for such periodic interviewing; convention and events. Convention (or habit) finds some organizations routinely surveying satisfaction on an annual basis (the arguably least preferable method), or perhaps quarterly. In other cases, major events (the spring industry conference; the end of the tourist season, and so on) can trigger administration of a satisfaction survey. Professionals who support periodic assessment will most likely do so out of a belief that their needs for information are relevant to these events and therefore the collection should be as contiguous to the event or time period as possible. Sampling only certain periods is, of course, subject to substantial bias from "coincidental contaminating events." For example, if the periodic measurement of satisfaction happens to coincide with a 'low fares" promotion, how representative will the measured satisfaction be of non-promotional fare performance?

Interval sampling also gives the salesforce or other service providers a calendar with which to allocate special treatment to customers. If the periods for customer satisfaction measurement are widely known, these periods can signal the time for enhanced servicing of customers. There are even those organizations who will ask their sales or marketing organizations to distribute questionnaires to their customers during these time periods. Such conduct is wide open to all sorts of bias. This practice should be discouraged and avoided!

There is an efficiency to mass distribution of surveys at only certain times of the year. The required infrastructure is much less. Such a periodic distribution can be more easily subcontracted. A research vendor, an interviewing firm or even a mailing house can be retained to handle the "wave" of interviews. It is essentially a "batch job." Another firm (or the organization itself) can be prepared to accept returned interviews, and tabulate the data. No ongoing organization or department really needs to be created.

Unfortunately periodic measurement of satisfaction also frequently leads to a corporate periodic focus on satisfaction. Without an ongoing program, without regular reports on satisfaction trends, satisfaction becomes something that is only considered once a year—during the appointed interval!

Interviewing Continuously

Although a more considerable undertaking, more and more organizations are moving to a continuous audit of satisfaction with their products, services, and servicing. Continuous measurement recognizes the ongoing importance of customer satisfaction. In addition, continuous measurements will not be nearly so influenced by momentary events (the so-called "contaminating events"). With a continuous measurement the satisfaction professional has a better chance of developing commitment to quality from the organization's entire workforce, since the measurement is always contemporary and will occur frequently. Workers throughout the organization are quite likely to have their customers' satisfaction reported to them on a monthly or quarterly basis. Continuous interviewing keeps an organization focussed on customer satisfaction not allowing it to be forgotten between survey waves.

Interviewing After "Moments of Truth"

Moments of truth is the concept given the service quality world by Jan Carlzon (past president of Scandinavian Airline System) in his insightful book of the same name (Carlzon 1985). Carlzon was able to identify service encounters in which SAS employees either lived up to or failed to meet customers' expectations. These moments Carlzon labeled "moments of truth." The term has come to be attached to any interaction in which the effectiveness of an organization is tested. Hence, claim settlement in the insurance business is a moment of truth. Likewise, buying an airline ticket on the telephone, or calling a customer service center for assistance are similarly moments of truth. Every moment of truth can be followed up with a satisfaction survey to determine how well the organization performed in this important interaction.

Organizations, sometimes even industries, have begun to examine their businesses from the customer's viewpoint, looking for the "moments of truth" that surround their dealings with customers. If you identify the important (this is not to suggest that some moments of truth are unimportant, but obviously some will be *more* important) moments of truth, surrounding your business, you will have a "road map" of critical performance events. And, as these moments of truth are engaged in by each of your customers, you have an ideal time to assess your customers' satisfaction with how well your organization conducted this important interaction.

Many organizations routinely sample customer satisfaction after each of several specific moments of truth. In the insurance business these moments might be: sign up (purchase); the billing process; making a claim; renewing one's coverage. One could sample on a quarterly (or more frequent basis) the satisfaction of a sample of those customers who experienced each moment of truth during the quarter.

FOLLOW-UP AFTER RESPONSE

It has earlier been suggested that much of the decline in response rates to satisfaction surveys can be attributed to the fact that in few satisfaction surveys are customers' responses ever actually acknowledged. Because more and more organizations are understanding the value of input from customers, the number of surveys each of us (as customers) are asked to complete is increasing exponentially. Unfortunately, many of the organizations just beginning to assess their customers' satisfaction may initiate their process without a proper understanding of the responsibility of satisfaction measurement. A result, it is feared, is a rapid decrease in CSM response rates. A sad result is a rising disenchantment with the satisfaction measurement process among customers on a global basis. Their responses are not acknowledged, their input appears ignored, and they fail to see improvement in the goods and services they have critiqued!

In order for satisfaction measurement to continue to flourish, we must establish a certain "code of conduct" for our survey work. An essential component of such a code would be the promise of an acknowledgement to each customer who completed or returned a questionnaire. The following "code" is respectfully submitted:

> I promise to respect the attitudes, suggestions, and requests of my customers. I understand my surveys impose on their valuable time. In consideration for this, I promise to attend to the information they provide. I acknowledge my responsibility to confirm to each participating customer I received their survey response, and if possible, I will strive to report to each and every customer what I have learned from their singular and joint response, and how I will act to improve my products, services and servicing in accordance with their views.
>
> I understand that without exercising this sort of responsibility, I am disregarding my organization's most precious asset—the commitment and loyalty of its customers.

Happily, such a code is in the best interests of *both* parties. The participating customer feels appreciated and is given hope that his comments will be used to improve the quality of the products or services delivered to him. And, the sponsoring organization is given the opportunity to subsequently survey its customers bonding them ever more closely to the brand.

The proverbial downside to this happy situation is the cost of the follow-up and acknowledgment process; a cost many marketing researchers and some corporate financial officers will dismiss as too high. The expense of follow-up is really an investment in the continued satisfaction of the customerbase that will pay handsome rewards in the future. Study after study confirms that properly attended customers will more than pay back any communication effort in their elongated lifetime and their expanded lifetime purchases (Vavra 1996, TARP various).

Here is a listing of the essential postsurvey activity the marketer ought to commit to.

1. Acknowledge each customer's survey participation. This can be as impersonal as a mass mailed, non-customized postcard acknowledging receipt of the mail questionnaire or telephone interview. But, ideally (and almost necessarily so for high-value customers) the acknowledgment should be:

- personalized
- and ought to express some sensitivity to the general tone of the customer's comments

2. Ideally customers should be told how their suggestions for improvement will be acted upon, or they should be thanked for their words of praise.

3. A thank you for the customer's participation. This can be in the form of some "value-added" product or activity. For example, a general report of generic findings from your survey; or a piece of your organization's affinity merchandise (a ball cap, letter opener, etc.) or some other special token of appreciation. Less desirable—especially for industrial customers—is a monetary incentive.

RECORDING YOUR SATISFACTION DATA

Just as important as properly collecting your satisfaction data is anticipating how you wish it stored in computer format. Do not ever turn this task over to a service bureau ("tab-house") without thoroughly considering the consequences of how your data should be entered into computer records. Failure to consider the storage format could render some future analyses completely impossible.

Customer Identification

Data in survey research projects is normally identified by an arbitrary questionnaire or respondent number, and by a record number (in cases where one respondent's data fills more than one record). So conventional survey research questionnaires typically have an ID number either preassigned (before distribution) or affixed as they are returned. The ID number identifies the record, but not usually the respondent who provided the information.

In contrast, it is the author's belief that *all responses* to a customer satisfaction survey ought to be attributed back to the *specific customers* who offered the responses and beliefs. Therefore, it is impractical to affix a customer-designator after the questionnaire is distributed or returned; the customer-designating information must be on the questionnaire to begin with. (The customized questionnaires discussed in Chapter 4, of course, answer this need directly by producing a specific questionnaire for each customer.) In automotive research the customer designator will invariably be the VIN (vehicle identification number) by which all automobile sales and claims are tracked.[1] In financial services the designator could be the customer's account number, allowing the responses to be linked to an addressable customer.

Sometimes customers will obliterate the designator—or perhaps fail to respond because it prevents their anonymity. Because some customers will desire to remain anonymous, it is a good idea to overtly acknowledge the questionnaire (or interview) is trackable to them, informing your customers you would like to identify their individual answers, but offering them the opportunity to respond anonymously, if they so desire by removing the designator.

Organizing the Data Layout

Data from questionnaires is stored in record format in computer files. Conventions, originating with the now-antiquated IBM punch card, set record length at 80 characters (or "columns"). With today's technology there are few such restrictions on record length. Some researchers still adhere to an 80-column format, which is also the typical number of columns easily displayed on a computer "character-oriented" CRT screen. However, with today's WYSIWYG Windows® programs, one can more easily "size" the screen's viewing area to display much longer record formats than the previous character-based programs allowed. And, most computer text editors allow horizontal scrolling across fields of many more than 80 characters. However, it is still a good idea to limit the total characters in a string to 60–100. If you have 230 characters of response codes, you could accommodate that in four lines of 60–70 characters. (You will need to allow some characters at the start of each record for customer ID and record number, followed by the data.)

Precoding the Questionnaire

Though it is becoming increasingly uncommon, if your satisfaction data will be manually data entered, it is advantageous to provide some entry information on the questionnaire to assist your data entry personnel. Usually such entry codes are placed next to where the interviewer or cus-

----

[1] Though the VIN is such a "natural" designator, automobile manufacturers encounter problems with how to identify owners of multiple models of their cars. Some have adopted unique customer numbers, in addition to the VIN!

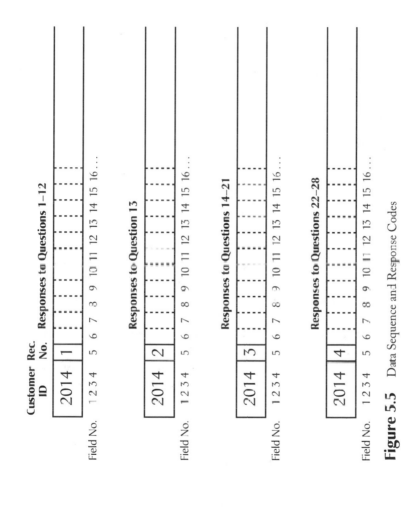

Figure 5.5 Data Sequence and Response Codes

219

5. How likely would you be to recommend our brand to your friends and business associates? Would you say you would (READ ALL RESPONSES, CHECK ONE)

17-1 [ ] Definitely recommend to a friend
  2 [ ] Probably recommend to a friend
  3 [ ] Might or might not recommend
  4 [ ] Probably not recommend to a friend
  5 [ ] Definitely not recommend to a friend

5. How likely would you be to recommend our brand to your friends and business associates? Would you say you would (READ ALL RESPONSES, CHECK ONE)

[ ] Definitely recommend to a friend   17-1
[ ] Probably recommend to a friend   -2
[ ] Might or might not recommend   -3
[ ] Probably not recommend to a friend   -4
[ ] Definitely not recommend to a friend   -5

Figure 5.6   Questionnaire Styles

tomer will enter answers. The codes will be of two types: *data sequence codes or character fields* and *response codes.* Data sequence codes tell your data entry people the exact record location for each response. Should they double up or skip an answer, they will quickly notice that and be able to identify the missing datum. Response codes are either symbolic or numeric representations you assign to each response option. They allow you to numerically process and quantify your customers' responses. In Figure 5.6, the "17" refers to the seventeenth character field (the location on the data record) , while the "1", "2", "3", and so on are response codes identifying the answer your customer has given.

By convention, data entry codes and response codes are placed along the right-hand side of the questionnaire form—though they can also be placed throughout the questionnaire. In self-administered questionnaires, it is a good idea to use a smaller typeface for these codes or to photographically "screen" the codes so they appear lighter in shade. This will help keep respondents from getting confused by the numbers.

Post-Coding Responses

For all closed-ended questions in your survey you will generally have assigned response codes to all anticipated answers. However, in some prelists, (for example, "What hotel chains have you stayed at during the last 12 months?") you may have prelisted a reasonable number of different chains, yet you probably have not listed all of the chains your customers have frequented. Anticipating this, you may have instituted an answer response of "Other—Please Specify." You will not know which hotel chains are volunteered until you receive your completed interviews back from the field. Once you have these responses, codes will need to be assigned to each additional hotel chain mentioned.

Of course when we ask an open-ended question, we anticipate having to code customers' responses. If your survey is a continuing survey, you will already have a preexisting code structure. But when initiating a survey, or asking an open-ended question for the first time you will need to establish codes for each response you wish to tally.

To establish a coding structure, you will generally select a sample of 25–50 returned questionnaires. Read through all of the answers to a particular open-ended question. Try to get an idea about the types of responses being given. Then, on a second reading, write down each new discrete thought to which you wish to assign a code. Each idea you want to tally will need its own, discrete code. A code should meet two criteria: the code should be unambiguous, it must represent one and only one idea or response; and each code should establish an analytically meaningful category, pertinent to your satisfaction survey.

Generally codes are numeric (though they could be alphabetic). Some satisfaction professionals will somewhat arbitrarily assign numeric, two-digit codes, say ranging from 1–99. The author prefers to assign codes in a systematic way. For example, codes under fifty might represent favorable responses, those over fifty, unfavorable. Within each run of fifty numbers, the decile value could represent the same performance attribute. Carrying this procedure further, the hundreds location (of the code) could represent a particular aspect of the product or service. In Figure 5.7, for example, the three-digit code "253" would represent a negative comment about cost related to the hardware. Structured codes like these make "nets" in cross-tabulations somewhat easier to produce. For example, a net of all "100" coded responses versus "200" coded responses tells us quickly the frequency of *product/equipment* comments compared to *hardware* comments. Similarly, a net on all 01–49 codes versus 50–99 gives us an immediate feeling for the quantity of *favorable* versus *unfavorable* comments.

As codes are established for each open-ended question, they must be retained in a codebook that will stay with your study from year to year. Each time you field your study, you will use the same codes where possible. But you will also need to keep an open mind to allow instituting new codes for new issues and points of view.

1___   Product/Equipment

Positive Comments

11 Quality
12 Reliability
13 Cost
14 Documentation
15 Size/Dimensions
16 Delivery/Issuance

Negative Comments

51 Quality
52 Reliability
53 Cost
54 Documentation
55 Size/Dimensions
56 Delivery/Issuance

2___   Hardware

Positive Comments

11 Quality
12 Reliability
13 Cost
14 Documentation
15 Size/Dimensions
16 Delivery/Issuance

Negative Comments

51 Quality
52 Reliability
53 Cost
54 Documentation
55 Size/Dimensions
56 Delivery/Issuance

3___   Software

Positive Comments

11 Quality
12 Reliability
13 Cost
14 Documentation
15 Size/Dimensions
16 Delivery/Issuance
22 Accuracy of Coding

Negative Comments

51 Quality
52 Reliability
53 Cost
54 Documentation
55 Size/Dimensions
56 Delivery/Issuance
62 Accuracy of Coding

Figure 5.7   A Hierarchical Coding Structure

Coding Conventions

Certain practices are advisable in establishing the numeric codes you will use for entering your data:

1. Use only one character per data location in your records. If a question prompts multiple responses, establish contiguous data locations for the maximum number of responses you anticipate receiving. (You will use the same response codes, either precoded, closed-ended codes or the open-end codes you have established, placing whichever ones apply in the response locations.)
2. For the most universal analysis of your data, use only numeric codes—not all computer programs will accept alphanumeric codes (that is, "a, b, c, d"). Avoid using any special characters (that is "@", "*").

3. Adopt a uniform, question-to-question convention for representing response conditions like: "no answer," "don't know," and "does not apply." Because computer programs vary in how they read blanks, it is best to enter a character in each data location of your customer records. If you mean zero, enter a "0". If the question is not answered, enter a code for "no response." Similarly establish discrete codes for "does not apply." As these codes will probably be numeric (that is, no answer = "9", does not apply = "8"), you will have to exclude these values from any numeric computations. Most computer analysis programs allow you to specify certain numeric values as codes for such missing values which are then excluded from the numerical analysis.

4. Make sure to make the data location fields wide enough to support all acceptable codes. For example if you have established three-digit codes for a particular question, make sure to provide three data locations in your record format for each response anticipated.

METHODS OF DATA ENTRY

Perhaps the greatest opportunity for error (of the many sources that exist) is in data entry. Yet, invariably little time is ever spent establishing quality procedures for this stage.

Data entry is usually accomplished by one of three different methods: (1) Data entry personnel transferring responses from a submitted form; (2) interviewers directly entering responses into a CATI interviewing system; and (3) respondents entering data directly into the system through computerized interviewing procedures (whether by diskette, by modem, through the Internet, and so on).

Each of these data entry methods offers opportunity for error and will require its own separate error-reduction (data verification) procedures.

By Data Entry Personnel

When data entry personnel will enter questionnaire-responses into computer files, instructions must be established to guide their data entry. Obviously, the most important instruction is the file-location for each question's response. This will be communicated by one of several different methods. Sometimes the data location will actually be printed on the questionnaire next to the response area (as shown in figure 5.6). Other times, the location will be shown by a physical template or a diagram visually showing data entry personnel where to enter each response. Increasingly, computerized data entry templates are being used (see Figure 5.8).

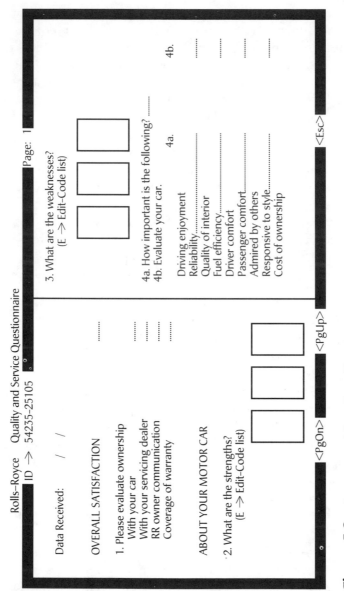

Figure 5.8 Computerized Data-Entry Template

When data locations are printed on the questionnaire, they typically refer to record locations. That is, "6–7" means a two-digit field beginning in the sixth location of the record and occupying space to the seventh location. (In the days of IBM punch cards and the 80-column data they supported, data locations frequently ran between 10 and 80 with the first 10 positions reserved for respondent number and the card serial number.) Today, with data records virtually limitless in length, these numbers can run consecutively from one to the final datum number.

Using data locations preprinted on the questionnaire requires that a data analysis plan be fully thought-out prior to printing the questionnaire. Though this adds a step to the questionnaire construction phase and may delay fielding, it is generally worth the extra effort. It usually results in reasonably well-organized data.

If a physical template or diagram is used, it will provide data entry personnel with locations in which to start major blocks of data. This template can be as simple as a "master questionnaire" with the data entry locations handwritten in. Sometimes the template is produced on transparency film. This type of template can simply be placed over each questionnaire to be entered and the data entry locations are identified next to the written answers.

Computer spreadsheet programs, database programs or even word processors can also be used to support data entry. Each of these programs may have proprietary or special input templates to assist you in controlling the way your data is entered.

Data entry by computer template is a reasonably new concept. The computer is programmed to assist the data entry person in his entering the information. The most useful templates actually emulate the layout and appearance of the questionnaire. In this way it is very easy for the data entry person to confirm that he is entering the right datum in the correct location. Additionally, computerized templates can be programmed with editing logic:

- checking that only legal codes are entered for each question;
- checking the consistency of information sequentially related to previous information;
- checking that contingent answers are filled in only for those customers who qualify to be asked the branch-pattern of questions.

A fringe benefit of template-guided entry is how it can obsolesce printed, precodes on questionnaires.

If you happen to omit space for a response as may happen, especially considering composite variables that are necessarily added only after some data has been initially analyzed there will be considerable difficulty finding room for these overlooked variable(s). Either the data will have to be shifted (manually or by the computer) to make room for the overlooked variable or the analytical team will have to suffer the inconvenience of having the overlooked variable placed at the very end of the data record.

Verification for Manually Entered Data

Data manually keyed-in should be subjected to some degree of verification. The most common verification procedure, dating back to a verifying IBM keypunch station, requires the same data to be entered twice in succession. In other words the data entry person enters the same data from a questionnaire two times. The second entry is used to "verify" the original entry. If a datum entered in the second round fails to correspond with the same datum from the first entry, the operator is alerted and he must reexamine his work to see whether the first entry was incorrect, or the second. Because the same data entry person reenters the same data, this method does not correct for entry person biases. That is, if the data entry person misinterprets a respondent's handwriting on the first entry round, it is likely she will similarly misread it on the second round.

The only way to minimize errors from entry person biases is to have different operators enter the same data in different rounds. This is, however, logistically difficult. It requires that the computer file containing first round responses be maintained with the physical questionnaires containing the first round data, so that another operator may reenter the data.

By Interviewers Directly Entering

Today a substantial number of telephone-administered satisfaction studies will be fielded with interviewers using CATI (computer assisted telephone interviewing). Such interviewers will read questions and their accompanying answer-grids directly from a computer's CRT screen to respondents. Because skip-patterns are automatically administered, CATI data probably is overall cleaner than data collected by other means. As respondents answer each question, the interviewer keys the answer directly into the computer. Some CATI systems will check for question-to-question logic, editing responses as the interview is conducted.

There is, however, virtually no way of guaranteeing that an interviewer who is told a rating of "5" actually enters a "5," since the data entered is the only physical record of the interview.

Two possible procedures exist to verify the accuracy of data directly entered by interviewers. One can recontact respondents and hope they remember what they told the original interviewer, though this procedure is admittedly subject to wide discrepancies. Alternatively, one could audio tape-record the original telephone interview, and rekey the customer's answers from the tape recording. Then, both records can be compared. In the event of a discrepancy, the tape may need to be reconsulted.

By Respondents Entering Their Own Responses

Self-administered surveys are becoming more and more common, especially those administered through electronic ports (computer terminals, the Internet, computer bulletin boards, and so on). Wherever a customer enters data directly into a database, there is no certain way to check for accuracy of data entry. A good rule of thumb is to echo a customer's responses to your most critical questions, asking the customer to verify her answer or to be certain that is the rating she wished to assign. Critical questions could also be asked twice, at different points in the interview, though this will be noticed by customers and may cause them more concern than it will aid the accuracy of your survey.

REFERENCES

Carlzon, Jan. *Moments of Truth*. Cambridge, MA: Ballinger Books, 1987.

Marketing Metrics. *InterviewDisk: Interviewing Software for the Personal Computer*. Paramus, N.J., (201) 599-0790.

Sawtooth Technologies. *Ci3 Software*. Evanston, IL, (847) 866-0870.

Technical Assistance Research Programs, Alexandria, VA.

Vavra, Terry G. "Score Your Customers by Satisfaction, Loyalty, Profitability and Potential" presented at National Center for Database Marketing, 18th National Conference, Orlando, FL Dec. 13, 1996.

APPENDIX TO CHAPTER 5:
SELECTING A RESEARCH PARTNER

Many satisfaction professionals will decide to form a partnership with a research vendor or satisfaction consultant to assist them in conducting and analyzing their survey. This Appendix briefly describes some of the questions one might ask in selecting that important partner. It also describes how to locate firms who are in business to assist in the conduct of satisfaction surveys.

Assessing the Capabilities of a Potential Vendor-Partner

As you review the capabilities of various research companies to become your potential partner in conducting your satisfaction process, you will want to assess:

- what it will be like to work with and depend on the vendor on a continuing basis;
- how trustworthy the vendor appears in its ability to represent your organization with your customers;
- how creative the vendor will be in helping you improve your process, rather than relying on an established process;
- and, how well the vendor will be working with tight deadlines, and requests for additional analyses, throughout the contract period.

A possible list of questions to ask potential suppliers is presented in Table 5A.1. A good test, however, is to ask potential vendors to demonstrate how they approach a problem you are facing. If you have an existing program, you could present a challenge or element of your process that you are currently trying to improve, and ask for suggestions. If you are creating a satisfaction program, perhaps you could ask potential vendors for their suggestions about how to deal with a particularly difficult aspect of your program-to-be. It is generally not fair to ask potential vendors to design an entire satisfaction measurement process for your situation. First, the vendor's creativity is one of the things you will be paying for, so they should not be expected to give this away free. Second, there will be too much about your organization, your category and your customers that potential vendors do not know, making the intelligent design of a program impossible prior to complete briefing.

Table 5A.1   Questionnaire for Potential Vendor-Partners

1. Does the consultant have experience with CSM programs of similar size, scope, and geography as your program?
2. Does the consultant have experience with CSMs for your offering: product or service, for your industry, for your status: profit, not-for-profit?
3. Is the consultant a full-service supplier, that is do they have qualitative and quantitative research capabilities, do they offer primary and secondary data gathering?
4. Can the consultant establish and maintain an "intelligent database" that will be necessary to drive the interactive correspondence with your customers, which is necessary to elicit high cooperation rates?
5. Can the consultant interact with your customerbase in a manner and style consistent with the way you interact with your customers?
6. Does the consultant have advanced analytic skills (multivariate statistics), exceeding simple, descriptive statistical capabilities?

Locating Companies Skilled in Conducting Satisfaction Surveys

There are several established directories of research and marketing services companies that are available to assist you in identifying potential vendors/consultants. Most of these directories list companies by their category or analytical expertise, to assist you in finding a compatible vendor. However, try not to be too parochial in your review of vendors. You may or may not want a company that specializes in your industry. Sometimes a vendor new to an industry can bring a fresh perspective to the formulation or administration of a program. You should probably value creativity, intelligence, and responsiveness over knowledge of your industry.

Table 5A.2 lists several available directories. Many of these are also now available on the Internet.

Table 5A.2 Vendor Directories

Directory	Sponsor/ Address	Telephone Number
AMA International Member & Marketing Services Guide	American Marketing Association 250 S. Wacker Drive, Suite 200 Chicago, IL 60606-5819 website: www.ama.org/msg	800-AMA-1150
IMRI Guide & International Directory	The Market Research Society 15 Northburgh Street London, EC1VOAH United Kingdom website: www.imriresearch.com	44-171-4904911
International Directory of Marketing Research Companies and Services Green Book	American Marketing Association/ New York Chapter 60 E. 41st Street, Suite 1765 New York, NY 10165 website: www.greenbook.org	212-687-3280
Marketing Tools Directory	Marketing Tools 127 West State Street, PO Box 68 Ithaca, NY 14851 website: www.demographics.com/directory	800-828-1133
MRA Research Services Directory Blue Book	Marketing Research Association 2189 Silas Deane Highway, Suite 5 Rocky Hill, CT 06067	203-257-4008
The Researcher's Source Book	Quirk Enterprises, Inc. 8030 Cedar Avenue, Suite 229 Bloomington, MN 55425 website: www.quirks.com/research/search.html	612-854-5101

CHAPTER 6

The Basic Tools of CSM Analysis

OVERVIEW

The effectiveness of any customer satisfaction program depends not only on how well the questionnaire is designed, and how professionally the data is collected, but also on how skillfully the collected data is analyzed. The first and most important step is to establish an analytical plan to guide the analysis. Otherwise, the sheer volume of the data, the multitudinous analytical opportunities available, and the relationships discovered in the analysis may seduce and confuse the analyst. The data plan should strategically focus on the primary objectives of the satisfaction survey; with this perspective understood, the plan will be more meaningful.

Satisfaction practitioners have developed a rich array of analytical procedures that are performed on satisfaction data. The origin of many of these procedures (like the *quadrant chart*) has been the work of individual analysts searching for appropriate tools to use in a specific study. Other procedures have been developed by one or more of the many research companies specializing in customer satisfaction research. Because these firms strive to distinguish themselves from their competition, they are motivated to develop new and better analytical tools. Only a small faction of the academic community has been active in developing methods of analysis, for all of the reasons described in Chapter 1.

We will discuss four data analysis categories:

1. basic (univariate and bivariate) numerical analysis;
2. advanced numerical (multivariate) analysis;
3. analysis of verbatim (open-end) question responses;
4. and graphical analysis.

We will cover all but the last topic in this chapter. Graphical analysis will be covered in Chapter 7.

Data should be analyzed on at least two levels, at the basic level (univariate or bivariate) for management reports and at a more advanced level (multivariate) for a better understanding of the data. The univariate or bivariate analyses (often conducted as "cross tabs") are the least complex methods of analysis. They display survey results in a simple, more direct perspective, which is ideal for reporting results. Multivariate analyses are concerned with uncovering complex relationships within the data or with determining causality between one criterion variable (often overall satisfaction) and a battery of other variables (performance attributes). These techniques are more difficult to explain in a management report and are often best used as the satisfaction professional's "toolkit" helping him or her better comprehend the structure of the data.

Establishing an Analytical Plan

Attempting to make some sense of the volume of data you will typically collect in a satisfaction survey is a little like being trapped in quicksand. The more you thrash about, the deeper embedded (and more hopeless) you become. So it is wise to have a well thought-out plan for your analysis before you begin. This is especially true since your management will, no doubt, be waiting for your results and will be intolerant of any forays into the data pursuing additional insights and hypotheses, which prolong the submission of your report. This is not to say that you cannot continue to "mine" your results after submitting your report, it simply recognizes the time demands on a satisfaction survey and on you as a satisfaction professional.

As with any social science research project, it is best—if not mandatory—to state your hypotheses up front, prior to conducting your survey. Your analysis should be guided by these postulated linkages. You should be mindful of not pursuing opportunistic relationships that your analysis discovers. Leave these as issues to be further investigated after you have investigated your primary, ingoing hypotheses.

A standard analytical process would be the following:

1. edit and code all open-ended questions;
2. run a frequency program (marginals) on all variables, especially your continuous ones to determine how you can categorize them for convenient display in crosstabs;
3. explore the relationships existing within multiple-scale questions, through multivariate analyses;
   - use factor analysis to better understand how your customers have used multiple-scale questions. This means that if three scales (of a battery of 10) all load on the same factor, they are representing the same quality. To separately report all three of them might accord the issue more prominence than it merits;
   - use multiple regression to derive the relative importance of each of your performance variables. You should use these importance weights whenever you list the variables, listing them in order of their importance.
4. identify the "banner" (with its banner-points) you wish to use for your crosstabs, and run the cross-tabulations;
5. list your performance variables by importance and calculate the change from your previous satisfaction measurement;
6. test each change to determine if it is a significant or non-significant change—refrain from reporting directional changes;
7. attempt to model overall satisfaction to the other variables in your survey, this will imply which variables are most closely related to overall satisfaction. These variables should be the ones on which you focus improvement efforts.

You may wish to customize your analytical plan to specific needs or interests you, your quality improvement team, or your management have. The important thing is to discipline your analysis with a plan. To do less, is to risk running through your data becoming "seduced" by perhaps trivial, inconsequential discoveries. Your goal is to stay focused on your primary informational objectives.

Basic CSM Analysis

Univariate Analysis

Univariate analyses as the name implies include a range of statistical tools for examining satisfaction variables *one at a time*. While this elementary analysis cannot explore correlations between measures like product quality and overall satisfaction, univariate analysis is nevertheless a valuable starting point for exploring the nature of satisfaction results returned by your survey. Often times satisfaction professionals are in such a hurry to explore the relationships among groups of variables they may skip this important basic step. Such an omission is unfortunate and unwise. Many a talented statistician will patiently sit constructing a frequency distribution or a scattergram of a variable or two to "get to know" his data before progressing to the more exotic forms of statistical analysis.

Marginal Analysis–Frequency Distributions

A good initial step is to run a frequency distribution program on each variable in the survey. This basic, descriptive analysis will provide you a frequency count or histogram of the responses to every question for which you request it. The programs that typically produce the frequency distributions also usually calculate a number of critical measures of your data like the mode, the median and the mean of the data, as well as measures of the skewness of the data and the variation or variance of the data. For now we will focus on the frequency array or histogram produced by such programs. Figure 6.1 shows the histogram displaying answers to an open-ended survey question, "*How many times in the last month did you call customer service?*" (See Figure 6.1).

Frequency distribution programs are an absolutely necessary prerequisite to specifying your crosstabs. They are sometimes referred to as "marginal runs" since the "count categories" of the frequency distribution are what would appear on a crosstab table as the question responses—on the left-hand *margin* of the crosstab table.

Continuous variables need to be categorized for more useful display as row "stubs" and possibly as banner points in your cross-tab analysis. The frequency counts of responses to the customer service question are shown in Table 6.1. The displayed frequencies and cumulative percentages help the satisfaction professional properly divide the open-end responses into more meaningful categories. (If the open-end responses were not simplified by categories, there would be as many rows

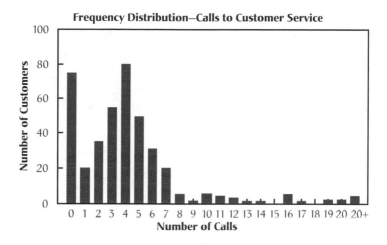

Figure 6.1   A Histogram or Frequency Distribution of Responses

(responses) in the cross-tab table as different frequencies were volunteered—there could be more stubs than would be useful.) Notice how in Table 6.2, the analyst has indicated collapsing the distribution into a small number of more useful categories (i.e. 0, 1–2, 3–4, 5–6, 7–10, 11–15, 16–20, >20). These categories will become the stubs for the question as it will be displayed in subsequent cross-tab tables.

Measures of Central Tendency

Consider a survey of 1000 customers in which each customer is asked 35 questions. That tallies to 35,000 data points! Because raw survey data becomes overwhelming so quickly, we have become accustomed to using certain measures like the *average* as a form of *data reduction*. The average is only one *measure of central tendency*, which helps us to depict the meaning conveyed in large volumes of data without pondering all of it.

Measures of central tendency are convenient numbers that attempt to describe entire sets of data in a single score. There are three commonly used measures of central tendency: the *mode*, the *median*, and the *mean*.

The Mode.   The mode is rarely used in customer satisfaction work. It represents the score that occurs with the greatest frequency. If your data are unimodal and symmetrically distributed, the score with the greatest frequency will probably be somewhere near the middle of the distribution. In such a case, the mode turns out to be a quick way to estimate the

Table 6.1 A Marginal Analysis Showing the Frequency Distribution of Responses to a Continuous Variable Question

Number of Calls to Customer Service

Response	Frequency	Percent
0	75	0.19
1	20	0.05
2	35	0.09
3	55	0.14
4	80	0.20
5	50	0.13
6	31	0.08
7	20	0.05
8	5	0.01
9	1	0.00
10	5	0.01
11	4	0.01
12	3	0.01
13	1	0.00
14	1	0.00
15	0	0.00
16	5	0.01
17	1	0.00
18	0	0.00
19	2	0.01
20	2	0.01
20+	4	0.01
Total	400	1.00

mean of the data. Of course data can have more than one mode. Such distributions are called bimodal (or trimodal). Consider a customerbase in which many are highly pleased, but an equal number of customers are likewise displeased. This data would have two modes, and then neither mode would be a useful summarization of the ratings of the customers.

The Median. While the median itself is not often used in satisfaction research, it will be useful to consider it and a special condition of its calculation. The median defines central tendency in a somewhat more definitive method than the mode. Where the mode was influenced by the shape of the data, the median more closely portrays the *distribution* of the data. The

Table 6.2   A Frequency Table to "Collapse" a Continuous Variable

Number of Calls to Customer Service

Interval	Response	Frequency	Percent	Cume Percent	Included Percentage
0	0	75	0.19	0.19	19%
1–2	1	20	0.05	0.24	14%
	2	35	0.09	0.33	
3–4	3	55	0.14	0.46	34%
	4	80	0.20	0.52	
5–6	5	50	0.13	0.65	21%
	6	31	0.08	0.73	
	7	20	0.05	0.78	
7–10	8	5	0.01	0.79	7%
	9	1	0.00	0.79	
	10	5	0.01	0.8	
	11	4	0.01	0.81	
	12	3	0.01	0.82	
11–15	13	1	0.00	0.82	2%
	14	1	0.00	0.83	
	15	0	0.00	0.83	
	16	5	0.01	0.84	
	17	1	0.00	0.84	
16–20	18	0	0.00	0.84	3%
	19	2	0.01	0.85	
	20	2	0.01	0.85	
20+	20+	4	0.01	0.86	1%
	Total	400	1.00	1.00	

median is defined as the score from within an *ordered distribution* of scores above which and below which an equal number of customers lie. The median is calculated by ordering all customers according to their ratings (scores) from lowest to highest. The median score demarcates that score below which 50 percent of your customerbase expressed a lower rating and above which 50 percent of your customerbase expressed a higher rating. It is the rating *exactly in the middle* of an ordered listing of all ratings!

In an ordered array of five satisfaction scores: 68, 71, 72, 75, and 76, it is easy to identify 72 as the median score. But in arrays of 500 or 1000

Table 6.3   Calculation of the Median

	Frequency	Cume Freq	Percent	Cume Percent	
48–50	2	2	0.67%	0.67%	
51–53	4	6	1.33%	2.00%	
54–56	11	17	3.67%	5.67%	
57–59	9	26	3.00%	8.67%	
60–62	17	43	5.67%	14.33%	
63–65	21	64	7.00%	21.33%	
66–68	16	80	5.33%	26.67%	
69–71	25	105	8.33%	35.00%	
72–74	31	136	10.33%	45.33%	
75–77	37	173	12.33%	57.67%	median = 76.14
78–80	36	209	12.00%	69.67%	
81–83	28	237	9.33%	79.00%	
84–86	23	260	7.67%	86.67%	80th centile = 84.39
87–89	17	277	5.67%	92.33%	
90–92	15	292	5.00%	97.33%	
93–95	5	297	1.67%	99.00%	
96–98	3	300	1.00%	100.00%	
99–100	0	300	0.00%	100.00%	
Total	300				

The Median is calculated as:

$$median = L + \left(\frac{.5N - cf_b}{f_w} \right) n_i$$

$$median = 75 + \left(\frac{(.5 \times 300) - 136}{37} \right) \times 3 = 76.14$$

The Eightieth Centile is calculated as:

$$eightieth \; centile = L + \left(\frac{pN - cf_b}{f_w} \right) n_i$$

$$eightieth \; centile = 84 + \left(\frac{.8 \times 300) - 237}{23} \right) \times 3 = 84.39$$

customers, with numerous customers awarding similar ratings, the median is not so easily identified. The first step in calculating the median, is to array ratings in an ordered frequency distribution. Cumulative frequency and percentage should be calculated. In Table 6.3, 300 satisfaction scores have been collapsed into intervals. Each individual rating, and each interval represents a continuum of scores. That is, the overall satisfaction score of 78 should be looked upon as representing a range of scores from 77.50 to 78.49; the interval 78–80 similarly represents a range of scores from 77.50 to 80.49. In this arrayed data, the satisfaction score dividing the sample's ratings exactly in half, is obviously somewhere in the interval, 75–77. (The prior interval, 72–74 accounts for 45.33 percent of the sample, and the interval 75–77 increases the cumulative percentage to 57.67 percent.)

To calculate the median, one could use any of the standard computer statistical packages, or the frequency distribution in Table 6.3 and the following procedure. Identify the interval immediately proceeding a cumulative percentage of 50 percent or more. The median is then calculated using equation 6.1:

$$mdn = L + \left(\frac{.5N - cf_b}{f_w} \right) n_i \tag{6.1}$$

Where: L = lower limit of interval containing the median

N = sample size

cf_b = cumulative frequency *below* the interval containing the median

n_i = size of the interval containing the median

f_w = frequency within the interval containing the median

The above formula is actually a special case of the calculation of *centile rank*. The median happens to occupy the 50th centile rank. Centile ranks are useful for identifying segments of the customerbase according to evaluations of a product or service. For example, if one wished to calculate the score below which 80 percent of one's customers scored, (to identify the 20 percent of the customers who expressed the highest satisfaction ratings) one would use an expanded version of equation 6.1, as:

$$Cp = L + \left(\frac{pN - cf_b}{f_w} \right) n_i \tag{6.2}$$

Where Cp = centile at the pth level (i.e. 10%, 20%, 30%, etc.)

L = lower limit of the interval containing Cp

p = percentage of f below Cp, expressed as a percentage (for the 80th centile, p = .8)

N = sample size

cf_b = cumulative frequency *below* the interval containing the Cp

f_w = frequency within the interval containing Cp

n_i = size of the interval containing Cp

Referring to the data in Table 6.3, and using the above formula, the eightieth centile can be computed and will be seen to fall at an overall satisfaction of 84.39.

The Mean. We are all familiar with the mean or arithmetic average. We utilize this measure perhaps without totally understanding its true virtues. Of all of the measures of central tendency, the mean is the most useful in satisfaction research. It can be considered as the *one* number in a distribution that best describes all of the numbers in that distribution. The mean, as a measure of central tendency, is analogous to the way the center of gravity best represents the distribution of weight throughout an object. Just as knowing the center of gravity allows one to "balance" an object, a mean offers a point of equilibrium in a distribution of scores.

The mean is calculated by a formula we all understand:

$$\bar{x} = \frac{\sum x}{N} \qquad\qquad (6.3)$$

Relationships Among the Measures of Central Tendency.

In a unimodal, perfectly symmetric distribution, the mean, median, and mode will all be aligned and equal. (To the extent these measures differ, as calculated from our own survey data, we can surmise our data departs from a truly "normal distribution.") That is because as a distribution departs from that of a relatively normal, bell-shaped curve, these measures will all begin to differ. The mode is most seriously affected by changes in the distribution—becoming essentially useless as any distribution approaches a rectangular or multi-modal distribution.

Two relatively ordinary deviations from a normal distribution are *skewness* and *truncation*. A *skewed* distribution has extreme scores on one end. Overall satisfaction will generally be skewed with a majority of higher ratings. The concentration is not what makes the distribution skewed, however. It is those few extremely low satisfaction ratings hanging out on the low end. Such a distribution would be considered skewed to the low end of your ratings.

Truncation occurs when a response scale imposes a limit below which the measured phenomenon actually peaks. For example, if you measured satisfaction on a scale from "Poor to Good," you would no doubt have a truncated distribution with an extremely high frequency of "Good" ratings. The high frequency at "Good" would be the result of there being no response position for those of your customers who considered your

Table 6.4   Two Distributions of Satisfaction Scores

	Company Stores	Franchise Stores
Mean	87	87
Median	88	88
Mode	87	87

service to be "Excellent." Their ratings would be clumped with those of your customers who thought your service was only "Good."

Measures of Dispersion or Variability

Despite their value, the measures of central tendency cannot tell us *everything* we need to know from samples of our customers. Imagine two sub-samples of customers, those served by "company stores" and those served by "franchise stores." Consider the measures of central tendency for the distributions of these two samples to be as shown in Table 6.4. Because the mean is less than the median, it may be concluded the distributions are skewed to their low ends by the occurrence of several extremely low satisfaction ratings. Also since the modes equal the means, we know the distributions have their highest frequencies towards the middle of their ranges; the distributions are unimodal. Skewness to the left-hand side of the ratings continuum (towards lower scores) is referred to as "negative skewness." Most customer satisfaction data is probably negatively skewed with a majority of higher scores, and a few outlier, low scores.

Concluding that these two customer groups had reasonably equal satisfaction ratings would be premature. In fact, there is more to ratings distributions than the measures of central tendency. Table 6.5 shows the raw data underlying these two distributions and representative histograms are shown in Figure 6.2

While this additional information does not contradict our earlier observations, it is also apparent there is more to be learned about these distributions. In the franchise store sample there are customers with lower satisfaction scores than among the company store customers. The major difference between the two groups of customers is that customers of the company store have more similar scores among themselves than do the customers of the franchise stores. Scores of the franchised stores' customers are less similar among themselves showing a wider distribution. There is a need for yet another statistic—a number that describes the

Table 6.5 The Underlying Satisfaction Scores

	Company Stores	Franchise Stores
70–71	0	3
72–73	0	2
74–75	0	1
76–77	0	2
78–79	2	3
80–81	7	4
82–83	7	7
84–85	14	11
86–87	19	16
88–89	20	16
90–91	14	12
92–93	10	10
94–95	6	8
96–97	1	3
98–100	0	2
	100	100
Mean =	**87**	**87**
Median =	**88**	**88**
Mode =	**87**	**87**

dispersion or "spread" of scores about our measures of central tendency. Such a measure can be called a *measure of dispersion or variability*.

The Range.   To make the reporting of the two groups of customers more useful, a simple measure of dispersion like the *range* of scores in each group could have been used. (See Table 6.6.) With the range added to the measures of central tendency, the two distributions can be more easily understood to be different, with the franchise stores' group having customers with lower scores and therefore a wider range of scores. In contrast, the narrower, more compact range of the company store customers suggests they are more homogeneous regarding measured satisfaction.

   Unfortunately, while extremely easy to calculate, the range is limited in its use as a measure of variability since it is based on just two numbers, the highest and lowest scores within a group. If either score is unusually divergent from the group's mean, the resulting range will imply a larger degree of dispersion than actually exists. The range fails to account for the *density* of scores (that is how they are distributed) *between* the two end points.

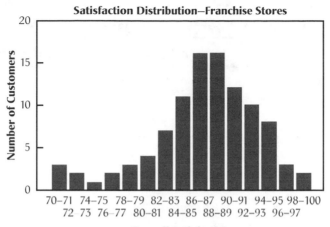

Figure 6.2   Samples from the Same Population

The Standard Deviation.   A measure of variability that does an excellent job of representing the distribution density of your satisfaction scores is the *standard deviation* commonly denoted by the lowercase sigma, σ. This measure is based on the departure (deviation) of the collected scores about their own mean. While it is easy to calculate, one must start with raw data, it cannot be easily extrapolated from the other aggregate measures. The formula for the calculation of the standard deviation is given in equation 6.4.

Table 6.6   Dispersion of the Satisfaction Scores

	Company Stores	Franchise Stores
Mean	87	87
Median	88	88
Mode	87	87
Range	18 (78–96)	28 (70–98)

$$\sigma = \sqrt{\frac{\Sigma\left(x_i - \bar{x}\right)^2}{n}} \qquad (6.4)$$

Where x_i = each individual score
x = the mean
n = the sample size

Equation 6.5 offers a computationally easier way to calculate the standard deviation from a small set of scores. This method is frequently used with manual spreadsheets and electronic calculators.

$$\sigma = \sqrt{\frac{\Sigma x_i^2}{n} - \bar{x}^2} \qquad (6.5)$$

Where x_i^2 = each score squared
$\bar{x}^2$ = the mean squared
n = the sample size

(While many formulae will show the denominator as $n - 1$, in actuality with large samples [n > 100], the impact of this adjustment is more trouble than it is worth.)

For data sets larger than 100 customers, you will probably wish to group your data into categories. Table 6.7 shows the satisfaction scores of 263 customers, categorized or grouped into class intervals of three points each (for example 48, 49, and 50). There are 17 intervals (Col. A) necessary to represent the customers' distribution of scores, from 48–50 with 2 customers (Col. B) to 96–98 with 3 customers (Col. B).

The worksheet in Table 6.7 can be used to compute both the mean and the standard deviation from such grouped data. The procedure is relatively easy:

Table 6.7 Calculating the Standard Deviation from Grouped Data

Category Width = 3

COL A	COL B	COL C	COL D	COL E	COL F	COL G	COL H
			Deviation of	Col D/			
		Interval's	Midpoint	Interval			
	Frequency	Mid-point	from X'	Width	Col B*Col E		
c_i	f	m	x'	x'/c_i	$f(x'/c_i)$	$(x'/c_i)^2$	$f(x'/c_i)^2$
48–50	2	49	−27	−9	−18	81	162
51–53	4	52	−24	−8	−32	64	256
54–56	11	55	−21	−7	−77	49	539
57–59	9	58	18	6	54	36	324
60–62	17	61	−15	−5	−85	25	425
63–65	21	64	−12	−4	−84	16	336
66–68	16	67	−9	−3	−48	9	144
69–71	25	70	−6	−2	−50	4	100
72–74	31	73	−3	−1	−31	1	31
75–77 $x' = 76$	37	76	0	0	0	0	0
78–80	36	79	3	1	36	1	36
81–83	28	82	6	2	56	4	112
84–86	23	85	9	3	69	9	207
87–89	17	88	12	4	68	16	272
90–92	15	91	15	5	75	25	375
93–95	5	94	18	6	30	36	180
96–98	3	97	21	7	21	49	147
99–101	0	100	24	8	0	64	0
Totals	**263**				**−124**		**3646**

The mean is calculated as:

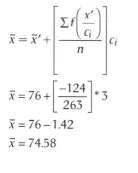

$$\bar{x} = \bar{x}' + \left[\frac{\sum f\left(\frac{x'}{c_i}\right)}{n}\right] c_i$$

$$\bar{x} = 76 + \left[\frac{-124}{263}\right] * 3$$

$$\bar{x} = 76 - 1.42$$

$$\bar{x} = 74.58$$

The standard deviation is calculated as:

$$\sum x^2 = \left[\sum f\left(\frac{x'}{c_i}\right)^2 - \frac{\left[\sum f\left(\frac{x_{i'}}{c_i}\right)\right]^2}{n}\right] c_i^2$$

$$\sum x^2 = \left[3646 - \frac{[124]^2}{263}\right] * 3^2$$

$$\sum x^2 = [3646 - 58.46] * 9$$

$$\sigma = \sqrt{\frac{\sum x^2}{n}}$$

$$\sigma = \sqrt{\frac{3587.54 * 9}{263}}$$

$$\sigma = 11.08$$

- identify the midpoint of each interval (Col. C)
- select the interval that *probably* contains the mean (any column will work, but the closer the interval selected is to the actual mean, the less adjustment will later be required)
- adopt the midpoint of the interval chosen as the *approximate mean, x'*
- calculate the deviation of each interval's midpoint from the approximate mean (Col. D)
- divide these deviations by the interval width c_i (Col. E)
- weight this deviation (Col. E) by the frequency within the interval f (Col. F)
- square both columns E and F

The mean is now calculated by equation 6.6:

$$\bar{x} = \bar{x}' + \left[\frac{\sum f \dfrac{x'}{c_i}}{n} \right] c_i \qquad (6.6)$$

Where x = sample mean to be calculated
  x' = approximate mean used for convenience
  $f(x'/c_i)$ = (Col. F) the deviation divided by the interval width weighted by the interval frequency
  c_i = the interval width
  n = sample size

The standard deviation may be calculated by equation 6.7:

$$\sum x^2 = \left[\sum f \left(\frac{x'}{c_i} \right)^2 - \frac{\left[\sum f \left(\dfrac{x_i}{c_i} \right)^2 \right]}{n} \right] c_i^2 \qquad (6.7)$$

$$\text{and } \sigma = \sqrt{\frac{\sum x^2}{n}} \qquad (6.7a)$$

Where $f(x'/c_i)^2 = $ (Col. H) the deviation divided by the interval width
 weighted by the interval frequency and squared

$f(x'/c_i) = $ (Col. F) the deviation divided by the interval width
 weighted by the interval frequency

$c_i = $ the interval width

$n = $ sample size

The standard deviation is the most useful parameter in economically describing the dispersion of our entire data set. For example, assuming our customers' satisfaction data are normally distributed, we can use the standard deviation to predict the proportion of scores that will fall within a specified range of the population mean. In fact, from knowledge of the normal distribution, we can say that 68 percent of all sample means will fall within plus or minus one standard deviation of the mean. Ninety-five percent of all sample means will fall within plus or minus two standard deviations of the mean. And virtually all (99.5 percent) sample means will fall within plus or minus three standard deviations of the mean.

Of course, most spreadsheet computer programs and database programs generally have functions to calculate the standard deviation (for example @STD in Lotus 123) so you will seldom have to calculate it manually. It is also a normal option for any frequency or descriptive statistics program in the widely available statistical packages (for example SAS, SPSS, SYSTAT and BMDP).

Other Measures of Extremeness

In satisfaction work we are striving not only to increase our customers' average satisfaction, but to totally satisfy as many customers as possible. A useful measure, then, is the use of *top box* and *bottom box* scoring, which has been borrowed from the marketing research community. Top and bottom box scoring is a measure of extremeness—how many customers have assigned the best or worst score to one's product, service, or servicing.

If we were measuring an overall satisfaction question on a 5-point scale, the top box would be represented by all of those customers assigning the highest score (say a "5"—*extremely satisfied*). As the number of scale positions is increased, the "top box" is generally expanded to the "top boxes"—perhaps not only those customers assigning a score of "10"—extremely satisfied, but also (because of the wider distribution of the ten points) those assigning scores of "9" and *possibly* scores of "8" as well.

The bottom box or bottom boxes can also be tallied to detect the number of customers totally dissatisfied, representing the other end of the score distribution. You might wish to try indexing the bottom box to the top box as an easy way of visualizing at least the tails of your satisfaction score distribution.

Top box scoring gives the organization a useful way of tracking the extent to which it is providing *complete satisfaction.* It is compatible in this way with the orientation of TQM objectives and gives the satisfaction professional a convenient way of reporting and tracking satisfaction.

Interpreting Response Levels

It is often said that one satisfaction survey (the first one administered) is not enough, it is only a beginning (or benchmark) from which to track the future movement of satisfaction. While monitoring change (hopefully improvement) of your satisfaction variables is important, it is not the only value of a satisfaction survey. You can, in fact, derive considerable knowledge from the first wave of a satisfaction survey. You will not only have an estimate of the general satisfaction of your customerbase, you will be able to explore the possible differences in satisfaction among different segments of your customerbase. If you have included competitors' customers, you will also know how you compare in satisfaction against those competitors. An additional insight will be what you will be able to learn about the importance of various performance attributes as they relate to your customers' overall satisfaction. Information on importance will help you better respond to improving overall satisfaction.

Ultimately, as you administer the second and successive waves of your satisfaction survey, you will be interested in the presence and significance of change. Your ability to interpret the *magnitude of change* will be critical to your response and action plans. Not all the changes in scores you observe (from one survey period to another, or between groups of customers) will be significant. Because of sampling error, sample statistics (the mean, and so on), which *appear* to have increased or decreased may not confirm actual change. The different levels may simply be the result of your having drawn samples of customers from different areas in your customer-population distribution. While the population's rating has remained invariant, your two samples appear to represent changed scores. Figure 6.3 shows a possible situation. While the distribution (and hence mean) of the population remains unchanged (shown by the single population distribution curve) you may have drawn samples from somewhat different areas of the population distribution. Your sample means, Period

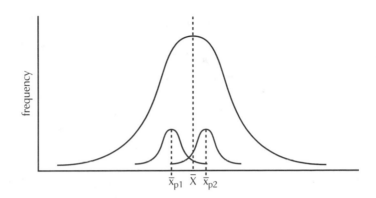

Figure 6.3   The Relationship Between the Population Mean and Means from Two Samples: Period 1 and Period 2

1 to Period 2 appear to show change. Yet they are both drawn from the same, stable population distribution; overall, ratings of satisfaction in your customerbase have not changed!

One can classify score changes as either statistically *significant* or *insignificant,* as either *substantial* or *inconsequential.* It is imperative that you understand the basics of significance testing so that you will be able to properly interpret change.

Key Concepts

The average of any performance measure or the average overall satisfaction as determined from a sample of your customers is a *statistical concept.* It is your best *estimate* of how all of your customers feel from your collected data, yet it is subject to the whims of sampling. Before you can report the level of satisfaction of your total customerbase to your management, you must be able to extrapolate from the sample score (or *statistic*) to a predicted value for your total customerbase. This process relies on your understanding of *sample size, tolerance of error* (confidence interval), and an accepted *level of significance.*

Sample Size.   The size of your sample has a substantial impact on the confidence you can place on a rating from your sample. As the size of your sample increases, approaching the size of your entire customerbase, you can more confidently generalize your sample's rating to your entire customerbase, because they are both essentially the same. Smaller samples determine the confidence with which you can generalize findings from the sample to your entire customerbase. Sample size is related to a concept called the *standard error of the estimated mean.*

Tolerance for Error. The tolerance for error (the confidence interval you select) has to do with the range of variation you are willing to accept around any sample statistic. In the case of a single measure, say an overall satisfaction rating of 7.0, there will be a confidence interval about that score. The confidence interval is a range about the satisfaction rating that will include a proportion of all means that might be sampled. The size of the confidence interval is related to the level of confidence you expect and to your sample size. To determine the range of satisfaction scores in your customerbase that could support a sample statistic of 7.0, you need to declare a level of statistical significance, coupled with your sample size.

Level of Statistical Significance. The final step is to decide on the level of significance you will accept for your analysis. The conventional practice is to use a 95 percent level of significance. This means that only 5 out of 100 times will you expect to be wrong in your determination of your customerbase's real score. While conventionality ordains this level, there is nothing magical about it. You could just as easily decide to use a 90 percent level of confidence. Recognize that if you stay with convention, you will probably not be asked any questions, but buck conventionality, by adopting a different level of significance and you will no doubt be asked to explain your decision.

Standard Error of the Estimated Mean. The standard error is actually the *standard deviation* of an implied sampling distribution of all sample means from a given population. The standard error describes the "degree of error" (departure from the population mean) to be expected in any one sample mean.

$$\text{standard error of the mean} = \sigma_{\bar{x}} = \frac{\sigma}{\sqrt{n}} \qquad (6.8)$$

Where σ = population standard deviation
$\quad n$ = sample size
$\qquad$ (When the population standard deviation is unknown, the sample standard deviation may be used as an estimate.)

When you are dealing with proportions rather than means, there is an equivalent standard error of the proportion, as specified in equation 6.9.

$$\sigma_p = \sqrt{\frac{p(1-p)}{n}} \qquad (6.9)$$

Where p = proportion measured
   n = sample size

Because the population of all possible means from any given distribution of scores is normally distributed, the standard error can be used to construct the confidence interval about any observed mean, or to test the mean for differences from other means. The same rule prevails, 68 percent of all sample means will lie within ± 1 standard error; 95 percent within ± 2 standard errors, and 99.5 percent within ± 3 standard errors.

The Normal Distribution.   Before proceeding to use these tools, we should quickly review the implications of what is known about normally distributed data.

Impact on Estimates

These parameters interact as demonstrated in Tables 6.8 A&B. Table 6.8A shows the impact on mean ratings, while Table 6.8B shows how these same parameters can impact proportional answers. First, dealing with mean ratings, compare the results in Examples 1 and 2. Between 1 and 2 the only difference is the size of the samples. When the size is increased from 500 customers to 1,000 customers, the confidence interval *decreases* from .4 to .28. By interviewing more customers you have narrowed the range within which the true mean satisfaction of your customerbase lies. However, an extra 500 interviews have narrowed your understanding of exactly where the population mean lies by only .12 units. Conversely, if you reduce your sample size from 1,000 customers to only 500 (for budgetary reasons), you will face the consequence of having to report to your management a wider confidence interval within which your customers' *actual* average satisfaction lies, and therefore a less definitive answer.

Comparing Example 1 with Example 3 shows the impact of settling on a less demanding level of statistical confidence. With the same sample size, but a reduced level of statistical precision (90 percent, instead of the traditional 95 percent), your confidence interval again decreases, from .2 to .165. (The lower precision level of 90 percent means you are willing to be wrong as many as 10 times out of 100 hence the confidence interval narrows.)

Table 6.8A   Sampling Ramifications for Mean Data

	Example 1	Example 2	Example 3	Example 4
Sample Mean (Overall Sat)	7.5	7.5	7.5	7.5
Standard Deviation	2.23	2.23	2.23	2.23
Sample Size	500	1,000	500	500
Confidence Level	95%	95%	90%	85%
Standard Error of the Mean	0.1	0.07	0.1	0.1
Calculated Tolerance	±.2	±.14	±1.65	±1.44
Confidence Interval	7.3–7.7	7.36–7.64	5.85–9.15	6.06–8.94

Table 6.8B   Sampling Ramifications for Proportional Data

	Example 1	Example 2	Example 3	Example 4
Sample Proportion (Sat "Top Box")	65%	65%	65%	65%
Sample Size	500	1,000	500	500
Confidence Level	95%	95%	90%	85%
Standard Error of the Mean	2.4%	1.7%	2.4%	2.4%
Calculated Tolerance	±4.8%	±3.4%	±3.96%	±3.46%
Confidence Interval	60.2%–69.8%	61.6%–68.4%	61%–69%	61.5%–68.5%

Table 6.8B similarly demonstrates the impact of sample size and confidence level on the confidence interval for proportion scores.

Interpreting a Single Metric Score

Let us assume, as we postulated earlier, that your survey determines an overall satisfaction rating of 7.5. What rating or range of ratings should you report to your management? To answer this question, you will need to use your discovered sample standard error and a level of statistical significance that you choose.

Using your measured rating, the standard error, and the level of confidence you have selected you can now identify the confidence interval within which your customerbase's mean overall satisfaction rating actually occurs, using *equation 6.8* and remembering from the normal distribution that 68 percent, 95 percent or 99.5 percent of all means will fall within the interval of 1, 2, or 3 standard errors of the mean.

In the example, with 7.5 as the mean satisfaction rating from 500 customers, and a standard error of the mean of .1, at the 95 percent statistical confidence level, the interval within which your customers' actual satisfaction would fall is limited by 7.3 to 7.7. In your report to management, your best answer is that your current satisfaction is within the range 7.3 to 7.7, or that satisfaction is 7.5 ± .2.

Interpreting a Single, Nominal Score

What if your report of satisfaction is a proportion, that is, that 65 percent of your sampled customers rated overall satisfaction with a "top box"— "extremely satisfied" rating? What can you say about the true proportion of your total customerbase? The same procedure applies, except you would now use *equation 6.9*, the standard error of proportions.

With 65 percent of your 500 sampled customers saying "extremely satisfied," and a standard error of the proportion of 2.4, you would report to management that at the 95 percent confidence level, actually 60.2 percent to 69.8 percent of your customers are "extremely satisfied." Or, you could report "extreme satisfaction" at 65 percent ± 4.8 percent.

Difference Between Two Subsamples

As you review the distribution of responses to your survey's questions, the next question you will find yourself asking (or being asked), is "How different is any particular variable (overall satisfaction, for example) across different groups of customers, say long-tenure customers versus new, or short-tenure customers?" Because this question deals with only one variable, it is a univariate analysis, but we need to expand our view of univariate procedures.

Two different tests of significance can be used depending on the metric of the variable. For continuous variables on which it is appropriate to calculate a mean, the t-test is the appropriate significance test to use to determine the similarity or difference between two subsamples. For nominal or proportional data, a test of the significance of the difference between proportions is required.

Differences on a Nominal Variable.   Let us say your data shows that 81 percent of your company store customers give an "extremely or somewhat satisfied" overall satisfaction rating, but only 76 percent of your franchise stores' customers rate overall satisfaction equally high. Are

these proportions significantly different, or are they differences we might expect to result from variations in sampling? The test for the significance of the difference of proportions will help us answer this question.

The formula for testing the difference of proportions requires that the difference be converted into a "z-score":

$$Z = \frac{p_1 - p_2}{\sqrt{\dfrac{p(1-p)}{n_1} + \dfrac{p(1-p)}{n_2}}} \tag{6.10}$$

Where $p = \dfrac{n_1 p_1 + n_2 p_2}{n_1 + n_2}$

p_1 = proportion in sample 1
n_1 = size of sample 1
p_2 = proportion in sample 2
n_2 = proportion in sample 2

The resulting Z score is interpreted according to one's need for statistical significance. If differences are desired at the 95 percent level of confidence, then a Z-score of 2 (actually 1.96) is required. A table of the normal deviate provides probability estimates for other Z scores. (See Appendix Table A.1.)

Profile Differences on Nominal Variables. When your data is only nominal, you will still have plenty of needs to compare customer groups. Consider a more complex comparison that might be made between two customer groups as illustrated in Table 6.9. Here, two groups of customers (long-tenure and short-tenure) are profiled according to their use of seven different descriptions of service in an adjective check list. You have read (or presented) a list of adjectives to your customers and asked them whether or not each adjective describes your product or service. The resulting score is simply a "yes" or "no" vote for each adjective; yes it "describes your service," no it does not. Your need is to determine the extent to which the differences are explainable by sampling variation alone, or do they indicate a very real difference in perceptions of the quality of service your customers have received?

The appropriate test to use is a chi-square test to determine how similar (or dissimilar) these two subsamples are with regard to their adjective assignments. The chi-square test compares the frequency distribution on a particular question across one, two, or multiple subsamples.

The formula for a chi-square analysis is:

$$\chi^2 = \Sigma \frac{(o-e)^2}{e} \tag{6.11}$$

Where o = the observed frequency in each cell
$\quad e$ = the calculated, expected frequency in each cell

To calculate a chi-square analysis by hand, you will have to calculate the expected values to compare with your observed values. The expected values are created by using the marginal frequencies to estimate the "expected" or "chance" frequency in each cell. In the outlined cell (Table 6.9B), representing "sometimes hurried" and "short-tenure customer," the expected value of 42.7 is calculated as follows. Take the row percentage (64/375) and multiply the column total of short-tenure customers, 250. The resulting frequency, 42.7 is your expected frequency for this cell. To calculate other expected frequencies, simply take the appropriate row percentage (row total/table total) times the column total. By summing Equation 6.11 over all pairs of observed and expected frequencies, a chi-square value is calculated.

You can look up the significance of the calculated value in any chi-square table (see Appendix Table A.2). Chi-square tables are organized by "degrees of freedom." You will need to calculate how many degrees of freedom your data has prior to entering the chi-square significance table. In general, the degrees of freedom are calculated by taking the number of rows in your table minus 1 times the number of columns also minus 1. In our example (Table 6.9) the degrees of freedom are (7-1)* (2-1) or 6.

If you use a computer program to calculate the chi-square value (most spreadsheet programs will do this for you), chances are the computer program will interpret the significance of the resulting chi-square value. The significance value will always be a decimal between 0 and 1. which will tell you the odds that the two distributions are different. That is, a value of .05 suggests that only 5 times out of 100 could the two distributions have come from the same population, and the distributions may be considered statistically different at the 95 percent level of confidence.

Differences on a Metric Variable.   When your response scale is interval or ratio-scaled you have the right to calculate means as a measure of response. Let us say you have asked your customers to rate their overall satisfaction on a 1 to 10 scale. Now you wish to determine if the satisfaction ratings from the two subsamples (long and short tenured customers)

Table 6.9A   A Chi-Square Analysis

Which of the following words describe our customer service?
(Number agreeing with an adjective check list.)

Adjective	Long-Tenure Customer	Short-Tenure Customer
Courteous	56	140
Helpful	48	103
Often rude	9	20
Sometimes hurried	26	38
Pleasant	61	167
Very businesslike	77	112
Hard to reach	6	5
	$n_L = 125$	$n_S = 250$

Table 6.9B   Calculating the "Expected Frequencies" for a Chi-Square Analysis

Adjective	Long-Tenure Customer	Short-Tenure Customer	
Courteous	56/65.3	140/130.6	196
Helpful	48/50.3	103/100.7	151
Often rude	9/9.7	20/19.3	29
Sometimes hurried	26/21.3	38/42.7	64
Pleasant	61/76.0	167/152.0	228
Very businesslike	77/63.0	112/126.0	189
Hard to reach	6/3.7	5/7.3	11
	$n_L =$	$n_S =$	$n_L + n_S = 375$

The X^2 value is calculated as:

$$\chi^2 = \Sigma \frac{(o-e)^2}{e}$$

$$\chi^2 = \frac{(56-65.3)^2}{65.3} + \frac{(48-50.3)^2}{50.3} + \ldots + \frac{(112-126)^2}{126} + \frac{(5-7.3)^2}{7.3} = 15.10$$

χ^2 = 15.10 with $(7 - 1*2 - 1) = 6$ degrees of freedom (exceeds the critical chi-square value of 12.59, therefore the customer groups may be considered statistically different)

are statistically different. In this case you would use a *t-test*. Most statistical software will offer a routine to calculate *t*-tests. It may be in a "stand alone" t-test program, or you may be referred to a one-way analysis of variance (ANOVA). To submit your data, you will need a "marker" in your customers' data file to indicate which group each of your customers belongs to. Some software is very choosy about what characters you can use as group markers, so make sure you consult your software manual before taking the time to mark your customers' records. The formula for calculating a *t*-score is:

$$t = \frac{\bar{x}_1 - \bar{x}_2}{\sqrt{\left[\frac{\sum x_1^2 - \frac{(\sum x_1)^2}{n_1} + \sum x_2^2 - \frac{(\sum x_2)^2}{n_2}}{(n_1 + n_2) - 2}\right] * \left[\frac{1}{n_1} + \frac{1}{n_2}\right]}} \qquad (6.12)$$

Where
- x_1, x_2 = means of first and second groups
- n_1, n_2 = sample sizes of first and second groups
- $\sum x_1^2, \sum x_2^2$ = sums of the squared score values from the first and second groups
- $(\sum x_1)^2, (\sum x_2)^2$ = squares of the sum of scores from first and second groups
- degrees of freedom = $(n_1 + n_2) - 2$

Table 6.10 shows how a *t*-test is calculated. To determine the significance associated with a particular *t*-value, you will need to consult a table of *t* values, entering the table at the row representing the degrees of freedom in your analysis, and the column representing the level of statistical significance you wish to use. If your calculated *t*-score exceeds the value in the table, your groups are significantly different (see Appendix A3). While it may be useful to know how to calculate a *t*-score, most software programs will not only calculate *t*-scores but will also interpret the statistical significance of the *t*-score for you.

The *t*-test is intended for pairs of means. When you have several subsamples whose differences you wish to test, a more effective test is the one-way ANOVA (analysis of variance). The ANOVA will first test if any two groups are significantly different. This will be indicated by a significant *F*-test. Then you may compare each pair of means using a *t*-test procedure to determine which pairs of means contributed to the significant *F*.[1]

----
[1] The reader is referred to basic descriptive statistics books for this procedure. You may refer to Bruning, James L., and B. L. Kintz. *Computational Handbook of Statistics*, for the procedure.

Table 6.10   A t-Test

West Coast Customers			East Coast Customers		
Customer ID	Sat. Scores		Customer ID	Sat. Scores	
	(x_1)	$(x_1)^2$		(x_2)	$(x_2)^2$
1	8	64	101	7	49
2	9	81	102	6	36
3	7	49	103	7	49
4	8	64	104	8	64
5	8	64	105	6	36
6	10	100	106	7	49
7	10	100	107	7	49
8	8	64	108	9	81
9	9	81	109	7	49
10	8	64	110	6	36
Σ	85	731	Σ	70	498
x_1	8.5		x_2	7	

The t-Test is calculated as:

$$t = \frac{8.5 - 7.0}{\sqrt{\left[\dfrac{731 - \dfrac{(85)^2}{10} + 498 - \dfrac{(70)^2}{10}}{(10+10) - 2}\right] * \left[\dfrac{1}{10} + \dfrac{1}{10}\right]}}$$

= 8.18 with (10 + 10) – 2 degrees of freedom (exceeds the critical t-value of 2.101 @ 95%, therefore the means may be considered significantly different)

Bivariate CSM Analysis

Cross Tabulations

The Method.   Cross tabulations (crosstabs) are one of the basic tools of conventional marketing research. While they may at first glance appear perplexing (see Figure 6.4) they are really a rather common sense cross categorization of data. They are not an analytical technique per se, they merely display the data. Some users would claim they can "test" various hypotheses based on the way they structure and produce crosstabs, looking for larger cell frequencies where issues or questions intersect. In this sense, crosstabs provide a very useful "overview" of one's survey results.

The portion of a crosstab shown in Table 6.11 simply depicts responses to one question, overall satisfaction, by responses to the classificatory

Medical Equipment Study

Question 2A: Please tell us how satisfied you are with the SERVICEABILITY OF PRODUCTS

	TOTAL	Marketing Region				Recommend Purchase		Influence		Experience	
		North	Central	South	West	Definitely	Prob/Undec	Very	Some-None	<10 yrs	10+ yrs
	(A)	(B)	(C)	(D)	(E)	(F)	(G)	(H)	(I)	(J)	(K)
TOTAL	100 / 100.0 / 100.0	35 / 100.0 / 35.0	20 / 100.0 / 20.0	15 / 100.0 / 15.0	30 / 100.0 / 30.0	53 / 100.0 / 53.0	47 / 100.0 / 47.0	39 / 100.0 / 39.0	61 / 100.0 / 61.0	17 / 100.0 / 17.0	82 / 100.0 / 82.0
TOTAL ANSWERING	100 / 100.0 / 100.0	35 / 100.0 / 35.0	20 / 100.0 / 20.0	15 / 100.0 / 15.0	30 / 100.0 / 30.0	53 / 100.0 / 53.0	47 / 100.0 / 47.0	39 / 100.0 / 39.0	61 / 100.0 / 61.0	17 / 100.0 / 17.0	82 / 100.0 / 82.0
1-Extremely Satisfied	25 / 25.0 / 100.0	9 / 25.7 / 36.0	6 / 30.0 / 24.0	2 / 13.3 / 8.0	8 / 26.7 / 32.0	22 / 41.5 / 88.0	3 / 6.4 / 12.0	8 / 20.5 / 32.0	17 / 27.9 / 68.0	4 / 23.5 / 16.0	21 / 25.6 / 84.0
2-Somewhat Satisfied	52 / 52.0 / 100.0	21 / 60.0 / 40.4	8 / 40.0 / 15.4	8 / 53.3 / 15.4	15 / 50.0 / 28.8	23 / 43.4 / 44.2	29 / 61.7 / 55.8	20 / 51.3 / 38.5	32 / 52.5 / 61.5	10 / 58.8 / 19.2	42 / 51.2 / 80.8
3-Neither Satisfied nor Dissatisfied	18 / 18.0 / 100.0	4 / 11.4 / 22.2	5 / 25.0 / 27.8	4 / 26.7 / 22.2	5 / 16.7 / 27.8	5 / 9.4 / 27.8	13 / 27.7 / 72.2	11 / 28.2 / 61.1	7 / 11.5 / 38.9	3 / 17.6 / 16.7	14 / 17.1 / 77.8
4-Somewhat Dissatisfied	4 / 4.0 / 100.0	1 / 2.9 / 25.0	1 / 5.0 / 25.0	1 / 6.7 / 25.0	1 / 3.3 / 25.0	2 / 3.8 / 50.0	2 / 4.3 / 50.0	-	4 / 6.6 / 100.0	-	4 / 4.9 / 100.0
5-Extremely Dissatisfied	1 / 1.0 / 100.0	-	-	-	1 / 3.3 / 100.0	1 / 1.9 / 100.0	-	-	1 / 1.6 / 100.0	-	1 / 1.2 / 100.0
Cannot Rate	-	-	-	-	-	-	-	-	-	-	-
MEAN	2.04	1.91	2.05	2.27	2.07	1.81	2.30	2.08	2.02	1.94	2.05
STANDARD DEVIATION	0.83	0.70	0.89	0.80	0.94	0.90					

Figure 6.4 A Sample Crosstab Table

259

Table 6.11   Looking for Relationships

	Reli-ability	Features	Service-ability	Retain Value	Easy to Use	Overall Satisfaction
Attribute Average	*7.4*	*7.7*	*5.8*	*6.9*	*5.5*	*8.1*
Customer						
10001	7	6	7	6	6	7
10203	8	7	5	8	6	9
11044	7	7	6	7	4	6
10445	6	8	5	7	6	8
22345	9	10	7	8	6	10
25600	8	8	7	8	5	9
30400	6	7	5	7	4	8
50505	8	9	7	7	5	9
60666	7	7	5	5	6	8
77500	8	6	7	6	7	7
Correlation with Overall Satisfaction	0.54	0.77	0.34	0.57	0.14	

question of location (west coast and north east). The crosstab table is merely a series of two-way data display tables linked by the column questions and headings (referred to as the "banner") tabulating the results of the same row-wise question, in this case overall satisfaction. (The row labels are generally referred to as "stubs.")

Traditional statistical software packages (SPSS, SAS, SYSTAT) have not produced "banner crosstab" tables, further mystifying the technique. While each of these packages has a "tables" or "crosstab" routine, generally this will allow producing only two-way tables (two variables cross-related) or three-way tables (two variables cross-related, for every value of a third variable). The beauty of the "marketing research" crosstab, is that answers to one survey question may be examined by many different other variables—*all on the same table*! Because the statistical packages lack such routines, you will have to buy a special, crosstab program or use a computer tab house that will produce (among other analyses) crosstab displays of your survey data (American Marketing Association, New York Chapter AMA).

Once a crosstab table is recognized for exactly what it is, it can be parsed into a series of row-column intersections or cells. These cells comprise the entire table. Generally, the column variables are instituted to represent characteristics of your customer base, *West Coast Customers* versus *East Coast Customers,* or *High-Value Customers* versus *Low Value Customers,* and so on. As such, it may be said that the columns represent "independent variables" or classifications while the row variables represent "dependent variables" or outcomes. ("Dependency" is not always strictly implied.) Of course the variables chosen for columns may have only one value or they may have multiple sub-values. Gender as a column variable would have only two values (*Male, Female*); while SIC codes could have an indefinite number of sub-values. The only limitation to the banner points is the number of columns that can be calculated and displayed on one page.

Most crosstab programs limit the total number of columns in a banner to 21 or 22. Recognizing that at least one column must be reserved for *Total Sample,* the satisfaction professional has approximately 20 columns across which to allocate classificatory variables. (Of course numerous crosstabs can be run, but the reader is urged to limit herself in the number of crosstab banners ordered. The analyst's burden—of structuring the results—increases geometrically with additional crosstab banners. There simply becomes too much data to humanly digest or synthesize!)

The Format.   There is a universal standard for how data is displayed in the cells of a crosstab table. The cell can contain up to four numbers, but frequently only the first three (from top down) are shown. The order and identity of these cell entries is depicted in Figure 6.5A. The topmost number in the cell should always be a whole number. This number represents the *frequency count* of those customers who fall into the cell demarcated by the banner column and the stub row. Referring to the outlined cell in Figure 6.5B, it can be seen that 15 of the 120 customers interviewed were from the West Coast and gave a satisfaction score of "somewhat satisfied."

The second number in the cell, usually containing a decimal value, is the *column percent* number. It is the proportion of those customers represented by the column who have responded (or can be identified) with the "stub" row value. Think of this percentage as an **incidence,** that is, the proportion of the column's customers who are represented by the row stub response. In Figure 6.5B, 21.4 percent of the West Coast's customers gave the response "somewhat satisfied." The third number, also a decimal value, is the *row percent* number. This number can be thought of as representing **composition**—that is for all customers offering the row

Raw Frequency
Column percent
Row percent
Table percent

Figure 6.5A   Components of a Crosstab Cell

	Total	Customer's Location	
	Customers	West Coast	North East
Total sample	140	80	60
No response	20	10	10
Total answering	120	70	50
Extremely satisfied	**45**	**30**	**15**
	37.5	42.9	30.0
	100.0	66.6	33.3
		25.0	12.5
Somewhat satisfied	**35**	**15**	**20**
	29.2	21.4	40.0
	100.0	42.9	57.1
		12.5	16.6
Somewhat dissatisfied	**25**	**10**	**15**
	20.8	14.9	30.0
	100.0	40.0	60.0
		8.3	12.5
Extremely dissatisfied	**15**	**5**	**10**
	12.5	7.1	20.0
	100.0	33.3	66.6
		4.2	8.3

Figure 6.5B   Sample Crosstab Table

answer, what proportion are represented by the column characteristic? In Figure 6.5B, the row percentage is 42.9 percent in the outlined cell. This means of all customers replying they were "somewhat satisfied," 42.9 percent came from the West Coast. (Note, if 70 of 120 reporting customers were from the West Coast, we would expect 70/120ths of all "somewhat satisfied" customers to be from the West Coast. How does the 42.9 percent compare with this expectation? Are there more or less "somewhat satisfied" customers from the West Coast than you had expected?)

If there is a fourth cell entry, this will be the *table percent* number. It displays the proportion of the total sample who are both stub and banner **qualified.** The table percent number can frequently help you make a point about the incidence or penetration of a particular set of conditions (the stub and banner characteristics). In Figure 6.5B, in the outlined cell, the table percent is 12.5 percent. This means of all reporting customers, 12.5 percent were from the West Coast *and* were "somewhat satisfied."

Ordering a Crosstab.   To produce a crosstab report, the satisfaction professional needs to go through five steps:

1. identify the questions to be used in the "banner" (column headings), and the appropriate way to divide responses to any continuous variable to be so used;
2. run frequency counts on all questions with continuous responses to identify appropriate categories for the "stubs" (row titles);
3. determine how to deal with missing data, overall and for specific questions/tables;
4. specify which individual tables in the crosstabs would benefit from "filtering." (Most tables will be reported for the total sample. But for some tables, reporting questions that are conditional, you may wish to "filter" the customers being tabulated to only those customers who qualify on the condition, (that is "have multiple insurance policies," "eat out 2+ times per week," and so on);
5. specify the overall appearance desired for each crosstab page.

Which Variables to Select for the Banner?   We have identified the banner variables as "classificatory" or independent variables, yet they need not be restricted to demographics. Often the greatest utility comes from crosstabs where the banner variables are "analytical." For example, one of the overriding questions of any satisfaction survey is "What distinguishes the satisfied from the dissatisfied customers?" So why not institute two columns of your banner for exactly that, *Satisfied Customers* versus *Dissatisfied Customers.* Notice that these categories need not be all inclusive of responses to the overall satisfaction question. For example, the *Satisfied Customers* column could be defined as "Top Box" customers (those giving an overall satisfaction rating of 10, 9, or 8) while the *Dissatisfied Customers* could be represented by those giving a particularly low satisfaction rating or "Bottom Box" (say overall satisfaction ratings of 4 or less). The banner points described in this way will ignore customers who awarded the product a satisfaction rating of 7, 6, or 5, but that's okay. The banner sub-points have been chosen to tease out the most information from the stubs by choosing extreme categories—very satisfied and very dissatisfied.

Dividing Continuous Variables.
Not all of your variables (for your banner or your stubs) will yield discrete categories: *East coast* versus *West coast*. The above example of dividing overall satisfaction ratings into two groups; satisfied and dissatisfied, shows how you will need to specify categories for those variables with continuous responses. For example, customers arrayed by their *Total Sales* or *Total HH Income* would both require categories to make the reporting useful. The satisfaction professional will arrive at appropriate categories by ordering a frequency count run (as described in Table 6.1), and then examining the results to identify meaningful points of division for the continuous variable.

Handling Missing Data.
No matter how hard your interviewers try to get answers from every customer or how committed your customers are to providing you with complete information in a self-administered survey, you will still have questions with missing data from some respondents. Missing data on crosstabs is best handled by instituting a row showing the frequency of "no answer" for each question. Then, the remainder of the table can be based on those who responded. This is appropriate for most cases except where a "no answer" is actually meaningful. For example, the number of customers who cannot specify the percent of their category requirements they allocate to you, may be a useful response and should be included in the distribution of answers. On the other hand, those customers for whom you lack an SIC code may not be relevant, since this is simply missing information with no informational value of its own.

Filtering.
There are certain crosstab tables whose value may be enhanced by examining them for levels of a third variable. (Remember, a crosstab table essentially shows the association between two variables, the column variable, and the row variable.) What if your column headings include High Value Customer/Low Value Customer and East Coast Customers/West Coast Customers, but you would like to examine the results of a particular question by High Value Customers in the East Coast. An economical way of doing this (without using a "nested" banner of value within location) would be to "filter" one or more tables by West Coast versus East Coast. For the tables you filter in this way, you will have a distribution of stub answers by value within location (see Figure 6.6).

Medical Equipment Study

Filter: Respondents from the "North" marketing region.

Question 2A: Please tell us how satisfied you are with the SERVICEABILITY OF PRODUCTS

Filter: Respondents from the "North" marketing region.

	TOTAL	Marketing Region				Recommend Purchase		Influence		Experience	
		North	Central	South	West	Definitely	Prob/Undec	Very	Some-None	<10 yrs	10+ yrs
	(A)	(E)	(C)	(D)	(B)	(F)	(G)	(H)	(I)	(J)	(K)
TOTAL	35 / 100.0 / 100.0	35 / 100.0 / 100.0	-	-	-	22 / 100.0 / 62.9	13 / 100.0 / 37.1	19 / 100.0 / 54.3	16 / 100.0 / 45.7	3 / 100.0 / 8.6	32 / 100.0 / 91.4
TOTAL ANSWERING	35 / 100.0 / 100.0	35 / 100.0 / 100.0	-	-	-	22 / 100.0 / 62.9	13 / 100.0 / 37.1	19 / 100.0 / 54.3	16 / 100.0 / 45.7	3 / 100.0 / 8.6	32 / 100.0 / 91.4
1-Extremely Satisfied	9 / 25.7 / 100.0	9 / 25.7 / 100.0	-	-	-	9 / 40.9 / 100.0	-	3 / 15.8 / 33.3	6 / 37.5 / 66.7	2 / 66.7 / 22.2	7 / 21.9 / 77.8
2-Somewhat Satisfied	21 / 60.0 / 100.0	21 / 60.0 / 100.0	-	-	-	11 / 50.0 / 52.4	10 / 76.9 / 47.6	12 / 63.2 / 57.1	9 / 56.2 / 42.9	1 / 33.3 / 4.8	20 / 62.5 / 95.2
3-Neither Satisfied nor Dissatisfied	4 / 11.4 / 100.0	4 / 11.4 / 100.0	-	-	-	1 / 4.5 / 25.0	3 / 23.1 / 75.0	4 / 21.1 / 100.0	-	-	4 / 12.5 / 100.0
4-Somewhat Dissatisfied	1 / 2.9 / 100.0	1 / 2.9 / 100.0	-	-	-	1 / 4.5 / 100.0	-	-	1 / 6.2 / 100.0	-	1 / 3.1 / 100.0
5-Extremely Dissatisfied	-	-	-	-	-	-	-	-	-	-	-
Cannot Rate	-	-	-	-	-	-	-	-	-	-	-
MEAN	1.91	1.91	-	-	-	1.73	2.23 F	2.05	1.75	1.33	1.97
STANDARD DEVIATION	0.70	0.70	-	-	-	0.77	0.44	0.62	0.77	0.58	0.69

Figure 6.6 A Filtered Crosstab Table

Appearance of the Tables.   Generally far less attention is spent considering how the crosstab tables will look than is warranted. This is probably because satisfaction professionals focus on selecting the banner variables, but then delegate the format to the crosstab house or computer programmer. This is generally a bad decision. The order of variables along the banner is very important; determining how easy it will be to use them. Also, the information contained on each page can help or hinder the page's utility. It is best to draw how you would like the banner to look, as well as to specify all of the information you would like included in the table.

Statistical Tests.   Many crosstab programs provide significance testing of means within their list of options. You will need to decide for which pairing of column means significance tests are useful. When you specify these columns, the program will compute a *t*-test for the column means and interpret the *t*-score's significance for you. In Figure 6.7, the columns headed customer status: current versus past, are subjected to *t*-tests. The Figure indicates that for this variable, the difference between these two groups' ratings is significant at the 95 percent level of confidence.

Correlation Analysis

One of your goals in interpreting your survey results will be to identify key areas for improvement. Be careful how you identify these key areas. Table 6.11 shows some average scores on several performance attributes, along with the overall satisfaction scores from 10 customers. Looking at the means suggests that "easy to use" may be causing the most problems since its mean is lowest of the five attributes. Can you depend on this sort of analysis to determine priorities for improvement? If you examine the rating profiles of the 10 customers, you are likely to draw a somewhat different conclusion.

   If you identify the two customers who gave the lowest satisfaction ratings (10001 and 77500) you will see their lowest attribute ratings are on "features." Similarly, the customer awarding the highest satisfaction score gives his highest score to "features." It appears that ratings of variables other than "easy to use" may be more related to overall satisfaction. Looking at individual cases like this can usually help you spot the problem areas. Yet when you have thousands of customers' responses and 20 or more attributes, eyeballing customers' profiles may be impossible. In the later case, correlation analysis can help you identify linkages between the performance attributes and overall satisfaction.

Medical Study

Please tell us how satisfied you are with the SERVICEABILITY OF PRODUCTS

	TOTAL	Marketing Region				Recommend Purchase		Influence		Experience	
		North	Central	South	West	Definitely	Prob/Undec	Very	Some-None	<10 yrs	10+ yrs
	(A)	(B)	(C)	(D)	(E)	(F)	(G)	(H)	(I)	(J)	(K)
TOTAL	100 / 100.0 / 100.0	35 / 100.0 / 35.0	20 / 100.0 / 20.0	15 / 100.0 / 15.0	30 / 100.0 / 30.0	53 / 100.0 / 53.0	47 / 100.0 / 47.0	39 / 100.0 / 39.0	61 / 100.0 / 61.0	17 / 100.0 / 17.0	82 / 100.0 / 82.0
TOTAL ANSWERING	100 / 100.0 / 100.0	35 / 100.0 / 35.0	20 / 100.0 / 20.0	15 / 100.0 / 15.0	30 / 100.0 / 30.0	53 / 100.0 / 53.0	47 / 100.0 / 47.0	39 / 100.0 / 39.0	61 / 100.0 / 61.0	17 / 100.0 / 17.0	82 / 100.0 / 82.0
1-Extremely Satisfied	25 / 25.0 / 100.0	9 / 25.7 / 36.0	6 / 30.0 / 24.0	2 / 13.3 / 8.0	8 / 26.7 / 32.0	22 / 41.5 G / 88.0	3 / 6.4 / 12.0	8 / 20.5 / 32.0	17 / 27.9 / 68.0	4 / 23.5 / 16.0	21 / 25.6 / 84.0
2-Somewhat Satisfied	52 / 52.0 / 100.0	21 / 60.0 / 40.4	8 / 40.0 / 15.4	8 / 53.3 / 15.4	15 / 50.0 / 28.8	23 / 43.4 / 44.2	29 / 61.7 f / 55.8	20 / 51.3 / 38.5	32 / 52.5 / 61.5	10 / 58.8 / 19.2	42 / 51.2 / 80.8
3-Neither Satisfied nor Dissatisfied	18 / 18.0 / 100.0	4 / 11.4 / 22.2	5 / 25.0 / 27.8	4 / 26.7 / 22.2	5 / 16.7 / 27.8	5 / 9.4 / 27.8	13 / 27.7 F / 72.2	11 / 28.2 I / 61.1	7 / 11.5 / 38.9	3 / 17.6 / 16.7	14 / 17.1 / 77.8
4-Somewhat Dissatisfied	4 / 4.0 / 100.0	1 / 2.9 / 25.0	1 / 5.0 / 25.0	1 / 6.7 / 25.0	1 / 3.3 / 25.0	2 / 3.8 / 50.0	2 / 4.3 / 50.0	-	4 / 6.6 / 100.0	-	4 / 4.9 / 100.0
5-Extremely Dissatisfied	1 / 1.0 / 100.0	-	-	-	1 / 3.3 / 100.0	1 / 1.9 / 100.0	-	-	1 / 1.6 / 100.0	-	1 / 1.2 / 100.0
Cannot Rate	-	-	-	-	-	-	-	-	-	-	-
MEAN	2.04	1.91	2.05	2.27	2.07	1.81	2.30 F	2.08	2.02	1.94	2.05
STANDARD DEVIATION	0.83	0.70	0.89	0.80	0.94	0.90	0.66	0.70	0.90	0.66	0.86

Comparison Groups: BCDE/FG/HI/JK
Independent T-Test for Means, Independent Z-Test for Percentages
Upper case letters indicate significance at the 95% level.
Lower case letters indicate significance at the 90% level.

Figure 6.7 A Crosstab Table with Statistical Tests

In the lower half of Table 6.11 Pearson Product Moment Correlations have been calculated for each pairing of attribute with overall satisfaction. More than the means, the correlation coefficients provide a good picture for you, of the attributes whose ratings are most highly related to overall satisfaction. The highest correlation coefficient is for "features," which would probably be your best starting point to increase overall satisfaction.

Risk Analysis

Correlation analysis is one method for sorting through your attributes to determine those that appear most related to overall dissatisfaction. Another method for accomplishing this is *risk analysis*. This is a handy technique that examines ratings on each performance attribute against overall satisfaction.

To conduct a risk analysis, it is necessary to "dichotomize" (divide into two groups) the ratings on each of your performance attributes and overall satisfaction, on an individual customer basis. You must examine the general distribution of performance ratings to decide what level you consider satisfactory. Let us imagine you have measured performance and satisfaction on a 1 to 10 scale. Most of your performance attributes have means in the 7s, as does your overall satisfaction rating. Using these averages, you could then score each customer as having a score at or above the mean, or below the mean on both the performance measures as well as overall satisfaction.

Now, you can develop a two-by-two table for each performance attribute compared to overall satisfaction. These tables will look like the table in Table 6.12A. The columns identify the two levels of overall satisfaction, low (less than the overall average of 7) and high (the average or higher). The rows identify levels of rating of the performance variables, in this case, "product reliability." Again, the average rating of the performance variable is used as a dividing point. The top row includes those customers giving product reliability a low rating (less than the average), the bottom row includes those customers rating product reliability high (at the average or higher). The table then shows how ratings on product reliability are related to overall satisfaction.

The uppermost left cell, low "product reliability" and low "overall satisfaction" shows the number of customers scoring both variables low. In this case, 48 customers (12 percent of the total customerbase) rated both product reliability and overall satisfaction low. Conversely, 18 percent (70 customers) gave product reliability a low rating, but nevertheless

Table 6.12A   A Risk Analysis Table for One Performance Attribute

	Overall Satisfaction Rating	
Rating on Product Reliability	*Low (< 7)*	*High (7+)*
Low (< 7)	48 (12%)	70 (18%)
High (7+)	37 (9%)	245 (61%)

Table 6.12B   A Summary Risk Analysis Table for All Performance Attributes

Performance Attributes	Risk Analysis Rating	
	Attribute Low/ Overall Low	*Attribute High/ Overall High*
Product Reliability	12%	61%
Product Features	5%	75%
Serviceability	22%	55%
Retains Value	18%	65%
Easy to Use	35%	30%

gave overall satisfaction a high rating (the top, rightmost cell). The lower right cell shows the proportion of the total sample who were apparently pleased both with product reliability and with overall satisfaction—giving each an above average rating.

It can be very useful to review all of the performance attributes in this sort of way to examine their relationship with overall satisfaction. Table 6.12B shows a listing of all of the performance attributes by their relationship with overall satisfaction. This sort of summary chart can provide useful insights into which performance attributes one ought to pay attention to first, in order to improve overall satisfaction.

Analyses to Help Identify Primary Issues or Causes

Pareto Analysis

Pareto Analysis is a technique for recording and analyzing information relating to the possible causes of a problem or general dissatisfaction. A

Pareto diagram is a special form of a vertical bar chart, which allows the causal information to be visually displayed. Because of its graphical nature, a Pareto analysis is both a useful diagnostic and reporting tool. The analysis often produces insights not previously considered. "First things first," is the thought behind the Pareto diagram; the properly constructed diagram should suggest which attribute or activity resources should first be concentrated on to produce the most substantial improvement in customer satisfaction. Very often the simple process of arranging data may suggest something of importance that would otherwise have gone unnoticed.

Because of its graphical and yet intuitive nature, Pareto Analysis is very often used by quality improvement teams, helping the team readily identify basic problems. The communication process between people takes on many forms, and Pareto diagrams are a form of language using a graphical display in a commonly understood format. Selecting classifications, tabulating data, ordering data, and constructing the Pareto diagram serves a useful purpose in problem investigation.

Pareto diagrams can also be used to illustrate progress. Comparing Pareto diagrams drawn at key milestones during the solution of a problem enables the effectiveness of the corrective actions to be evaluated. Changing conditions may cause a reordering of the data classes. These changes can be highlighted by using colors or transparent overlays, or by presenting the diagrams in sequence.

The Basics of Pareto Analysis.   Analysis often reveals that a small number of failures are responsible for the bulk of quality problems. In many situations, a similar pattern becomes apparent when we look at the relationship between numbers of items and their contribution to the extent of a problem. This pattern has been referred to as the "80/20 rule" and shows itself in many different ways. For example, 80 percent of the telephone calls you receive, probably come from 20 percent of your friends or coworkers. Building on this understanding, Juran reportedly created the so-called "Pareto Principle" named after the Italian economist (Juran 1975). (Pareto had observed that the majority of his country's wealth was owned by relatively few people.[2]) In TQM studies Pareto

----

[2]Interestingly, though seldom discussed in satisfaction literature, Pareto may have been one of the first theoreticians to be concerned with satisfaction! In his economic discussions, he maintained that consumer satisfaction with products could not be measured directly, but rather consumers could only be expected to rank products in order of their preference for them. When two products were perceived as equal, Pareto developed the notion of "indifference."

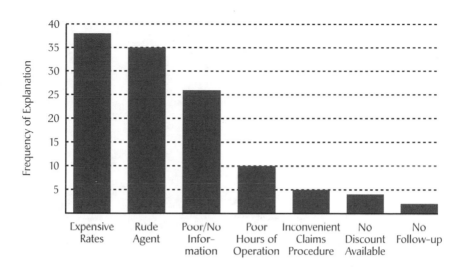

Figure 6.8   A Pareto Analysis of Responses to a Question Exploring the Overall Satisfaction Rating

Analysis was implemented with the understanding that a few basic problems generally could be found that were responsible for lagging quality.

Similarly, 80 percent of a company's failure costs probably result from 20 percent of its problem areas. The 80/20 principle does not mean that exactly 80 percent of the total problem is caused by exactly 20 percent of the features, but that there is generally a similarly large imbalance between severity and the number of causes. In other words, among the wide range of problems that your organization may be faced with, there are a few vital ones that must be tackled immediately, and many others that can be dealt with later. Pareto Analysis shows at a glance which problem areas can be regarded as the *vital few* needing immediate action, and which problem areas are the *useful many* to be dealt with over time.

Figure 6.8 shows a Pareto analysis of open-end answers to a question following up the overall satisfaction question, "Why are you this satisfied/dissatisfied?" The greatest number of explanations, about 38 percent, deal with comments about "rates." The next most frequent explanation concerns the "agent." Then there is a slight gap, followed by "information." The remaining explanations constitute the "useful many." It is clear that attention should be directed at the first three explanations (the "vital few"). The figure shows how vividly a Pareto chart displays underlying problems and can help focus remedial efforts on the most appropriate ones.

In most cases the identification of the "vital few" does not come as a complete surprise. On the contrary, some of the problems on the list will have long been notorious, but the big accomplishments of the Pareto Analysis are that:

- some notorious problems are confirmed as belonging to the "vital few";
- some problems, previously not notorious, are identified as belonging to the "vital few";
- the "useful many" are identified;
- the priority for sorting out problems is established.

There are five steps to creating a Pareto Analysis:

1. List the activities to be analyzed;
2. Calculate frequencies of occurrence for each;
3. Rank the activities by occurrence;
4. Draw the Pareto chart based on frequency;
5. Interpret the results.

Draw a bar chart to illustrate the relative frequencies of each activity. The vertical scale will show the number (occurrence) of each activity, and the horizontal scale will show the categories. When there are a significant number of minor activities, they can be combined into an "Other" category to simplify the chart.

Once the activities are plotted by frequency of occurrence, it may be desirable to introduce costs or severity of the activities. This will change your Pareto diagram considerably. To accomplish this, the data must be weighted by the cost or severity of each activity.

Root Cause Analysis[3]

Cause and Effect Analysis is a technique for identifying the possible causes of a problem. It is also a visually effective way of organizing and recording the causes as they are suggested. The method is also called the "fishbone" diagram because of its similarity to a fish's skeleton, or the "Ishikawa" diagram after Professor Ishikawa, who made the analysis an important tool for the Japanese Quality Movement. (See Wilson, Dell, and Anderson [1993] for a more complete discussion of this technique.)

----

[3]Descriptions in this and the preceding section have adapted material from the excellent TQM manual, *Strive for Perfection*, prepared by Rolls-Royce Motor Cars, Crewe, England. Appreciation is expressed to Rolls-Royce.

Cause and Effect analysis is appropriate for a variety of needs:

- Defining a problem
- Identifying possible data requirements
- Identifying possible causes
- Developing objectives for solutions
- Narrowing down causes

Because the results of satisfaction surveys involve measurements on numerous variables, resolving a reported problem can often appear difficult, unmanageable, even insoluble. One way of beginning to break down such problems into smaller, more easily handled chunks is to explore some of the possible causes by using Cause and Effect diagrams. Cause and Effect Analysis can be used in conjunction with Pareto Analysis and Brainstorming as an interactive process.

Another aspect of Cause and Effect diagrams is their ability to show progress in solving a problem. One can tell at a glance how thoroughly a problem has been investigated by the development of the fishbone. A Cause and Effect diagram that shows a substantial number of possible causes, indicates that a problem is in the process of a thorough investigation. On the other hand a bare Cause and Effect diagram may indicate that the problem was not significant, or that the solvers of the problem were not exhaustive in their search for possible causes.

Many organizational problems seem at first to be simple to solve. It is quite usual for a problem symptom to be recognized and relevant action taken at once to solve it. Too often, however, the remedy is not effective because it is either directed at the wrong cause, or there may be multiple causes. Methods used for solving problems should be capable of identifying all the causes. For remedial action to be effective, it is necessary that all possible causes be identified.

A Cause and Effect diagram is constructed in the following sequence:

- **Preparation**   Having decided that you wish to use Cause and Effect Analysis make sure that you are thoroughly prepared. The technique involves Brainstorming and you must be familiar with how that works. The section on Brainstorming also contains useful hints on how to select your participants.
- **Start the Diagram**   Establish what the problem, or effect, is. Start the diagram by putting this in a box, and draw a process line pointing to the box.

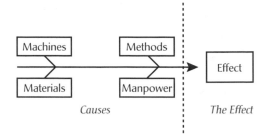

Figure 6.9   Basic Structure of the Root-Cause or Fishbone Diagram

- **Identify Major Causes**   There are at least three ways to do this:
  - brainstorming to identify possible causes
  - using a provocative structure to stimulate identifying causes, consider the "4M" approach—Machines, Methods, Materials, and Manpower;
  - or alternatively the "PEMPEM" approach—Plant, Equipment, Materials, People, Environment, and Methods.

These major cause categories are written in boxes on either side of the process line and the boxes are connected by lines slanting towards the main line. Now you are ready to identify all of the possible causes falling into each of the major (boxed) causes (see Figure 6.9).

- **Identify All Possible Causes**   Use brainstorming to generate lists of causes and relevant causal information down to each rib of the diagram. All the causes and information are examined, and related to one or more of the major causes. Causes and information can be subdivided to show as accurately as possible the various elements of each. Links should be drawn between causes and information that are interrelated.
- **Incubate the Ideas**   As in brainstorming, incubation can produce valuable hindsight additions to the diagram.
- **Evaluate and Analyze the Possible Causes**   At this point creative thinking becomes less important than analytical thinking. The groups of causes and information identified on the fishbone must be thought of, at this point, as theories about causes. These theories have to be tested by logical analysis to make certain they are valid. This analysis should also reveal just how the causes provoke the effects; this will assist in devising appropriate remedies.

Tips for Cause and Effect Diagramming

To successfully create a cause and effect diagram, the following guidelines should be adopted:

- When constructing Cause and Effect diagrams, focus on the most essential factors;
- Ideally, create your fishbone diagram as a team effort, the possible insights will increase as different points of view are included in your team.
- Create your fishbone diagram using the basic approach of "brainstorming" to ensure that all the causes are considered. All members must feel free to express their ideas. The more ideas mentioned, the more comprehensive the diagram will be; one person's idea may trigger someone else's.
- The aim in Cause and Effect diagramming is not to apportion blame but to create a solution-oriented atmosphere. Focus on solving problems rather than how they came about in the first place. The past cannot be changed—only the future can be affected by eliminating the *causes* of undesired problems.
- Do not "overload" any one fishbone diagram. If a cluster of causes begins to dominate the diagram, consider isolating that cluster on a separate diagram.
- Construct a separate diagram for each problem. If the problem definition is not specific enough, some major categories of the diagram may become overloaded and it may be necessary to redefine the problem.
- Look out for and examine closely the relationship between causes—this is where unexpected solutions are likely to turn up.
- Circle the most likely causes. This is usually done after all possible ideas have been posted on the Cause and Effect diagram, and each idea has been critically examined.

A completed cause and effect diagram will look something like Figure 6.10. In this example, from Wyckoff (1983), Midway Airlines has identified reasons to explain why its planes were leaving late from the gate. Once all possible causes had been identified, a Pareto analysis was conducted. Four of the causes accounted for over 85 percent of all late departures. These causes became Midway's focus of attention.

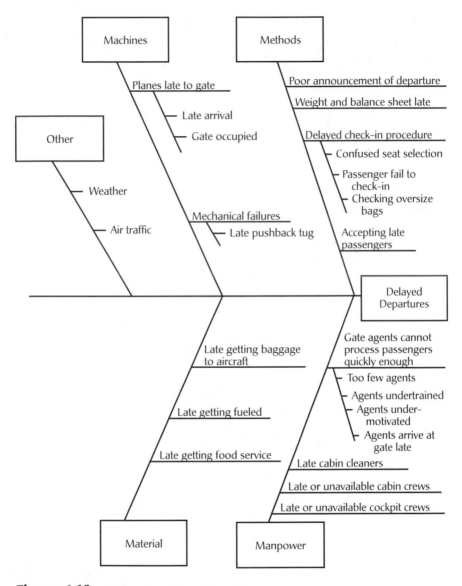

Figure 6.10   A Completed Root-Cause Diagram

Reprinted with permission from Wyckoff, D. Daryl, "New Tools for Achieving Service Quality," *The Cornell HRA Quarterly*, November 1984, pp. 78–84.

SPECIAL TOOLS FOR VERBAL ANALYSIS OF CSM DATA

The Voice of Our Customer

One of the continuing objectives of satisfaction research is to listen to customers. For that reason, as we have established earlier, it is always a good idea to ask at least two open-ended questions allowing your customers to raise their own issues stated in their own terminology with their own solutions or requests. Unfortunately, very frequently such responses will be tabulated by assigning them already established codes or categories, which may be in existence from previous surveys. By categorizing open-end responses with existing categories, each individual customer's outlook or specific meaning can be lost. So, while we initiate our open-end questioning with the desire to hear the current customer's "voice," we end up homogenizing his or her idiosyncratic response(s) into existing category(ies) whose general meaning may lose the intensity and flavor of the individual customer's verbatim.

The author believes improving the way in which open-end responses are analyzed is the greatest overall improvement that can be made to satisfaction surveys. And, while the practicality of summarizing open-ends through code structures is understood, it is also possible to maintain the integrity of open-ends by entering them, in their entirety, into a computer file. A number of analyses can be applied to this file.

Verbatim Analyzer®

First of all, the satisfaction professional must commit to preserving the integrity of all (or the most useful) open-end responses by data entering them into computer files. They should, of course, be placed in a relational data file indexed to the main data file, if not made an integral part of it. Data entering open-ends from self-administered questionnaires (especially computerized ones) will be relatively easy. Paradoxically, many CATI implemented surveys still use paper and pencil to capture long open-ends. These will be costly and sometimes complicated to link to individual customers' records. Remembering the potential value of having the complete open-ends available should hopefully sustain the satisfaction professional through the complications and costs of retaining them.

Frequency Count—Freq. order the most descriptive words

Word	Frequency
UNUSUAL	6
DELICIOUS	4
CHEESY	4
EXPENSIVE	3
GREASY	3
CHEDDARY	2
FATTENING	2
UNNATURAL	2
SPECIAL	2
CRUNCHY	2
USELESS	1
FLAVORLESS	1
INNOVATIVE	1
SCRUMPTIOUS	1

Keyword Search—Interest in product: expensive

#22009 Probably too *expensive*. Cheddar and Bacon sounds like it would have a tart or bitter flavor. Bacon is too *expensive*.

#14044 I like the taste of Oscar Mayer Bacon but it's too *expensive* to eat that often. It cooks great in the microwave and that is why I like it.

#93871 It would be good crumpled on a salad or on in omelet. It might be too *expensive*. Bacon is already too *expensive*.

#78144 Too *expensive*. I raise pigs and don't buy any pork products. I am a vegetarian.

#30003 Too *expensive*. But might become a fad that I would have to try since everyone else was trying.

What do you like about product—sorted by gender and age

SEX   = 1—Male
AGE   = 1—18–24 Yrs
  #10010 The possible taste combination.
  #21968 Nothing.
  #77776 The taste is great and it's easy to serve. Neat clean and less of a mess. Not melted cheese on plates running off of burgers.

SEX   = 1—Male
AGE   = 2—25–34 Yrs
  #14041 Intriguing, Innovative idea.
  #54328 The bacon taste.
  #67031 Not messy on Bacon Cheeseburger.
  #77871 How humorous the concept is.

Figure 6.11   Verbatim Analysis

Once the open-ends are data entered, consider these opportunities implemented either with existing software (like Verbatim Analyzer) or custom-programmed software:

- Conduct a frequency count on words, phrases, or concepts to identify the most commonly volunteered issues. This sort of listing can become input for a Pareto analysis.
- Search customers' responses for the occurence of keywords in context (KWIC), you will learn much more reading how an issue is alluded to in the customers own perspective and wording.
- Build tables of the occurrence of keywords tallied by customer classifications (for example *East coast* versus *West coast* customers).
- Sort open-ends (in their entirety) by various classifications of your customers, for example, long-tenured vs. new customers.

The author has personally introduced the use of open-ends into several customer satisfaction surveys. In the Owner Satisfaction Programme conducted for Rolls-Royce Motor Cars, Mr. Paul Beart of Rolls-Royce says verbatims "emotionalize the numbers and data of a customer satisfaction programme." In the Rolls-Royce factory in Crewe, England, customers' appropriate comments are posted every quarter in the factory's main departments: Engine Build, Paintshop, Woodshop, Upholstery Shop, and so on. Because the comments are linked to each motor car's VIN (vehicle identification code) workers in the factory can relate the comments to a specific motor car they helped build. Trained in total quality management, the workers readily accept the value and insight offered in the owners' reactions.

THE PROBLEM OF MISSING DATA

Assume Missing Data Is Random

There are two types of missing data: nonrandom and random. Nonrandom omissions occur when a particular type of customer decides not to provide certain information. For example, maybe dissatisfied customers are reluctant to personally criticize their sales representative. So, rather than give harsh ratings on sales reps' performance they simply skip over the rating, leaving it blank. This is *nonrandom missing data* because its omission is *systematically related* to some other characteristic of your customerbase. On the other hand, the occasional skipping of a question by customers hurrying to complete their questionnaire, is an example of *random missing data*. It is assumed such omissions are randomly distributed throughout all of the questions in your survey, in a more or less random fashion.

We will only address ways of dealing with random missing data. If you wish to test whether missing data in your customers' returned questionnaires is randomly distributed or not, refer to tests described by Anderson, Basilevsky, and Hum (1983). Generally, if the missing values are scattered throughout the data file and not concentrated among any small group of customers nor specific questions, you may consider the omissions to be random.

Missing data is important to our analysis of satisfaction data because many of the statistical packages that will be used for analysis will automatically delete all cases with missing values. This generally means a substantially smaller customerbase for the analysis than responded to the survey. And, if some values are desired to be calculated for each responding customer, it will be unacceptable to have some customers excluded from analyses because they have some data values missing.

Three Options

There are three actions to be taken with missing data: delete the cases with missing values, replace the missing values with "neutral values," and estimate the missing values (Anderson, Basilevsky, and Hum 1983).

Delete Customers with Any Missing Data

Because satisfaction professionals try so hard to maximize the response to a satisfaction survey it is disappointing to have to consider deleting some customers' responses simply because they have left some questions unanswered. But in cases where a customer fails to answer a substantial number of questions, it is probably best to exclude this customer from analysis. Of course you should consider omitting from your analysis any questions on which nonresponse is particularly high. Regarding customers, (or cases) an alternative rule to consider (if you are prepared to use one of the following replacement rules) is to delete only those customers who fail to answer more than a minimum number of questions. You can establish a minimum number, say 75 percent. You should also reject any customers who fail to answer very important questions, like overall satisfaction, which may ultimately end up as criteria (dependent variables) in subsequent analyses (Mullet 1994).

Replacement with Neutral Values

"Neutral values" are replacement values that attempt to preserve the average response or "status quo." These values can be calculated in one of two ways. The method some statistical packages offer is to use the total sample's average (of all customers who did answer) as the replacement for an omitted variable. The other option, is to calculate the average (of those questions answered) individually for each customer and then replace missing questions with the respondent's *own average*. This method is especially appealing because it tends to maintain the respondent's individual answering tendencies. In either case, the thought is that replacement by such averages will minimally disrupt the analysis of the total sample's data by other statistical techniques.

Estimation by Case

In this procedure, an estimation procedure, like regression analysis will be used to statistically estimate the missing values based on a regression model built from relationships in the surrounding data. First, customers are generally clustered into groups whose response profiles are roughly similar. Then, a regression model can be built to estimate a customer's missing data, using the relationship of his other supplied values to other variables' values from the remainder of his cluster. While this will be a tedious process, in some cases it may be warranted to preserve numbers or data from specifically important customers.

REFERENCES

American Marketing Association. *Marketing News: Directory of Software Suppliers.* Chicago, 1996.

American Marketing Association, New York Chapter. *The GreenBook Directory of Research Techniques and Suppliers.* 1996.

Anderson, Andy B., Alexander Basilevsky, and Derek P. J. Hum. "Missing Data: A Review of the Literature," in Peter H. Rossi, James D. Wright, and Andy B. Anderson. *Handbook of Survey Research.* New York: Academic Press, Inc., 1983.

Bruning, James L., and B. L. Kintz. *Computational Handbook of Statistics.* 4th Ed. New York: Longman, 1997.

Dow-Jones. *American Demographics: Directory of Software Suppliers.* Ithaca, NY, 1996.

Juran, J. M. "The Non-Pareto Principle: Mea Culpa," *Quality Progress.* May 1975, pp. 8–9. (Also reprinted in: Juran, J. M., *Juran on Quality by Design.* New York: The Free Press, 1992, pp. 68–71.)

Mullet, Gary M. "Regression Regression." *Quirk's Marketing Research Review.* October 1994, pp. 12–15.

Wilson, Paul F., Larry D. Dell, and Gaylord F. Anderson. *Root Cause Analysis.* Milwaukee, WI: ASQC Quality Press, 1993.

CHAPTER 7

The Basic Graphical Tools for CSM Reporting

OVERVIEW

One of the biggest downfalls of customer satisfaction measurement is its failure to get properly communicated to operational management. Often the failure is a result of the way in which the information has been presented—it is not user friendly. Customer satisfaction information, to really help improve products, services, and processes, must be communicated to multiple layers within an organization. It requires—more than any other type of information—a compelling yet simple reporting mechanism.

Graphical techniques are frequently the answer. The adage, "A picture is worth a thousand words" is true in satisfaction work, but only as long as the picture is *carefully chosen* and *thoughtfully drawn*. Unfortunately, some pictures (graphs) employed in CSM reports today, are so confusingly assembled or are so poorly thought-out, they literally require a thousand words of explanation! When properly executed, graphical presentations can be a substantial aid with which to communicate customer satisfaction results. Unfortunately little has been written or discussed about this very important topic. This chapter will reveal numerous methods for communicating specific messages via graphical techniques.

A Philosophy of Graphical Reporting

Too often satisfaction results are graphed without a careful plan for exactly what needs to be communicated. The result is almost always a misconceived graph type, and displayed findings, which are either difficult to understand or which fail to communicate the main finding.

Tufte (1983) in what many consider the seminal book on statistical graphing, identifies several objectives of business graphics:

- to show the data;
- to induce the viewer to think about the substance (of the graphic) rather than about the methodology, design, or production technology of the graphic design;
- to avoid distorting what the data have to say;
- to present many numbers in a small space;
- to make large data sets coherent;
- to encourage the eye to compare different pieces of data;
- to reveal the data at several levels of detail, from a broad overview to the fine structure;
- to serve a reasonably clear purpose: description, exploration, tabulation, or decoration;
- to be closely integrated with the statistical and verbal descriptors of a data set.

It is important that the satisfaction professional have a lexicon of graph types at his disposal and that he astutely select each graph to maximally accomplish the above objectives. And, a revolution is at hand. Where previously a satisfaction professional may have had to hire and work through a charting specialist to produce graphs, today with a wide range of personal computer graphing software available, most often the satisfaction professional (or someone on his staff) will interact directly with the charting program. While this may be more efficient, unfortunately the expertise previously contributed by the chartist is today often missing. This means satisfaction professionals (and the vendors who work for them) must become more astute users of the computer graphing software.

Establish a Goal for Each Graphic

It is not simply a matter that each section or chapter of your satisfaction report ought to have a "mandatory" graphic. The thought should rather be, given the idea(s) that needs to be communicated by a set of particular

Table 7.1   Graph-Types Associated with Major Graphing Goals

Magnitude	Thermometer Charts
	Bar Charts
	Radar (Spider) Charts
Growth, Trends, and Change	Line Graphs
	Area Graphs
	Scattergrams
Composition	Pie Charts
	Stacked Bar Charts
Order, Sequence, or Flow	PERT Charts
	Flow Diagrams
	QFD Grids

findings, can graphics enhance the communication of the idea(s) beyond what a written description can accomplish? If the answer is no, then graphics should probably be avoided. But very often the answer will be a resounding "yes." In these cases the task is threefold:

- to clearly have a goal in mind;
- to then select the most appropriate graph-type to accomplish the goal;
- and then to configure the graph in the most compelling way possible.

There are at least four specific purposes graphs can provide for the satisfaction professional: depicting magnitude, tracking growth/change, displaying composition, and establishing order, sequence, or flow. Table 7.1 identifies the graph-types most often associated with each of these purposes.

Unfortunately there is little assistance in how to choose a graph-type to be found in the manuals accompanying most computer graphing programs. The trouble with these manuals is that rather than discussing the purpose of general graph-types, they invariably tend to describe specific graphs—kind of like describing the execution, without mentioning the strategy involved!

Depicting Magnitude

Graphs are terrific aids in helping management visualize aspects of magnitude, like customers' perceptions of an organization's absolute *performance* and its performance relative to goals or competition. If we have several attributes on which we have assessed our organization's performance, a graph can help management visualize not only the rank order of performance (from best performance to worst), but also clusters of attribute performance levels; the top third, the middle third, and the bottom third. Graphs of the importance ratings assigned performance attributes can similarly help; consider dichotomizing or trichotomizing importance ratings. It will help your management conceptualize product or service attributes (or other issues) in terms of the levels of expectations, importance, or performance.

Tracking Growth and Change Information

Change is one of the key findings of any customer satisfaction survey. Beyond numerical change scores (expressed as a percentage of the base number), graphs can depict *change* most easily and most dramatically. And, unlike numerical change scores, which essentially apply only to pairs of scores, a line graph can show trends across a virtual infinity of measurement points.

Depicting Composition

When you wish to show how a number of elements (say customer groups) combine to form a total, you are dealing with a goal of portraying *composition*. Composition graphics will always show how a collection of items (customer groups, categories of answers to an open-end question, and so on) add up to the total, 100 percent.

Establishing Order, Sequence, or Flow

Nothing is quite so effective in communicating the demands of a time schedule as a flow chart. The satisfaction professional will benefit from flow and sequence charting at two opposite ends of his process: the organization, gathering, and analysis of data and the implementation of action plans to help solve customers' problems and improve satisfaction. Flow charts, PERT, or CPM (critical path method) sequence charts, or QFD (quality function deployment) grids can each be an effective planning tool in the CSM process.

Combinations

It is often the case that you will wish to accomplish more than one of these goals with one particular graph. There is no easy answer here. For example, what about current performance as a bar chart with some indication of trend or change? Such combined goals stretch the capabilities of current graph-types. We will offer some examples during our discussion.

Add Value to Your Graphs

It is likely all of us have seen graphs where the components of the graph have simply been "stripped" from a crosstab or a questionnaire with little or no thought given to the order in which the components are listed or organized. Such a graph is a waste of the viewer's time because of the effort the viewer must assert to "unravel" the information and restructure it to be more informative. (For examples of poorly designed graphs see Figure 7.1.) The horizontal bar chart in Figure 7.1A has not been ordered from most to least frequent problem; the viewer must organize the problems for herself. The vertical, clustered bar chart (Figure 7.1B) is guilty of trying to communicate too many things in one graphic. There is the overall trend in satisfaction across the years, the trend of each region, and the comparison of regions within each year and by growth trend. What is the viewer's understanding? Probably the viewer leaves the graphic completely confused and frustrated!

There is almost always the opportunity to make the information conveyed in a graph or chart more useful by purposefully organizing it prior to graphing it. For example, one might simply reorder the performance attributes so they appear in descending order of performance. Or, one might reorder the list of customer groups to better represent tenure or location. Always question the order or position in which information is entered in a graph to determine if there is not a more meaningful way to display the information.

Keeping Graphics Simple

Like so many things, we seem to have a need to over complicate our use of graphs. Many times a simple graph will be more useful than a complicated one. The author is often struck by his own zeal to concoct relatively exotic graphs, which, though they make a cogent point, are so complicated, the average manager is put off by the effort required to fully comprehend them. That is not to say that new and complex graphs ought not to be tried, indeed they should. But the manner in which a new or complex graph is presented can make or break the idea. In this chapter we will examine several relatively new ideas for communicating CSM results. But remember, for all but the most simple of

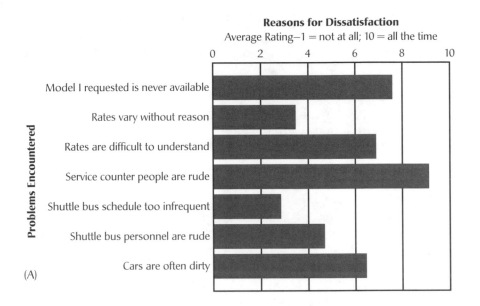

(A)

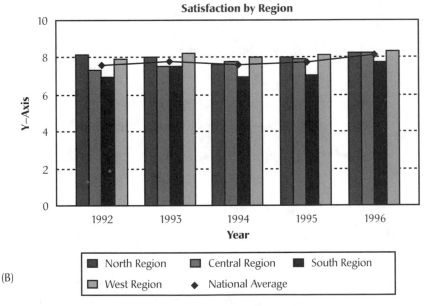

(B)

Figure 7.1 Examples of Poor Graphs

graphs, the typical audience will need to be helped along in understanding the graphic display itself.

The first rule of graphing, then, must be to attempt to keep our graphs as simple as possible to make the point we wish to communicate. If our point requires a more complex graph, the graph ought to be "built" sequentially in front of the audience, to increase the likelihood of their understanding it. That means if a graph shows multiple effects, or uses multiple scales, such a graph ought to be sequentially constructed with an accompanying dialogue so the audience understands the final display, as a result of having witnessed the individual components being assembled.

Label and Orient Your Graphs Carefully

Too often, report graphics will be poorly labeled. It is worth every bit of time it takes to properly identify and label your graphs. This means a clear and unambiguous title, well-identified axes, and a properly identified legend.

Titles.   Your titles should tell the reader or viewer exactly what commodity is being graphed and which customer groups or operating units are being compared.

Axes.   The horizontal and vertical axes (if your graph uses axes) should be clearly labeled. It is also a good idea to maintain a similar scale for axes among all of the graphs in your report since your audience will invariably transfer their understanding of your first graph to others you present. Also, consider long and hard before you use truncated axes (axes that begin at a value greater than zero). Very often graphing programs will automatically truncate axes to make graphable results more visible. This can, however, result in potential misunderstanding. Consider the two graphs in Figure 7.2. The graph in Figure 7.2A suggests a much more dramatic improvement in satisfaction, because the vertical axis has been truncated and starts at a value greater than zero. The more appropriately scaled graph, in Figure 7.2B, offers the viewer a more realistic idea of the true degree of improvement.

Legends.   Legends help assign identities to bar colors or types, but are somewhat inconvenient in that the reader or viewer has to refer from the graphic to the legend and back again. It is preferable, to somehow directly label the identity of bars or performance measures. Try using your corporate color or logo to help the reader immediately identify representations.

Figure 7.2A   Example of a "Truncated" Vertical Axis

Figure 7.2B   The Correct Depiction

Data Table.   Some computer graphing programs provide an option to produce a data table that appears directly beneath the graph. This table, containing exact values, is often a very handy reference for those who wish numerical precision alongside a graphical depiction of results (see Figure 7.3).

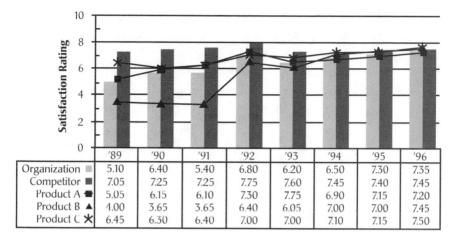

	'89	'90	'91	'92	'93	'94	'95	'96
Organization	5.10	6.40	5.40	6.80	6.20	6.50	7.30	7.35
Competitor	7.05	7.25	7.25	7.75	7.60	7.45	7.40	7.45
Product A	5.05	6.15	6.10	7.30	7.75	6.90	7.15	7.20
Product B	4.00	3.65	3.65	6.40	6.05	7.00	7.00	7.45
Product C	6.45	6.30	6.40	7.00	7.00	7.10	7.15	7.50

Figure 7.3   A Data Table Incorporated into a Chart

Overcoming the "Rainbow Effect"

It is assumed that much of your graphing will be completed using graphing packages for the personal computer. While such programs have made business graphing available to a much larger user group than has ever before been possible, there are several unfortunate consequences to this widespread availability. Prior to the graphing packages, if one needed a chart, he would seek out the assistance of a graphic artist. Now whether or not this artist totally understood the numbers she was graphing, she brought to the assignment artistic training that taught her the appropriate typefaces to use and a good sense of the use of color.

With today's graphing software available to everyone, we have graphs being produced by people untrained in the artistic side of things. Just as the advent of word processors—with availability to unlimited typefaces—brought forth a sea of documents crowded with far too many different (and sometimes terribly gaudy) fonts, so too does the advent of graphing programs yield graphs with far too many colors and very often with incompatible color schemes. Poorly produced charts often resemble a garish rainbow of colors unleashed in one graph.

Color is most effective when it is used sparingly. If overused, it can confuse, even "blind" a viewer. A second rule of graphing, then, is to use color sparingly and with total purpose in mind. Never use color simply because it is available!

Assign Universal Meaning to Specific Colors

Color in a business graphic can not only make a chart more aesthetically attractive, it uniquely can convey some basic meaning as well. If one sees a bar chart with some red bars coupled with some green bars, the immediate assumption would be that the green-colored bars represented some basically good outcomes, while the red-colored bars would probably be understood to convey poor outcomes or trouble areas. If there were more green bars than red, the viewer would most probably conceive an overall positive outcome; if the red bars outnumbered the green, the same viewer would be alerted to a deteriorating situation. All of this communication occurs simply on the basis of the astute use of colors!

Because of their inherent, almost universal meanings, watch your use of the red and green colors, and their companion color, orange. It is probably a good idea to withhold these three colors from representing any particular customer group, using them instead to convey direction and severity of outcomes.

In its handbook on the use of color, Hewlett-Packard (1991) suggests using the color wheel (see Figure 7.4) to select appropriate colors and shades for graphing. It offers the following guidelines for the selection of particular colors:

- Do select one color or hue from the wheel to unify all of your graphics (your organization's logo color is often very appropriate). Varying the lightness or darkness of this color allows for differentiation and variety.
- Do not select opposite or complementary colors; this will distract the audience's eye, because of the severe contrast. If you must use complementary colors, do adjust the saturation or value of one of the colors to achieve greater visual harmony.
- Do try to select colors adjacent on the color wheel, this creates visual harmony in your graphics.
- Do achieve contrast by selecting hues with one or two colors between them. Try to use darker colors in the background and brighter colors in the foreground.
- Do keep in mind that black and white are colors too. As you design with color, plan your use of black, white, and other colors accordingly.

If you assign one group of colors to certain customer types or performance attributes in one chart, do not change the color assignments later. Instead, maintain the same color representation throughout your graphs. You will find your management picks up on the color assignment

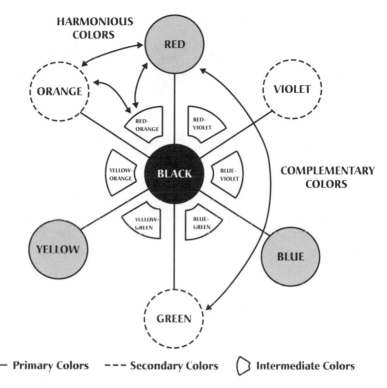

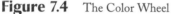

Figure 7.4   The Color Wheel

convention quite easily and is then aided throughout the remainder of the report. (It is amazing to see how many times reports are compiled with color graph after color graph in which colors are seemingly randomly assigned on a graph-by-graph basis with absolutely no rationale or established color key. In these cases, the chartist has failed to recognize the value of a uniform color key.)

Frequently your color graphs will ultimately be photocopied in black and white, so it is very helpful if you also assign a unique texture or shading pattern to each customer group and color as well. Then, as the color charts are black and white photocopied, the shading or texture pattern will nevertheless convey the meanings the colors had originally represented.

Increasing the Appeal of Graphs with Symbols

All of your graphs and charts can be made more personal and more interesting by including symbols in your graphs. One of the most compelling modifications you can make, is to replace the innocuous bar in bar charts with symbols (or stack or row of symbols) that are more relevant to your organization. For example, a bar can become a line of cars, a stack of money—bills or coins. Even without taking the time to fill the entire bar, a symbol can placed at the end of each bar to add to the "visualness" of your graphic (see Figure 7.5).

What to Graph?

For response scales within a customer satisfaction survey there will be numerous different quantities that can be graphed. For example, means of numerical ratings, top box scores on response scales, percent (of excellent) scores, and so on. There is no right or wrong answer. The satisfaction professional must decide which is most meaningful for his particular management. An important point: once a decision is reached, the adopted convention should be used consistently throughout the report or results presentation. Avoid switching carelessly from graphing means to top-box percentages and back again.

How to Create Graphs

We've alluded to computer graphing software without being specific. There are three classifications of computer programs the satisfaction professional can use to produce striking charts and graphs. The programs are:

- graphing programs (Harvard Graphics®, Freelance®, PowerPoint®, and Correl Draw®)
- spreadsheet programs (Lotus 123®, Excel®, Quattro®)
- statistical packages with graphing routines (SPSS, SYSTAT, SAS, BMDP, and Statgraphfix)

These programs are all capable of generating most of the graphs and charts shown in this book. Some will do so with less work, some will be more compatible with the professional's other software—particularly the word processor used. It is generally a good idea to stay within the same "family" if you wish good "portability." For example, a graph that is created for inclusion in the written report must be able to be imported into the word processing document. At the same time, the professional might also wish a full-color transparency to be made of the chart for a presentation. Usually, if you create a graph in a graphing program (or possibly a spreadsheet program) you will have the maximum flexibility of being able to both include the graph in your report as well as to create stand-alone transparencies, slides, or even electronic slide shows.

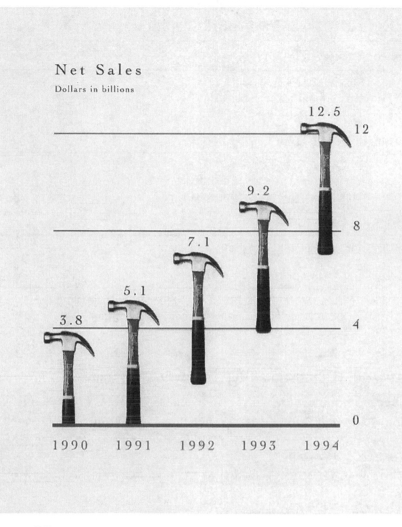

Figure 7.5   Enhancing Graphs with Symbols and Logos

Reprinted with permission, The Home Depot Inc., *1995 Annual Report*, Atlanta.

Table 7.2   Uses for Report Graphics

Depicting Magnitude

Identifying Attribute Importance
Reporting Performance on Attributes
Isolating Key Driver Attributes

Tracking Growth, Trends, and Change

Showing Growth in Overall Satisfaction
Monitoring Change on Performance Attributes
Monitoring Change of Attribute Importance

Displaying Composition

Depicting the Composition of the Customerbase

Establishing Order, Sequence, or Flow

Planning the Steps and Timing Involved in the Conduct of a CSM Process
Charting Remedial Actions to be Taken to Improve Satisfaction

THE USES FOR GRAPHS IN CSM

Earlier the four general roles for business graphics were identified, demonstrating: magnitude, trends and change, composition, and order or sequence. In this section we will examine more closely the graphing opportunities in satisfaction reporting. Table 7.2 reviews one or more applications within each of the four roles.

Reporting Importance

One of the most important results of most customer satisfaction programs is the discovery of priorities—usually customers' priorities. The relative importance weights customers assign to various internal procedures, to product attributes, or to their own requirements all help us focus a response in accordance with the importance of the issues. So the communication of discovered importance weights is one of our most important analytical and reporting goals. Numerical lists can obviously communicate the same information, but probably not as vividly as some of the graphical techniques we discuss here. For purposes of comparing three charts for graphing importance, we will use the data in Table 7.3.

Table 7.3 Importance of Service Attributes

Ltr.	Attribute	Total Customers	Northeast Customers	Central Customers	South Customers	West Customers
A	Reasonable rates	9.2	9.0	9.2	9.0	9.4
B	Accurate billing statements	8.3	8.7	8.7	9.0	8.9
C	Speedy claims service	8.4	8.6	8.0	8.3	8.6
D	Policies with relevant coverage	7.6	7.1	7.1	8.5	7.8
E	Simple application process	7.2	7.2	7.9	6.8	6.8
F	Timely billing statements	6.7	8.8	6.1	6.0	6.0
G	Knowledgeable reps	6.4	7.3	6.1	5.7	6.6
H	Financial strength of carrier	6.0	6.4	5.9	5.9	5.6
I	Understanding my needs	5.4	5.7	4.6	5.5	5.9
J	Convenient hours of operation	4.3	4.0	4.5	3.9	4.6

Question: *Using a scale from 1 to 10, where 1 represents "not at all important" and 10 represents "extremely important," please rate the importance of each of the following characteristics of automobile insurance and automobile insurance carriers.*

Source: From *Attitude Measurement for Marketing Strategies.* Reprinted with permission.

This data represents importance judgments of 10 service characteristics collected from four different customer groups, in this case defined by the area of North America in which they reside/conduct business.

"Thermometer" Charts

A unidimensional scale showing the relative position of each of several product attributes, can be aptly described as a "thermometer" chart. Just as our body temperature describes the health of a human being, the relative "temperatures" or importance ratings can depict the health of an organization. The author believes that "temperature" as a real life analog helps most people understand exactly what is portrayed in this simple, yet very important chart type. Figure 7.6 shows a typical thermometer chart, this one shows the importance ratings the total customerbase (in Table 7.3) accorded the service attributes.

To construct a thermometer chart, one need only produce ratings for each of the items to be plotted. The scale to be used can be average ratings on a 1–10 scale (for example, financial strength of carrier—6.0) or the ratings could be rescaled as percentages of perhaps an ideal score (for example, financial strength of carrier—60 percent). In a later chapter we will discuss Thurstone scaling as an easy way to derive comparable importance weights for graphing in a thermometer graph.

The thermometer chart is best when depicting one group, the total customerbase (as above), for example. When you wish to display relative importance ratings among several groups, you could use multiple, side-by-side thermometers, but a bar chart may be a better choice.

Bar Charts

Bar charts are ideal for depicting the relative importance ratings between several groups, for example the four sales territories in Table 7.3. To create such a chart, the formal request to a graphing program is for a "clustered bar" chart. Figure 7.7 shows a bar chart for relative importance ratings between two of the four customer groups, *West Customers* versus *Northeast Customers*.

Notice that as the length of the bars for any one attribute become more different in length, this will trigger questions of statistical difference. For example, considering *"timely billing statements,"* are the two sales territories significantly different? One must be prepared within a clustered bar chart to indicate where the depicted differences *are* statistically significant. In the example this is accomplished by adding a simple asterisk for each

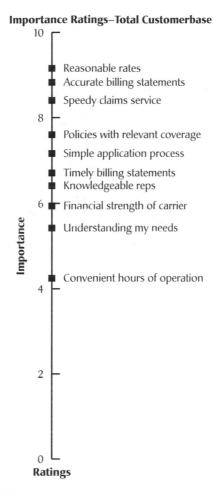

Figure 7.6   A Thermometer Chart

difference that is statistically different. Of course, as the number of groups to be compared exceeds two, the depiction of significant differences becomes much more difficult.

Vertical or Horizontal Bar Charts?

The author personally favors horizontal bar charts. They are easily placed within report text (because of their compatibility with "portrait" printing). And, they allow more space along the left-hand margin for attribute labels.

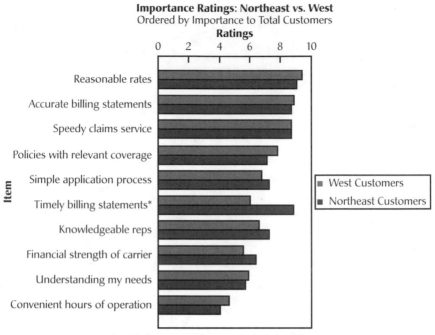

Figure 7.7   A Bar Chart for Importance Ratings Among Customer Groups

Radar Charts

"Radar" or "spider" charts are a relatively new graphic to customer satisfaction. Depending upon your organization, they may be easily understood, or not. Engineering-oriented organizations seem to pick up on them most easily. They are a variant on the bar chart. Figure 7.8A shows a how a radar chart would display the importance weights for the Total Customer group. A radar chart can also be used to compare findings among groups, as among the four sales territories listed in Table 7.3. Figure 7.8B shows a comparison of the attributes' importance as judged by the four customer groups. As the number of groups to be compared exceeds four or five, radar charts tend to become somewhat more confusing.

Notice there is a vector for each attribute. The vectors originate from the origin. Each attribute's score is indicated on its vector. The scores are usually joined by a line, forming an ellipsoid. The extent to which the ellipsoids representing different groups overlap or depart offers vivid proof of the similarities or differences between the groups being compared. This

Importance Ratings—Total Customers

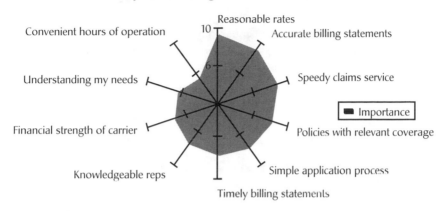

Figure 7.8A   A Radar or Spider Chart for Importance Ratings

Importance Ratings by Customer Group

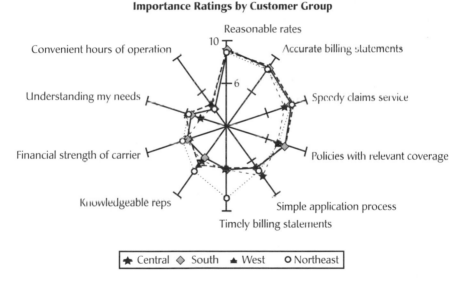

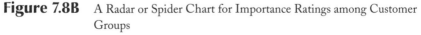

Figure 7.8B   A Radar or Spider Chart for Importance Ratings among Customer Groups

method of identifying "profile differences," using the ellipsoids, is a bit easier than attempting to identify profile differences in a conventional clustered bar chart. This ease of comparison causes some professionals to prefer radar charts.

Reporting Performance

Rating *performance* is the other most important aspect of customer satis-faction programs. It is critical because beyond the measurement of overall satisfaction, some performance measurements must be taken to link over-all satisfaction to specific areas of manageable improvement. While bar and spider (radar) charts are, again, very useful graphics, it may be con-fusing for your audience if you use the same type chart for two different quantities (importance *and* performance). On the other hand, sometimes this can work very nicely.

Bar and Radar Charts

Just as bar charts and radar charts were used to depict the relative impor-tance of various issues of a product or service, they can similarly be used to show the relative performance of an organization on a battery of per-formance attributes. In Table 7.4 we have reported perceived perfor-mance on the service characteristics whose importance was reported in Table 7.3. Figure 7.9 uses a bar chart to depict perceived performance on the ten performance attributes (Table 7.4) for our organization.

Indicating Change

Once performance has been plotted, a frequently asked additional ques-tion, is "*How* has performance changed from the last measurement?" This creates the need for a combination graphic showing both current perfor-mance and portraying change from a previous measurement. The easiest way to answer this question is to institute a separate column at the side of the bar chart to symbolically show direction and magnitude of change. One can use arrowheads (pointing up for increases, down for decreases), plus and negative signs, or even numerical change scores (for example: +5 percent, −15 percent). Managers who will be viewing such combined charts will have to be "trained" first to look at the current performance (the length of the bar) and then, secondarily, to look at the change indi-cator (See Figure 7.10).

Bar Charts—Against Goals

As performance is assessed, there will undoubtedly be goals against which it is to be measured. These goals may have been set by manage-ment (that is, "We should attain performance ratings on all attributes of a minimum 7.5 on a 10-point scale," or "We will strive to attain a 'com-pletely satisfied' rating from at least 50 percent of our customers"). The

Table 7.4 Performance on Service Attributes

Ltr.	Attribute	Our Organization	Competitor A	Competitor B	Competitor C
A	Reasonable rates	8.6	7.4	8.2	7.2
F	Accurate billing statements	8.7	6.7	9.0	8.9
H	Speedy claims service	7.6	7.0	8.3	8.6
G	Policies with relevant coverage	9.1	8.1	8.5	7.8
C	Simple application process	8.2	7.9	8.6	8.6
B	Timely billing statements	8.8	6.6	8.2	8.0
I	Knowledgeable reps	7.3	8.3	9.2	7.9
D	Financial strength of carrier	7.4	8.1	8.4	7.6
E	Understanding my needs	7.7	7.2	8.2	8.6
J	Convenient hours of operation	9.0	7.1	8.5	7.7

Question: Using a scale from 1 to 10, where 1 represents "poor" and 10 represents "excellent," please rate the performance you've experienced from our company on each of the following characteristics of automobile insurance and automobile insurance carriers.

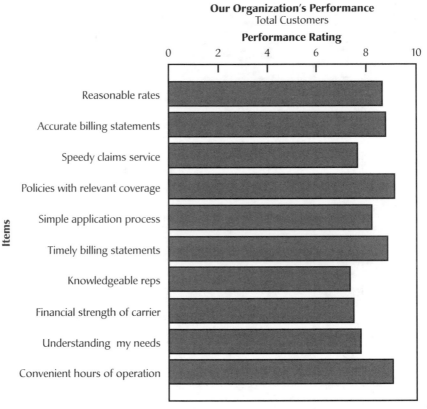

Figure 7.9   A Bar Chart Depicting Perceived Performance

goal could be the previous period's measurement, in which case the objective might be to "score no lower than the previous score, possibly higher." In Figure 7.11 a goal of "a minimum of 8.0 on all performance attributes" has been identified by a solid grid-line at 8.0. This chart format makes it clear, not all performance ratings have achieved the sought standard.

Comparative Bar Charts—Against Competition
When measurements of competitors' performance are available, this competitive data makes an excellent pairing with the organization's own performance rating data. Figure 7.12 depicts our organization's performance against that of two competitors, A and B. Again, be prepared for

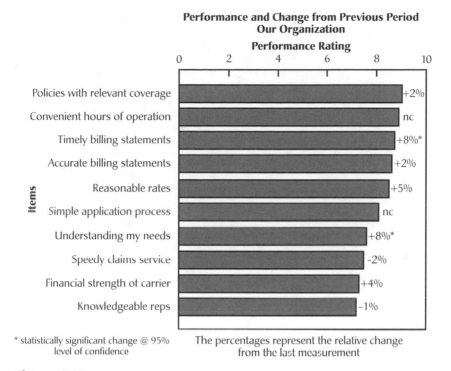

Figure 7.10   Performance Change

the question of statistical significance (of the difference between the scores). It is a good idea to anticipate the question, by adding a significance test to the graph.

Reporting Change

"One thing is certain, change is inevitable," so the saying goes. And so it certainly is with customers' ratings and their satisfaction with our products and services. Their expectations are constantly heightened both by our own improvements and by the challenges of our competitors' improvements and enhancements in their products, their services and the servicing they offer. Customers' consequent ratings of our performance are apt to change based on their higher level of expectations.

The measurement of change and the consequent depiction of change becomes, then, one of the most important discoveries from each fielding of your customer satisfaction survey. (If your are measuring satisfaction continuously—as has been advocated in this book—you probably

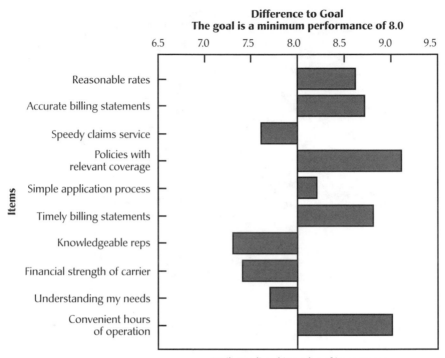

Difference to Goal
The goal is a minimum performance of 8.0

Figure 7.11   A Bar Chart Showing Performance Against Goals

will not want to report change on a continuous basis, but rather may wish to accumulate enough data over several weeks or months and report change on a quarterly basis. If you do otherwise, you may find smaller samples of returns providing a rather "bumpy" up and down story.)

Line or Trend Charts

The most common chart for depicting change or a trend in the level of data is the line chart (see Figure 7.13). Because the horizontal axis is used for time periods, the line chart can summarize scores over a fairly substantial time period. The line chart is also easily adapted to comparing satisfaction scores between different organizations. Different line-types and symbols can be used to represent each organization or customer group to be compared (see Figure 7.14).

Figure 7.12 Comparative Performance

Bar Chart for Changes

When it is necessary to show changes on a battery of items (like performance attributes), a bar chart showing deviation from the previous score may be a very effective display. There are essentially two ways to do this.

Deviations from the Past. One can institute an arbitrary "past performance" axis, which will represent each variable's previous (but admittedly different) performance score. Then, the bars will represent either positive or negative shifts from the previous score. Ideally, positive shifts should be colored green to show improvement; negative shifts red to show deterioration. Attributes should be ordered (top to bottom) according to their current performance or importance scores. But the problem

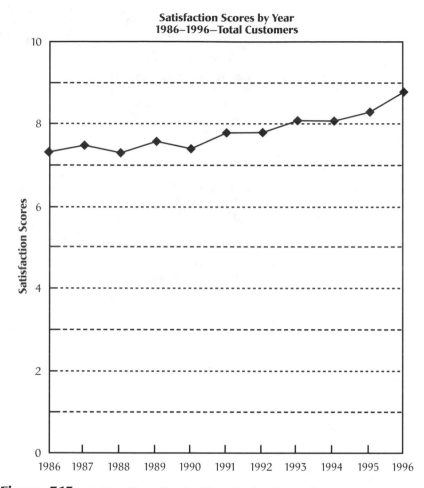

Figure 7.13   A Line Chart Showing Trend in Satisfaction Data

with this format is its inability to show exact levels of performance of each of the attributes, since deviations are all shown from the arbitrary "previous score axis" (see Figure 7.15).

Stacked Bar for Increases/Decreases.   A stacked bar can correct the problem of the arbitrary previous score axis, by actually plotting the previous performance and then showing the improvement as a green added bar segment, or as a red segment showing decrease (see Figure 7.16).

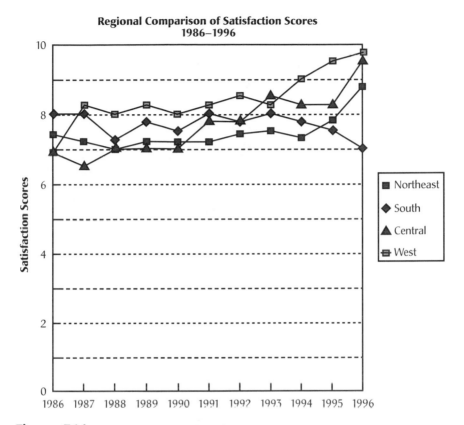

Figure 7.14   Line Chart Comparing Groups

Box and Whisker Charts

Probably one of the most informative charts, albeit somewhat complex, is the "box and whisker" or the "hi-lo-close" chart. This graph happily displays current level and then, perhaps a range that accounts for previous scores. The "box" (or the lo-hi range) shows the confidence interval about the previous period's mean, while the "whisker" or "close" shows the current score. When the "whisker" exceeds or lags the box, a significant increase or decrease is identified. All of this occurs in a framework displaying all of the performance attributes, scaled by their current performance, so their relative performance is directly readable (see Figure 7.17).

To remind viewers of the relative importance of the graphed performance attributes, they could be ordered on the vertical axis by importance or by current performance (our choice in Figure 7.17).

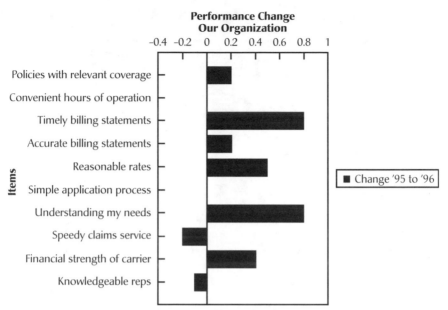

Figure 7.15   Bar Chart Comparing Performance against the Past

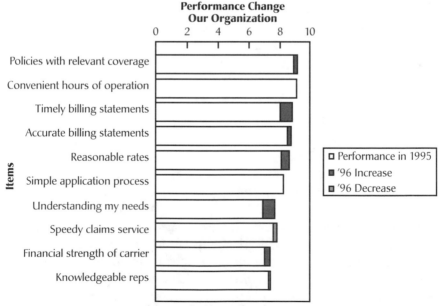

Figure 7.16   Stacked Bar for Change Scores

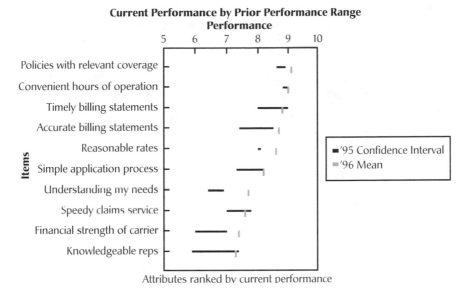

Figure 7.17   Bar and Whisker Chart for Change

GRAPHS DEPICTING ACTIONABILITY

The Quadrant Chart

For every satisfaction survey that has been fielded and has collected the simultaneous measurements of product/service attribute importance and performance, there has been the managerial question of how to allocate remedial attention and resources. The quadrant chart, first suggested by Martilla and James (1977), has been universally employed as an excellent answer to this question. The typical quadrant chart is formed by creating a grid represented by importance ratings on the vertical axis and performance ratings on the horizontal axis. This chart is generally subdivided by drawing a vertical line at the average performance rating for all attributes and a horizontal line at that point on the vertical axis representing the average importance rating given the attributes. Four sectors or "quadrants" are formed by these two lines.

As one plots each attribute into this gridwork, the following logic is applied. If the organization is truly listening to its customers, then attributes ought to be delivered in proportion to their importance. That is, attributes plotted by their importance and performance ratings ought to

Table 7.5   A Prototypical Quadrant Chart

Importance

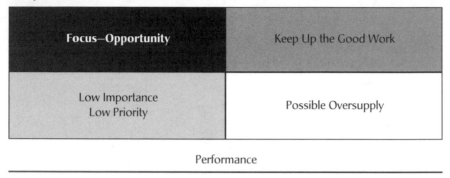

Focus—Opportunity	Keep Up the Good Work
Low Importance Low Priority	Possible Oversupply

Performance

form a "regression line" running from the lower left to the upper right. Attributes lying on (or near) this imaginary line would verify that they were perceived as delivered (performed) roughly proportional to their judged importance by customers. This happy condition describes an intelligent and responsive organization.

In actuality, while *some* attributes may lie on such an imaginary regression line, a great many attributes' importance and performance ratings will cause them to be plotted somewhere else in the two-by-two grid. Each of the quadrants has been described and carries a normative action strategy. These descriptions and strategies are shown in Table 7.5.

Those attributes lying in the lower left or upper right are in "okay" quadrants. In these quadrants performance is roughly proportional to importance. The requisite action for attributes in these two quadrants is to maintain their current levels of delivery. They are perceived to be supplied in proportion to their importance.

The two remaining quadrants offer opportunities for action. The lower right quadrant is labeled "oversupply" because attributes located in this quadrant are being delivered to a much greater extent than their judged importance warrants. If possible, performance on these attributes should be relaxed. This is an area where, quite possibly, more is being spent in time, money, or resources than is warranted by customers' expressions of importance. If possible, resources should be withdrawn from these variables to be applied elsewhere.

Finally, there is the upper left-hand quadrant. Here very important attributes are perceived as being underdelivered. Attributes in this quadrant signal an opportunity for improvement. But, one must be careful to determine *what type* of improvement is required. Customers' perception of under delivery may, in fact, be a "factually correct" perception.[1] If we can verify we are failing to offer as much of the attribute as is desired (for example, we are supplying less than competitors), then our mandate is to increase our performance on these attributes. Such a problem is clearly a *"product/service" problem.* But, what if we are reasonably certain we are supplying as much (or possibly more) than our competitors? If this is the case, we have a *"communication" problem.* That is, customers have apparently not been made aware of our delivery of these attributes to the point they credit us fairly for our performance. In these cases we must increase our customers' awareness of our delivery through the "management of evidence" (Vavra 1995).

In Figure 7.18 the ten attributes of Tables 7.3 and 7.4 are plotted according to the importance and performance scores reported in the Tables. Managers and quality improvement teams readily embrace quadrant charts because they logically identify courses of action with which to increase overall satisfaction.

The Competitive Quadrant Chart

The traditional quadrant chart is basically an "internal" analysis. That is, it looks at the organization's perceived performance in isolation from the category or the marketplace. A competitive quadrant chart can involve performance in a category in such a way as to show attributes whose *relative performance* is lacking.

A competitive quadrant chart is formed by again plotting importance on the vertical axis, but by replacing absolute performance on the horizontal axis with comparative performance. To plot a competitive quadrant chart, one requires judgments not only his organization's performance, but judgments of competitors' perceived performance as well. Generally, the crosshair on the horizontal axis will represent parity performance, a level at which our performance is equal to either the average of all competitors or the "best of class" competitor. Movement to the

----

[1]We are respecting the recognition that whatever customers perceive, is, by definition the reality with which the organization must deal. However, sometimes customers' perception(s) will be *consistent* with fact, other times *inconsistent* with fact. The extent to which customers' perceptions are consistent or inconsistent with fact determines *how* the organization must deal with them, not whether or not the organization accepts them.

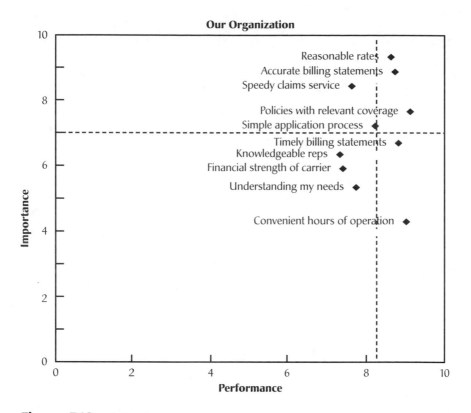

Figure 7.18   A Quadrant Chart

right of the crosshair will indicate attributes where the organization's performance is superior to that of competitors, to the left, attributes whose comparative performance is inferior to competitors. Figure 7.19 replots the attributes of Figure 7.17 with the data on competitors' performance shown in Table 7.4.

By creating a competitive quadrant chart, the satisfaction professional can identify attributes, improvement on which is dictated by the performance dynamics of her category. The competitive quadrant chart also identifies attributes on which there is leverageable superiority.

Leverage Analysis

Actionability is all about prioritizing. Simple customer judgments of attribute importance offer one way of prioritizing our attention and remedial

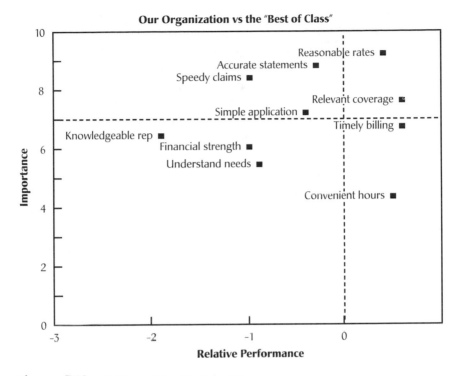

Figure 7.19   A Competitive Quadrant Chart

actions. A model developed by Kano (see Chapter 9 for a discussion) suggests another way of prioritizing based on importance. However, when one prioritizes based on importance alone, one may be overlooking other aspects of the market situation that could also help establish prioritization.

Leverage analysis builds on the priorities established by customers' importance judgments, adding the consideration of comparative performance in the marketplace. That is to say, if two attributes were about equal in performance, but our organization was perceived as comparatively disadvantaged in one and at parity on another, it would probably behoove us to focus on improving that attribute on which we were perceived as disadvantaged. So the goal in leverage analysis is to weight an attribute's importance by the competitive leverage to be gained by improving in that attribute. In Table 7.6 it is reasonably easy to see that while customers judge "reliability" to be the most important attribute, there is relatively little advantage to be gained from focusing on it, given the relative parity in the marketplace on "reliability." There is far more leverage to be developed by tackling the somewhat less important issue of "customer service," given our organization's perceived inferiority on this issue. The third attribute, "safety," has two disadvantages: it is lower in importance ratings and our organization already is perceived to be comparatively stronger on safety.

Table 7.6 is a worksheet for developing leverage ratings.

Expectational Analysis

The Dutch economist, Van Westendorf, created a very intriguing questioning scenario to help ascertain customers' expectations about prices. To ascertain customers' price sensitivities, Van Westendorf suggested asking three questions. The first ascertaining the lowest price at which a minimally functioning product entry could be purchased. The second identifying the highest price a customer would tolerate paying. And the third question eliciting the price the customer most likely expected to pay. This model has been adapted to attribute performance in a product or service category:[2]

- *minimal performance*   What is the absolute lowest level of performance a customer would accept, below which the product or service would be considered unfit for purchase?
- *superior performance*   What is the level of performance customers would consider "world class" performance? Generally customers can only imagine the conditions of superior performance. Occasionally they can reflect on their dealings with another organization in an entirely different category and translate the service they have received into the present category.
- *acceptable performance*   What is the level of performance customers most likely expect to receive? This level represents a realistic compromise from their perceptions of superior performance, since they are likely to excuse the supplier from achieving truly superior performance, though they would still desire it.

----

[2]The work on the expectation scale described here was developed with Douglas Snadecki (IBM Consulting Group) and Alan Ivey (Liberty Mutual Insurance Company). Their input and creativity is gratefully acknowledged.

Table 7.6 Example of Leverage Analysis

		Performance Ratings of			
Attribute	Importance	Our Organization	Organization A	Our Advantage/ Disadvantage	Attribute's Leverage
Reliability	3.5	7.5	7.4	0.1	0.35
Customer Service	3.1	6.9	8.1	-1.2	-3.72
Safety	2.9	7.5	6.6	0.9	2.61

Leverage = Importance × Advantage/Disadvantage

Our Organization's Leverage for Reliability $3.5 \times .1 = .35$

Our Organization's Leverage for Customer Service $3.1 \times -1.2 = -3.72$

Our Organization's Leverage for Safety $2.9 \times .9 = 2.61$

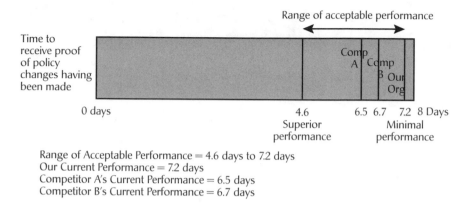

Range of Acceptable Performance = 4.6 days to 7.2 days
Our Current Performance = 7.2 days
Competitor A's Current Performance = 6.5 days
Competitor B's Current Performance = 6.7 days

Figure 7.20   A Competitive Leverage Chart

   These three levels of performance can be operationalized using a sequence of questions similar to the following:

1. What is the lowest level of performance on this attribute that you would *tolerate* before you would consider buying a different brand or switching to a different provider? (If the product were a computer monitor, the attribute might be screen pitch, in which case, .31mm might be the minimal resolution that would be tolerated.)
2. What is level of performance would you consider as superior? (In the monitor example, .22mm might be considered "superior" performance.)
3. What level of performance do you perceive you are currently receiving? (It is likely the customer would report a current resolution of .28mm.)

   Given this information, the analyst is in the fortunate position of being able to map out these various levels of expectation. These diagrams, arraying performance from minimal to superior describe a "spectrum" of performance, hence they have been given the name, "spectrum charts." Figure 7.20 shows the spectrum chart resulting from the hypothetical data collected above. The focus, of course, is on how close to superior our organization's ratings are.

   Beyond the graphical approach, there is a way to quantify the relationships depicted in the spectrum chart. A numerical concept called the "performance ratio" has been conceived. This ratio describes how much of the way from minimal to superior performance a brand or organization has progressed on a specific performance attribute. On the measure, 0 percent would indicate performance only at the *minimal* level; 100 percent would indicate performance at the *superior* level. Any number in between would suggest opportunity to improve ultimately reaching 100 percent and superiority. Table 7.7 shows how performance ratios may be calculated and compared.

There is value in comparing one's performance ratios with competitors in the category, or with the market in general. An "action standard" of 75 percent or higher and a lead of 25 percentage points or more has been established to identify performance that is advantaged enough to be considered "leverageable" against competition. In Table 7.7, our performance ratio for time to assess damage is 1.08. This ratio exceeds 75 percent and we lead competition (60 percent) by at least 25 percentage points. This attribute is identified as a leverageable point for us.

REFERENCES

Hewlett-Packard. *A Guide to Using Color.* Camas, WA, Part No. C2113-90030, 1991.

Martilla, John A., and John C. James. "Importance-Performance Analysis," *Journal of Marketing.* Vol. 41, no. 1 (January 1977): 77–79.

Tufte, Edward R. *The Visual Display of Quantitative Information.* Cheshire, Connecticut: Graphics Press, 1983.

Vavra, Terry G. *Aftermarketing: How to Keep Customers for Life Through Relationship Marketing.* Burr Ridge, IL: Irwin Professional Publishing, 1995.

Table 7.7 The Performance Ratio

Metric		Acceptable		Ratings		Performance Ratio*		Leverage
		Minimum	Superior	Our Organization	Best of Class	Our Organization	Best of Class	
Waiting time for Rep to return calls	hours	36	4	2	4	106%	100%	both
Waiting time to receive proof of coverage	days	10	4	5	3	83%	117%	boc
Time for company to assess damage	days	30	5	3	15	108%	60%	us
Number of conversations to fully understand options and coverage	conversations	4	1	3	3	33%	33%	neither

*Performance Ratio $= 1 - \left[\dfrac{current - superior}{minimum - superior} \right]$

DISCOURSE: DISCUSSING AND ACTING ON THE FINDINGS

The phase that is missing in all too many satisfaction measurement processes is this phase, the phase in which the information gleaned from the survey process is properly analyzed and then placed into a quality improvement process that involves top level management. The goal is to not let the survey be the end of a program, but rather the start of a quality improvement initiative in which specific managers or departments take ownership of the identified problems or opportunities and address them as challenges to improve.

This phase also marks the reinitiation of the Discovery and Design phases readying the process for its next fielding.

findings
Discourse

CHAPTER 8

Advanced CSM Analysis

OVERVIEW

Beyond the more intuitive world of univariate and bivariate analysis (discussed in Chapter 6), is a whole constellation of statistical techniques that have been developed to deal with *groups of variables*, hence their name, *multi*variate techniques. While they can be intimidating to read about and learn, the satisfaction professional of today should be verbally comfortable with at least five of the more commonly used multivariate techniques. Although he may choose not to conduct any multivariate analysis himself, a basic understanding of the methods will still help him determine when a particular technique could be useful, and what to expect from applying the technique. This knowledge will make the satisfaction professional a better *customer* of a statistical consultant's collaboratory work.

We will also take an "excursion" into an exciting new way to look at CSM data. Though most satisfaction professionals deal with satisfaction data as if it were "flat" (two-dimensional), it is no more flat than is our world. It is always composed of several different "modes" or planes. In this chapter we will examine different "modes" of customer satisfaction data. The "modes" or dimensions include, but are not limited to, customers, attributes, brands (or competitors), and measurement occasions. The modes conceptually combine to form a cube or geometric figure of higher dimension. Though easy to consider, the resulting datacube is unfortunately never directly analyzed. Conventionality has dictated that the different dimensions of the datacube be compressed and the data looked at in easier to handle two-dimensioned arrays. When the data cube is compressed for analytical or reporting convenience, it is valuable to remind ourselves of the dimension(s) that have been hidden in the compression.

MULTIVARIATE ANALYTICAL TECHNIQUES

Multivariate techniques can be divided into two basic groups: techniques for exploring *relationships* and techniques for determining *dependency*. Figure 8.1 shows this division and some of the techniques appropriate to each need. Exploring the relationships in your data has to do with how the questions in your survey may be related; aligning themselves to address basic characteristics. Or, relationships can describe the different, basic customer-types in your customerbase (that is, how customers may be combined into segments with similar needs, likes, etc.). Determining the dependencies in your data addresses the important question of how easily one (or more) questions can predict the level of another question. The most obvious example of this investigation is the search for performance variables that are "key drivers," those performance attributes whose ratings are most closely related to customers' overall satisfaction.

Multivariate Analysis to Explore the Structure of Data

In this section we will discuss three multivariate techniques (factor analysis, cluster analysis, and multidimensional scaling) that are useful for describing the relationships existing among things, be they questionnaire scales, customers, or competitive brands or products.

Factor Analysis

The Method.   Factor analysis is a statistical procedure that "decomposes" a data matrix into its bare *structural* essentials. The technique is based on an assumption first tackled by psychologists in intelligence testing, that

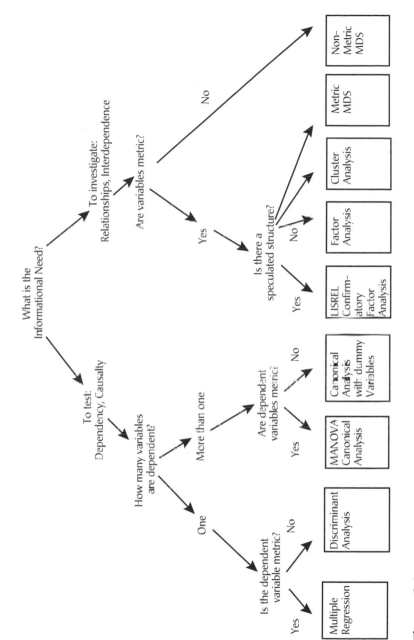

Figure 8.1   A Map of Multivariate Techniques

325

although they asked people multitudinous questions to measure intelligence, there would probably be a basic set of aptitudes discovered. Factor analysis was originally used to identify the basic modes of intelligence and how many questions might be measuring the same aptitudes and might, therefore, be redundant. The method decomposes any data matrix into roots (*eigenvalues*) and factors (variable *loadings* on the factors). The roots tell us how many basic dimensions (aspects of evaluation) there are in our data. The related factor loadings describe each dimension in terms of our original performance attributes. The loadings show which attributes are together measuring the same aspect of our product or service.

With today's statistical computer packages it is very easy to conduct a factor analysis on *any* data set, yet because of the number of issues that ought to be addressed in properly specifying the factor analysis, and the complexity of the interpretation of results, it is advantageous to know something of the mechanics of the analysis.

There are two basic factor analytic models, *principal components* and *factor analysis*. The primary difference between the models is that principal components (the model most often implemented by statistical packages) assumes 100 percent of the variance of the model can be assigned to "common" factors. Factor analysis, the alternative model, allows the existence of "unique" factors and thus relaxes demands made on the decomposition, requiring that less than 100 percent of the variation need be accounted for. Generally "communalities" are estimated for each variable (the amount of variation each variable has in common with all of the other variables in the system). The factor analytic model is only held responsible for accounting for the amount of variation represented by the level of communality, no more. The differences between the models is not widely understood. To make matters more confusing, principal components as an analytic procedure is normally executed within the "Factor Analysis" program of most of the major statistical packages.

The principal components model is probably the most meaningful for the satisfaction professional. Typically, we will have many more variables to measure than the customer has dimensions of appraisal. Further, it is likely that the performance attributes we utilize are all related to each other, reducing the likelihood of unique factors. The principal components model can help us better understand our customers' points of view, by combining our performance attributes into basic evaluative dimensions just as customers have combined them in their evaluations. These combinations of attributes (factors) show us how constrained (or simplistic) our customers' view of our product or service really is.

Decisions You Will Have to Make.   While the purpose of this book is not to teach advanced statistics, it will still be desirable for you to know some of the basic considerations in ordering a factor analysis of your data. There are a few questions you will have to answer as you order a factor analysis:

1. What form do you want your data matrix in for the factoring process?
   - There are essentially only three possibilities. The most common input matrix is a correlation matrix of the variables. However, because the correlation matrix removes two valuable pieces of information (the mean and the actual variance), it sometimes produces less interesting solutions.
   - A variance-covariance matrix is the second form of input matrix. Only the mean, or level has been removed from the data to produce this matrix, and the analysis is sometimes more useful.
   - Finally, if the scales are all in the same metric (for example, 1–10 ratings) and have approximately level means, the third form of input matrix can be used, a simple cross-products matrix.
   - Note: Not all statistical packages allow the researcher to choose the form of input matrix to be used. If you must use a correlation matrix your analysis will not be flawed, it may simply lack some information that might have been offered by factoring one of the other input matrices.
2. How many factors do you wish to retain?
   - You may have a hypothesis about how many basic dimensions your customers will use to evaluate your product/service. If so, it is fair to ask the analysis to attempt to collapse the variables into that dimensionality space.
   - Otherwise, you can use one of two methods to allow the structure of the data to determine the dimensionality of your factor analysis. The most common decision rule, and one implemented by almost all factor analytic packages, is the "eigenvalue = 1" rule. The logic here is that no additional factors ought to be retained after the last factor accounts for a variation of only 1 (essentially the amount of variation attributable to just one variable).
   - The final method of determining the number of factors is referred to as the "scree test." *Scree* is a term for the clutter of boulders at the bottom of a mountain or steep cliff. To use the scree test, one plots the magnitude of the successive eigenvalues (roots) of the

decomposition against their root number. The resulting line graph will take the form of a steeply descending line. At some root number, the line will break and level off. It is at this point that the number of roots (factors) is identified.

3. Do you wish your factor solution rotated to simplest structure?

   - A factor solution is indefinite, that is it is always subject to some transformation. A number of procedures have been designed to rotate the factor solution to "simplest structure." Simple structure is usually defined by some objective criterion. An additional judgment is whether the satisfaction professional requires the factors to be uncorrelated ("orthogonal") or will allow correlation among them ("oblique"). Conventionally orthogonal rotations have been used because of their relatively easier interpretation. Cooper (1994) argues for an oblique solution, reasoning that while the original derivation of factors appropriately demanded independency that, in terms of factor composition, independency may be an unrealistic constraint.

   - The most common orthogonal rotation criterion is the *varimax* rotation. The varimax rotation attempts to rotate the factors in a way such that a maximum amount of variation is allocated to the first and each successive factor. This often results in a preponderance of attributes assigned to the first factor.

   - An increasingly popular rotation is the *equamax* criterion. The equamax rotation spreads variation across all retained factors in an "equal as possible" way. Because it produces a solution with attributes fairly evenly divided across factors, it may be more useful (than the varimax rotation) in customer satisfaction surveys.

4. Do you want to produce factor scores?

   - Factor scores are a way of creating a raw data file for your customers, which includes the calculated scores on the discovered factors for each customer. The scores approximate how your customers might have rated your product/service if you only asked them to rate your product/service on the discovered factors rather than on the raw variables that they originally answered.

   - Factor scores are useful if you will be clustering your customers, looking for basic types of customers. These groupings can be based on how they rated your product/service. In this case, factor scores are the better variables with which to cluster your customers rather than the original variables since the original variables are intercorrelated.

Using Factor Analysis to Simplify Your CSM Surveys. The value of factor analysis for the satisfaction professional, is the technique's ability to simplify the large evaluative datasets we collect from customers. If we administer 30 performance attributes, because our exploratory research and internal discussions have identified 30 questions, we are no doubt overcomplicating a decision that the customer probably makes using far fewer evaluations. Principal components can help us test this notion and identify exactly which fewer evaluative dimensions customers actually use. With this knowledge, it is customary to consider reducing the 30 attributes (originally asked in your questionnaire) to a smaller number. The way in which the attributes loaded on the factors would identify attributes that best represented the basic, evaluative dimensions, and could, by themselves, represent yet other attributes, which loaded on the same factors.

An Example of Factor Analysis Applied to Customer Satisfaction Data. To demonstrate factor analysis and the other multivariate tools in this chapter, we will use the medical equipment data in Table 8.1. The 15 performance attributes (1a–1o) represent different operational aspects of a piece of medical equipment. Even though the satisfaction measurement team may have done everything possible to try to eliminate redundancy, the measures still may be correlated among themselves, such that a smaller number of performance attributes would have exhaustively captured customers' true feelings about the medical product.

Submitting the ratings of 100 customers on these 15 attributes to a factor analysis will help determine how much correlation exists among them. The goal is both to understand which attributes are used by customers to apparently convey the same judgment, and how many major judgments (items of information) are contained in the performance ratings. The SPSS factor analysis routine was used for this solution. Figure 8.2 shows the output that begins with a listing of the variables, their means and standard deviations. The next section of output confirms the value of factoring this data. The "Communalities" are the amount of variation each variable has in common with all others.[1] These communalities, all above 0.6, suggest a substantial amount of intercorrelation among the ratings on these performance variables. Their magnitude confirms the

----

[1]Communalities are essentially the R^2s when each variable is used as a dependent variable and all other variables are used as independent variables to predict the other variable.

Table 8.1   Medical Equipment Satisfaction Data

Item No.	Positions	Question No.	Contents	Abbreviation
1	1–4		ID Number	
2	5	1a	Salespeople's professionalism	CSR's Prof
3	6	1b	Salespeople's follow-up/ responsiveness	Res Foll-up
4	7	1c	Accuracy of invoicing	Inv Accur
5	8	1d	Ease of operation	Ease of Op
6	9	1e	Product features	Prod Feat
7	10	1f	Product reliability	Prod Rel
8	11	1g	Product durability	Prod Dur
9	12	1h	In service support	In-serv Sup
10	13	1i	Training materials	Trng Mat
11	14	1j	Consultant's competence	Cons Comp
12	15	1k	Consultant's professionalism	Cons Prof
13	16	1l	Biomedical engineering training	Bio Eng Trng
14	17	1m	Spare parts availability	Prts Avail
15	18	1n	Phone support availability	Supp Avail
16	19	1o	Factory repair quality	Repr Qual
17	20	2	Overall satisfaction	
18	21	3	Recommend purchase of XYZ's products	
19	22–23	4a	Purchase process	
20	24–25	4b	Order Process	
21	26–27	4c	Products	
22	28–29	4d	Educational Support	
23	30–31	4e	Biomedical Engineering Support	
24	32–33	4f	Technical Support	
25	34	5a	Influence	
26	35	5b	Years Experience	
27	36	6	Job Title	
28	37	7	Cluster membership	
29	38	8	Satisfaction group (for discriminant analysis)	
30	39–45		Region	

decision to employ factor analysis as a useful way to eliminate this intercorrelation.

To determine the number of factors, the "eigenvalue = 1" criterion was used. The eigenvalues (or "roots") begin with 6.786, which accounts for 45.2 percent of the total variance, and end with the fourth root, of

Table 8.2   Interpreted Factor Loadings

Factor 1	Factor 2	Factor 3	Factor 4
Consultant's competency	Invoice accuracy	Product reliability	Biomedical engineering training
Consultant's professionalism	CSR's professionalism	Product durability	Spare parts availability
Training materials	Responsiveness of follow-up	Ease of operation	Factory repair quality
In-service support	Phone support availability	Product features	
Consulting and In-Service	*After-Sale Follow-Up*	*Product Features and Reliability*	*Repair Support*

1.090. The four factors have been rotated with the equamax routine, to increase the utility of the factor "loadings." Factor loadings—the correlation of each attribute with the four factors—are displayed in their rotated form in the lower portion of Figure 8.2. The program has sorted and ranked the attributes according to which factor they load on. (An attribute or variable is said to "load" on that factor with which it has the highest correlation—simply examine each variable's row to identify the highest entry.) The first four attributes, beginning with *Consultant Competency* and ending with *In-Service Support* all comprise the first factor. The composition of each of the three remaining factors is similarly shown.

These four "factors" may be considered as *evaluative dimensions*. They summarize the major ways the 100 customers evaluate or judge the medical apparatus. To make the factors more useful for discussion, it is possible to label or name each of the four factors as has been done in Table 8.2. This is a subjective process. One simply looks at the attributes that compose each factor and selects a word or concept that seems to summarize the array of attributes. For example, in Table 8.2 the first factor has been labeled a *"Consulting and In-Service"*. These services are typically important with medical products, and their combination on the first factor underscores this importance.

```
------------------------- FACTOR ANALYSIS -------------------------
```

Analysis number 1   Listwise deletion of cases with missing values

	Mean	Std Dev
CSR's Professionalism	1.75000	.70173
Responsiveness of Follow-up	1.97000	.84632
Invoice Accuracy	1.88000	.74237
Ease of Operation	1.50000	.65905
Product Features	1.69000	.74799
Product Reliability	1.59000	.87727
Product Durability	1.83000	1.01559
In-service Support	1.82000	.73002
Training Materials	1.89000	.75069
Consultant Competency	1.75000	.62563
Consultant Professionalism	1.70000	.62765
Biomed. Eng. Training	2.09000	.73985
Spare Parts Availability	1.95000	.77035
Phone Support Availability	1.83000	.72551
Factory Repair Quality	1.89000	.66507

Number of Cases =   100
Final Statistics:

Variable	Communality	*	Factor	Eigenvalue	Pct of Var	Cum Pct
CSR's Prof	.79831	*	1	6.78636	45.2	45.2
Res Foll-up	.78209	*	2	1.85322	12.4	57.6
Inv Accur	.71990	*	3	1.46268	9.8	67.3
Ease of Op	.63901	*	4	1.09040	7.3	74.6
Prod Feat	.66863	*				
Prod Rel	.80055	*				
Prod Dur	.77223	*				
In-ser Sup	.74121	*				

Figure 8.2   Output from a Factor Analysis

With the simplification offered by the factor analysis, the satisfaction professional might choose to eliminate some of these variables the next time she fielded this survey. The decision of which variables to eliminate is as much art as science. One should retain those variables that have particular relevancy to the organization, or for which a department is directly responsible. The key criterion in retention is how actionable each of the retained variables are.

Variable	Communality	*	Factor	Eigenvalue	Pct of Var	Cum Pct
Train Mat	.79299	*				
Cons Comp	.83977	*				
Cons Prof	.82620	*				
Bio Eng Trng	.74289	*				
Prts Avail	.70474	*				
Supp Avail	.64301	*				
Repre Qual	.72113	*				

EQUAMAX   rotation   1 for extraction   1 in analysis   1 - Kaiser Normalization.
EQUAMAX converged in 7 iterations.

Rotated Factor Matrix:

	Factor 1	Factor 2	Factor 3	Factor 4
Consult Comp	.86679	.24743	.15776	.04837
Cons Prof	.84421	.27568	.17461	.08386
Train Mat	.81912	.22910	.24071	.10773
In-ser Sup	.73595	.35175	.24323	.12926
Inv Accur	.28449	.77545	.17510	.08354
CRS's Prof	.34676	.77054	.12979	.25979
Res Foll-up	.32964	.76754	.23682	.16803
Supp Avail	.23961	.68423	.18876	.28600
Prod Rel	.23134	.15952	.04081	.12094
Prod Dur	.33412	.04185	.79525	.16255
Ease of Op	.13203	.16038	.74844	.18894
Prod Feat	.01145	.48490	.65772	.02771
Bio Eng Trng	.09160	.01208	.04361	.85583
Prts Avail	.04530	.22081	.08235	.80446
Repre Qual	.04976	.18811	.25003	.78788

Cluster Analysis

The Method.   In its basic analytical perspective, cluster analysis is very similar to principal components analysis; both techniques seek to form combinations of things. In principal components one is combining variables that measure similar phenomena, in cluster analysis one is generally seeking to combine customers who view things similarly. That is to say, the technique scans the ratings profiles of all customers looking for customers whose rating profiles are similar. If such "mirror customers" are found, they will be clustered together as similar. The goal in cluster analysis is to form clusters from customers so there is as much similarity within and as much difference between clusters as is possible.[2]

There are two generally recognized approaches to cluster analysis: *hierarchical clustering* (also referred to as linkage procedures) and *nodal procedures* (iterative partitioning methods). (Interestingly, factor analysis can also be used for customer clustering—by factoring a matrix of correlations or cross products among customers. The use of factor analysis is not, however, recommended because of its mandate to form clusters (factors), which are orthogonal (uncorrelated) with one another, a somewhat unrealistic supposition for customer segments.) Of the two main clustering methods, the nodal method is the more practical for customer satisfaction work.

Nodal clustering programs are Euclidean distance oriented.[3] First, a space of as many dimensions as there are attributes is created. Each customer is represented in this space by the ratings he or she has given on the attributes included. (In a space of as many dimensions as attributes, each customer can be represented by a single point in this multi-dimensioned space with coordinates defined by the ratings given on each attribute.) At this point, a number of cluster centroids are arbitrarily established. Then, distance measurements are calculated for each customer from every cluster centroid. The algorithms strive to assign each customer to that cluster with whom the customer's distance is least. Customers are assigned and reassigned and cluster centroids recalculated, until some homeostasis is achieved. Some nodal methods work on the basis of minimizing the "between versus the within cluster" sum-of-squares ratio.

Of all the available nodal clustering procedures, perhaps the most popular and readily available, is the "k-means" procedure. As a nodal method, the "k" in k-means specifies how many clusters are anticipated. Rather than testing to see how many clusters can be formed, the k-means

---

[2]For a more complete description, the reader is directed to Aldenderfer and Blashfield, *Cluster Analysis,* or other texts on cluster analysis.

[3]There are several different conceptualizations of distance. The "Euclidean" model is most frequently used, and is defined as the square root of the sums of the squared differences of the coordinates for two products or entities on each considered dimension.

procedures are oriented to simply allocating customers to the number of clusters specified by the satisfaction professional.

Decisions You Will Have to Make.   To conduct a smart cluster analysis of your customers, be prepared to answer the following questions as you order a clustering analysis:

1. Which variables to use for clustering?
   - While this is a major consideration in social research projects, it becomes trivial in satisfaction work. One will generally select all of the variables in a particular "battery" of the questionnaire. For example, if one is looking for customer segments based on similar importance profiles, the attribute importance question is the appropriate list of variables for input to the clustering exercise.
   - As a general statement, use all of the variables that make sense to you.
   - It is always a good idea to make sure the variables are all of a similar metric (as will likely be the case in importance judgments). Ideally all should be interval or ratio scaled. It is difficult to combine metrics (that is, some interval scaled items, some nominal)
2. What processing is necessary for the variable responses?
   - As input to a clustering algorithm, your customers have to be represented in some form of similarity-dissimilarity mode. You may have to transform your raw scores to create such measures of similarity.
   - One of your first considerations is how similar is the metric of your variables? In importance judgments within a satisfaction survey all variables will be very similar, perhaps answered on a 1–10 response scale. But if your input variables vary between concepts like income, age, and satisfaction, then you will need to consider ways of making the metric of the input variables consistent.
   - Many clustering programs may anticipate variables of disparate metric and will offer as a common practice, data standardization. As we have said earlier, standardization removes two elements of information: level and dispersion. Both of these may be important in identifying satisfaction cluster membership. Try not to have your data standardized.

3. What form do you want your data matrix in for the clustering process?
   - You have less control over the type of matrix used to represent your customers in a cluster analysis than you have for variables in a factor analysis. You may have to accept the matrix suggested by the clustering procedure you use.
   - If your data is all interval or ratio scaled, you can use distance measures or correlation coefficients, if your data is only classificatory you will have to adopt a matching coefficient (Sokal and Sneath 1984). If your data is mixed, consider Gower's coefficient (Churchill 1992).
4. How many customer-clusters do you expect?
   - Unlike factor analysis in which you are given some help in determining the number of factors that is appropriate to retain, in many cluster analysis solutions there is no such help. You have to decide how many clusters you expect, a priori.
   - Chances are you will have some in-going idea about the composition of your customers. While there may be no one configuration that is totally right, you can try out several, based on different ways of viewing your customers. One or more of these configurations will probably produce a satisfactory solution.

Using Cluster Analysis to Identify Benefit Segments of Customers. Probably one of the most beneficial applications of cluster analysis in customer satisfaction work is to identify clusters of customers who allocate importance to performance attributes in similar ways. At some point in your work, if you collect importance judgments from your customers of the performance attributes in your survey, you will want to investigate the existence of "benefit segments." Benefit segments are groups of customers who allocate importance to performance attributes in a similar way, yet a way different from other groups of customers. One can well imagine a group of customers who might place high importance on after-sale service. Another group might accord higher importance to a wide array of features. Still others might accord the most importance to products that are easily upgradeable. By clustering your customers based on the importance weights they assign to performance attributes, you will be able to discover how many such groups of like-minded customers exist in your customerbase, and which performance attributes they idiosyncratically value.

An Example of Cluster Analysis Applied to Customer Satisfaction Data. To demonstrate cluster analysis, we will use the medical equipment data again. In addition to including the performance ratings of the equipment on the performance attributes, the dataset also includes customers' judgments of the importance of the 15 product attributes. To simplify collecting this information, the six attribute-groupings were used (4a–4f). Customers were asked to use a constant sum procedure in which they divided 100 points across the six groupings of performance attributes. It is these six importance weights we will use to attempt to cluster the 100 customers into groups who weight the groupings in similar manners. The resulting clusters can be referred to as *benefit clusters;* each cluster will contain customers who placed a similar value on the performance attribute groups—a value that is conceivably different from the importance weights other customer groups assigned.

The grouping importance ratings of the 100 customers were submitted to the "Quick Cluster" algorithm of SPSS. Figure 8.3 shows the results. We have requested a three cluster solution, so the output begins by showing the starting configuration it has used for the three clusters.[4] Once the program has reached a stable cluster assignment (in this example after only three iterations), it lists the customers by their cluster membership. (Cluster membership identifiers are also customarily written to a data file, which can be appended to customers' records in your customerbase.)

The "Final Cluster Centers" shows the importance ratings given the six attribute groupings by the customers actually comprising each of the three clusters. The analysis reports how many customers were assigned to each group; in this case 44 were assigned to cluster one, 13 to cluster two, and 43 to cluster three. Table 8.3 shows how the importance rank-order of the attribute-groupings changes considerably across the three customer clusters. It appears Cluster 1 is oriented to the entire product and support experience, hence our label the *holistic customer.* Notice how much more equally the importance points are distributed across all six attribute groups by this cluster's customer than any other cluster. Cluster 2's customer has been labeled, *support oriented,* while Cluster 3 places over half of all importance points on the product itself—clearly oriented to the *product's performance.*

----

[4]The analyst may provide his own starting configuration. Clustering results are said to be sensitive to the initial configuration. So if you have an idea about how your customers may cluster, it is fair to input this as a starting point.

```
------------------------- QUICK    CLUSTER -------------------------
Initial Cluster Centers.

Cluster   Bio Eng Sup   Ed Sup   Order Proc   Products   Purch Proc   Tech Supp
   1        5.0000      20.0000   10.0000     10.0000     50.0000      5.0000
   2        5.0000      10.0000    5.0000      5.0000      5.0000     70.0000
   3        1.0000       1.0000    1.0000     95.0000      1.0000      1.0000
-------------------------------------------------------------------
```

Convergence achieved due to no or small distance change.
The maximum distance by which any center has changed is 1.2879
Current iteration is 3

Minimum distance between initial centers is 80.0000

Iteration	Change in Cluster Centers		
	1	2	3
1	41.8319	39.6921	38.8522
2	1.0426	4.9387	.6029
3	.4999	1.8263	.0000

Case listing of Cluster membership.

LNAME	Cluster	Distance
Murray	1	14.866
Tinaya	1	20.814
Stage	3	2.200
Quens	1	41.624
Lagroon	3	10.814
Manuel	1	10.225
Ellington	1	20.643
Savoca	1	17.698
Ellis	3	17.618

Figure 8.3   Output from a Cluster Analysis

Table 8.3   Customer Benefit Clusters Interpreted

Cluster 1	Cluster 2	Cluster 3
26.3 Products	33.0 Technical support	59.4 Products
16.4 Educational support	23.7 Biomedical engr. supp.	9.6 Educational support
15.8 Technical support	15.0 Educational support	9.4 Biomedical engr. supp.
15.7 Biomedical engr. supp.	9.7 Order process	9.3 Technical support
13.8 Purchase process	9.2 Purchase process	6.4 Purchase process
12.3 Order process	8.4 Products	6.3 Order process
The Holistic Customer	*The Support-Oriented Customer*	*The Product Performance Customer*

LNAME	Cluster	Distance
Estrada	2	21.395
McClone	1	9.098
Paulsen	3	12.425
Petermeier	1	10.323

Final Cluster Centers

Cluster	Bio Eng Sup	Ed Sup	Order Proc	Products	Purch Proc	Tech Supp
1	15.7273	16.4318	12.3182	26.3864	13.7500	15.8182
2	23.7692	15.0000	9.6923	8.4615	9.2308	33.0000
3	9.3721	9.5581	6.2558	59.4186	6.3721	9.3256

Analysis of Variance.

Variable	Cluster MS	DF	Error MS	DF	F	Prob
Bio Eng Sup	1146.3793	2	48.939	97.0	23.4247	.000
Ed Sup	535.5949	2	58.261	97.0	9.1929	.000
Order Proc	400.4046	2	23.427	97.0	17.0910	.000
Products	18498.5561	2	131.795	97.0	140.3584	.000
Purch Proc	596.1929	2	40.975	97.0	14.5501	.000
Tech Sup	2809.6263	2	50.041	97.0	56.1464	.000

Number of Cases in each Cluster.

Cluster	unweighted cases	weighted cases
1	44.0	44.0
2	13.0	13.0
3	43.0	43.0
Missing	0	
Valid cases	100.0	100.0

Multidimensional Scaling (MDS)

The Method.   Multidimensional scaling or perceptual mapping (as it is frequently called) is a way of viewing how customers "organize" a category and the competitors in it, both in the perceptual framework they institute and how they position competitors within the framework. The many techniques for MDS typically work on data of much lower metric than that usually collected through satisfaction surveys, but some versions will operate quite nicely on the rich (highly metric) data produced by the typical satisfaction survey.[5]

----

[5]There are also procedures for producing perceptual maps from some of the other techniques described here, most notably factor analysis and discriminant analysis.

One of the best uses for MDS is to visualize how customers position the competitors in a category, and particularly how competitors are seen as interrelating one to another. The MDS technique produces a minimum-dimensioned space within which all of the competitors are depicted. The key learnings for the satisfaction professional are:

- the number of dimensions required to adequately reproduce customers' ratings of competitors;
- the identities of these dimensions (what performance characteristics do they embody?);
- and the location of each of the competitive brands or organizations within the space.

The issue of the dimensionality of the map is similar to that addressed in the interpretation of a factor analysis. It has to do with how many basic distinctions customers use to mentally compare the competitors in a category. For example, customers might only use *price* and *features* to distinguish among four competitors. In this case a two-dimensioned space would be adequate to display feelings about the four competitors. A MDS solution can help one quickly identify the advantages and disadvantages of your offering. Repositioning strategies are often formulated as a result of viewing the perceptual map produced by a MDS solution.

Decisions You Will Have to Make.   Perceptual mapping, like factor and cluster analysis requires the analyst to make several decisions prior to conducting the analysis. The decisions you will have to make include:

1. What data will you submit to the MDS program.
   - Perceptual mapping programs work with all kinds of data. Some programs require a square, symmetric matrix of similarities/dissimilarities (sort of like a correlation matrix) between the brands/organizations in the category. Other programs will accept attribute ratings of the various competitors.
2. How many dimensions do you want in your final map?
   - Some mapping programs assist the analyst in understanding what dimensionality will best represent the information contained in the original input data, others require the analyst to make an a priori judgment. While this sounds tautological, some MDS algorithms will provide a criterion measure to show how easy or

difficult it was for the algorithm to represent all competitors within the dimensionality specified by the satisfaction professional. With such a criterion, the map which was easiest for the algorithm to fit, is presumably the most appropriate representation.
3. How to interpret the dimensions in the MDS solution
   • The satisfaction professional will need to either become creative in intuitively labeling the dimensions based on the characterizations of the products/brands most correlated with each dimension or employ additional analytical programs to interpret the dimensions.

Using MDS to Depict Your Organization and Competitors.
There are two ways to employ the benefits of MDS in helping you to visualize the understandings you collect in your customer satisfaction survey:

• with your current data you can either:
  • process the information to conform to the input requirements of most MDS programs, or
  • utilize factor analysis or discriminant analysis to produce a similar perceptual mapping representation for you.
• by collecting some additional data in your survey, you will have preference or similarity data, which can be input directly into an MDS program.

An Example of Multidimensional Scaling Applied to Customer Satisfaction Data.
To utilize perceptual mapping, similarities data was collected from the medical equipment customers. There were six competitors in the category. Pair preference judgments or pair dissimilarity judgments are an easy yet effective method with which to collect dissimilarities data. However, pairs increase dramatically as the number of competitors in a category increases. In the present case, five competitors means there are 10 possible pairs of competitors (5 × 4/2). Because 10 judgments were considered too many for each customer to make, the pairs were divided to 2 split-sample conditions of 6 pairs each. Each customer was randomly given one of the split-samples, 6 pairs in all.

The customers were asked to rate the similarity of the competitors in each pairing. Similarities were collected on a ten-point scale with 1 representing "identical" and 10 representing "totally different." The

K Y S T   MULTIDIMENSIONAL SCALING - PC-MDS VERSION
WRITTEN BY JOSEPH B. KRUSKAL, FOREST W. YOUNG, WITH JUDITH SEERY

ANALYSIS TITLE: Similarities of Competitors in the Medical Equipment Field

INPUT PARAMETERS:

MAXIMUM DIMENSIONS	3	MINIMUM DIMENSIONS	2
DIMENSION DECREMENT	1	MINIMUM STRESS	.01000
SCALE FACTOR GRADIENT	.00000	STRESS STEP RATIO	.99900
MAXIMUM ITERATIONS	50	COSINE OF ANGLE BETWEEN GRADIENTS	.66000
AVERAGE COSINE OF ANGLE	.66000	NUMBER OF PRE-ITERATIONS	1

EUCLIDEAN DISTANCE	TORSCA INITIAL CONFIGURATION
STRESS FORMULA 1	NO WEIGHTS AFTER DATA
TIES PRIMARY	MONOTONE MODEL
UPPER HALF MATRIX	ASCENDING DATA
NOT BLOCK DIAGONAL	ALL PLOTS OF FINAL CONFIGURATION
DIAGONAL ABSENT	ALL SCATTER PLOTS OF DIST VS DHAT
SPLIT BY DECK	ROTATE FINAL CONFIG. COORDINATES

PARAMETERS: 5   1   1   TITLE: (4F4.1)

HISTORY OF COMPUTATION: N= 5 THERE ARE   10 DATA VALUES, SPLIT INTO 1 LIST(S).
DIMENSION(S) = 2   ZERO STRESS WAS REACHED
THE FINAL CONFIGURATION HAS BEEN ROTATED TO PRINCIPAL COMPONENTS.
THE FINAL CONFIGURATION OF 5 POINTS IN 2 DIMENSIONS HAS STRESS OF .000 FORMULA 1
WAS USED.
THE FINAL CONFIGURATION APPEARS:

	1	2
XYZ	-1.016	-.035
Comp1	-1.136	-.151
Comp2	.028	.312
Comp3	1.157	.307
Comp4	.967	-.432

Figure 8.4   Output from an MDS Analysis

data was averaged over all 100 customers, resulting in the five-by-five dissimilarities matrix shown in Table 8.4. Notwithstanding the metric, this table is very much like a correlation matrix. The entry in each cell represents the similarity (low numbers, 1–5) or dissimilarity (high numbers, 6–10) of each pair of competitors. This matrix was submitted to KYST, a multidimensional scaling program (Smith 1987).

The primary output of the program is the perceptual "map" depicted in Figure 8.4. The number of dimensions is usually a judgment the satisfaction professional must make, though some programs offer a "stress" factor to tell how hard or easy it was for the program to force the competitors into the map. We have only asked for two dimensions. Looking at the map, one can see the location of Company XYZ, in the

DIMENSION 2 (Y-AXIS) VS. DIMENSION 1 (X-AXIS)
```
        *....*....*....*....*....*....*....*....*....*....*....*
 3.000**                            |                       **  3.000
 2.769**                            |                       **  2.769
 2.538**                            |                       **  2.538
 2.308**                            |                       **  2.308
 2.077**                            |                       **  2.077
 1.846**                            |                       **  1.846
 1.615**                            |                       **  1.615
 1.385**                            |                       **  1.385
 1.154**                            |                       **  1.154
  .923**                            |    Comp 2             **   .923
  .692**                            |                       **   .692
  462**                             |                       **   .462
  .231**                            |         Comp 3        **   .231
  000** - - - - - - - - - - - XYZ - - - 0 - - - - - - - - - - - - - - - - -**   .000
 -.231**                Comp1       |                       **  -.231
 -.462**                            |                       **  -.462
 -.692**                            |                       **   .692
 -.923**                            |                       **  -.923
-1.154**                            |    Comp 4             ** -1.154
-1.385**                            |                       ** -1.385
-1.615**                            |                       ** -1.615
-1.846**                            |                       ** -1.846
-2.077**                            |                       ** -2.077
-2.308**                            |                       ** -2.308
-2.538**                            |                       ** -2.538
-2.769**                            |                       ** -2.769
 3.000**                            |                       ** -3.000
        *....*....*....*....*....*....*....*....*....*....*....*
      . -3.3333.   -2.0000.    -.6667.    .6667.   2.0000.   3.3333
    -4.0000     -2.6667    -1.3333     .0000   1.3333    2.6667    4.0000
```

Table 8.4   An Input Matrix for a MDS Analysis

	Company XYZ	Competitor 1	Competitor 2	Competitor 3	Competitor 4
Company XYZ	0	3.6	6.7	6.3	4.4
Competitor 1	3.6	0	6.3	8.8	6.3
Competitor 2	6.7	6	0	8.3	7.4
Competitor 3	6.3	8.8	8.3	0	7.1
Competitor 4	4.4	6.3	7.4	7.1	0

left half of the map. Its competitors are located throughout the space depicted by the map. A number of conclusions can be drawn from the map:

1. XYZ's closest competitor is Comp1. Its almost identical position (to XYZ) in the map denotes customers' perceptions of the high similarity of the two companies.
2. Two other competitors (comp 2 and comp 3) occupy the upper right-hand quadrant, suggesting these two are also perceived as similar.
3. Comp4 has the lower right quadrant by itself, though this may represent a less than ideal positioning.

To get the most use out of a perceptual map, the satisfaction professional must be able to identify the axes of the space that help describe each competitors' placement in the space. Sometimes identification of the axes is accomplished intuitively. ("The vertical axis must represent price since we're at one extreme and our low-priced competitor is at the other!" "Maybe the horizontal axis represents distribution from broad to exclusive because two of our competitors, each of whom focuses on one type of distribution or the other, are at opposite ends of the horizontal axis!")

Beyond an intuitive identification, performance attributes can be regressed into the map, if ratings on the performance attributes are available for at least one other competitor in addition to our organization.[6]

Multivariate Analysis to Determine Causality

The second family of multivariate techniques is directed at determining the dependency of one or more variables upon other variables. These techniques have substantial value to the satisfaction professional. In this section we will briefly review two techniques for determining dependency: multiple regression and discriminant analysis.

Multiple Regression

The Method.   Most of us have heard of regression and perhaps some have even used it. Multiple regression is, of course, the multi-variable analog for linear regression. The technique allows us to calculate weights (coefficients) describing the relationship of each of several independent variables to a variable labeled the *dependent variable*—the variable we wish to explain based on ratings on the other, *independent variables*.

----

[6]Inserting properties can be accomplished using the computer program, PROFIT, part of the PCMDS package (Smith 1987).

Multiple regression computer programs are readily available (including being offered in the three most widely used computer spreadsheet programs). These programs generally require fewer decisions to be made than any of the techniques we have so far described. So it is very easy to conduct a multiple regression analysis. But again, the value of your analysis will depend in no small part on your general understanding of the technique, its capabilities and its limitations.

Decisions You Will Have to Make.   You will mostly have only to describe where your data is and which variable you wish to specify as the dependent variable. A general requirement is that you have data from at least two and a half times as many customers as you have independent variables. That means if you have 30 performance variables you want to specify as independent variables, you will need data from at least 75 customers, a modest requirement. Other decisions you will have to make include:

1. Specifically which variables do you want to specify as your independent variables?
   - In a determination of "key drivers" the independent variables will likely be all of your performance attributes. One note of caution. The independent variables are truly meant to be independent; including *independent of one another*. When customers answer a number of performance attributes together, there is usually some correlation built into their ratings. This introduces a problem in multiple regression called "multicollinearity." There are procedures for overcoming it. We will discuss this more below and in Chapter 9.
2. Do you want to use a constant, or do you wish a solution that goes through the origin?
   - The existence of a constant, A_0, suggests there will be some baseline level in the dependent variable, even when all independent variables are zeroed out. In satisfaction models this is a difficult position to defend, but allowing a constant is common.
3. How to deal with missing data
   - In Chapter 6 we reviewed three options to deal with missing data. Two additional considerations in regression analysis: make sure to exclude any customers who fail to answer the dependent variable, and consider excluding questions from your analysis with a high nonresponse rate.

Using Regression Analysis in Customer Satisfaction Projects.   One of the most valuable applications of multiple regression in customer satisfaction is the determination of "key drivers." In this application, multiple regression is used to determine the relative weight each performance attribute's ratings have on overall product/service satisfaction. Those attributes whose regression coefficients are largest can be considered the most important performance elements in creating overall satisfaction. Hence the designation, *key* drivers (of satisfaction). It must be mentioned that this investigation is fraught with mathematical danger, mostly because of the high likelihood of the existence of *multicollinearity* in your satisfaction performance ratings. Multicollinearity is the term for the condition of non-independent, independent variables in a regression model. When the independent variables (performance ratings) are correlated among themselves, this will artificially inflate the results of the regression model. (See MacLauchlan 1992, Grisaffe 1993, and Mullet 1994.)

In examining a regression analysis, there are three things to look at:

- R^2 the coefficient of determination
- the regression coefficients (b's) for each independent variable
- an F-test reporting the significance of the model

The R^2 is a measure of how well the total model (in our case, overall satisfaction as a function of the performance attributes) works. It is interpreted as the proportion of variation in the dependent variable (overall satisfaction) that is accounted for by the group of independent variables (performance attributes) we have selected. Normally, one would hope to see R^2 above 0.5. But beyond the level, you would like to know the amount of variation accounted for was statistically different from zero. To determine this, there is a test of significance for R^2. The test, which is an F-test, describes if the independent variables, as a group, are significantly related to the dependent variable. Most computer programs calculate and interpret the F-value for you.

The *regression coefficients* describe the importance of each attribute in predicting the dependent variable. The coefficients can be interpreted as the amount by which the dependent variable would be expected to change if the appropriate independent variable changed by one unit. Regression coefficients are subjected to tests of significance also to determine if they are statistically greater than zero. Typically a t-test is calculated for each independent variable's regression coefficient.

Those independent variables whose coefficients are not statistically significant, may just as well be removed from the model; they contribute nothing to overall satisfaction.

Sometimes, when the independent variables are comprised of disparate scaled items (that is, dollars, years, and housing units), the independent variables will need to be standardized to facilitate comparisons. Regression coefficients based on standardized data, are called *beta coefficients*. Because customer satisfaction data will usually be composed of judgments gathered on similar response scales (for example 1–7 rating scale, 1–10 rating scale), the satisfaction professional will usually not have to standardize the data in his analysis.

When your regression analysis is to be performed on an extensive list of attributes, which are likely to be intercorrelated, one analytical option is to consider *stepwise multiple regression*. In this approach the satisfaction professional lets the computer select those independent variables that are "best." However, the procedure is only applicable when the professional lacks an in-going model of the structure of his data. The value of the stepwise procedure is that it produces a relatively parsimonious model (it will include only those independent variables that are significantly related to the dependent variable) and it virtually eliminates multicollinearity in the final model. Unfortunately, several issues minimize its practical value: the technique has demonstrated instability in split-half tests; it may exclude key independent variables, and the statistical tests accompanying standard regression analysis are no longer valid due to the stepwise procedure's selection processes.

An Example of Regression Analysis Applied to Customer Satisfaction Data.   A good use of regression analysis is to investigate within your satisfaction data how one variable may be "explained" by others. In this case we will use a regression model to explore how customers' willingness to recommend is related to the 15 performance attributes. In this analysis, willingness to recommend is the dependent variable and the 15 performance attributes are the independent variables. Figure 8.5 reproduces the results of this analysis.

Because several of the performance variables are correlated with one another, in a straight regression model with all 15 attributes, only one variable's coefficient was significant. To attempt to control for the multicollinearity, a stepwise regression model was employed. The fourth and final step from this analysis is shown in Figure 8.5. In this fourth

**** MULTIPLE REGRESSION ****

Equation Number 1   Dependent Variable. .   Q4

Variable(s) Entered on Step Number
   4. .   Supp Avail

Multiple R	.71240
R Square	.50751
Adjusted R Square	.48677
Standard Error	.53548

Analysis of Variance

	DF	Sum of Squares	Mean Square
Regression	4	28.07020	7.01755
Residual	95	27.23980	.28673

F =   24.47401   Signif F = .0000

Variables in the Equation

Variable	B	SE B	Beta	Tolerance	VIF	T	Sig T
Resp/Foll-up	.185456	.087903	.209987	.523318	1.911	2.110	.0375
Prod Rel	.308641	.070171	.362243	.764314	1.308	4.398	.0000
Cons Comp	.209155	.103280	.175067	.693709	1.442	2.025	.0457
Supp Avail	.186448	.092822	.180974	.638636	1.566	2.009	.0474
(Constant)	.066692	.181580				.367	.7142

Equation Number 1   Dependent Variable. .   Q4

Variables not in the Equation

Variable	Beta In	Partial	Tolerance	VIF	Min Toler	T	Sig T
CSR's Prof	.043178	.035775	.338086	2.958	.338086	.347	.7293
Inv Accur	.064612	.062326	.458262	2.182	.384540	.605	.5463
Ease of Op	-.031260	-.036708	.679114	1.473	.523231	-.356	.7225
Prod Feat	.106273	.118331	.610598	1.638	.508775	1.155	.2509
Prod Dur	.049967	.039502	.307799	3.249	.307799	.383	.7024
In-ser Supp	-.069471	-.066035	.444992	2.247	.444992	-.642	.5227
Train Mat	-.049780	-.046552	.430690	2.322	.430690	-.452	.6524
Cons Prof	.084300	.063717	.281359	3.554	.281359	.619	.5374
Prts Avail	.023498	.030395	.824017	1.214	.519739	.295	.7688
Bio Eng Trng	-.016924	-.023283	.932107	1.073	.517279	-.226	.8218
REpr Qual	-.079413	-.099191	.768554	1.301	.518387	-.966	.3363

Figure 8.5   Output from a Multiple Regression Analysis

step, four variables are included in the model; *responsiveness of follow-up, product reliability, consultant's competency and phone support availability.* Each is significant as denoted by the t-test values shown and their significance levels.

Discriminant Analysis

The Method.   Discriminant analysis is somewhat related to multiple regression. The purpose of the technique is to make a prediction, but instead of predicting the level of a continuous variable, like overall satisfaction, the predictor variable is simply a classification, like whether a customer is a member of the group "satisfied customers" or oppositely a member of the group "dissatisfied customers." Discriminant analysis can be a useful technique to help you determine which performance attributes best discriminate satisfied from dissatisfied customers.

A commonsense answer to this question might be drawn directly from your crosstabs. Take any set of variables and array the variable means for the groups whose membership you wish to predict. Chances are the variables with the greatest difference in means (between the two groups) might be more discriminating. (The problem here is that the variables do not act independently, we desire a measure of the variables' simultaneous effect to take account both of their interrelationship and any information they share.)

Decisions You Will Have to Make.   Using discriminant analysis requires some degree of creativity. You will have to identify a classificatory variable to be used as your dependent variable. This may need to be created for the analysis. For example, if you were to use discriminant analysis to discriminate between satisfied and dissatisfied customers, you would need first to decide what level of satisfaction you were willing to consider "satisfied." Assuming you had measured overall satisfaction on a 1–10 scale you would have to create the nominal variable, "sat group", with two classifications: "satisfied" and "dissatisfied". Then, you'd have to code each of your customers as belonging to one of the two groups. (Though you will recognize ordinality in this particular example, there will be many more cases where the group definition will not be easily ordered, for example: "west coast customers," "central customers," and "east coast customers.")

Using Discriminant Analysis in Customer Satisfaction Projects.
Let us assume you have collected your satisfaction measurement data. While you may have explored the data using other statistical techniques, a question you may have asked yourself might be, "Which performance attributes discriminate best between satisfied and dissatisfied customers?" Or you might ask, "Considering two customer groups, new and tenured customers, what are their major differences in perceived

performance?" Discriminant analysis can answer these types of questions, helping you identify issues, elements of service performance or product characteristics that maximally differentiate the groups you've selected.

A discriminant analysis produces several outputs:

- a discriminant function
- a test of statistical significance
- discriminant coefficients
- a classification table

The test of significance for discriminant analysis is the Mahalanobis D^2 statistic, a squared distance measure similar to the standard Euclidean distance measure. It describes the distance from each customer to the customer's assigned group mean. The F-statistic is used to test the significance of the D^2 statistic and is routinely output by most statistical packages. The D^2 gives a measure of the overall significance of the model, that is, how well the battery of independent variables discriminate the condition you're attempting to predict.

Discriminant coefficients are interpreted much the same way as are regression coefficients. A small coefficient suggests little influence on the classification, a large one substantial influence. Each represents the relative contribution made to the classificatory discriminant function by a one-unit change in the independent variable.

The discriminant function describes a linear combination of scores or ratings such that the derived weights maximally discriminate between the groups being compared. When the discriminant function is applied to the attribute mean ratings for each group, the group's discriminant score is calculated. By similarly weighting each customer's scores, one can assign individual customers to one or another group, based on which group's score the individual customer's score is closest.

Assigning individuals to the classificatory groups, after the analysis helps produce the classification matrix (sometimes called a "confusion matrix"). This is a table with as many rows and columns as there are groups. Typically, predicted group classification defines the columns, actual group membership the rows. The diagonal describes the proportion of each group correctly classified. There are numerous ways to interpret the classification rate of the matrix. The most reasonable way (for groups of equal or unequal size) is the proportional chance criterion:

$$\textit{chance criterion} = \alpha^2 + (1 - \alpha)^2 \qquad (8.1)$$

α = proportion of customers in Group 1
$1 - \alpha$ = proportion of customers in Group 2

To be fairest to the evaluation, a population for discriminant analysis is frequently divided into two samples: the analysis sample (upon which the analysis is created) and the hold out sample, a sample used to test the classificatory precision of the discriminant function.

While our discussion has suggested application primarily to a two-group situation, discriminant analysis can accommodate more than two groups. The analysis is only slightly more complex than that described here. You should consult a good statistical textbook for further assistance.

An Example of Discriminant Analysis Applied to Customer Satisfaction Data.

Very often in a customer satisfaction survey there will be a curiosity to know which of the performance attributes are most associated with satisfied customers. (This is similar to a question addressed in Chapter 9, the identification of *key drivers*. It can be argued, however, that the question is a bit different, and often both analyses will be conducted.) To investigate the linkage between satisfied customers and the performance attributes, the medical equipment of customers were split into two groupings; one with very high satisfaction scores (50 customers) and the other with very low scores (15 customers). There were 35 customers who had given moderate satisfaction scores. For purposes of this analysis they were set aside.

The 65 customers and their satisfaction scores and ratings on the performance attributes were submitted to the discriminant analysis routine in SPSS. Figure 8.6 shows the output. The program initially confirms the number of cases submitted and their two categories: 0-low satisfaction and 1-high satisfaction. Because there are only two groups, only one discriminant function is identified. The variables' correlations with the function are shown in the middle of the page. Notice that *Responsiveness of Follow-Up* is the most correlated, with *Invoice Accuracy* and *Product Reliability* being next most highly correlated. Three variables, *Repair Quality*, *Parts Availability*, and *Biomedical Engineer Training* are almost independent of the satisfaction classification. (All three of these performance attributes have very modest correlations with the discriminant function.)

The output ends with a classification or "confusion" matrix. This matrix shows how successful the function's weights are in correctly classifying customers as either high in satisfaction or low in satisfaction. In the case of the present analysis, the function was able to successfully classify 97 percent of all customers (see also Table 8.5).

------------------D I S C R I M I N A N T   A N A L Y S I S------------------

On groups defined by STSFIED

      65 (Unweighted) cases were processed.
     0 of these were excluded from the analysis.
      65 (Unweighted) cases will be used in the analysis.

Number of cases by group

            Number of cases

SATISFIED	Unweighted	Weighted Label
0	15	15.0
1	50	50.0
Total	65	65.0

Canonical Discriminant Functions

Fcn	Eigenvalue	Pct of Variance	Cum Pct	Canonical Corr	After Fcn	Wilks' Lambda	Chi-square	df	Sig
:					0	.250206	76.894	15	0000
1*	2.9967	100.00	100.00	.8659 :					

  * Marks the 1 canonical discriminant functions remaining in the analysis.

Pooled within-groups correlations between discriminating variables and canonical discriminant functions

(Variables ordered by size of correlation within function)

Res Foll-up	.63517	Prod Dur	.45024	Cons Prof	.36282
Inv Accur	.58644	Cons Comp	.41224	Ease of Op	.30178
Prod Rel	.56600	In-serv Sup	.41184	Repre Qual	.18543
CSR's Prof	.54380	Prod Feat	.40409	Prts Avail	.17754
Supp Avail	.47670	Trainng Mat	.36758	Bio Eng Trng	.09229

Canonical discriminant functions evaluated at group means (group centroids)

Group	Func 1
0	3.11153
1	-.93346

Classification results–

	Actual Group	No. of Cases	Predicted 0	Group Membership 1
Group	0	15	13	2
			86.7%	13.3%
Group	1	50	0	50
			.0%	100.0%

Percent of "grouped" cases correctly classified: 96.92%

Classification processing summary

      65 (Unweighted) cases were processed.
     0 cases were excluded for missing or out–of–range group codes.
     0 cases had at least one missing discriminating variable.
      65 (Unweighted) cases were used for printed output.

Figure 8.6   Output from a Discriminant Analysis

Table 8.5   A Discriminant Analysis Classification Matrix

Actual Classification	Predicted Classification		
	Group 1	*Group 2*	*Total*
Group 1	13/86.7%	2/13.3%	15
Group 2	0/0%	50/100%	50

An Alternative Procedure: Stepwise Discriminant Analysis.

Generally when discriminant analysis is used, it is assumed that the variables identified to the analysis are the best set of variables for discriminating the cases. The traditional discriminant model attempts to fashion a discriminant function using all of the submitted variables. There are times in satisfaction research, when the professional's only reason for selecting a group of variables is that prima facie they make sense. This is a situation where some testing may be valuable.

When it is not totally clear that a set of variables is the best set, a variant of discriminant analysis, *stepwise discriminant analysis* may be applied. Stepwise discriminant analysis not only builds a discriminant function, it does so by selecting candidate variables from a list of possible discriminating variables. Starting with no variables in the model, the analysis proceeds to both add and remove variables so as to maximally discriminate between the specified groups. The procedure would be extremely useful were it not for its susceptibility to multicollinearity and the all too frequent occurrence of multicollinearity within satisfaction data.

When multicollinearity exists, the set of variables selected by the model cannot be trusted, nor can the discriminant coefficients. It has been suggested, however, that where multicollinearity is a population-based phenomena, which will not vary group by group, that the impact of multicollinearity may be somewhat lessened. In any event, it is always interesting to see the results of a stepwise discriminant analysis. It would be a good rule of thumb to always accompany the analysis, however, with a correlation matrix of the relationships among the variables to see how appropriate or inappropriate the procedure may be.

Other Advanced Multivariate Techniques

The field of multivariate analysis continues to grow in capabilities. Several relatively new procedures promise considerable value for the satisfaction professional. Each of these techniques is reasonably complex, however.

For this discussion, we will briefly review the techniques and how they might assist the satisfaction professional. To implement any of these procedures, the professional is probably best advised to seek help from a statistical consultant.

Confirmatory Factor Analysis

Factor analysis as we have discussed it has been purely exploratory—seeking possible relationships among variables and measures that have been collected. Traditional factor analysis procedures have frequently been criticized as statistical "fishing expeditions," explorations absent any preconceived theory about why and how measured phenomena ought to relate. A newer form of factor analysis, called confirmatory factor analysis has been developed by Joreskog and Sorbom, (1989) and others. Confirmatory factor analysis starts with an analyst's hypothetical model of how variables or constructs are thought to relate. The procedure is capable of conducting tests to see if the hypothesized structure is upheld by the collected data.

Joreskog's statistical package for confirmatory factor analysis, LIS-REL (*l*inear *s*tructural *rel*ationships) is widely available and has become the generic term for the procedure.

Structural Equation Modeling

Related to confirmatory factor analysis (and often implemented by it) is the practice of structural equation modeling. Building on the "path models" of the past—largely a result of regression modeling, structural equation models extend confirmation to an entire process model. The satisfaction professional may have a model of satisfaction such as that proposed in Chapter 1 (p. 37). Structural equation modeling is an analytical procedure for testing to see just how well the observed data confirms the model and its relationships. In this way structural equation modeling advances the satisfaction professional's understanding of the base process by which satisfaction is formed in his product or service category. The procedure represents a responsible search for confirmation of a process model which may be described to an entire organization.

Structural equation models are built to identify structural relationships among constructs in a model, like those depicted in Figure 8.7A.

There are two basic types of constructs depicted in the model, *endogenous constructs* those that are affected by other constructs within the model, and *exogenous constructs* those outside the model that are not affected by other model constructs. Constructs may be either observable

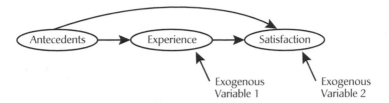

Figure 8.7A   A Structural Equation Model

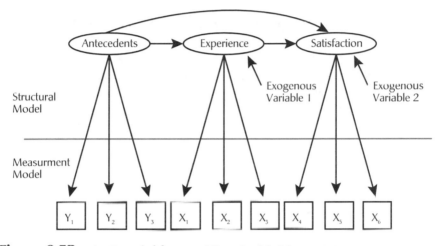

Figure 8.7B   An Extended Structural Equation Model

(gender, age, income) or unobservable (expressed overall satisfaction, judgments of product reliability, features, and so on). A satisfaction professional's model will always have constructs of the latter variety. This complicates the model. Extending the model previously examined (in Figure 8.7A), we have the model in Figure 8.7B. This extended model has two submodels, the *structural model* represented by the relationship between the unobservable constructs, and the *measurement model,* consisting of indicator variables that operationalize the constructs. The measurement model is similar to a conventional factor model where various unobservable constructs are thought to be represented by their appropriate indicators (for example: performance attributes). The structural model is closer to a conventional linear equation or path model, representing relationships among specified constructs.

While it might seem appropriate to estimate each of the models separately (creating factor scores for the measurement model by a factor analysis) and then using those scores to estimate the structural model, it is actually more efficient to test both submodels simultaneously.

Probit Modeling

Probit modeling, though at present infrequently used in satisfaction surveys, would seem to have some valuable application. Given a customer's scores on a series of performance attributes, probit analysis can produce a probability function describing the likelihood of the individual customer belonging to a particular group of customers, for example, those "completely satisfied" (8 or higher on a 10-point scale, "extremely satisfied" on a five-point verbal scale, and so on). This could have substantial value where not all customers can be included in the formal satisfaction measurement program, yet it is desired to identify both dissatisfied and satisfied customers. By asking only a few, key questions, a probit analysis might be able to produce a probability for each customer's satisfaction level.

Probit analysis may sound similar to discriminant analysis, but its purpose is to assign a probability to a customer's state, not assign the customer to a group.

CSM Data Is Three-Dimensional

Customer satisfaction data, like our world is never two-dimensional. Instead, it consists of many dimensions or modes. All too often however, in our analyses, we treat this data as if it were flat, reducing the several dimensions into a two-dimensional array, generally a customers-by-attributes matrix. To force the data into this two-dimensioned matrix, some important information is lost as one or more additional dimension(s) is/are reduced to averages: that is, the average customer; the average competitor; the average occasion, and so on. In this section we will explore some of the analytical opportunities hidden in the different "planes" of the satisfaction data cube.

Conventions

As we reference a data matrix, the matrix will always be considered to be a rectangular matrix of dimensionality $n \times m$. Customers will always be represented as rows of the matrix, and by the subscript n. Attributes (m) will form the columns of the matrix. The typical satisfaction data matrix is shown in Figure 8.8.

The single plane or "wafer" will usually contain data from a sample of customers rating a company or organization on various performance

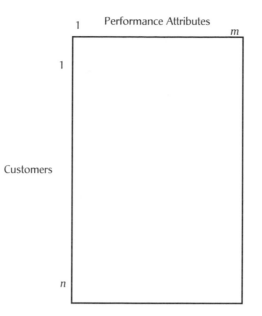

Figure 8.8   The Satisfaction Data Matrix

attributes. To analyze the information we will generally calculate means or average scores for each of the attributes. This reduces the data matrix to a row vector of means (see Figure 8.9A).

When one looks at a conventional CSM analysis in this way it becomes rather clear how disregardful our traditional univariate analyses really are. We have totally ignored any variation or information contained in the customer-to-customer differences that exist in the raw data. Using the average customer vector of attribute averages, disregards the information about *individual differences* contained in the original data. If we have suspicions about customer differences, we may explore this in relatively trivial ways. For example, knowing we have long-term customers and short-term customers we may form averages for each such a priori customer subgroup (see Figure 8.9B). While respecting basic differences in customers, such investigations, motivated by a priori segments hardly exploit all of the information collected in the raw data. Because such investigations rely on the current understanding of the customerbase, rather than exploring new opportunities, they tend to perpetuate the current corporate mindset. As a satisfaction professional, try to use your data to update or enhance your organization's view of the market. Do not wholesale adopt conventional thinking unless, of course, it is verified by *your* data.

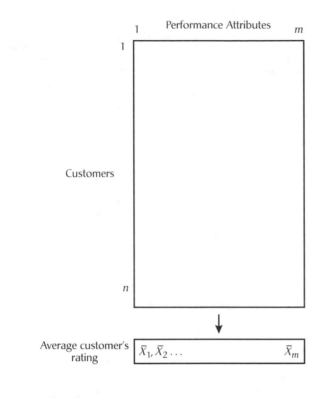

Figure 8.9   Illustrations (A) and (B) of Averaging the Satisfaction Matrix

The Dimensions of Satisfaction Data

As we have already said, the data from a satisfaction survey is far more complex than we generally realize. So accustomed are we to seeing tables or grids reporting averages, that we may fail to remind ourselves that hidden within the average is a distribution of scores or points of view. Let us quickly review the dimensions of a typical satisfaction dataset and identify how we may currently be concealing or recognizing the complexities. Often, "digging into the data" can provide enormous insights and opportunities for better strategic planning.

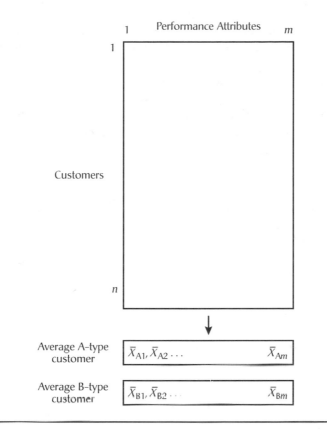

Units of Observation

Customers. We seem aware of the possible differences existing among our customers. The identification of customer "benefit segments" is one way in which we are attempting to explore individual differences existing within our customerbase (as was demonstrated in this chapter's section on cluster analysis, p. 333).

Attributes. Somehow we seem less likely to aggregate attributes, though factor analyses of attribute ratings help to identify dimensions of attributes that measure or represent similar qualities or issues.

Competitors.   Competitors are frequently thrown together to represent the "market" even though we are cogently aware of *their* many differences.

Observations.   And, while most customer satisfaction surveys are launched as continuous, recurring surveys, sadly the only time we generally see historical or longitudinal data is in a trend chart of overall satisfaction. Needless to say, such a summary chart can hide all sorts of dynamics in the underlying data.

How the "Data Cube" Helps

It is proposed that customer satisfaction data should be acknowledged to always contain more than two dimensions. Further, it is recommended that these additional dimensions be explored rather than being dismissed by being "averaged over." If we throw out the traditional two dimensioned data matrix and adopt a cube instead, we will be reminding ourselves of the multi-modal nature of all satisfaction data. As we collapse across one mode or another, we must be mindful that we are disregarding the information (specifically the variation on the data) that may exist in that mode. Any measure of central tendency used to collapse the mode for future analysis, will necessarily conceal the variation that exists.

While there are a few analytical models that handle multi-mode data, generally the complexity of these procedures will overwhelm the satisfaction professional. It may even be difficult to find a consultant adept in some of the more exotic techniques.[7] Consequently we shall advocate utilizing two-dimensional tools for the analysis of multi-mode data. This means the data cube will necessarily be reduced to a two-dimensioned table. However, unlike conventional analyses, we will now be mindful of the underlying complexity of the data from which the two-dimensioned array was produced.

Ways of Analyzing the Data Cube's Information

Consider the satisfaction data cube shown in Figure 8.10. Looking at the first plane, we see the two, expected dimensions: customers and performance attributes. This first plane, the A plane will usually be associated with the satisfaction professional's organization or brand. But, we acknowledge there are additional brands on which we could have data, we have the

----
[7]The reader is referred to Arabie, Carrol, and Desarbo—"Three-Way Scaling and Clustering," Ledyard Tucker—"The Extension of Factor Analysis to Three Dimensional Matrices," and Donald Campbell—"Convergent and Discriminant Validation by the Multitrait Method Matrix."

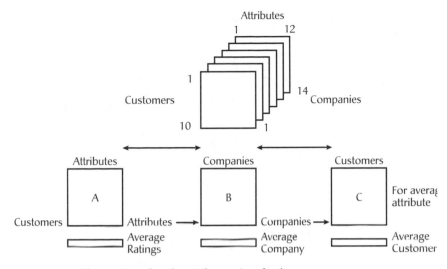

Plane A: Describes the attribute ratings for the average company
Plane B: Describes the company ratings for the average customer
Plane C: Describes the customers for the average attribute

Figure 8.10   The Data Cube and Its Three Planes (or Faces)

third dimension shown in the diagram; companies. The data cube described here includes:

- 10 customers;
- 12 performance attributes; and
- 14 companies.

Figure 8.10 shows how the data cube can be collapsed to form two additional separate two-dimensional matrices (planes B and C). It is our contention that each of these matrices should be fully analyzed.

By the "Average Competitor"

Wafer or plane A contains ratings of the "average company" on the 12 attributes attributable to the 10 customers—since this matrix has been formed by collapsing over the company dimension. Averages formed on the columns produce average attribute ratings, allowing the attribute ratings to be compared for the highest and lowest scores.

If this A plane were to be factor analyzed, the resulting factors would represent evaluative dimensions of attributes.

By the "Average Customer"

Wafer or plane B contains ratings by the "average customer" for the 14 companies on the 12 attributes. Column averages from this matrix produce average company ratings, identifying the highest and lowest rated companies. Factoring this matrix would produce company factors—groupings of companies that tended to be rated similarly on the 12 attributes.

By the "Average Attribute"

Wafer or plane C contains ratings on the "average attribute" for the 14 companies as awarded by the 10 customers. Column averages in this matrix represent average customers, showing the customers with the highest to lowest overall ratings. A factor analysis of this matrix would produce customer factors, similar to the benefit clusters formed by cluster analysis on page 338.

AGGREGATED ANALYSES VERSUS DISAGGREGATED ANALYSES

Most customer satisfaction reports are conducted at the aggregate or total customerbase level. While such a macro picture is needed and is useful, the aggregate report can hide important dynamics in the scores of individual customers. In this section we will briefly review the value of looking at report data at the individual level. We will see that "still waters can run deep."

Figure 8.11 shows a reasonably optimistic trend line for overall satisfaction. Consecutively, over the years depicted, this company's overall satisfaction has increased by 6.9 percent. Generally this would be welcome news for most satisfaction professionals. But if one were to take a closer look at the data, specifically looking at how individual customers or customer segments in the customerbase were scoring the company, the interpretation might be somewhat less optimistic.

The fact of the matter is, that while overall satisfaction does continue to increase, some very real weaknesses may be visible in the customerbase, if *individual* customers' growth over the years is similarly inspected. In Table 8.5 the two customers scoring the company highest in the first year (customers 2 and 8) are an interesting place to start our closer inspection. Customer 2's ratings actually decrease over the five years studied! This customer ends up in year five with the lowest satisfaction rating. Customer 8's ratings over the five years do not decrease, but their growth (2.5 percent) is far lower than that of the total sample. Customer 7 represents another concern. This customer's scores are not improving or declining.

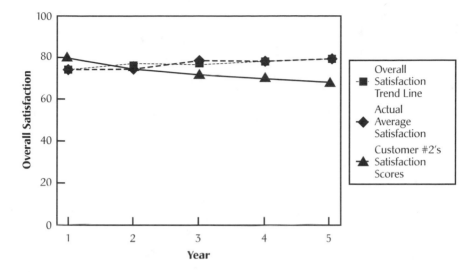

Figure 8.11   Trending Aggregate and Individual Data

While it cannot be denied that growth in the overall satisfaction trend is a very acceptable goal, it is also wise to attach a corollary goal; that individual customer's scores should not decrease, but that a majority of them should similarly increase. A summary table for this sort of analysis is depicted in Table 8.6. Though 70 percent of the customers' satisfaction ratings have increased, this analysis shows that 30 percent have either declined (10 percent) or remained level (20 percent). You may wish to consider framing an action standard based on this analytical perspective. Such a goal might be to create increased ratings among 75 percent or more of your customer base, with no (or a minimal number) decreasing in their ratings.

REFERENCES

Aldenderfer, Mark S., and Roger K. Blashfield. *Cluster Analysis.* Beverly Hills, CA: Sage Publications, 1984.

Arabie, Phipps, J. Douglas Carroll, and Wayne DeSarbo. *Three-Way Scaling and Clustering.* Newbury Park, CA: Sage Publications, 1987.

Campbell, Donald, and Donald W. Fisk. "Convergent and Discriminant Validation by the Multitrait-Multimethod Matrix." *Psychological Bulletin.* Vol. 56 (1959): 81–105.

Table 8.6   Individual Trend Data

Year	Customer Number										Average
	1	2	3	4	5	6	7	8	9	10	
1	78	80	70	75	70	78	72	80	72	74	74.9
2	80	75	67	75	72	80	72	83	74	70	74.8
3	83	72	79	87	85	83	72	79	74	75	78.9
4	80	70	87	73	80	80	72	84	77	78	78.1
5	85	68	85	80	83	78	72	79	80	83	79.3
Average Five Year	81.2	73	77.6	78	78	79.8	72	81	75.4	76	
Outcome	+	–	+	+	+	nc	nc	–	+	+	

Churchill, Gilbert. *Marketing Research: Methodological Foundations,* Fifth Edition, Chicago: Dryden Press, 1991.

Cooper, Lee G. "Tracking the Components of Customer Satisfaction." Working Paper, Anderson School of Management, University of California, Los Angeles, 1994.

Grisaffe, Doug. "Appropriate Use of Regression in Customer Satisfaction Analyses: A Response to William MacLauchlan." *Quirk's Marketing Research Review.* (February 1993): 10–17.

Hauser, John R. "Comparison of Importance Measurement Methodologies and Their Relationship to Consumer Satisfaction." *MIT Marketing Center Working Paper 91–1,* 1991.

Joreskog, K. G., and D. Sorbom. *LISREL 7: A Guide to the Program and Applications,* Chicago: SPSS Inc., 1989.

MacLauchlan, William. "Regression-based Satisfaction Analyses: Proceed with Caution." *Quirk's Marketing Research Review.* (October 1992): 10–13.

Miller, John A. "Studying Satisfaction, Modifying Models, Eliciting Expectations, Posing Problems, and Making Meaningful Measurements," in Keith H. Hunt (ed), *Conceptualization and Measurement of Consumer Satisfaction and Dissatisfaction.* Bloomington, IN: School of Business, Indiana University, 1977, pp. 72–91.

Mullet, Gary M. "Regression, regression." *Quirk's Marketing Research Review.* (October 1994): 12–15.

Smith, Scott, *PCMDS Multidimensional Statistics Package,* Provo, UT: Brigham Young University, 1987.

Sokal, R., and P. Sneath. *Principles of Numerical Taxonomy.* San Francisco: W. H. Freeman, 1963.

Tucker, Ledyard R. "The Extension of Factor Analysis to Three-Dimensional Matrices." in Frederiksen, N. and H. Gulliksen (eds.) *Contributions to Mathematical Psychology.* New York: Holt, Rinehart and Winston, 1964.

Computer Diskette Offer

To receive a DOS/Windows 3.1/95 diskette containing:

- the medical equipment data used in this chapter;
- .WK4 (Lotus 123®) spreadsheets and graphs for all charts shown in this book;
- confidence interval and significance-testing spreadsheets

send a check or money order (payable to Marketing Metrics, Inc.) for $15 to:

Improving Diskette
c/o Marketing Metrics, Inc.
305 Route Seventeen
Paramus, NJ 07652

This diskette is offered on an "as provided" basis, we cannot provide computer technical support for these files.

CHAPTER 9

Monitoring Changes in Performance

OVERVIEW

Ongoing customer satisfaction programs face the difficulty of "keeping up with changing times." The issues and attributes that were pivotal to customers in one time period will likely change. As they do, the established CSM program can become irrelevant and out of date. It is important to have in place a process for anticipating *changes in customer requirements,* and for incorporating new perspectives into the ongoing customer satisfaction program.

Many different elements of the environment influence changes in customer requirements, including:

- industry changes
- competitors' changes
- changes occurring within the customerbase
- cultural or country-wide differences between customers

This chapter will provide the specific tools needed to keep a CSM relevant to the customerbase. We will emphasize change, rather than constancy. In situations where a marketing research perspective thwarts flexibility by arguing for an unchanged questionnaire, the needs of the customer must be placed ahead of the analyst's needs for a stable analytical framework. Openness and updatedness have to be the keywords of customer satisfaction measurement.

CHANGES IN CUSTOMER REQUIREMENTS

In Chapter 3 we introduced the concept of customer requirements. As you can imagine these requirements are constantly undergoing change. In order to understand how they change, it will be useful to identify some of the factors that influence their formation. The factors can be classified as *internal*—those under the control of the organization and *external*—those factors outside of the organization and beyond its control.[1]

Factors Under Company Control

Perceived Quality Experienced

Past experiences with the product, or other products offered by the same company will influence a customer's requirements regarding a future purchase. Some customer service professionals suggest that customers' attitudes are preconditioned based on their past experiences, and that they enter into a purchase decision with a degree of cynicism (Nykiel 1992). On the other hand, good experiences in the past can develop loyalty. Customers, out of loyalty, may always buy one brand or model of a product, and temper their requirements to meet what they normally experience with that product. Over time this could lead a customer to develop a relatively idiosyncratic list of expectations, becoming almost a "niche customer."

A frequent airline traveler becomes loyal not only out of a preference for the brand of service, but also because of the frequent traveler miles offered by the airline. In some cases, the incentive miles may cause a customer to overlook an incident of poor service from a flight attendant in an effort to keep his commitment to that airline not inconsistent with his more general experience. Alternatively, customers who give such a large amount of business to an airline may develop exceedingly high requirements of that airline. For example, a business traveler may become

----

[1] I am indebted to a former colleague of mine at Marketing Metrics, Ms. Kelly Uscategui for many of the ideas in this section.

so accustomed to being "upgraded" to a first-class seat with a coach class fare, she may come to require that the airline upgrade her ticket on each and every flight.

Marketing Message

Customer requirements are also affected by the company's initial marketing message. Promises of "quality service" may lead customers to select one brand over another, and will certainly raise requirements once that brand has been purchased. Alternatively, if a brand is positioned as a "no frills" brand, with services reduced in an effort to reduce costs, the customer's requirements may be accordingly adjusted downward.

Price

The price charged for a product will certainly influence customers' requirements. It is important that price be set in accordance with the organization's strategic positioning. Prices can often be set too low or too high, and will present the possibility that a customer either feels that the product is underpriced or that, if offered at a the higher price, it is a poor value (Berry and Parasuraman 1991).

Environment in Which the Product/Service is Consumed

The physical environment in which the product is delivered will help establish requirements of customers as well. Customers, for example, expect that an establishment with a new, modern waiting area will possibly add that expense to the service or product price. Management hopes the newer surroundings will make the delivered product or service worth a higher price. Baker (1986) describes the physical environment in which services, in particular, are delivered as being made up of three elements:

- *Ambient factors*—background conditions that exist below the level of immediate awareness, and that draw attention particularly when they are disagreeable. Such ambient factors could include obnoxious background music or noise.
- *Design factors*—visual stimuli that are noticeable to customers, such as the comfort of waiting room furniture, or the architecture of an office.
- *Social factors*—people present in the environment, including customers and employees. The image of a company can be greatly influenced by the atmosphere created by not only its employees, but also the type of clientele it attracts.

Product Information

Through customer education programs and printed information available on products, customers have become more knowledgeable regarding the selection in the marketplace; how products and services work; and what ingredients are included (Hinton 1991). Thus, customers' requirements can become both more sophisticated and informed than ever before. Consider how consumer knowledge regarding automobile safety systems has increased during the past decade, and how this increased knowledge has led consumers to specifically desire automobiles that are available with air bags and other safety systems. The requirements are not only higher, they are more specific.

Encounters with Organization Personnel

The initial experience with organization personnel will shape the customer's future requirements in using the product or service. If an initial experience is poor, customers may enter the relationship with a degree of skepticism, and the organization may have to meet tougher future requirements.

Organization/Brand Reputation

The reputation of an organization or product in its industry is one of the few aspects of the product or service of which a potential customer can have knowledge prior to experiencing it. Customers will enter the purchase decision with some requirement regarding the credibility or trustworthiness of the provider based largely on this reputation (Zeithaml, Parasuraman, Berry 1990).

Factors Beyond Company Control

Degree of Involvement in the Purchase

When customers spend considerable effort in making their purchase decision, including the selection of the brand and product, they enter the relationship with relatively high requirements that the product perform well. They desire confirmation that their choice is a good choice (Richins and Bloch 1988).

Environment in Which the Product/Service is Consumed

For some products, such as the food and service in a restaurant, the environment in which the product is delivered is the same as that in which it is consumed. In most circumstances, however, the customer consumes an organization's product or service in an environment that is completely out of the control of the organization. The particular nature of a customer's environment will impact his requirements of the product. For example, a customer who will be eating his breakfast during his morning commute may require that a product, perhaps a breakfast sandwich, be convenient to hold and not require the use of a knife and fork. Alternatively, a customer who consumes her breakfast once she arrives at the office may require that it keep its flavor for enough time for her to arrive at the office.

Customer Interpretation of the Marketing Message and Product Information

Despite the intended message provided by the marketer regarding the product's value, functionality, convenience, and so on, the customer will invariably interpret the message according to her own frame of reference. This interpretation will influence the customer's requirements regarding advertised aspects of the product. Consider, for example, how a term such as "convenient hours of operation" can be interpreted quite differently by different customers. For a customer who works 9 to 5, convenient hours may be open until 10 P.M. Alternatively, a customer who works the night shift might consider early morning (7 A.M.) or late night hours (10 P.M.–2 A.M.) as "convenient."

Events Precipitating Change

Experienced Satisfaction/Dissatisfaction

Once a customer has experienced satisfaction with a product over time, he will be more likely to require the same or higher levels of performance in the future. Alternatively, if dissatisfaction has occurred, requirements may be adjusted downward. For example, if a customer encounters canceled airline flights during an important trip, the requirement for the next trip may be that the flights simply depart. If the same customer has had extremely good experiences flying, with no cancellations or delays, he may require that the airline continue to deliver the same or even a higher level of service.

The Economy

The economy obviously impacts customers' ability to pay for or willingness to expect certain products. Using the airline example once again, a business customer whose employer has imposed spending restrictions may now require that the airline offer discounted fares on travel rather than frequent flights during convenient hours. The customer's desire for convenient flights may still exist, however, his priorities may have shifted. Alternatively, if the economy experiences growth, and spending is less restricted, the customer may shift his priorities once again.

Competition

When new competitors enter any industry, introducing more fully featured products or services, the new choices will once again impact current customers' requirements. Competition does, after all, create a "frame of reference" for products and services. And, sometimes influence can come entirely from outside the immediate product or service category when a customer is exposed to a capability in another category that somehow influences requirements in the present category. For example, ATMs in the banking industry may start customers thinking about how they should alternatively be able to buy movie or theater tickets in the entertainment industry.

Changes in the Customer's Environment and Lifestyle

Any change in a customer's lifestyle will evoke changes in his or her requirements of consumer products purchased. Growth in family size, divorce, marriage, and entering college are all examples of how consumers' environments may change. With each type of change, customer requirements of some products will necessarily change.

For business customers, environmental change comes in different forms. However, the impact on requirements is similar. Miller (1985) describes an industrial customer's environment as having three change variables:

- *Dynamism*—growth opportunities and innovation and technological changes in the industry;
- *Heterogeneity*—wide range of customer types which require diversity in production;
- *Hostility*—competition and legal or political constraints in the industry.

Result

With each source of change, customers' requirements will be affected. For example, when business customers experience rapid technological change, they will most likely require that many of the products they purchase demonstrate a similar degree of innovation. Consider a personal computer sales company that, as a result of competition and greater sophistication among its customers, must offer next day delivery in order to remain competitive. The courier service it selects to deliver its computers will most likely be under scrutiny to offer innovations in tracking services, or lower rates based on volumes, and so on. The courier's standard delivery service may no longer be adequate to meet the requirements of the PC company that has experienced such a change in its own environment.

A Prototypical Monitoring Program

Because sources of influence and change are all around, requirements are likely to rapidly shift. Astute organizations will create monitoring programs to reevaluate the appropriateness of their current understanding of customer requirements. These monitoring programs can accomplish two purposes: confirm the present requirements and explore the existence of new requirements.

Step One: Reconfirm the Dimensions/Requirements

As described previously, under our discussion of the process for discovering customer requirements, factor analysis can be used to generate groupings of attributes based on the performance ratings assigned to those attributes. The attribute factors, as we have previously explained, identify major perspectives of evaluation of a product or service.

By factoring performance (or importance) ratings, this first step provides the organization a view of the endurance of existing evaluative factors showing that some attributes that were previously considered similar, are still combined with other attributes to represent the same dimension. Alternatively, it may be found that some different attributes have "entered" existing factors suggesting that the ways in which the product or service is judged have changed.

By regularly applying factor analysis, companies can periodically monitor how customers describe their products. This knowledge can help quality improvement teams understand how improvements in one aspect of a product might contribute to higher satisfaction with a general requirement. For example, using the personal banking example described in Chapter 3, during one period the issue *access to account information* may have been considered to be a component of the **Secure Transactions** requirement. When a factor analysis is undertaken during a subsequent period, *access to account information* may be found to have become part of the **Accessibility** requirement. The company may conclude that, if **Accessibility** is found to be of higher priority than **Secure Transactions,** efforts should perhaps be directed at ensuring customers access to account information.

Step Two: Establish Priorities for Performance Attributes

This pursuit is best known as a "key driver analysis." Customer satisfaction measurement programs regularly provide feedback on how a company's product is performing, and how satisfied customers are with specific product attributes. From this list of attributes, management must determine the areas in which quality improvement resources should be focused. That is, on which attributes will improvements trigger the greatest response in terms of improved overall satisfaction. This prioritization step can be accomplished in a number of ways, some *explicit,* and some *implicit.*

The explicit methods for prioritizing performance attributes require customers to provide an evaluation of the importance of the issues separately from their performance ratings. Some specific techniques include:

1. **Paired comparisons of requirements,** in which customers are given pairs of issues and asked to select that which is most important. This technique can be problematic when the number of attributes is high. Customers can become fatigued if they are asked to judge a large number of pairs, and the participation rate will suffer.
2. **Rank ordering of requirements,** in which customers are asked to rank order issues in order of their importance. With large numbers of attributes, modifications on the technique can be applied (see our discussion of the sequential pile sort later in this chapter).

The results of these techniques can be analyzed using statistical techniques such as Thurstone's Case V (See Nunnally 1978 or Guilford 1954). The result will be an ordering of requirements, and an assignment of ordinal weights for each. The distance between weights can be interpreted to show differences in requirement importance.

Step Three: Compare Performance Measures to the Structure of the Data

The derived importance (by either implicit or explicit methods) provide a measure of the general priority among the overall requirements. But before adopting these weights without reservation, it is important to reflect them against what is known about the structure of the data. In Chapter 8 we discussed how a factor analysis can provide the satisfaction professional with an understanding of the structure of his data. The factor analysis produced groups (factors) of measurement attributes that appeared to measure the same issue, concern, or need. The number of factors identified provided an understanding of the number and type of basic views that customers brought to the evaluation of a product or service category.

It is useful to compare the key driver analysis against the factoring to make certain that each factor or grouping of attributes is represented among the key drivers. It may be that one factor or issue is overrepresented among the key drivers. In this case, the factor analysis could mediate the key driver analysis and suggest that not all of the key drivers representing the same issue necessarily be carried forward.

Step Four: Explore the Information Provided through Other Sources

It is important to escape the myopia of one's current system. Do not hesitate to look outside your current process for other sources of insight. Other input and feedback from customers such as customer mail, verbatim responses to open-ended questions, and periodic discussions with both customers and employees can produce good insights.

Customer mail: Although customer mail and/or complaints compiled by a help center will represent the opinions of only the most vocal or aggressive customers, they can nevertheless be valuable sources of issues concerning all customers. If a large percentage of complaints pertain to a product aspect that is not included in the ongoing customer satisfaction questionnaire, management should take the complaints as a clue to explore the issue in more depth with customers and employees. If the issue is further confirmed, it should be a candidate for inclusion in a revised satisfaction interview.

Verbatim responses to open-ended questions: When customers are asked to evaluate their experience with a product, they typically put themselves in a frame of mind to consider all aspects of the product that contribute to their overall experience. Even if customers are not asked to provide numeric evaluations on a particular issue, if that issue is of concern to the customer, he or she may be inclined to provide a comment regarding the issue if given the opportunity. For example, if a customer's automobile does not contain an airbag, there may be no question regarding the safety system on the automobile company's questionnaire. However, if the customer is concerned about having an airbag, she may provide a written comment in a space requesting additional comments.

Periodic discussions with employees: Once a company's management determines that certain issues are perhaps of importance to customers, it is appropriate to explore those issues in greater detail with employees who are in direct contact with customers.

DIFFERENT VIEWS OF SATISFACTION

As a satisfaction questionnaire is being assembled, there may be some debate about whether "overall satisfaction" should be measured, separately by itself. Those satisfaction professionals who choose not to measure overall satisfaction as a separate rating will generally create a variable they believe represents their customers' overall impression of their product or service. This variable is *generally* a composite created from all of the individual performance attribute ratings. It is often referred to as an *index of satisfaction,* it can also be called a "CSI" (customer satisfaction index).

The Index of Satisfaction

The index of satisfaction, as used by many satisfaction professionals, is really a misnomer since the variable they refer to is not a number "indexed" to any specific base number. The measure is really much better described as a *composite measure of satisfaction.* It is merely an aggregation of all performance attribute ratings, generally averaged to keep the same metric as the individual attribute scores.

While the index will sometimes be used in place of collecting a measure of overall satisfaction, if you collect the overall measure there is still some value in constructing an index of satisfaction. You would generally simply total and average each customer's performance attribute ratings. This measure becomes a new datum for each customer's data record. You will have to create a storage place for the measure in your data file once you calculate it.

Some might suggest a simple average would not do justice to what might be known about the performance attributes. Table 9.1 shows how an index of satisfaction might be calculated in several different ways.

Table 9.1 Calculating the Index of Satisfaction

	Column A Total Sample	Column B Customer 1	Column C Customer 1	Column D Customer 1	Column E Customer 1
	Importance Weights*	Ratings	Index 2	Importance Weights	Index 3
Attribute 1	0.05	7	0.35	0.1	0.70
Attribute 2	0.2	10	2	0.09	0.90
Attribute 3	0.15	6	0.9	0.13	0.78
Attribute 4	0.13	6	0.78	0.09	0.54
Attribute 5	0.08	9	0.72	0.12	1.08
Attribute 6	0.08	8	0.64	0.1	0.80
Attribute 7	0.12	9	1.08	0.08	0.72
Attribute 8	0.05	5	0.25	0.15	0.75
Attribute 9	0.05	7	0.35	0.05	0.35
Attribute 10	0.09	7	0.63	0.09	0.63
Total	1	74	7.7	1	7.25

Satisfaction Index 1 (unweighted) — 7.4
Satisfaction Index 2 (weighted – population weights) — 7.66
Satisfaction Index 3 (weighted – customer's weights) — 7.25
Overall Satisfaction Rating — 7

*Index 1 is a simple average of the ratings in Col B
Index 2 is a weighted average using the total customerbase's importance weights (Col A)
Index 3 is a weighted average using the individual customer's importance weights (Col D)

377

Column B is a simple average of the scores over the 10 performance attributes. But what if the judged importance of the attributes is known? Should not each attribute's score be weighted by its importance in the calculation of the index? (Column C shows an index weighted to the population's importance weights.) Ideally, if weighting were to be employed, the importance weights could even be at the individual customer level. Column E shows a weighted index built on Customer 1's own importance weights.

Many practitioners point out that a composite measure will be more statistically reliable than any single measure. Hence, in trending, the composite measure may be a better choice.

Other Satisfaction Indices

Other practitioners, like Digital Equipment Corporation, have devised special weightings of their satisfaction distribution and have referred to these weighted averages as a *customer satisfaction index* (Dandrade 1994). In particular, a formula is advocated that assigns the following weights to the five response levels ("very satisfied," "satisfied," "neither satisfied nor dissatisfied," "dissatisfied," "very dissatisfied") on Digital's corporate-wide satisfaction measure:

> *add all of the percentages of responses reflecting satisfactory (very satisfied, satisfied, neither satisfied nor dissatisfied) ratings*
> *subtract five times the "very dissatisfied" score*
> *subtract two times the "dissatisfied" score*

This produces an index that can range from 100 to −500. The formula consciously overweights dissatisfaction to focus business units on improvement.

A more ambitious customer satisfaction index is the multiple-measure described by Kessler (1996). Touting the simplicity of one number as a score of overall performance, Kessler suggests combining reasonably diverse measures like: customer satisfaction, supplier satisfaction, internal performance metrics, and market indicators (price advantage/disadvantage, market share) into one weighted index or number. She shows the advantage of this in cross-competitor comparisons (assuming all of the data can be gathered for competitors).

Trending the Index Against Overall Satisfaction

There are at least two ways to use the composite satisfaction index if you calculate one. The most common use is to longitudinally plot index

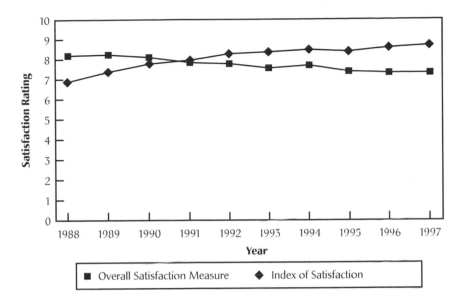

Figure 9.1   Trending Overall Satisfaction against an Index of Satisfaction

scores against overall satisfaction measure scores. The assumption is the composite, index score describes how well an organization is doing, based on *its* definition of performance (represented by the battery of performance attributes administered in the questionnaire).

On the other hand, the explicit measure of overall satisfaction describes how "globally acceptable" an organization is considered by its customers. In Figure 9.1 the index of satisfaction trend line is climbing, indicating the organization is doing a good job on those things being specifically measured. Yet, in the same time frame, the overall, explicit satisfaction measure is decreasing, showing increasing displeasure of the customers. The paradox depicted in Figure 9.1 suggests several possible explanations. It may be the performance attributes being measured include the following:

- The measured performance attributes include issues no longer relevant to the customerbase and therefore not totally correlated to customers' overall satisfaction
- The measured performance attributes fail to include new issues that have recently become relevant to customers
- Customers are less willing to rate *specific* products/services high for fear that these specifics may subsequently be neglected

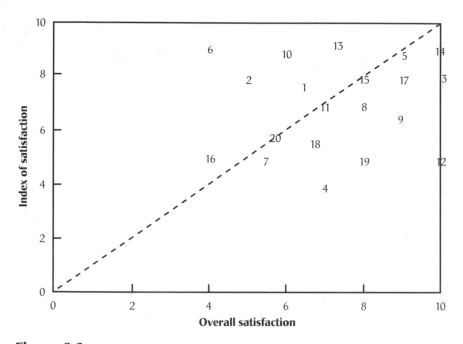

Figure 9.2   Plotting Individual Customers by Their Overall Satisfaction and Index of Satisfaction

- It is conceptually easier to be more critical of specific issues as compared to the broader concept, "overall satisfaction." There is often a bias toward positive scores on broad, affective concepts like "overall satisfaction"
- The placement of the "overall satisfaction" question in the questionnaire may have biased responses. For example, by placing the question at the beginning of the interview, specific criticisms may not yet be "top-of-mind." Whereas placing the overall satisfaction question at the end of the questionnaire stimulates a more thorough critical appraisal.

Consider another way of utilizing the information in these two measures. If you were to create an "X-Y" plot of each customer's joint scores, you would have a picture of how well the two measures agreed across your customerbase, and you would have a valuable way of segmenting your customers. Look at Figure 9.2, which shows 20 customers who have been plotted according to both their overall satisfaction measure and the composite index of satisfaction calculated for each. A plurality of points lie on or near a regression line from lower left to upper right. For these customers, the two scores are closely aligned. But now consider the customers whose scores do not agree. Those customers in the upper left have higher index scores than overall satisfaction scores. These appear to be the first customers who may recognize there are additional performance issues besides the ones currently being measured. These customers would be good ones to interview to attempt to understand what additional performance measures need to be audited.

Customers in the lower right have higher overall satisfaction scores than their index scores. These customers may represent a loyal following (perhaps advocates) who despite their loyalty for the brand (and hence high overall satisfaction), are objective enough to recognize some opportunities for improvement on an attribute by attribute basis.

Kano Analysis

Satisfaction professionals are frequently confronted with the need to interpret customers' ratings of attribute importance. The fact of the matter is, that in rating the importance of various performance attributes, customers may be communicating several different reactions, all related to importance and their requirements, yet vastly different in how each reaction ought to be responded to.

Professor Noriaki Kano and some associates, reasoned that cus tomers might be communicating different levels (or types) of importance in their *explicit* judgments of importance (Kano 1996).[2] An illustrative example Kano offers is satisfaction ratings for a ballpoint pen. If the ink flow of the pen is poor, Kano suggests the customer will express considerable dissatisfaction. Yet, if the ink flows adequately, paradoxically it is likely the customer will not express extreme satisfaction, because the customer *expects* a ballpoint pen to adequately dispense ink. Ink flow is a mandatory function.

The valuable insight in this line of reasoning is that often our measures of explicit importance fail to distinguish the performance attributes that are important, but *expected* (from all competitors), versus those that are important and may be used to differentiate one organization's offering from another's. This means we may inadvertently load up our satisfaction

----
[2]Professor Kano's ideas were originally published in Japan in 1984. He has spoken on his view of differences in attribute importance numerous times in the United States, but the first fully translated version of his original paper is only recently available in a collection of papers edited by Dr. John Hromi.

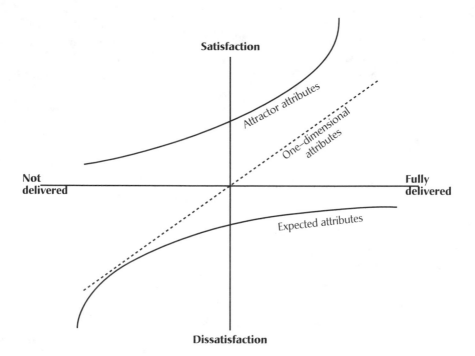

Figure 9.3   Kano's Three Definitions of Quality

surveys with important but expected attributes failing to leave adequate room for important and potentially differentiating attributes.

Kano's ideas suggest a hierarchy of importance:

- *expected*, basic attributes—These attributes could be rated as "important," but they are totally expected. They define activities or functionality the customer expects. They establish "thresholds" of acceptability.
- *one-dimensional* attributes—These are articulated needs, what customers will say they need. Satisfaction increases linearly as these attributes are more fully delivered.
- *attractor*, delighter attributes—These attributes are unexpected, but if offered generate "delight" and surprise the customer. They can act to attract customers from one brand to another.

Kano depicts the responsiveness of each of the three importance types according to the diagram shown in Figure 9.3. The responsiveness of the *expected* attributes plateau showing diminishing returns to satisfaction, beyond their initial contribution. The *one-dimensional* attributes create satisfaction in proportion to their delivery. But, the *attractor* attributes show significant contributions to satisfaction.

Kano and his associates' suggestion for identifying how customers view the importance of various performance attributes is less established. They suggest asking customers two questions about each attribute. Using the attribute "picture quality" of a television, the questioning would proceed:

1. How would you feel if the TV picture was poor? (for example, there was a ghost image or shadow)
2. How would you feel if the TV picture was good? (for example, there was no ghost image or shadow)

Answers to both of these questions for each performance attribute are displayed in a symmetric table, using as many rows and columns as there are stubs in the satisfaction rating scale for Questions 1 and 2 above. Let us assume a five-point Likert response scale: extremely satisfied, somewhat satisfied, neither satisfied nor dissatisfied, somewhat dissatisfied, and extremely dissatisfied. Kano quantifies the number of customers in each of the 25 cells and then classifies each performance attribute according to which of the 25 cells has the highest frequency of customers (see Figure 9.4).

Alternative analytical procedures are being developed. For example, Harvey Thompson (IBM Consulting Group) has created an analytical procedure to identify Kano's three types of attributes. Explicitly derived importance weights must be gathered for the attributes to be examined. Subsequently importance weights are also derived implicitly, based on the attribute's correlation with an external satisfaction criterion like overall satisfaction. (A procedure like the "key driver" process described in the next section is ideal.) Then, each attribute is plotted in a two dimensioned importance grid. (See Figure 9.5.) Explicitly derived weights define the horizontal axis, implicit weights define the vertical axis. Thompson's reasoning is as follows. Those attributes for whom the explicit and implicit weights agree (lower left and upper right) are the one-dimensional importance attributes; either very unimportant or very important. Attributes falling in the upper left (those whose explicit importance is low, but whose ratings are highly related to implicitly derived satisfaction) are considered Kano's "attractor" attributes. These may identify possibly valuable competitive strategies. Attributes falling in the lower right represent "must be" attributes.

If the Attribute Didn't Work:

If the Attribute Worked Well:	Extremely Satisfied	Somewhat Satisfied	Neither Satisfied Nor Dissatisfied	Somewhat Dissatisfied	Extremely Dissatisfied
extremely satisfied			A	A	O
somewhat satisfied	R	R	I	O	M
neither satisfied nor dissatisfied	R	R/I	I	I	M
somewhat dissatisfied	R	R/I	R/I	R/I	
extremely dissatisfied	R	R	R	R	

Legend

O   One-dimensional evaluation; satisfaction when fulfilled, dissatisfaction when unfulfilled.

A   Attractive evaluation; satisfaction when fulfilled, no feeling when unfulfilled.

M   Must-be evaluation; no feeling when fulfilled, dissatisfaction when unfulfilled.

I   Indifferent evaluation; no satisfaction or dissatisfaction regardless of fulfillment or unfulfillment.

R   Reverse evaluation; dissatisfaction when fulfilled, satisfaction when unfulfilled.

S   Skeptical evaluation; suggests questions are not fully understood.

Figure 9.4   Kano's Classification Procedure for Attribute Importance

Implicit, Derived Importance

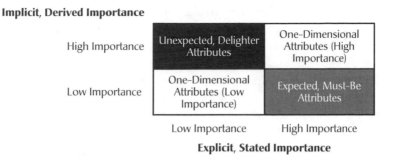

Low Importance   High Importance

Explicit, Stated Importance

Figure 9.5   Identifying Kano's Importance Types

Appreciation is extended to the IBM Consulting Group for this analytical insight

KEY DRIVER ANALYSIS

In all customer satisfaction work there is the need to assign priorities to those issues that are measured. Without prioritization, one is helpless to know how best to effect improvement. Priorities, expressed by customers, provide the information required to correctly organize improvement efforts. So it is no surprise that a substantial amount of effort in customer satisfaction programs is directed at assigning priorities to the performance attributes, for the implementation of improvement programs. "Key drivers" has become a keyword in the CSM community and the key driver identification task has become a critical component of every satisfaction professional's toolkit. *Key drivers* is the name given to performance attributes whose ratings disproportionately effect overall satisfaction. If the key drivers are known, then any key driver whose performance scores are substandard assumes priority for improvement efforts.

The Recurring Need to Reassess—Periodically

Given the dynamic world of customers and the nature of competitors, no category or industry stands still for long. In fact, change is almost constant. This being the case, it is difficult for any satisfaction professional to imagine that he knows the most current key drivers in his category. He may well have identified key drivers a year ago, but that information is probably already stale. So there is need for constant reassessment. Most established satisfaction programs regularly revisit key driver ascertainment.

The major problem with reassessment is its cost and its impact on the customerbase. Key driver studies are a fairly rigorous examination of customer-defined priorities. While it is possible to consider incorporating the key driver study within the satisfaction survey, most satisfaction professionals tend to favor focus. They feel the satisfaction survey is already long, multifaceted and complex; to add a key driver task would make the survey even more tedious. Those who favor a separate key driver survey like the focus of the separate survey on establishing priorities, and customers seem to appreciate this focus as well.

While the concept of key drivers is both intuitive and simple; unfortunately operationalizing a key driver identification procedure is far from easy. There are two approaches: the *implicit derivation* methods and the *explicit derivation* methods. Each is frequently practiced, but each has its drawbacks and problems.

Implicit Methods for Identifying Key Drivers

Implicit methods of key driver identification can be thought of as indirect assessment methods; they try to imply priority weights from existing information collected in the satisfaction survey. Typically implicit methods use mathematical procedures to help derive the importance weights.

The Advantages and Disadvantages of Implicit Identification

One of their biggest drawbacks is that implicit methods are constrained by the information that is currently being collected. As customer priorities shift substantially, new issues should probably be added to the questionnaire. But, implicit methods will not pick this up, because they have only the current body of issues to deal with.

On the positive side, implicit methods make absolutely no additional demands on the customerbase. So the satisfaction professional does not have to worry about tiring customers out with multiple pleas for information and assistance.

Implicit methods are also quick; the data already exists, an analysis can be completed very quickly and with very little extra cost.

Regression Analysis

Because key drivers are, by definition, those performance attributes most closely related to overall satisfaction, regression analysis is the ideal multivariate tool with which to explore this model of dependency. Specifically the model tested is shown in equation 9.1.

$$Y = A + b_1 x_1 + b_2 x_2 + b_3 x_3 + \ldots b_n x_n \qquad \text{Eq. (9.1)}$$

Where:

Y = overall satisfaction

A = a constant

b_1 = regression coefficient for performance attribute 1

x_1 = mean of performance attribute 1

From our discussion of regression analysis in Chapter 8, the reader may remember the regression coefficients for each performance attribute will describe the relative importance of each in influencing overall satisfaction. Those attributes with the largest (and significant) coefficients will be the key drivers.

Figure 9.6 shows output from the SPSS multiple regression routine for the medical equipment data. All 15 variables have been entered into the model regressed against overall satisfaction as the dependent variable. (This is a somewhat risky step. Ratings on performance attributes in most customer satisfaction surveys are frequently intercorrelated. That is, the independent variables [the performance attributes] are not independent of one another. This condition produces multicollinearity and multicollinearity will not only inflate the derived R^2 but will also confound the determination of which variables are significantly correlated with the dependent variable.) Notwithstanding the possibility of multicollinearity, the 15 variables have been introduced into the model.

The regression output shows a significant model (the ANOVA table has an F-value of 9.96, which is highly significant). There are four variables whose t-score is statistically significant. These variables are identified in the lower portion of the output. They are: *responsiveness of follow-up; invoice accuracy; product reliability;* and *phone support availability.* (It is always interesting when after-sale, support services define customer satisfaction. This may imply a category in which most of the competitive products are functionally equal, but after-sale service is the key differentiator.) In addition to the support services, one product attribute, *product reliability,* is also significantly related to overall satisfaction. To increase overall satisfaction in the following time period, it is reasonable to focus one's improvement efforts on one or more of these four attributes.

Explicit Methods for Identifying Key Drivers

Explicit methods of key driver identification (as previously summarized) entail specific data collection for the purpose of identifying priorities of importance; these are the direct methods of key driver determination.

***** MULTIPLE REGRESSION *****

Listwise Deletion of Missing Data

Equation Number 1   Dependent Variable..   Q2AOVERSAT

Block Number 1. Method: Enter

| OPPRF6 | OPFUP7 | OPACCR9 | PDEASE10 | PDFEAT11 | PDRELI13 | PDDURA14 | ESINSR16 |
| ESTRN17 | ESCOMP19 | | ESPRF20 | BSAVSP25 | BSAVTR22 | BSAVTR22 | TSPHN27 | TSQLRP29 |

Variable(s) Entered on Step Number

1.. Factory Repair Quality
2.. Consultant Competency
3.. Product Features
4.. Invoice Accuracy
5.. Product Durability
6.. Spare Parts Availability
7.. Biomed. Engrng. Training
8.. Ease of Operation
9.. Phone Support Available
10.. In-Service Support
11.. Follow-up/Responsiveness
12.. Training Materials
13.. CSR's Professionalism
14.. Product Reliability
15.. Consultant Professionalism

Multiple R   .80012
R Square   .64018
Adjusted R Square   .57593
Standard Error   .52261

Analysis of Variance

	DF	Sum of Squares	Mean Square
Regression	15	40.81813	2.72121
Residual	84	22.94187	.27312

F =   9.96351   Signif F = .0000

Equation Number 1   Dependent Variable..   Q2AOVERSAT

------- Variables in the Equation -------

Variable	B	SE B	Beta	Tolerance	VIF	T	Sig T
CSR's Prof	-.098262	.141749	-.085921	.278828	3.586	-.693	.4901
Resp Foll-up	.258434	.113747	.272539	.297690	3.359	2.272	.0256
Inv Acc	.292486	.110295	.270563	.411497	2.430	2.652	.0096
Ease of Op	.070505	.109411	.057900	.530589	1.885	.644	.5211
Prod Feat	.021658	.101027	.020186	.483107	2.070	.214	.8308
Prod Rel	.241940	.118265	.264474	.256296	3.902	2.046	.0439
Prod Dur	-.054628	.098924	-.069131	.273323	3.659	-.552	.5823
In-Serv Supp	.076918	.124393	.069969	.334544	2.989	.618	.5380
Train Mat	-.145207	.126885	-.135829	.304070	3.289	-1.144	.2557
Cons Comp	.149539	.173261	.116578	.234787	4.259	.863	.3905
Cons Prof	.075218	.176793	.058827	.224054	4.463	.425	.6716
Prts Avail	.067769	.092501	.065052	.543314	1.841	.733	.4658
Bio Eng Trng	.048352	.097426	.044576	.530986	1.883	.496	.6210
Supp Avail	.213689	.107117	.193183	.456787	2.189	1.995	.0493
Repr Qual	-.107722	.115531	-.089273	.467284	2.140	-.932	.3538
(Constant)	-.309879	.232812				-1.331	.1868

Figure 9.6 Output from a Key Driver Multiple Regression

The Advantages and Disadvantages of Explicit Identification

Explicit methods require that a whole survey effort be mounted to collect new data. As such, they incur extra costs and may annoy customers who find they are contacted more than once a year, to respond to questionnaires that do not appear all that different.

The opportunity of explicit techniques is that the satisfaction professional essentially starts with a "clean slate." Current issues may be included, new issues may be trialed, there is even the opportunity to allow customers to add issues at the time of information collection.

Most Frequently Used Procedures

There are several different ways to collect the data required for a discriminating key driver exploration. But the overriding requirement among all of these methods is that they require customers to make *tradeoffs* in their evaluative judgments. A simple importance rating scale (1–7, "not at all important" to "extremely important") will be unsatisfactory in helping to identify key drivers. Using such a scale, customers would be free to rate many, if not all, performance attributes as "extremely important." Yet the organization has limited resources with which to improve its product/service offering. It must know exactly which attributes are *the* most important.

Judgment tasks that require customers to trade-off one attribute against another are the best way to collect importance data, which embodies this critical notion of prioritization. Several different tasks for collecting trade-off judgments have been used and advocated. We will review a number of the techniques and then develop a preferred method.

Constant Sum.   Constant sum techniques present a list of attributes to customers and then ask them to describe the importance of the attributes by allocating a fixed number of points across the list of attributes. Customers may assign as few or as many points to each attribute as they like. The more points they assign, the more importance they are ascribing an attribute. The only constraint is that the total of all assigned points must equal the fixed number of points with which they started out. Figure 9.7 shows a typical constant sum question.

Constant sum tasks are fine when the number of attributes to be evaluated is reasonably small, usually 10 or less. (This is a condition most key driver studies will not be able to easily meet, as there are inevitably 20–30 attributes being considered.) Constant sum tasks also seem to work best in situations where the customer can see the allocation task (in personal or self-administered surveys), they generally do not work well in telephone surveys.

Please divide 100 points among the following 10 descriptions of an automobile according to how important each description is to you personally in choosing a brand of automobile. You may assign as many or as few points to each descriptor as you like. Please see that your final assignments add to 100, no more!

Engine Performance	_____
Fuel Consumption	_____
Road Holding	_____
Heating/Air Conditioning	_____
Quality of the Interior	_____
In-car Entertainment System	_____
Paintwork	_____
Braking System	_____
Electrical System	_____
Transmission	_____
TOTAL	**100**

Figure 9.7   A Typical Constant Sum Question

Constant sum results are tabulated by simply averaging the points assigned to each attribute, and then ordering the attributes from the one with the most points to the one with the fewest points.

Rank-Ordering.   Customers may be presented with a list of performance attributes and asked to rank them from the most important to the least important attribute. Though this is a straightforward request, the process becomes tedious for customers as the number of performance attributes exceeds 10 to 15.

A secondary disadvantage is that the quality of data produced by this task is really only ordinal. Though an attribute may be considered more important than another, the distance or amount of that superiority will not be captured nor will it be identifiable.

Pair Preference.   Pair preference tasks are an eloquently simple way to collect trade-off judgments. All customers know they "can't have everything." So, when presented with a pair of performance attributes and asked to identify which attribute is most important, most customers will readily comply. The judgments presented to customers, as pairs, are very easy to comprehend and respond to.

The primary problem with pair-preference judgments is how the number of pairs geometrically expands as the number of performance attributes to be judged expands. If there are 10 attributes there are 45 pairs, but if the number of attributes doubles to 20, the number of pairs quadruples to 190! This is the major problem with pair-preference judgments. There are ways of working around this difficulty, but none are perfect. The most common solution is to "split-sample" the pairs. This means that in the case of 45 pairs, no customer is presented with all 45, but that each individual customer might be randomly presented with one-third, or 15 pairs. The data from all participating customers is aggregated and averaged and is generally quite robust. But, it is very easy to exhaust a sample of customers. For example, if you were evaluating 20 attributes, and had 190 pairs, if you decided to ask customers to react to no more than 20 pairs, and if you required at least 50 customers to evaluate each pair, you would require a total sample of 10 groups of 50 customers each, or 500 customers in all!

You might have some concerns about your ability to suitably randomize your customers among those 10 groups, such that there were no systematic biases between the groups, which might influence their preference judgments. It also bothers some people, that each customer is exposed to only a subset of the attributes. It is likely that a particular customer might see less than half of the total performance attributes being judged.

The presentation of attributes within each pair should always be controlled (for example, no attribute should always be listed first). And, pairs should obviously be randomized in presentation. This type of task works particularly well in computer-administered versions.

Once you have collected the preference judgments, this data is typically analyzed by a statistical routine called Thurstone's Case V. See the next section for a discussion of the Case V technique. This procedure is a very simple, yet eloquent method for metricizing the ordinal data.

Hybrid Techniques.   Because of the shortfalls of the constant sum and pair preference techniques, the author has developed an explicit judgment procedure we will call *sequential pile sorting*. This procedure will provide trade-off judgments, and yet has the advantage of presenting all attributes to all participating customers.

To conduct a sequential pile sort, each of the performance attributes to be prioritized should be assigned a classification code and printed on a sort card. Each participating customer receives a full deck containing all performance attributes to be prioritized. The cards can be accompanied by a "sort board." The sort board identifies how many piles are to be initially created and provides a space for the cards assigned to each pile. The number of piles designated on the sort board will depend on the total number of performance attributes to be judged. The more attributes, the more piles necessary. Generally you will want enough piles so that when the attributes are evenly sorted across the piles, there will be a maximum of 15 attributes in each pile. Piles may be labeled, "the most important attributes," "the second most important attributes," and so on.

After the attributes have been assigned to the piles, customers are asked to re-examine each pile and to rank the attributes within the pile according to the relative importance of these attributes. They, of course, proceed from one pile to the next until they have ranked the attributes within every pile. The end result of the pile sort and ranking is an overall ranking of the total set of attributes. This task works well either when self-administered or administered by an interviewer. In the case of self-administration it is necessary to provide customers some way of recording their orders. Customers can be asked to bundle the piles with rubber bands, place separate piles in supplied envelopes, or they can be given a response sheet on which to list the numbers of the attributes in the order in which they had been sorted. Interviewers can use similar recording methods. A sample sortboard and instruction set are shown in Figure 9.8.

Thurstone's Case V Analytical Technique

A convenient and insight-provoking method of analyzing pair-preference and rank-order judgment data is a procedure called *the Law of Comparative Judgment*. The procedure was developed by the psychometrician L. L. Thurstone. One special analytical case of the methodology, which Thurstone called the Case V method is easiest to use. The Case V method provides a procedure for metricizing the pair-preference data of the original pair-proportions matrix. The procedure is available in several statistical packages, including PCMDS (Smith 1987), though it can also be accomplished quite handily in a spreadsheet (see Guilford 1954, 159).

Data from the pair-preferences is assembled in a *proportion matrix*. This is a square matrix with performance attributes describing both the columns and rows (see Table 9.2). Entries in each cell represent the proportion of the customerbase preferring the column attribute over the row attribute. The diagonal is judgmentally filled with 50 percent.

A typical computer solution for Thurstone scaling is shown in Figure 9.9. In this case we have used the four performance attributes found in the implicit regression analysis to be the most important. By collecting pair-preference data from customers on the importance of each of these four attributes, we will have better information about their true importance. The frequency matrix at the top of the analysis is the data which is input to this program. The program first echoes the proportion matrix

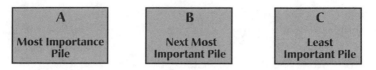

INSTRUCTIONS:

Please open the white envelope labeled **Envelope 1**, which includes 13 cards, each card describing a different service or feature that XYZ might offer to customers like you. Please read the feature/service described on each card.

Please sort the cards into three piles based upon the importance of each feature to you personally. You should place the four most important features in Pile A, the four next most important features should be placed in Pile B, and the five least important features should be placed in Pile C. You may place the piles on the three spaces above. When completed, you should have three piles containing 4–5 cards in each.

Now examine the four cards you have placed in Pile A. Please sort them in order of preference, placing the card describing the feature that you consider most important on the top of the pile. Similarly sort in order of importance the four cards in Pile B and the five cards in Pile C.

Next, number the cards in descending order of importance (for example, cards in Pile A = 1 to 4, cards in Pile B = 5 to 8 and cards in Pile C = 9 to 13. Card 1 should be the most important feature and Card 13 should be the least important).

Please keep the cards in order after you have ranked them.

Place each stack of cards in descending order in the envelopes labeled with the same letter as the pile: A, B, and C.

Thank You once again for your participation

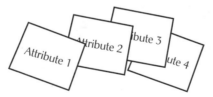

Figure 9.8   A Sequential Pile Sort Sortboard

(previously described in Table 9.2)—the input for the analysis. The matrix shows the number of times each attribute was preferred over every other. For example, in the first column headed "Inv Accur," we can see *invoice accuracy* was preferred over "Prod Rel" (*product reliability*) only 28

Table 9.2   Preparing Data for a Thurstone Analysis

	Attribute A	Attribute B	Attribute C	Attribute D
Attribute A		# people ranking B higher than A	# people ranking C higher than A	# people ranking D higher than A
Attribute B	# people ranking A higher than B		# people ranking C higher than B	# people ranking D higher than B
Attribute C	# people ranking A higher than C	# people ranking B higher than C		# people ranking D higher than C
Attribute D	# people ranking A higher than D	# people ranking B higher than D	# people ranking C higher than D	

times. The Case V procedure calculates a scale value for each performance attribute. The scale values represent each attribute's comparative perceived preference or value. The "final scale values" calculated here are shown at the bottom of the analysis. *Product reliability* receives the highest importance weight, of .455. (It should be noted that the analysis does not imply that *invoice accuracy*, scored 0.0 has no value. As the least favored attribute it is simply assigned a 0.0 value.) Convention suggests the attributes and their scale values be depicted in a thermometer scale, as is shown in Figure 9.10. And the scale values so produced are metrically superior to traditional ordinal scale values.

The method produces "interval-scaled" data which, beyond *order*, captures *degree* of superiority. The derived scale displays the property of equal intervals, characteristic of interval scales. In Figure 9.10, *Product Reliability* is shown to have the greatest importance of all four attributes, with a score of "4.6." It would be inappropriate to claim this attribute is "twice as important" as Phone Support Availability (2.8). However, it is appropriate to conclude that *reliability's* importance (4.6) is greater than the sum of the importance of both *phone support* (2.8) and *follow-up/responsiveness* (.5).

Consequently, *product reliability* should warrant as much attention or resources as both *phone support* and *follow-up/responsiveness* receive, together. In the thermometer display of Figure 9.10, there is no concrete meaning or definition of the zero point. The attribute values can be rescaled in relation to a reasonable zero point, often referred to as a "point of indifference."

Thurstone's Case V also permits us to give quantitative meaning to the *differences* among scale values. That is, by comparing the differences

THURSTONE CASE 5
PC-MDS VERSION

ANALYSIS TITLE:MEDICAL EQUIPMENT ATTRIBUTES—JUDGED SIMILARITIES

NUMBER OF RESPONDENTS = 96.
NUMBER OF STIMULI   = 4
LOW LIMIT OF P   = .0250
HIGH LIMIT OF P   = .9750

INPUT IS FREQUENCY MATRIX

FREQUENCY MATRIX - NUMBER OF TIMES STIMULUS (J) (COLUMN) IS PREFERRED
OR RATED OVER STIMULUS (I) (ROW)

	InvAccur	Res Foll	SuppAvail	Prod Rel
InvAccur	.0000	60.0000	64.0000	68.0000
Res Foll	36.0000	.0000	60.0000	68.0000
SuppAvail	32.0000	36.0000	.0000	56.0000
Prod Rel	28.0000	28.0000	40.0000	.0000
SUMS	96.0000	124.0000	164.0000	192.0000

PROPORTION MATRIX—FREQUENCY MATRIX DIVIDED BY NUMBER OF
RESPONDENTS

	3	4	2	1
3	.0000	.6250	.6667	.7083
4	.3750	.0000	.6250	.7083
2	.3333	.3750	.0000	.5833
1	.2917	.2917	.4167	.0000
SUMS	.5000	.7917	1.2083	1.5000

THETA FOR P MATRIX

	3	4	2
4	37.7612		
2	35.2643	37.7612	
1	32.6878	32.6878	40.2029

Figure 9.9   Thurstone Scaling Output

Z MATRIX – STANDARD NORMAL DEVIATES CORRESPONDING TO THE ENTRIES IN
THE PROPORTION (P) MATRIX
**** INDICATES CORRESPONDING PROPORTION IS ABOVE THE HIGHER LIMIT OR
   BELOW THE LOWER LIMIT OF P

	3	4	2	1
3	**********	.3190	.4310	.5487
4	−.3190 **************		.3190	.5487
2	−.4310	−.3190 **************		.2107
1	−.5487	−.5487	−.2107 *************	
SUMS	−1.2987	−.5487	.5393	1.3080

ZD (COLUMN DIFFERENCE) MATRIX
ENTRIES ARE DIFFERENCES BETWEEN THE INDICATED COLUMN ENTRIES OF
THE Z MATRIX
**** INDICATES A MISSING ENTRY IN EITHER COLUMN OF THE Z MATRIX

	4-3	2-4	1-2
3	**********	.1120	.1177
4	******************		.2297
2	.1120******************		
1	.0000	.3380***********	
SUMS	.1120	.4500	.3473
N	2	2	2
MEANS	.0560	.2250	.1737

*****FINAL SCALE VALUES*****

STIMULUS #	3	4	2	1
SCALE VALUE	.0000	.0560	.2810	.4547

STIMULI	SCALE
InvAccur	.000
Res Foll	.056
SuppAvail	.281
Prod Rel	.455

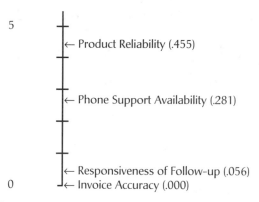

Figure 9.10   Thermometer Diagram of Thurstone Scale Values

in the scale values, or "overall importance" of one pair of attributes versus the differences in values of another pair of attributes, we can determine how much greater the difference is between one pair and another. For example, using Figure 9.10, the difference between the importance of *reliability* and *phone support* is approximately three times the difference between the importance of *follow-up* and *invoice accuracy*.

How Many Key Drivers to Retain

In using any of the above procedures, the result will be a vector of importance weights with a weight for each of the performance attributes tested. The satisfaction professional will need to examine the vector of weights to determine a cutoff value, which will identify the most important attributes, the *key drivers*. This determination is generally not very clear-cut, and requires some decision criteria.

There are three different techniques that may be used:

- *Plot the weights.* When the importance weights are plotted, they will form a line chart similar to the "scree test" mentioned in our discussion of factor analysis (Chapter 8). The plotted line will generally have an initially steep descent, and then at some point it will level off. The attribute immediately preceding this leveling can be considered the last of the key drivers.
- *Calculate first differences.* Similar to the scree plot, but numerical in nature, first differences are simply the difference in magnitude between each successive pair of importance weights. The attribute proceeding the minimization of "first differences" is chosen as the last of the key drivers.

- *Common sense and intuitive judgment.* There will be times when the objective measures described above may not clearly suggest a course of action. At other times, you may wish to override the objective process to maintain an attribute that you know to be of concern to your management or customers. Do not be afraid to impose your judgment in the decision process.

A Recommended Procedure

The choices in Key Driver determination offer some happy solutions. Rather than having to choose between the methods, the skilled satisfaction professional can actually conduct more than one. Many CSM programs today, incorporate periodic *implicit* determinations with less frequent *explicit* explorations. So, for example, one might implicitly review key drivers on a quarterly basis. And as long as no substantial differences are noticed, an explicit determination might be scheduled for every other year. Such a schedule maintains vigilance, yet minimizes additional costs and imposition on customers.

KEEPING YOUR CSM QUESTIONNAIRE UP-TO-DATE AND RELEVANT

It has been said many times throughout this book that one of the most important perspectives associated with a customer satisfaction study is to keep the process open. Open to new issues, open to new interpretations, open to change. As customer requirements have been noted to have changed and as key drivers have exchanged priorities, the satisfaction professional will need to modify the questionnaire or interview to reflect these new priorities. This will require at least two support systems.

Organizational Support

First, the satisfaction measurement and the quality improvement teams will need to be supportive of change. They must not only accept change themselves, but they must be prepared to defend change to the organization at large. Too often departments or individuals "adopt" certain measures. They understandably become distraught when the measures are no longer collected. But they must be helped to understand that the priority in the satisfaction process is to measure relevant not historical issues. Far too many marketing research "tracking studies" have retained questions simply out of respect for a 10–20 year historical trend line.

Logistical Support

Second, logistics must be in place so the mechanical construction of a revised questionnaire and the supporting data files do not prohibit change and modification. The database-driven questionnaire we described earlier is easily reprogrammed to include new questions and variables. So flexibility is the rule. The satisfaction professional must be ever proactive. She must cleanse passé issues out, welcome new issues in.

Using Database-Driven Questionnaires

If the interview is assembled in real time according to the fields active in the database, then the interview will always be consistent with the current information needs. This means that a database program or a smart word processor template with conditional fields will collect the appropriate questions from a separate question-database, and will organize these either as a telephone script or as a printed questionnaire.

References

Baker, Julie. "The Role of the Environment in Marketing Services: The Consumer Perspective." in *The Services Challenge: Integrating for Competitive Advantage,* eds. John A. Czepiel, Carol A. Congram, and James Shanagan, Chicago: American Marketing Association, 1986.

Berry, Leonard L., and A. Parasuraman. *Marketing Services: Competing Through Quality.* New York: The Free Press, 1991.

Dandrade, Robert. "Loyaltizing: A White Paper." Digital Equipment Corporation, 1994.

Green, Paul E., and Donald S. Tull. *Research for Marketing Decisions.* Englewood Cliffs, NJ: Prentice Hall, 1975, pp. 184–191.

Guilford, J. P. *Psychometric Methods.* New York: McGraw Hill, 1954, p. 159.

Hinton, Thomas D. *The Spirit of Service: How to Create a Customer Focused Culture: A Customer Service Strategy for the New Decade and Beyond.* Dubuque, IA: Kendall-Hunt Publishing, 1991.

Kano, Noriaki, Nobuhiko Seraku, Fumio Takahashi, and Shinichi Tsuji. "Attractive Quality and Must Be Quality," in Hromi, John D. (ed.). *The Best On Quality.* International Academy for Quality, Vol. 7, Milwaukee, WI: The Quality Press, 1996.

Kessler, Sheila. *Going for the Gold.* Milwaukee: The Quality Press, 1996.

Miller, D. "The Structural and Environmental Correlates of Business Strategy." *Strategic Management Journal.* Vol. 8, no. 1 (1985).

Nunnally, Jum C. *Psychometric Theory.* New York: McGraw-Hill, 1978, p. 58.

Nykiel, Roger. *Keeping Customers in Good Times & Bad.* Stanford, CT: Longmeadow Press Publishing, 1992.

Richins, Martha L., and Peter H. Bloch. "The Role of Situational and Enduring Involvement in Post-Purchase Product Evaluation." *Journal of Consumer Satisfaction, Dissatisfaction and Complaining Behavior.* Vol. 1, 1988.

Smith, Scott. *PC-MDS Multidimensional Statistics Package,* Provo, UT: Brigham Young University, 1987.

Zeithaml, Valerie, A. Parasuraman, and L. Berry. *Delivering Quality Services.* New York: The Free Press, 1990.

CHAPTER 10

How to Achieve "Buy-In" of CSM Results

OVERVIEW

It is being said with greater and greater urgency, that customer satisfaction surveys are only valuable if the uncovered desires of customers are adequately communicated and acted upon throughout the organization. The information must be communicated not only to those who have the power to change processes, but also to those individuals who actually carry out the processes. But communicating the often complex message of customer satisfaction findings is no easy task.

Communication is only the first step. Very often managers receive CSM information but are unable to understand how they can remedy the discovered dissatisfactions or problems. Too often, a product or a service seems so entangled in various operations throughout the organization that to effect a change would require substantial rethinking/reengineering of numerous complex operations.

Today more and more thought is being devoted to making CSM results actionable. Managers of marketing regions or retailing sites frequently ask what might be the consequences of some improvement in one or more of the included attributes. If the CSM professional lacks the ability to answer this question, the program is threatened. A major innovation that promises assistance in such cases, is the "what if" analysis. A what if analysis can help managers see the probable impact of improvements in any number of performance attributes. Such a demonstration can win these managers over as supporters of the program, by showing them how the model can help them to improve their ratings situation. Rather than a "report card" the satisfaction program becomes a guide for improvement.

THE RELATIONSHIP BETWEEN SATISFACTION AND PROFITABILITY

Although few will question the advisability of striving for higher satisfaction to keep a business viable or make it even more successful, recently investigations have been launched to definitively prove that increases in satisfaction actually do lead to increases in profitability and success. At the same time, the literature is becoming filled with discussions that argue that while satisfaction may be a necessary condition, it may by itself, *not be* a sufficient condition to retain customers (Vavra 1995, Pruden, Sankar and Vavra 1996). Not disregarding this important insight, it is still likely that a more satisfied customerbase will buy more products/ services and buy them longer, than a dissatisfied customerbase.

The linkage between profitability and satisfaction can be explained either through methods of inference or empirical proof. In either case, defining exactly what is meant by "profitability" will become a major "stumbling block" in this endeavor. Most organizations will have a difficult time identifying specific customer-by-customer profits. Some may have an idea of which customers are high cost or low cost to service, and certainly sales records will be available to document changes in sales: increasing sales, level sales, or declining sales. But having a "bottom line" on a customer by customer basis will be extremely rare.

Inferential Procedures

Inferential methods for testing the relationship between profitability and satisfaction are so named because they link satisfaction only with intentional data. Intentional data includes: attitudes about one's likelihood of continuing to buy or one's likelihood of increasing one's share of requirements purchased from a particular organization. Such analyses are typically demonstrated in the aggregate, as Figure 10.1 shows. In this figure,

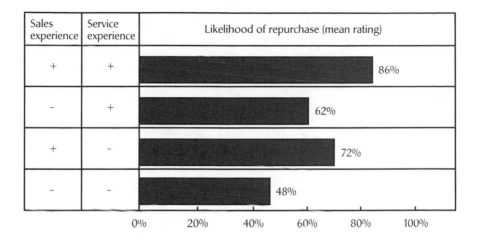

Sales experience	Service experience	Likelihood of repurchase (mean rating)
+	+	86%
–	+	62%
+	–	72%
–	–	48%

0%   20%   40%   60%   80%   100%

Figure 10.1   A Comparison of Satisfaction and Repurchase Likelihood

the value of customers who are satisfied with both sales and service (for an automobile manufacturer) is clearly evident. Of these customers, 85 percent express the likelihood of purchasing another of the manufacturer's automobiles.

Of those customers dissatisfied with both sales and service, there is only a 35 percent likelihood they will repurchase. So satisfaction has a very real consequence for customers' intended future purchase behaviors. However, as we have already established, the relationship between satisfaction and future purchasing behavior is complex; high satisfaction is no guarantee the *individual* customer will necessarily repurchase.

Empirical Procedures for Linking Satisfaction to Profitability

Despite the irrefutable evidence provided by the inferential methods, pressure is increasing to demonstrate the satisfaction-profitability linkage empirically. Empirical methods use actual known spending, demonstrated longevity, or some other objective measure of customer or account value. Because this investigation deals with causality, correlation or regression analysis is a likely tool for this analysis. Two procedures can be envisaged for analytically relating satisfaction to profits. These methods may be described as:

> **longitudinal**—looking at the movement of aggregate customer satisfaction and aggregate profitability over time; or

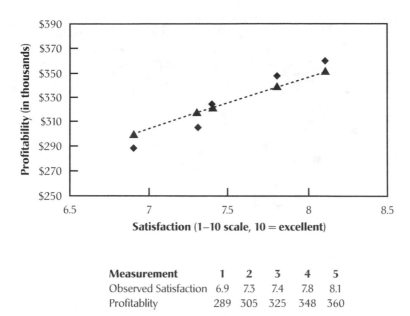

Measurement	1	2	3	4	5
Observed Satisfaction	6.9	7.3	7.4	7.8	8.1
Profitablity		289	305	325	348	360

Diamonds denote the actual satisfaction-profitability data point, triangles identify the trend-line (profitability = 43.44 × satisfaction, 0 intercept)

Figure 10.2   A Sample Satisfaction-Profitability Trend Chart

cross sectional—looking at the pairings of profitability and satisfaction from many different customers at any one point in time.

In both of these perspectives, the major problem is to identify a suitable variable to represent profitability.

Longitudinal Methods

The longitudinal methods attempt to demonstrate a relationship, over successive measures, between aggregate, organization-wide performance and the various observed levels of satisfaction. These methods will be most relevant to organizations that have recently employed customer satisfaction, and have witnessed increases in their satisfaction ratings. Figure 10.2 shows how five measurements of satisfaction and fiscal performance have been correlated with a trend-line establishing the relationship. With the trend line as plotted, each increase of one point in satisfaction suggests an increase in profitability of $43,000. Of course, we must not assume a completely linear relationship. It is likely that financial performance will relate to increases in satisfaction in a diminishing-returns model. Stated another way, the higher the starting level of satisfaction, the less the incremental financial performance is likely to respond to additional increases in satisfaction.

The viability of this form of linkage analysis will be dependent upon the ability to find a suitable measure of aggregate-level profitability for the vertical axis. Possibilities include:

- organization-wide profits
- sales levels
- account growth (incremental sales)
- market share
- aggregate estimate of share of customers' requirements

Cross-Sectional Methods

The cross-sectional approach assumes the organization's customers' satisfactions will be distributed over a range wide enough to allow comparison against each customer's purchases, profitability, share of requirements, or some other measure of business success at the customer level. This analysis takes place at one point in time, as opposed to the longitudinal analysis, which requires measurement points over several different points in time.

Because satisfaction measures are maintained at the individual level, any linking procedure necessarily will require performance data at the individual or account level as well. It is surprising how few organizations can derive a measure of profitability for individual customers or accounts. Any company depending upon direct marketing is likely to have appropriate metrics, as are not-for-profits and charities. These businesses have all learned over the years to reinvest only in those customers who create profits.

With the account-by-account performance information collected, compare the satisfaction scores for each of these accounts with the performance information. In Table 10.1 we have assumed a performance measure of change in sales. This performance measure is then correlated with the concomitant change in satisfaction score from the same period. Table 10.1 shows that for every unit change in satisfaction scores, sales may be expected to change by 19.8 units! This type of analysis should be compelling proof to even the most hardened skeptic of the importance of improving customer satisfaction.

Table 10.1   A Cross-Sectional Analysis Linking Profitability to Satisfaction

	Satisfaction Scores			Sales		
Customer	*1995*	*1996*	*Change*	*1995*	*1996*	*Change*
135	7.1	7.1	0.0	80	82	2
141	6.7	6.2	−0.5	60	50	−10
165	8.0	8.5	0.5	110	130	20
173	8.8	9.1	0.3	25	55	30
210	7.2	7.8	0.6	10	15	5
215	7.9	8.0	0.1	63	73	10
252	7.0	6.9	−0.1	61	46	−15
307	7.8	7.3	−0.5	33	33	0
388	7.6	8.1	0.5	26	32	6
420	7.9	7.9	0.0	60	67	7

Regression Output

Constant	3.71
Standard Error of Y Estimate	11.12
R Squared	0.36
Number of Observations	10
Degrees of Freedom	8
X Coefficient(s)	19.83
Standard Error of Coefficient	9.44

Planning for the Future

As the customer satisfaction field continues to increase in its sophistication and its desire to positively impact organizational survival and success, it will be critical for all organizations to better identify the returns they derive from each customer they service. To this end, satisfaction professionals should be requesting as much organization-wide performance data (in return for their supplying satisfaction information) as possible. Most organizations these days are accumulating substantial bodies of "internal metrics"; unfortunately this information is frequently "siloed" within operating areas or divisions. It is invaluable to establish a central "warehouse" of this vital information, making it available to the customer satisfaction effort as well as other internal groups. These data will help build a case for the relationship between satisfaction and profitability within the organization. If such an organization-wide effort is unrealistic, do not overlook the opportunity for maintaining your own database of internal metrics (from information supplied to you, or that you have independently collected) to contrast with your satisfaction results.

Do not ever fool yourself into thinking your management is so totally committed you will never need proof of the value of your satisfaction improvement efforts. There is a day in the life of *every* satisfaction program when someone in the organization will question the return on the investment. Be prepared for this day!

ORGANIZING FOR IMPROVEMENT

So vast and all-encompassing (of various departments and areas within an organization) will be the results of a customer satisfaction survey, that unless a formalized procedure is in place for reacting to the findings, they will probably not be widely utilized. This is because no *one* department owns (nor could act on) all of the findings of a customer satisfaction survey. Without an implementation process in place, the naive organization that simply fields a survey of customers, will find the results of a survey to be overwhelming. There will simply be too many different departments to involve, too many different processes to modify or to influence for one, isolated effort to effect. Even if the satisfaction process reports directly to the COO, it will be difficult to fashion the improvement plans and to allocate responsibilities.

But in organizations where an implementation process has been considered *before* the customer survey is fielded, then the results will not be so overwhelming. Hopefully an implementation task force (a Quality Improvement Team) will have been formed. This team should have representatives of each of the many departments and processes that may need to be altered. Each representative will be responsible for taking information back to his area prompting remedial actions to improve overall satisfaction.

A secondary benefit of having an implementation program in place is the continuity and continuous focus the implementation task force affords the customer satisfaction process. Rather than being a once-a-year, "on the bookshelf" project, the customer satisfaction process is given an ongoing life.

Illustrative of how quality review processes can be established to receive results from a continuing customer satisfaction is the process created by the Cellular Infrastructure Group of Motorola. The process is convened every six weeks. Here is a brief overview of the process:

The Motorola Cellular Infrastructure Group (CIG) Quality Review meeting is a vehicle by which the organization reviews the continuing progress of the quality system. It provides a forum through which all the functional groups of CIG present to senior management their quality, customer satisfaction data, and plans for improvement. These reviews also provide opportunity for cross-fertilization of ideas and serve to routinely refocus the organization on quality and customer issues.

This procedure applies to Quality Review meetings held in Motorola's CIG at the group level.

- The meetings are attended by the executive vice president and general manager of Motorola CIG, his direct reports, and their major managers.
- Each meeting begins with a presentation on the current level of performance of Motorola CIG's products and services. This ensures that the meeting maintains a customer focus.
- The presentations also include Customer Satisfaction Improvement Plans and goals with specific metrics to monitor these goals.
- The general manager is responsible for setting the overall focus and direction of the meeting. In addition, the general manager provides assistance in resolving critical issues. The general manager also assigns action items to resolve the critical issues and makes recommendations for improvement in products, procedures, and organizations.
- The Quality Organization is responsible for providing Motorola CIG with an unbiased view of the quality of its products and services.
- Each functional organization is responsible for creating improvement plans to address the areas identified by the CIG Quality Management Program. They present these plans during each of their respective presentations at each meeting.
- Suppliers of Motorola CIG are also part of the Quality Review meeting. Each participating supplier presents metrics and quality improvement plans identified by Motorola CIG. Each supplier presentation begins with action items from the previous meeting (if any). All action items are required to be completed by the next scheduled Quality Review meeting.

Motorola CIG customers periodically attend the Quality Review. CIG customers are considered the best source of feedback for proposed quality improvement programs. During the meeting, customers are invited to provide immediate feedback on quality improvement plans in addition to validating customer perception data from the satisfaction survey process. The Quality Review also serves to provide customers with an awareness of quality improvement efforts throughout Motorola CIG (Motorola CIG 1996).

METHODS FOR DIRECTING CHANGE FROM CSM RESULTS

Quality Function Deployment

There is a generally evolving belief in the management of technology that cooperation and communication among engineering, R&D (the technical planners), manufacturing (the builders), and marketing (collectors of customer information) leads to better product improvements and more acceptable new products (Griffin and Hauser 1992).

Evidence shows if engineering and manufacturing and R&D fully understand customers' needs and if marketing has explored how customer needs can be fulfilled by product or service changes, then a product or service is more likely to be profitable (Cooper 1984; Souder 1988; Pinto and Pinto 1990).

Quality Function Deployment (QFD) is the process that brings these traditionally isolated departments together and structures the information in such a way that it can be productively acted upon by all. QFD helps interpret how product characteristics and servicing policies affect customer preference, satisfaction, and ultimately sales. One discrete advantage QFD has over any other similar processes is its visual or grid format that participating parties find easy to understand.

A simple QFD diagram is shown in Table 10.2. The grid is formed with customer needs as rows and operating areas or departments as columns. Then in each cell of the grid, the relationship between the need and the department is quantified, from open (no relationship) to a gradation of relationship (weak to strong). This is a very simple way of allocating ownership of problems to operational areas within the organization.

The grid is organized in five sections: Needs, Importance, Responsibility, Perceptions, and Action. The customer requirements are listed in order of their importance weights shown in the second column. The perceptions section shows the client's perceived delivery of each requirement as well as the delivery by two competitors (A and B). For each requirement a competitive gap is formed in the Perception section. The highest

Table 10.2 A Quality Function Deployment Grid for a Ski Resort

Customer Requirements/Needs	Imp.	Engineering	Design Team	Grooming Staff	Base Management	Lodge Management	House Keeping	Marketing	Our Rating	Competitor A	Competitor B	Competitive Gap	Import Gap	Priority
		Responsibility							Customers' Perceptions				Action	
Upkeep/Condition of Base Station	0.20				■			○	6.9	7.7	7.5	-0.8	-0.17	2
Number of Trails	0.18	■	■						7.5	7.7	6.9	-0.2	-0.04	4
Condition of Trails	0.13		○	■					8.3	7.1	6.4	1.2	0.16	
Cost of Week Package	0.10				○	○		■	6.3	7.5	8.0	-1.7	-0.17	2
Lift Lines and Capacity	0.09	■							8.6	8.1	5.9	0.5	0.05	
Cleanliness of Lodge Rooms	0.08						■		9.0	4.9	7.0	2.0	0.16	
Quality of Lodge Restaurants	0.07					○			6.7	8.8	7.1	-2.1	-0.15	3
Comfort of Lodge Rooms	0.04								8.8	6.3	7.6	1.2	0.05	
Quality of Food at Base Station	0.04				■				7.8	8.4	5.0	-0.6	-0.02	5
Trail Signage	0.04		○	○					4.0	7.8	8.8	-4.8	-0.19	1
Spaciousness/Comfort of Lodge	0.02					○		○	8.9	6.6	7.3	1.6	0.03	
Spaciousness/Comfort Base Station	0.01				○				7.1	7.9	6.7	-0.8	-0.01	6
	1.00													

Key: ■ Strong Relationship
○ Weak Relationship

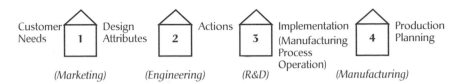

Figure 10.3   The Houses in the House of Quality Process

Adapted from: Griffin, Abbie, and John R. Hauser, *The Voice of the Customer,* Cambridge, MA: Marketing Science Institute, 1992.

performing competitor's score is subtracted from our oganization's delivery score, to form a "competitive gap." When this number is positive it signifies a requirement on which we are superior. Such requirements are leverageable strengths. Negative competitive gaps indicate requirements on which a competitor is perceived as superior. These requirements are weaknesses and are candidates for improvement. But the order by which they should be improved is taken from the importance weights. Each competitive gap is multiplied by the requirement's respective importance weight. The largest negative term in this second to the right column indicates that one requirement on which improvement efforts should first be directed. In Table 10.2 this is *trail signage*. The *upkeep/condition of the base station* is the next requirement on which improvement efforts should be focused. The Responsibility section of the grid tells us that the design team and the grooming staff should take the responsibility for improving the first requirement (*trail signage*), while base management should be responsible for improving the *upkeep/condition of the base station.*

The "House of Quality"

A more complex QFD process is the *House of Quality,* first practiced at Mitsubishi's Kobe shipyards in Japan in 1972. The process was later adopted by Toyota in the late 1970s, and by Xerox and Ford in the United States in 1986. Griffin and Hauser (1992) report its use by over 100 U.S. firms by 1991.

The "House of Quality Process" is actually a series of four "houses," each one connecting two of the four input areas (customer needs, design attributes, R&D actions, and manufacturing implementation). See Figure 10.3 for a representation of the four different houses. The most widely used and discussed (in a customer satisfaction context) is the first house, linking customer needs to design attributes (engineering's measures of product performance). This linkage essentially answers how added customer satisfaction can be engineered into the product or service.

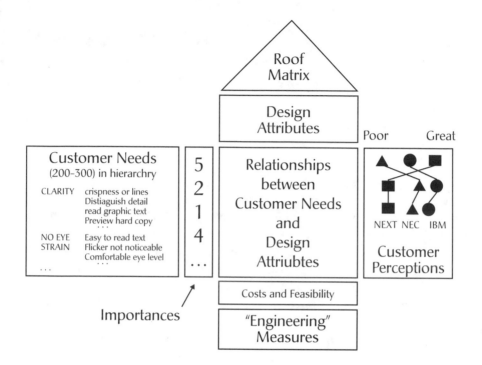

Figure 10.4   An Overview of the House of Quality Process's First House

Reprinted from: Griffin, Abbie and John R. Hauser, *The Voice of the Customer*, Cambridge, MA: Marketing Science Institute, 1992, page 6.

The House of Quality is composed of seven areas or components. These areas are identified in Figure 10.4 and are discussed below.

Customer Needs

A customer need is a description, in the customer's own words of the expected benefit of the product or service. Typically the needs are stated in consumers' terminology stressing not a particular technology or process, but how the product or service is desired to be experienced. The focus on the consumer's experience, rather than on technology or measurement has proven, Griffin and Hauser assert, to be one of the keys to the success of QFD. Focusing on technological solutions too early on, may cause one to overlook more creative solutions, which may be more readily available. As an example, responding to customers' desire for clearer print characters, Hewlett Packard engineers rearranged the pattern of dots on the page, in creating the LaserJet III, rather than focusing on newer technology to increase the number of dots on the page. Following the later solution would have meant clearer print, but at a greater cost and with a more extensive delay getting to market. Instead, Hewlett Packard introduced the LaserJet III quickly and at a price lower than that of its predecessor, the LaserJet II.

Because an explication of customer needs (or requirements) will generally yield a list of 200–300 needs, the QFD procedure requires that the list of needs be made more manageable. Typically this is accomplished by establishing a hierarchy within the needs. The most important needs, those labeled primary, are also understood to be strategic needs. These needs provide the product development team with basic design objectives.

Primary needs are elaborated by means of secondary, or "tactical needs." The secondary needs help the design team understand how the customer judges the basic or primary needs. They help the product development team focus their efforts on more detailed benefits that fulfill the strategic direction of the primary needs. Each primary need should be elaborated by three to 10 secondary needs. The secondary needs are closest to our performance attributes.

Tertiary needs, also considered to be "operational needs," provide the detail helping engineering and R&D to develop engineering solutions that fully satisfy the secondary needs.

Importance Weights

Customer needs are not equal. The House of Quality requires priority weights be assigned to the primary needs to help direct attention at those needs that are considered the more important. A substantial portion of Hauser and Griffin's work has investigated how to most accurately assess these weights. In Chapter 4 we have reviewed this work. Although we have taken the position that trade-off tasks are the logically superior method with which to assign weights, Hauser and Griffin (1992) in their work have found an explicit importance rating (1–10 importance rating for each attribute) is the measure most highly correlated with overall satisfaction.

Customer Perceptions

Customer perceptions are formal comparisons on primary and secondary needs, of how category competitors currently perform. Knowledge of which products/brands are perceived to best satisfy each need, can give engineering and R&D some useful insights into how to best address satisfying a particular need. Customer perceptions are measured using conventional marketing research measures of product performance. This would generally take the form of asking customers to rate the performance of each of the competitors in the category.

Segmentation   It is important to recognize that the importance weights assigned to the basic needs will not be uniform across the customerbase. Instead, it is quite likely that there exist segments of the customerbase for whom the primary needs have relatively different importance weights. When segments differ substantially, a decision may need to be made as to the customer segment or segments on which to focus. If more than one segment is to be addressed, a separate QFD analysis will have to be pursued for each segment.

Design Attributes

With the customers' needs listed, the product development team will list those measurable design aspects of the product or service that, if modified, would affect customers' perceptions of delivery on that performance attribute or need. It is not uncommon for one design attribute to influence more than one customer need.

Engineering Measures

These are specific measurements on each design aspect of the existing products—objectively measuring the performance of both the organization's product or service and those of competitors. Goals may be established for each measurement, based either on intuition or by reviewing customers' perceptions of the operation of the competitive offerings. If, for example, customers unanimously report superior performance by a specific competitor, engineering would wish to examine the competitor's solution to the problem, and their objective performance. This examination may suggest ways in which the current product or service can be modified for improved serviceability.

Relationship Matrix

The core of the house, the relationship matrix, relates customer needs to the design attributes. This matrix shows which design attributes influence which need and by how much. The nature of the relationship can be scored from strong to weak, identifying those design attributes most closely related to any specific customer need. However, because there will be an extremely large number of linkages, it is desirable to focus only on the very strongest linkages. Most QFD practitioners attempt to leave 70 percent or more of the cells in the relationship matrix blank. If more relationships were to be acknowledged, the process could easily become unmanageable—that is, too many design attributes would appear to need modification to improve a customer need.

Roof Matrix

Design attributes will quite frequently overlap or interact. The "roof" of the House of Quality identifies these relationships. The relationships between design attributes may be direct, a lighter car door means less pressure to close it, or indirect, as with computer battery life, longer life means a heavier battery (the opposite of what is desired both by customers and designers).

DISSEMINATING THE FINDINGS OF YOUR CSM

Written Reports

All too often, written reports become the artifacts of customer satisfaction surveys rather than action plans and reference tools for quality improvement. Make sure the reports you write and disseminate do not simply adorn the office shelves of your executives. Strive to make your reports valuable planning and reference tools.

Organization

Your written reports should probably include at least the following sections.

- Executive Summary/Improvement Plan—This section should be the "call to action." Any executive reading this section should emerge with a clear understanding of exactly what the organization needs to do to improve customers' satisfaction. Ideally the plans should be allocated by operating area or department.
- Key Trends—There will be a certain number of measures which your management is keen on reviewing on a continuous basis. Obviously, overall satisfaction is one of these measures. But there will be others, idiosyncratic to each organization and industry. Make sure these measures are clearly displayed as trends with an appropriate narrative, suggesting the ramifications of each depicted trend.

- Detailed Discussion of the Findings—There will be some readers of your report who will wish to examine how you have arrived at your conclusions. For these readers, the detailed discussion section should provide a complete explanation.
- Description of the Methodology—Do not fail to describe exactly which customers you are interviewing, how they are selected, when you interview them, and how you collect data from them. The more open your process is, the more easily it will elicit trust. The better understood the process, the more likely you will be to receive suggestions for improving it from one measurement wave to another.
- Appendix—The Appendix is a good place to locate all those things that might be questioned at some time or another, but which would only encumber the more actionable sections of your report with superfluous detail.

Contents

Generally, charts and graphs with a minimum of discussion are the most action-oriented way to communicate your survey's findings. Each organization will, of course, have its own "style sheet" and preferences. Also, it is a good idea to encourage your Quality Improvement Team to review your proposed contents, keeping open to their specific needs and suggestions.

Management Presentations

Beyond the written report, it is invaluable to schedule a presentation of your survey's findings. In a face-to-face discussion, it is far easier for executives to ask questions and form a consensus of agreement with your results. You should probably use such a personal meeting to elicit reactions from your management. This way you will know what each executive thinks about your satisfaction process.

"Frontline" Reports

Although policy-makers' support of a satisfaction program is important, their decisions can often run amuck on the floor of the factory or on the frontline in contact with customers. Without buy-in and understanding from the workers or service providers themselves, it may not be clear why processes or procedures need to be changed. In the absence of such understanding, the "tried and true way" may be reverted to.

Where successful satisfaction improvement programs have been executed, in almost every case the workforce will have been involved in the process. Without their meaningful involvement, the satisfaction program simply is reacted to as management's current fad or scheme. The pervasiveness of the program and the organization's commitment to it, may be transparent unless the workforce is meaningfully engaged in the change.

When you are able to parse customers' reactions out to a specific department or work area, create graphs or other visual displays to be disseminated to the departments. The supervisors or foremen in these areas (if they have been properly involved in improvement training) will readily embrace the information and should post it (alongside displays of internal metrics) to show department members customers' reactions to their department's contribution or output. This tactic has been implemented very satisfactorily by Rolls-Royce Motor Cars. In its factory in Crewe, England, each department foreman maintains a TQM bulletin board. Posted on the board, every month, are internal department metrics as well as the most recent satisfaction metrics (relevant to their area) as well as comments from customers collected in the satisfaction program.

Feedback to the Customer

Although much customer satisfaction information is appropriately disseminated within an organization, all too frequently the opportunity (or obligation) to communicate the findings back to customers is totally overlooked. Many companies will blush at the thought of exposing customer complaints to other customers. Yet, it has been found that this sort of openness for the satisfaction process creates immediate credibility for the process and produces invaluable support and cooperation for future waves of the program. When customers see that an organization is actually disseminating and acting on the information collected in the satisfaction measurement process, they are likely to become longtime supporters of the program. It becomes clear to them that their information is being used to increase the quality of those products and services on which they depend.

The Cellular Infrastructure Group of Motorola is exemplary in sharing the results of its customer satisfaction process with customers. Not only are recent survey results (and their attendant action plans) published in every quarterly newsletter, but customers are also invited to attend the Quality Review Meeting held every six weeks in Arlington Heights, Illinois. No customer of this organization could ever demean the satisfaction process by grumbling about the organization's lack of attentiveness to customer feedback. There is evidence everywhere as to how satisfaction measurements are being used!

THE "WHAT–IF" ANALYSIS

When quality and satisfaction improvement depend upon business units or affiliated businesses (dealers or franchisees) to improve their individual actions or performance, it may be difficult to properly educate and motivate these units to take the most appropriate corrective actions. Verbal cajoling and threats are often the only ammunition available. A "what-if" analysis using satisfaction data can perform an invaluable service working with such units to build constructive, remedial action plans.

The Value of Participation

Most of us are given to criticizing and distrusting plans in whose creation we have not been involved. We distrust and therefore often resist or even sabotage these plans. When a major organization's survival depends on the constructive reaction of independent business units (dealers, franchisees, and so on) to the implications of customer satisfaction data, a new tact must be employed. The best tactic is to attempt to establish "buy-in" or involvement from the operating units in any remedial plan established. This suggests such a plan should be formulated in "plain view" of the operating unit and, ideally, with input from its staff.

A modern customer satisfaction survey with information on both customers' ratings of performance as well as the importance of performance attributes is an ideal platform from which to build such a joint plan.

The Process

The author has had much success with a process referred to as a "What-If" Analysis. It is based on a real-time spreadsheet, which is capable of generating current satisfaction scores, for all operating units. This means a computer model with a relatively substantial database capability is required, since the satisfaction survey results must be stored and available to the model.

Table 10.3 shows how the spreadsheet looks initially. The Planner shown in Table 10.3 is for Office A, which currently has an overall satisfaction score of only 72 percent against a national average of 80 percent. National management would surely like Office A to improve its performance to at least equal that of the national average.

The What-If Analyst/Planner shows that in the most recent satisfaction survey, Office A was scored highest by its customers for: *understanding customers' financial goals, timeliness of investment transactions,* and *frequency of contacts.* Each of these received a "totally satisfied" rating from 90 percent or more of the Office's customers. On the other hand, the Office's lowest

Table 10.3 The What-If Planner—Beginning Grid

Weight	Attribute	Office A	National Average	Performance Gap	Action Plan
6	Expertise in various investment products	72%	80%		
9	Quality of advice	68%	72%		
6	Understanding of your financial goals	95%	95%		
9	Supplying investment research	79%	95%		
3	Follow-up on problems	60%	83%		
2	Invitation to investment seminars	45%	85%		
12	Monitoring the performance of your portfolio	78%	90%		
6	Frequency of contacts with you	90%	96%		
3	Timeliness of investments transactions	90%	85%		
4	Responsiveness to inquiries	55%	60%		
17	Investment performance	50%	57%		
8	Offering new investment ideas	75%	84%		
11	Reviewing your portfolio	86%	88%		
4	Professionalism in interaction with you	53%	76%		
	Customer Satisfaction Index	72%	80%		

ratings were on *invitation to investment seminars, investment performance,* and *professionalism.* How can Office A improve its ratings, and the sponsoring organization's satisfaction ratings as well?

Without the help of the What-If Planner, improvement plans would be difficult to establish and might not be readily understood by those expected to effect the improvements. What the Planner does is to demonstrate in real time the probable impact of any combination of improvements. Generally the executives of Office A would first be encouraged to identify a plan they would suggest as a good remedial step. Their plan should contain:

- the attributes on which they recommend focusing improvement efforts,
- target ratings for each of these attributes during the next survey period.

A formulated plan can actually be evaluated by the Planner. It will take the current performance levels of the remaining attributes, multiplied by their importance, plus the new target levels of the attributes identified in the Office's plan multiplied by the importance of these attributes and will calculate a new CSI score for the Office. This new CSI score is held for the next step of the What-If process.

The spreadsheet model knows the importance of each of the 14 performance attributes to the Office's customers. (These importance weights are shown in the left-most column labeled "Weight," but would generally not be displayed to the Office executives.) First, the spreadsheet model calculates performance gaps—the discrepancy between the Office's current satisfaction rating and the national average. Then each performance gap is weighted by the importance of the associated attribute. The three attributes with the largest weighted scores are selected as key to the most effective improvement plan. (By virtue of their large weighted score, these attributes offer the largest improvement potential to the Office's overall satisfaction score.) Then the attributes are sorted, placing the target attributes at the top of the list. Very often the spreadsheet's choice of attributes is much different from those chosen by the local executives. The respective improvements to the overall CSI ratings are compared. Generally the model's plan will offer the greatest improvement. The model's selection criteria is explained to the Office's improvement team, which can be a learning process for them.

Table 10.4 shows the completed action plan. The model has identified: *monitoring portfolio performance, supplying investment research,* and

Table 10.4 The What-If Planner—With a Recommended Action Plan

Weight	Attribute	Office A	National Average	Performance Gap	Action Plan
12	Monitoring the performance of your portfolio	78%	90%	12%	90%
9	Supplying investment research	79%	95%	16%	95%
17	Investment performance	50%	57%	7%	57%
4	Professionalism in interaction with you	53%	76%	23%	53%
2	Invitation to investment seminars	45%	85%	40%	45%
8	Offering new investment ideas	75%	84%	9%	75%
3	Follow-up on problems	60%	83%	23%	60%
6	Expertise in various investment products	72%	30%	8%	72%
9	Quality of advice	68%	72%	4%	68%
6	Frequency of contacts with you	90%	96%	6%	90%
11	Reviewing your portfolio	86%	88%	2%	86%
4	Responsiveness to inquiries	55%	60%	5%	55%
6	Understanding of your financial goals	95%	95%	0%	95%
3	Timeliness of investments transactions	90%	85%	-5%	90%
	Customer Satisfaction Index	72%	80%		76%

investment performance as the three most important performance attributes on which to improve in order to most improve the Office's next period Customer Satisfaction Index.

LINKING SATISFACTION TO EMPLOYEE COMPENSATION

Many feel that until satisfaction scores come full circle to being used in employee reviews and compensation, they will be perceived as only a gimmick or a fad. And, indeed, more and more organizations are moving to the point of incorporating their satisfaction scores in employee reviews. William M. Mercer, Inc. (1995) reported in 1995 that 10 percent of a national sample of 453 mid- to large-size companies made salesforce rewards partly contingent on customer satisfaction. An additional 10 percent in this survey said they planned to implement a satisfaction component in annual rewards within a year. The primary objective given for the implementation was to reduce customer attrition (Lissy and Morgenstern 1995). Mentzer, Bienstock and Kahn (1995) in a 1994 survey of executives of 124 major U.S. companies found 41 percent of the firms linking top management's performance evaluations to CSM results. CSM was tied to compensation for 35 percent of top managers, but for only one-quarter of middle-level managers.

While movement is occurring, this is a delicate issue and one that must be approached with tact and objectivity.

The Rationale

By linking some of employees' compensation to customer satisfaction, many believe, an organization's commitment to satisfaction is made more obvious. Making some portion of each employee's pay dependent upon customer satisfaction, will likely heighten awareness of and involvement in efforts to improve satisfaction. Joe Nacchio, former CEO of the Baldrige-winning CCS Division of AT&T, has observed, "It wasn't until AT&T CCS tied bonuses to customer satisfaction that employees became aware of the objective of customer satisfaction" (Kessler 1996). In this way, customer satisfaction is no longer simply a lofty corporate goal, it becomes something every employee should be concerned with. In focusing each individual employee more closely on customer satisfaction, the actions of the organization are brought closer to the needs of individual employees.

In order to successfully link satisfaction to compensation, here are some steps that should be undertaken:

- Build awareness of the customer satisfaction process—make sure employees can find out how they (or their department) are/is being evaluated.
- Establish an objective administration process for the survey, free from internal biases. Generally, having the program administered by an external, third party, provides this sort of assurance.
- Establish a good communication program for disseminating the results of each measurement period.
- Involve employees in creating and improving a quality improvement plan.

The Objectives

Employees must constantly alternate their attentions between doing things that influence sales in the present period versus doing things that will influence sales in the future; and between taking care of currently satisfied customers versus taking care of currently unhappy ones. The preoccupation of American workers and management appears to be focussed on increasing current sales and maintaining the satisfaction of those customers who are currently satisfied.

Such focussing represents trade-offs that both workers and managers have made, perhaps instinctively, maybe in the belief that their organization would wish them to behave in this manner. The trade-offs have severe long-term implications and often management is not fully aware of the extent to which such trade-offs are being made. Introducing customer satisfaction into the incentive program is one way to help focus workers on the long-term and on those customers who may currently be at risk.

In a model-oriented, but pragmatically based discussion of satisfaction-based incentive programs, Hauser, Simester and Wernerfelt (1994) position satisfaction measurement as one of the best indicators of effort expended (by employees) to affect (either preserve or increase) long-term sales. They conclude that customer satisfaction measures are more effective and will result in greater profitability for the sponsoring organization, when:

- both customers and noncustomers are measured—creating a market-view of the organization (rather than the view of customers which is admittedly biased to those who have self-selected themselves as current customers);

- the difference in measurement precision between measuring the satisfaction of customers and noncustomers is adjusted for;
- customers' satisfaction is weighted according to their switching costs, the lower the switching costs, the higher the weight for customer satisfaction (this avoids the bias of interviewing only "hostaged customers");
- satisfaction measures are disaggregated as far down as possible, down to the individual, if possible, to reflect the impact of each employee's actions.

How to Execute a Plan

The best motive for linking some part of compensation to customer satisfaction is to reward improvement. Linking compensation to satisfaction will fail if the link is viewed as a way of punishing poorly performing departments or individuals. If you plan to institute a satisfaction-incentive program, follow these suggestions for an effective initiation:

- properly explain the mechanics of the system as envisaged;
- post satisfaction ratings frequently making sure everyone understands the measures;
- allow for employee input and possible modification;
- ideally, allow employees to select or not select participation in the satisfaction-linked incentive program;
- trial the program for six months (for information and learning purposes only), then put the full program into operation;
- try to trace satisfaction scores down to individual employees— incentive programs work best when people feel personally in control;
- position the program not as a competition among individuals, but rather as an effort to encourage each employee to realize his/her full potential in achieving customer satisfaction for the organization.

Some Risks

Unfortunately, not every attempt to link satisfaction to compensation will immediately result in improved customer satisfaction. Several automobile companies have found that when they related customer satisfaction scores to dealer compensation and car allocations, the dealers found a way to *improve the scores* they received without necessarily improving their customers' satisfaction! A typical action was to "help" their customers complete the CSI questionnaire mailed by the manufacturer. The assistance rendered was always to suggest, to those customers who would listen, that the dealership be given only the highest scores! This advice was often given free of charge, and might even carry some form of incentive with it.

REFERENCES

Berry, Leonard L., and A. Parasuraman. *Marketing Services: Competing Through Quality.* New York: The Free Press, 1991.

Cooper, Robert G. "New Product Strategies: What Distinguishes the Top Performers?" *The Journal of Product Innovation Management.* Vol. 2 (1984): 151–64.

Griffin, Abbie, Greg Gleason, Rick Preiss, and Dave Shevenaugh. "Best Practice for Customer Satisfaction in Manufacturing Firms." *Sloan Management Review* (Winter 1995): 87–98.

Griffin, Abbie, and John Hauser. *The Voice of the Customer.* Report No. 92–106. Cambridge, MA: The Marketing Science Institute, 1992.

Hauser, John R., Duncan I. Simester, and Birger Wernerfelt. "Customer Satisfaction Incentives." *Marketing Science.* Vol. 13, no. 4 (Fall 1994): 327–50.

Kessler, Sheila. *Measuring and Managing Customer Satisfaction: Going for the Gold.* Milwaukee: ASQC Quality Press, 1996.

Lissy, William E., and Marlene L. Morgenstern. "More Firms to Link Sales Rewards to Customer Satisfaction." *Compensation & Benefits Review.* Vol. 27, no. 3 (May/June 1995): 12–13.

Mentzer, John T., Carol C. Bienstock, and Kenneth B. Kahn. "Benchmarking Satisfaction." *Marketing Management.* Vol. 4, no. 1 (Summer 1995): 41–46.

Mercer, William M., Inc. and Sales & Marketing Management Magazine. "Survey of Customer Satisfaction and Sales Compensation." New York, 1995.

Motorola Cellular Infrastructure Group, Personal communication, 1996.

Nash, Matthew J. "Closing the Customer Satisfaction/TQM Breach." *ASQC Quality Congress Transactions.* Boston: ASQC, 1993.

Pinto, Mary Beth, and Jeffrey K. Pinto. "Project Team Communication and Cross-Functional Cooperation in New Program Development." *The Journal of Product Innovation Management.* Vol. 7 (1990): 200–12.

Pruden, Douglas R., Ravi Sankar, and Terry G. Vavra. "Customer Loyalty: The Competitive Edge Beyond Satisfaction." *Quirk's Marketing Research Review.* (April 1996): 24, 49–53.

Rust, Roland T., Anthony J. Zahorik, and Timothy L. Keiningham. "Return on Quality (ROQ): Making Service Quality Financially Accountable." *Journal of Marketing.* Vol. 59 (April 1995): 58–70.

Souder, William E. "Managing Relations Between R&D and Marketing in New Product Development Projects." *The Journal of Product Innovation Management.* Vol. 5 (1988): 6–19.

CHAPTER 11

Globalizing Satisfaction Measurement

OVERVIEW

In today's multinational marketplace, corporations can hardly afford to disregard the market potential of other countries. Likewise, if these same corporations fail to measure the satisfaction of *all* of their constituent customers, their continued success is in jeopardy. Customer satisfaction measurement in the 1990s and beyond is truly a global concern. But, expanding a customer satisfaction program to encompass customers in other countries and cultures is not an easy process. Special talents and routines must be adopted if the CSM professional is to successfully measure, track, and compare satisfaction in the international marketplace.

This chapter considers some of the more important concerns for conducting CSM studies across different cultures in many different countries and in many languages, to produce survey results that are interpretable and useful for a global management team. The key perspective is to *act globally while thinking locally.*

THE SPECIAL CHALLENGES OF INTERNATIONAL MEASUREMENT

Culture has been shown to impact perception, learning and memory, problem solving and cognition (Cole and Scribner 1974). It is reasonable, therefore, to consider that culture could possibly influence the satisfaction expressed by customers of a multinational company. These differences could arise from:

- different expectations;
- different ways of evaluating performance;
- the different use of response scale formats; and
- being influenced differently by the number of response positions in any question scale.

Without a better understanding of the absence or presence of cultural bias and its magnitude and direction, the analysis of multinational data will be difficult and prone to error.

Understanding Cultural Differences

Toward Opinion Research in General

The various cultures of the world are all undergoing their own experience curves with regard to opinion research and measurement. It is fair to say the United States is probably the most advanced culture with regard to opinion measurement. In the United States we are probably surveyed so much we have become blasé to additional surveys. In other cultures the act of an organization communicating with its customers for purposes of improving its products or services may be very novel, if not downright unbelievable!

Toward Satisfaction Measurement

Similarly, most other cultures lag the United States in measuring customers' satisfaction with products and services. Japanese engineers and R&D departments have learned the importance of building products and services to meet customer requirements, but the thrust of Japanese research seems oriented to more qualitative explorations oftentimes in shopping malls and at trade expositions rather than to surveying individual customers in their homes through mail or by telephone.

The European countries are becoming exposed to satisfaction measurement, but customers are still not polled at the rate of U.S. customers. So, for most of the world's cultures satisfaction surveys will still be somewhat of a novelty. This means a tremendous advantage for those companies first implementing the appropriate processes. It also means heightened cooperation and response rates (among customers) for these, still novel, surveys. But some learning must also take place. Customers must be told how their feedback will benefit the sponsor-company and themselves ultimately, in the form of improved products, services, and accompanying servicing.

The Comparability of Cross-Cultural Attitudes

The primary motivation for conducting a multicountry satisfaction survey is, no doubt, to compare an organization's performance across the various regions or countries in which it operates to assure delivery of uniform quality. To accomplish this goal, it is critical that the satisfaction survey design, process, and data be as comparable across countries as possible. But is this a realistic goal? To make comparisons possible, a number of sources of variation must have been controlled. Consider diversity from language, from differing levels of literacy, and from possible differences in the equivalence of the constructs measured.

These issues raise the question of whether similar survey designs are usable or relevant in different sociocultural environments. Pike (1966) has labeled this question the "emic-etic dilemma."

Emic Measures

Because various cultures develop their own sociocultural behavior patterns and values, it is likely that attitudinal and behavioral phenomena will be expressed in very different ways. Given this diversity, the satisfaction professional responsible for a multicultural survey should ideally develop measures and scales unique to each culture to be covered. This is the *Emic* approach. It is based on the recognition of differences between cultures and on the acknowledged importance of honoring each culture's idiosyncracies.

However, the likely goal of multicultural satisfaction surveys, as has already been observed, is to facilitate comparison across countries. Emic surveys conducted within different cultures would defy easy comparison; to compare results from such studies would require a qualitative analysis

Table 11.1   A Comparison of Etic and Emic Measures

Characteristic	Approach	
	Emic	Etic
Perspective taken by researcher	Studies behavior from within the system	Studies behavior from a position outside the system
Number of cultures studied	Examines only one culture	Examines many cultures, comparing them
Structure guiding research	Structure discovered by the analyst	Structure created by the analyst
Criteria used to compare behavior in the culture(s)	Criteria are relative to internal characteristics	Criteria are considered absolute or universal

Source: Berry, John W., "Introduction to Methodology," in Triandis, Harry C., and John W. Berry (eds), *Handbook of Cross-Cultural Psychology, Vol. 2: Methodology*, Boston: Allyn and Bacon Inc., 1980.

or a highly subjective interpretation. If, on the other hand, the *same* question were asked in each of the cultures in which satisfaction was to be measured, comparison would be very easy. The practice of adopting a uniform question across cultures is the *Etic* approach (see Table 11.1).

Etic Measures

Etic constructs are fabricated on the belief (or hope) that there are certain industry requirements, values, and behaviors that transcend culture, such that relatively universal models of evaluation may be developed and used. These "pan-cultural," culture-free measures promise easy comparison and hence the opportunity for cross-cultural analyses. However, be warned, if the Etic approach is practiced in an unchecked manner, it can most assuredly lead to an abuse of the measures—imposing them on multiple cultures without the adaptation or cultural sensitivity that might be desirable or even necessary. Triandis (1972) has labeled this possible abuse, the "pseudo-etic" approach (conducting a study in an etic fashion when the emic approach was needed).

Countries Versus Cultures

Obviously one must not make the mistake of using countries as the predominating unit of analysis. In many, many different countries, multiple cultures prevail. The multicultural phenomenon is not only true in Middle and Far Eastern countries, consider Belgium and Switzerland. To equate countries and cultures is to grossly oversimplify the issue. The satisfaction professional's job is only intensified by this need to appreciate which of his markets are typified by multiple cultures, and then to assign a cultural heritage to each of his customers in those particular markets.

Establishing Equivalence

One of the most important considerations in conducting a multiple culture satisfaction survey, is the concept of *equivalence.* Equivalence covers all of the issues that yield comparable results across different cultures. Many of the constructs measured in satisfaction surveys have been defined and operationalized in the United States. There is the possibility that these constructs will be applied to other cultures without any guarantee that they are transferable or even applicable.

The concept of equivalence is important since it can be used to free satisfaction research from cultural bounds. However, typically the only aspect of equivalence that has concerned cross-cultural researchers is linguistic equivalence. In this section we will identify six forms of equivalence that should be considered prior to rolling a survey out internationally (Yu, Keown and Jacobs 1993; and Mintu, Calantone and Gassenheimer 1994).

Construct Equivalence

Construct equivalence is the most basic concern. The satisfaction professional must ask herself, "Does the phenomenon actually exist in other cultures?" It should not be assumed that other cultures have equivalent concepts or behaviors, without exploring their existence through qualitative research. Construct equivalence can be divided into three subcomponents:

Conceptual Equivalence. Many concepts are cultural bound. For example, the concept of "indifference" may or may not exist in another culture. If a question allows the response of "indifference" and this emotion is lacking or uncomfortable within a culture, then collected data may be flawed.

Functional Equivalence. The notion of functional equivalence addresses the similar function that products or services are expected to deliver across various cultures. In industrial products, functional equivalence is more likely due to the technical nature of the products. But consumer goods may vary in their sameness of functionality. Consider the bicycle. In some cultures the bicycle serves the function of almost purely recreation while in other cultures the functions of transportation and delivery would be more appropriately linked to a bicycle.

Category Equivalence.   Category equivalence has to do with how objects, stimuli, and behaviors are grouped together within different cultures. This will influence how issues are mentally considered. Category equivalence, quite possibly, also may influence customers' reactions to scalar questions making scales with fewer response positions more applicable in some cultures, scales with more numerous response positions more applicable to other cultures.

Measurement Equivalence

Measurement equivalence can also be decomposed into several sub-components.

Scalar Equivalence.   Does a chosen scale function equally well in different cultures? There is ample reason to believe that scales that are readily accepted in one culture may not work equally well in others. The satisfaction survey professional is warned not to casually apply scales across cultures without first testing their acceptance. This holds true even among Western cultures, which might be assumed to share methods and ideas. For example, while Americans are quite at home with a 1 to 5 numerical scale where 1 means "poor" and 5 means "excellent," Germans would likely be confused, expecting the "poor" alternative to have the higher numerical representation of 5 with 1 meaning excellent.

Item/Linguistic Equivalence.   It is critical that the items in a questionnaire be translated in an accurate manner so that the linguistic meaning remains similar across cultures. We will consider several ways to increase the accuracy of translations in a later section of this chapter.

Sample Equivalence

International marketing research can be plagued with a lack of equivalence in the consumers included in various cultures. Within international customer satisfaction surveys, however, there is more likelihood of a homogeneous sample across cultures because of the universal requirement that each survey participant must, necessarily, have chosen, purchased, and used a product or service for his opinions to be included. Care should be taken to use the same definition of "current customer," to the extent that an organization's customerbases in various cultures provide roughly equivalent customer data.

Survey Design Considerations

In national research, satisfaction professionals are accustomed to deciding on the field method as a function of the interview length, the turnaround required and cost. In international satisfaction projects, other considerations may arbitrate these three common factors. Certainly the development and efficiency of communication infrastructures will limit the acceptability of mail, telephone, fax, and Internet surveys. Lower interviewer labor costs and customers' preference for a personal visit from an interviewer increases the appeal of personal interviewing.

Mail Surveys

While mail surveys universally will be the least expensive field technique, the quality of local mail services will impact the effectiveness of this field method. The usual caveats still prevail. Response rates will be low, the quality of responses from self-administered questions will be less than if administered by interviewers, and turnaround time (time into and out of the field) will be lengthy. And, in some cultures where surveys are still more of a novelty than an accepted practice, customers' lack of familiarity with questionnaires and how to answer questions will likely produce poor quality data. Customers' inability to understand complex questions, to understand response options, or their propensity to answer sparsely to open-end questions, may all reduce the quality of the data collected by mail. Certainly response rates will suffer in cultures unaccustomed to self-administered surveys or where illiteracy is widespread.

The lack of a good customerbase may also constrain the use of mail surveys. For a mail survey to be a viable option, the customerbase must contain good address information. This unfortunately seems rarely to be the case. Very often, international addresses challenge the database structure instituted in the United States or United Kingdom. So, even if proper information is originally collected, its integrity may be damaged as it is forced into the traditional three database fields of street, city, and state.

Mail will generally be more successful among industrial customers since many businesses are accustomed to receiving international mail and may have simplified their mailing address to accommodate incoming mail. Also mail delivery to businesses may be more reliable than to residences. Mail-delivered surveys to businesses still, however, face the formidable challenge of being routed to the appropriate decision maker if his/her name is not known to the survey sponsor.

In consumer surveys, mail will face even more problems. Mail delivery in many countries is fraught with problems—either in the inefficiency of the distribution system or the lack of delivery directly to the dwelling unit. (Mail is still delivered to a box in a central post office in many cultures.) Mail delivery will generally be skewed to more economically developed, affluent neighborhoods in all emerging cultures, hence the possibility exists of a biased sample.

Traditionally the extensive delivery and return times have been major drawbacks for mail surveys. There are new signs of hope, however. The rapid growth of private, international delivery systems (FedEx, DHL, Airborne, and so on) offer new hope for international mail. Also, at least two domestic carriers' efforts to develop international delivery and return systems promise new avenues. Both the United States Postal Service and Britain's Royal Mail are engaged in developing exciting new international mail services. The advent of international business reply mail service as sponsored by these two postal services (USPS and the Royal Mail) also promises a major boost to international mail satisfaction surveys.

Telephone Surveys

The major advantages of domestic telephone surveys—widespread, efficient geographic coverage; quick turnaround; and the ability to conduct all interviewing from one, central, well-monitored facility are beginning to apply to today's international satisfaction surveys.

While some countries' telecommunications infrastructures are still evolving, most developed countries have a reasonably high coverage by telephone. Certainly in industrial surveys the penetration of telephones in businesses is almost universal, except for some very small businesses and craftspeople. The advantage of being able to screen for the decision maker (if his/her identity is not already known in the customerbase) makes interviewing by telephone particularly attractive.

With the advent of multilingual telephone field services, not only in Europe, but also in the United States, and with costs of international calling continuing to decrease, telephone interviewing becomes increasingly more attractive as a field procedure. In central facilities, calls can be carefully monitored and changes to the questioning process, if necessary, may be instituted immediately. Because most of the telephone field services will utilize CATI interviewing, the data will probably be more clean and error-free than when entered in a separate step.

In consumer satisfaction surveys, telephone interviewing may still encounter some problems dealing with telephone ownership. When the customerbase is affluent, this will be less a concern. As with volunteering information through mail surveys, interviewing by telephone will necessarily require a customerbase relatively comfortable conducting business by telephone.

Of course, the conventional caveats of telephone interviewing prevail. The interviews will need to be short, generally under 20 minutes. Questions and response scales must be kept as simple as possible.

Personally Administered Surveys

Personal interviewing has been the dominant field method outside the United States for a number of years. Although telephone interviewing is on the rise, personal interviewing still commands a significant share of international fieldwork. The reasons for personal interviewing's dominance are several. First, the costs of labor in other countries are more reasonable. And, considering the advantages of personal interviewing (like higher cooperation rates and generally better quality data), it becomes a more attractive field procedure.

The major drawback is the availability of qualified and well-trained personal interviewing field staffs. Unlike in the United States, personal interviewing subcontractors are not prevalent. This has led many companies and research organizations to develop their own interviewing staffs in various countries.

Personal interviewing will be quite effective in conducting industrial satisfaction surveys. Cooperation rates will surpass those for mail surveys and the personal interview format allows for more detailed information to be collected than by either mail or telephone. The advantage of a personal interviewer to further probe some questions, and to clarify answers to others produces richer quality data. The personal interviewer, sent to a customer's office, may also create the perception of the company's care for the customer and demonstrated courtesy. One must be careful, however, that chosen interviewers represent the sponsor-company professionally.

Personal interviewing for consumer surveys will be somewhat more difficult. The likely geographic dispersion of customers will increase travel costs. Individual customers may also be less comfortable allowing an interviewer into their homes. In certain countries, particularly Latin American and Middle Eastern countries, interviewers may be held in suspicion—as possibly governmental tax inspectors or collectors. Gender will also play a role. Interviewers in the Middle East are invariably males.

If there is a need to interview female heads of household, these interviews will necessarily have to be conducted in the evening hours when the male head of household is also present.

Considerations in Writing Questions

Demographics

While age and gender are universally recordable, even items as simple as marital status, income, education, occupation, and dwelling unit pose problems that may not be immediately obvious. With the universal rise in cohabitation, and with some cultures condoning polygamy, assessing marital status can be a challenge. ESOMAR has recommended a three-item scale: 1–married/living together; 2–single, and 3–widowed/divorced/separated.

Income poses a greater problem due to the wide variations in standards of living between cultures. Some have approached this problem by reporting income in a quartile-basis within each country. Those in the same income quartile between cultures can be inferred to possess the same degree of relative prosperity; an easier comparison than trying to compare levels of absolute income or wealth. Education should probably be handled in a similar manner since educational systems vary widely. (There are few analogs to the U.S. system of grade, high school, college, post-college.) The number of years of schooling or the age at which full-time education was completed are two, more universal education measures.

Occupational categories, at least major categories, appear relatively universal. In particular: farm-worker, industrial worker, blue-collar worker, office worker, white-collar worker, self-employed, lower and upper management, and professional all appear to have universal meaning.

Dwelling unit is a harder classification to operationalize universally. In most Western cultures dwelling units are primarily apartments of single or multiple story houses. Other cultures impose radically different units, from huts in Africa to one story, business and living quarters units in Far Eastern cultures. Very often not only the primary family unit resides there, but the extended nuclear family as well (parents, grandparents, siblings, and their families). Consequently dwelling unit has to be questioned with some degree of thought.

Purchase/Consumption Behavior

While purchasing, consuming, and usage behaviors are equally important to consumers and organizations around the world, their manifestation may not be directly similar from one culture to the next. Sociocultural differences may influence the processes leading to purchase behavior as well as the specific purchase made. Most certainly the determinants influencing the purchase decision and the process may be different.

For example, the appropriateness or relevance of different products or services may be markedly different by culture. While self-indulgent products reign in more developed, Western cultures, purchases in other European cultures may be more characterized by self-denial or the Protestant ethic. Basic cultural values will impact on the motivation driving product or service acquisition.

The way in which purchases are made will certainly vary depending upon the acceptance or rejection of credit spending. And the distribution networks vary markedly across cultures. Mass merchandisers and supermarkets serve American households' weekly shopping trips, with considerable storage of items at home. In contrast, in European and Far Eastern cultures, where in-home storage space is precious, and the desire for fresh items is stronger, household shopping will occur on a daily basis, often at small, neighborhood convenience stores or boutiques.

Product categories will also vary across cultures, preventing an easy comparison of evoked sets. For example, while in some cultures household appliances (like a washing machine) will be compared among manufacturers of that appliance, in other cultures the evoked set may not only include appliance brands, but domestic help as well as professional washerwomen. Packaged pasta in the United States will be compared among other brands of packaged pasta. In Italy packaged pasta may compete with homemade and specialty store fresh pasta (Douglas 1983).

While global brands (Kellogg, Nestle, Cadbury) are growing in importance, in many cases local brands may predominate product categories. And the market for consumer packaged goods is not totally universal. Some cultures still prefer fresh fruits, vegetables, and meats to prepackaged varieties.

Attitudes and Psychographics

The value of supplementing customers' perceptions of product performance with information about them as individuals is beginning to be accepted within the CSM community. However, the information that needs to be collected to provide such insight, is more difficult to collect in a cross-national survey. Of all of the types of questions subject to cultural influence, those related to attitudes, lifestyles, and individual value-systems may be most susceptible to cultural interpretation and differences.

In industrial satisfaction surveys it would generally be useful to know the extent or degree of purchase influence exerted by the individual survey respondent. Yet measuring the degree of influence may require great sensitivity to the ranges of acceptable behavior within each culture. Responses that are appropriate for one culture may be unthinkable or perceived as negatively aggressive in other cultures. To be sure of a question's appropriateness, the following sequence should be followed:

1. identify relevant attitudinal or life-style constructs within each culture to be surveyed. These can be surmised by studying the culture, examining quantitative data, or by conducting focus groups.
2. even when similar constructs are found to exist, they may need to be operationalized somewhat differently.

While a US executive may unabashedly agree to the statement: *I make the purchase decision myself* a counterpart in another culture (e.g. Japan) may feel less arrogant agreeing to the statement: *After consulting with my team, I make the purchase decision.*

While these statements are different, the wording of the second may be necessary to "allow" members of another culture to admit to their behavior.

Relatively similar cultures—westernized, industrial nations probably have many values in common. However, the satisfaction professional is well-advised to make allowance for country or culture-specific concepts, as well as country or culture unique measures of these concepts.

Choosing Scales and Question Types that Work Best Internationally

Using a well-planned and thorough research design, Yu, Keown and Jacobs (1993) investigated the cross-cultural application of three different scale formats and two different scale widths across four cultures. Of primary importance, the four cultures responded significantly differently on all but one of the scales, showing that it is not easy to find a universal scale type. The project showed Likert scales and the semantic differential to be far more culture-bound than was previously thought (it had been claimed that the Likert scale was fairly etic-culture free). In this research the only method not subject to emic (culture-bound) limitations was a rank-ordering task.

Comparing response positions, the number of scale points produced inconsistent results across the four cultures studied. The researchers' one permissible conclusion, the number of response positions offered *is sensitive* to cultural heritage. While Chinese and Japanese cultures appeared indifferent to a change between 5-point and 4-point Likert scales, Koreans and Americans tended to give more extreme answers when presented with the 4-point format. In contrast, the wider semantic differential scale with eight response positions produced more extreme scores. Because of a lack of pattern in the results, the authors were unable to make any steadfast recommendations about the better scale format or the ideal number of response positions to use in cross-cultural research. Their work, however, warns the satisfaction professional to generalize scale types only after considerable investigation.

THE ROLE OF TRANSLATION

While English is becoming the international language of business, U.S., U.K., and Canadian companies are well-advised not to impose English language questionnaires on their international customers. And, in consumer products, there is no option for the use of English questionnaires in countries where the native language is other than English.

The point made, that global customers should be surveyed in their own native tongue, the importance of translation is clearly evident. Occasionally the situation may arise in which the sponsor-company believes it can adequately translate a questionnaire into another language, in-house. This is probably a bad decision. Although professionally translated questionnaires should be distributed within the company to employees who speak the various languages into which the questionnaire has been translated, this should be done primarily to check the accuracy of translation for technical terms and processes. Rarely will an in-house translation meet the rigor of the sequence to be described below.

There are a number of different translation procedures that have been used.

Direct Translation

In direct translation bilingual translators translate the original (base) questionnaire into the other, required languages. This is the simplest, most economical, and fastest translation procedure. Unfortunately, direct translation can produce a "pseudo-etic" questionnaire when the translators are not equally adept in both languages or when they are less familiar with the idiomatic expressions and colloquialisms in one of the languages. This has been discovered in one direct translation of a satisfaction survey from English to Italian. The Italian questionnaire, it was later discovered, asked customers' "sexual satisfaction" with an automobile! Other examples of poorly rendered idioms abound in the general marketing literature including: the translation of a U.S. airline's "rendezvous lounge" into Portuguese for "prostitution chamber"; and Coca Cola's slogan, "brings good things to life," into Chinese with idiomatic meaning, "brings back the dead"!

Back Translation

To avoid these problems of direct translation, a procedure widely advocated is the process of "back translation" (Brislin 1970). In back translation a questionnaire is translated from the base language to a second language by a bilingual who is a native speaker of the second language. Then, the translated version (in the second language) is submitted to a translation back into the base language by a bilingual who is a native speaker of the base language.

Although back translation is more rigorous than direct translation, it does not always work. Several reasons related to the linguistic habits of the translators are to blame. First, bilinguals usually adopt their own rules for translating idioms—these rules may or may not correspond with usage conventions of the second language's population. They may also adopt a set of rules for translating terms that do not have direct equivalents. Hence, *amigo* may be translated as "friend." And, since the bilinguals (involved in the translation) know both languages, they may be able to make better sense out of a poor translation than the target customers will be able to do.

The final problem with back translation is that it starts with the assumption of a base questionnaire. To the extent that concepts described in this questionnaire are not transferable, the translated questionnaire will be pseudo-etic.

Decentered Translation

An approach that offers to solve many of these problems, is the so-called "decentering translation process" (Triandis 1972). Decentering requires successive translations and retranslations, with terms and concepts modified along the way, so that the final questionnaires employ terms and phrasing equally meaningful in both the base and second language. The major drawback of this process is its time-consuming and tedious nature.

Parallel Translation

A reasonable compromise may be a translation process referred to as "parallel translation" (Frey 1970). In this procedure, a committee of translators, all equally conversant with the languages involved, compares translated versions. Alternate wording, terms and phrases can be discussed until the committee is comfortable that near equal meaning has been achieved. While this procedure is reasonably quick, critics argue there are no formal rules governing the gerrymandering of wording and terms. Hence, it is feared that the strongest personalities (rather than the best translations) will win out.

Regardless of the specific translation process employed, it is crucial to the success of the survey that the satisfaction professional confirm for herself the quality of the translation. Unfortunately there are no criteria for assessing the adequacy/quality of translations. Douglas and Craig (1983) suggest four steps of evaluation:

1. evaluation of a translated questionnaire by monolinguals attesting to its comprehensibility and clarity;
2. evaluation of a translated questionnaire by bilinguals searching for possible errors of meaning;
3. testing customers' abilities to answer questions about the content of the translated questionnaire and/or their ability to perform any tasks required by the questionnaire;
4. testing both the base and translated questionnaires on bilingual customers to see if the questionnaires elicit the same patterns of response.

Table 11.2 offers a familiar, four-point Likert-type scale translated into five languages.

THE LOGISTICS OF A WORLDWIDE SURVEY

The logistics of any domestic satisfaction survey tend to surprise many survey professionals. But when a survey is rolled into more than one country or culture, the logistical concerns multiply geometrically. The question becomes how to control, oversee, and stimulate all at the same time.

Table 11.2   Translations of a Satisfaction–Dissatisfaction Scale

English	Very Dissatisfied	Somewhat Dissatisfied	Somewhat Satisfied	Very Satisfied
French	Très Mécontent	Un peu Mécontent	Un peu Satisfait	Très Satisfait
German	Sehr Unzufrieden	Etwas Unzufrieden	Etwas Zufrieden	Sehr Zufrieden
Spanish	Muy Insatisfecho	Algo Insatisfecho	Algo Satisfecho	Muy Satisfecho
Italian	Mólto Insoddisfàtto	Piuttòsto Insoddisfàtto	Piuttòsto Soddisfàtto	Mólto Soddisfàtto

Source: Marketing Metrics, Inc.

International Field Services

There are a growing number of telephone interviewing services in both the United States and Europe that are staffed and capable of conducting interviews around the world. Their interviewers are usually well-trained and will generally be native speakers of the non-English languages in which they interview. These facilities offer a valuable resource to the satisfaction professional considering telephone interviewing for his survey. The facilities are generally CATI-equipped and are centrally monitored. They are quite responsive and can even aid in the translation of questionnaires into non-English languages.

Prior to the appearance of these multilingual interviewing services, the only option was to find subcontractors in each country or culture in which the survey was to be fielded. The resulting amalgam of field services was not only difficult to coordinate, but quality control no doubt suffered. Now a single interviewing facility can conduct all of the interviews from one central location. This also gives the satisfaction professional the opportunity of observing the interviewing or of monitoring on-going interviews from essentially anyplace in the world by telephone.

Controlling Multi-Country Studies

There are three basic organization structures with which international satisfaction surveys may be administered globally: centralized, coordinated, and decentralized.

Centralized Administration

In this organizational perspective, the headquarters satisfaction officer will be responsible for all global satisfaction efforts. One or more field-work subcontractors will be retained to conduct the customer interviews. Then, all data processing and analysis will be handled at headquarters or by one analytical firm. In the centralized format, headquarters sets the survey objectives, writes the questionnaires, oversees data collection, and processes and analyzes the data.

Centralized administration offers the greatest control over an international survey. It also ensures comparability of the data across countries, and it may be the least expensive administrative format.

Centralized administration runs the risk of imposing an ethnocentric bias on the survey, possibly creating a psuedo-etic interview. Headquarters will strive for a uniform survey design with minimal adaptation to local countries' conditions. Local operating units may feel left "outside the loop" and may be resentful of the process. More serious than that, they may actually have trouble implementing results from the survey out of a lack of familiarity or understanding with the issues covered. They are almost certain to complain about the centralized survey's insensitivity to their local conditions and market factors.

Coordinated Administration

In a coordinated administration, corporate headquarters will participate in the design of the survey and the specification of informational objectives. An external research organization will be retained to finalize the study design, to oversee administration of the survey, to coordinate field-work, and to process and analyze the data.

Involving a third party for its specialized expertise is a good idea, especially when the headquarters' satisfaction staff may not be large enough to fully coordinate the international project. However, the third party can mean that relationships with local operating units are strained even more seriously than in the centralized plan. It will be advisable to include local management in reviewing the design and questionnaires at the local level. There is even the possibility of involving local management in overseeing data collection.

If, however, local concerns are given too much voice, then the comparability of the data and results will be impaired.

Decentralized Administration

In a decentralized administration, corporate headquarters establishes the objectives, in broad terms, but delegates the implementation of the satisfaction survey to the local operating units. In this format, the headquarters satisfaction officer has the least control over satisfaction measurement efforts. Local units will even be empowered to retain their own research agencies for purposes of finalizing the questionnaire, collecting data, processing responses, and analyzing the data.

There is the strong likelihood that the decentralized format will arrive at a more etic-questionnaire. To the extent that local issues are catered to, the survey results will defy easy comparison across markets surveyed. One way of instituting some standardization would be to set up a coordinating committee with representatives from each local operating unit, so that potential modifications to the questionnaire and/or survey process may be shared, discussed, and possibly adopted on a wider basis.

Decentralization will also have its problems meeting deadlines for completion of fieldwork, analysis of data, and submission of final reports—because of the number of different local research agencies conducting the work. Even the final reports themselves, originating in many different local units and research subcontractors, will likely be difficult to uniformly assimilate. It is, however, true that decentralization should result in the greatest support and understanding at the local level.

Table 11.3 profiles the two extreme positions, decentralized and centralized administration.

ANALYZING INTERNATIONAL DATA

As the survey professional completes an international satisfaction survey, management will want to see how the various market regions (generally countries) compare in their abilities to satisfy their customers. This comparison may be motivated by a desire to allocate resources such that underperforming regions may catch up, or it may be motivated by the desire to reward region management teams that are currently excelling. In either case, the satisfaction professional will want to offer scores that are as comparable as possible.

When two scores differ, for example,

$$S_{country\ A} < > S_{country\ B}$$

there are several, possible sources for this difference:

Table 11.3   Advantages of Centralized and Decentralized Survey Administration

Centralized Administration	Decentralized Administration
High consistency of processing and analysis across the countries, data is comparable	Recognizes differences between countries, procedures modified to accommodate differences, data more relevant within the country
Better adherence by field force to a standard format	Each market establishes its own, customized format
Faster response times, changes implemented quickly and uniformly	Local operating units involved in structure and conduct, feel more involved
Reports easily contrast and compare market regions	Corrective actions easier to implement in individual markets due to local operating unit's familiarity with the issues
More likely to meet completion deadline	Coordination and on-time completion problematic

- real differences in the performance experienced in country A versus country B. (This is the difference management is interested in. This can be addressed with changes in strategy or resource allocation.)
- differences arising from a cultural difference in expectations or in the way performance is evaluated;
- differences from error.

The satisfaction professional needs to be able to assure his management that reported differences are, indeed, the result of actual performance differences.

The Issue of Cultural Biases

As a customer is asked to rate his or her satisfaction with an organization's performance, he or she will engage in a series of steps to answer the question:

1. the customer must form or recall a perception of the organization's actual performance (to serve as the basis for the satisfaction evaluation);

2. the customer will invariably compare what he or she experienced against what he or she expected would/should happen;
3. the customer must then translate the performance-expectation ratio into a response on the rating scale provided.

Culture can play a role in each of these steps. To the extent that members of one culture approach the evaluation differently than members of another culture, there will be a cultural bias that can distort true performance evaluations.

Testing Your Data for Cultural Biases

The satisfaction professional must address three questions concerning cultural bias:

1. Do customers use the rating scale provided in approximately the same way?
2. Do the concepts measured have the same meaning across the cultures and, if they are combined into evaluative dimensions (or factors) is this structure the same?
3. Are the importance weights the customers attach to the different factors the same across cultures?

While the satisfaction professional's hope is an affirmative answer to all three questions, the wisest policy is to remain skeptical and to conduct some investigation prior to reporting cross-cultural results to management.

The first step is to determine if cultural bias appears to be present in your data. This test can be conducted in varying levels of sophistication; while it may not be necessary to use a more sophisticated test, we will describe two levels of tests.

1. Comparison of Grand Means

Let us assume a satisfaction survey with 30 performance attributes administered in three different cultures. Because the sponsoring organization is selling the same product or service in all three cultures, and has essentially the same marketing and support organizations in place in all three cultures, it is not unreasonable to expect the mean of attribute means across cultures to be approximately equal.

To test this null hypothesis, attribute ratings are averaged within each culture, and then an average of these averages is calculated (see Table 11.4). If the grand means are not significantly different, it is fair to conclude there are no cultural biases operating. If, however, one culture's grand mean is significantly higher or lower than the other two, cultural

Table 11.4   Comparison of Culture Grand Means

Attribute	United States Mean	Brazil Mean	Japan Mean
Attribute 1	7.5	7.9	6.8
Attribute 2	6.8	8.2	7.2
Attribute 3	7.7	7.9	6.9
Attribute 28	8.1	8.8	7.5
Attribute 29	7.5	8.1	6.8
Attribute 30	7.0	7.9	6.2
Grand Mean	7.7	8.1	7.1

Difference United States to Brazil, ns
Difference United States to Japan, ns
Difference Brazil to Japan, significant @ 95%

bias can not be ruled out. Unfortunately, neither can performance superiority or inferiority be positively excluded as well.

2. MANOVA Test of Variance

Multivariate Analysis Of Variance (MANOVA) is a way of testing the equivalency of multiple attributes within two or more classificatory variables (in our case countries). The model determines not only if the countries are equal or unequal, but also identifies those specific performance attributes that are most responsible for any discovered differences. A multivariate model can be productively employed to detect both the presence or absence of overall differences by culture and to identify those performance attributes on which significant differences occur.

How to Deal with Culturally Biased Data

If you verify that your cross-cultural data appears to incorporate cultural biases, there are several ways of handling your data, before reporting them side-by-side.[1] Two of the procedures detailed are from research conducted by Larry Crosby (1992). Each of these methods requires some transformation of the original data.

----

[1] To avoid a "head-on" comparison of scores from different cultures, which may be culturally biased, one can advocate: benchmarking improvement within each culture, or maximizing performance vis-à-vis competitors within each culture.

Table 11.5A   Calculating the Correction Factor

Country	Grand Mean	Correction Factor	The Calculation
United States	7.7	0.0	
Brazil	8.1	-0.4	(7.7–8.1)
Japan	7.1	0.6	(7.7–7.1)

Adapted from examples provided by Crosby, Lawrence A., "Toward a Common Verbal Scale of Perceived Quality," in *Marketing in the New Europe*, (45th ESOMAR Congress, Joint Session on the Race Against Expectations), Madrid, Spain: The European Society of Marketing Research, 1992.

Table 11.5B   Recalibrating Individual Attribute Ratings

Performance Attributes	U.S. Score	Brazil			Japan		
		Raw Score	Correction Factor	Adjusted Score	Raw Score	Correction Factor	Adjusted Score
Personal service	8.1	8.5	-0.4	8.1	7.1	0.6	7.7
Marketing plans	7.7	8.6	-0.4	8.2	7.2	0.6	7.8
Service accuracy	7.6	8.0	-0.4	7.6	6.9	0.6	7.5

Mean Score Adjustment

This method is a rather intuitive comparison of grand means across cultures. (*Grand means* are the average of all performance attribute means as shown in Table 11.4.) With grand means formed, one country is selected as the "base country" (for U.S. multinational firms, this would probably be the United States). Each other country's grand mean is compared to that of the base country, and a correction factor (the difference between each culture's grand mean from the base country's grand mean) is calculated. This "correction factor" can then be applied to any set of means for comparison between the cultures (see Table 11.5A & B).

The selection of items on which to form the grand mean is critical. If attributes are selected on which real differences might occur, this correction will only hide these important differences.

Scale-Point Usage Correction

While Method 1 works fine on mean scores, Crosby (1992) points out that many organizations state their action standards in terms of percent

Table 11.6   Scale Response Usage across Cultures

Grand Distributions**

Rating of	USA Grand Distribution	Brazil Grand Distribution	Weight*	Japan Grand Distribution	Weight*
10	18.0%	20.0%	0.9	10.0%	1.8
9	21.0%	24.0%	0.88	14.0%	1.5
8	18.0%	22.0%	0.82	20.0%	0.9
7	16.0%	18.0%	0.89	22.0%	0.73
6	13.0%	10.0%	1.3	12.0%	1.08
5	6.0%	3.0%	2	8.0%	0.75
4	4.0%	1.0%	4	5.0%	0.8
3	3.0%	1.0%	3	4.0%	0.75
2	1.0%	1.0%	1	3.0%	0.33
1	0.0%	0.0%	1	2.0%	0.05
Total	100.0%	100.0%		100.0%	
Mean Rating	7.7	8.1		7.1	
Correction Factor		−0.4		0.6	

*Weight calculated by dividing Base country's score by the second country (18%/20% − .9 for Brazil's "10" ratings)

**Distribution of ratings over 30 performance variables

of their customers giving a "top-box" or "top-two-box" score. He suggests a reasonably simple recalibration of the *distribution of scores* across cultures as a way to generate "culturally free" distributions.

By comparing the grand distributions of scores across the rating positions by culture, Crosby advocates weighting a response in a second culture inversely proportional to the odds of that response being given in the second culture relative to the odds of the response being given in the base culture. Table 11.6 shows that while U.S. customers used a "10" rating 18 percent of the time, the Brazilian customerbase used the "10" rating 20 percent of the time. The "10" rating in Brazil should probably be devalued, because of the Brazilian customers' apparent greater likelihood of awarding it. If we divide the U.S. proportion (18 percent) by the Brazilian proportion (20 percent) we derive the recalibration weight for Brazil's 10-ratings of 0.9.

Once the recalibration weights are computed for each point on the response scale, the responses to any one question may be reweighted to reflect a distribution similar to the base country's. Table 11.7 shows how such a recalibration might be applied to responses to the question, "Rate

Table 11.7   Distribution Recalibration

Responses to the question, "Rate the resolution of the screen display"

| | USA | Brazil | | | Japan | | |
	Actual	Actual	Weight Factor	Recalibrated	Actual	Weight Factor	Recalibrated
Rating of 10	25.0%	29.0%	0.9	25.4%	0.2	1.8	31.1%
9	17.0%	27.0%	0.88	23.0%	0.18	1.5	23.3%
8	20.0%	18.0%	0.82	14.3%	0.16	0.9	12.4%
7	18.0%	12.0%	0.89	10.4%	0.14	0.73	8.8%
6	12.0%	6.0%	1.3	7.6%	0.12	1.08	11.2%
5	6.0%	6.0%	2	11.7%	0.1	0.75	6.5%
4	1.0%	2.0%	4	7.8%	0.06	0.8	4.1%
3	1.0%	0.0%	3	0.0%	0.04	0.75	2.6%
2	0.0%	0.0%	1	0.0%	0	0.33	0.0%
Rating of 1	0.0%	0.0%	1	0.0%	0	0.05	0.0%
Total	100.0%	100.0%		100.0%	100.0%		100.0%
Mean Rating	7.7	8.1			7.1		
Correction							
Factor		-0.4			0.6		

Adapted from examples provided by Crosby, Lawrence A., "Toward a Common Verbal Scale of Perceived Quality," in *Marketing in the New Europe*, (45th ESOMAR Congress, Joint Session on the Race Against Expectations), Madrid, Spain: The European Society of Marketing Research, 1992.

the resolution of the screen display." While only 20 percent of the Japanese sample scored the resolution a "10," when the score is recalibrated, it becomes 31 percent!

Ipsatization

Ipsatizing or "centering" of data has been used by psychometricians when they wish to combine subjects whose scores, for whatever reason, may not be of a similar metric. It involves calculating a mean for a unit of evaluation, and then subtracting the mean (generally construed as the "level" of the data) from each, individual score provided by the unit of evaluation. (The "unit" could be a customer, a customer-type, or a culture.) In this procedure, ipsatizing disregards the "validity" of the metric difference; the goal is simply to compare among nearly similar groups. Leung and Bond (1989) review four different views they suggest be considered for cross-cultural data. Some of these views involve ipsatizing with means created in various ways.

Collecting External, Expectations Data

Crosby (1992) suggests an independent method for investigating cross-cultural biases. He proposes collecting auxiliary data from customers across cultures for a calibration exercise. The data would have to do with expectations. Ideally, expectations would be assessed across a number of different "domains" (Crosby has previously used: sports, the arts, education, science, and services). The goal is to see how forgiving or demanding customers in each culture would be to various levels of performance in each domain. For example here are three scales he proposes be administered to collect these cultural "expectations":

1. (Education domain) *By the time a student is 10 years old, she will be fluent in two languages.*
2. (Sports domain) *A competitive figure skater falls once in an otherwise flawless skating routine.*
3. (Service domain) *Your arrival by air on a one hour flight is delayed 15 minutes.*

For each performance description, a quality evaluation is asked for using the same rating scale on which the organization's performance will ultimately be assessed. Substantially different quality ratings on these uniform performance descriptions would be used as proof not only of cultural bias, but the direction and degree of the bias.

While this procedure is interesting, it calls for the collection of additional information from customers (which may appear superfluous to them) and measurement error could still account for some of the observed variation in scores.

REFERENCES

Brislin, R. "Back Translation for Cross-Cultural Research." *Journal of Cross-Cultural Psychology.* Vol. 1 (1970): 185–216.

Cole, Michael, and Sylvia Scribner. *Culture and Thought: A Psychological Introduction.* New York: John Wiley and Sons, Inc., 1974.

Crosby, Lawrence A. "Toward a Common Verbal Scale of Perceived Quality." in *Marketing in the New Europe.* (45th ESOMAR Congress, Joint Session on the Race Against Expectations). Madrid, Spain: The European Society of Marketing Research, 1992.

Detweiler, Richard A. "Culture, Category Width, and Attributions: A Model-Building Approach to the Reasons for Cultural Effects." *Journal of Cross-Cultural Psychology.* Vol. 9, no. 3 (September 1978).

Douglas, Susan P., and C. Samuel Craig. *International Marketing Research.* Englewood Cliffs, N.J.: Prentice-Hall, Inc., 1983.

Frey, F. "Cross-Cultural Survey Research in Political Science." In Holt, Robert W., and John E. Turner (eds.), *The Methodology of Comparative Research.* New York: The Free Press, 1970.

Leung, Kwok, and Michael Harris Bond. "On the Empirical Identification of Dimensions for Cross-Cultural Comparisons." *Journal of Cross-Cultural Psychology.* Vol. 20, no. 2 (June 1989): 133–51.

McCort, Daniel John, and Naresh K. Malhotra. "Culture and Consumer Behavior: Toward an Understanding of Cross-Cultural Consumer Behavior in International Marketing." *Journal of International Consumer Marketing.* Vol. 6, no. 2 (1993).

Mintu, Alma T., Roger J. Calantone, and Jule B. Gassenheimer. "Towards Improving Cross-Cultural Research: Extending Churchill's Research Paradigm." *Journal of International Consumer Marketing.* Vol. 7, no. 2 (1994).

Pike, Kenneth. *Language in Relation to a Unified Theory of the Structure of Human Behavior.* The Hague: Mouton, 1966.

Samiee, Saeed, and Insik Jeong. "Cross-cultural Research in Advertising: An Assessment of Methodologies." *Journal of the Academy of Marketing Science.* Vol. 22, no. 3 (Summer 1994): 205–17.

Triandis, H. C. *The Analysis of Subjective Culture.* New York: John Wiley and Sons, 1972.

Yu, Julie H., Charles F. Keown, and Laurence W. Jacobs. "Attitude Scale Methodology: Cross-Cultural Implications." *Journal of International Consumer Marketing.* Vol. 6, no. 2 (1993).

APPENDIX

Table A.1 Z-Values Representing Areas under the Normal Curve

z	.00	.01	.02	.03	.04	.05	.06	.07	.08	.09
0.0	.0000	.0040	.0080	.0120	.0160	.0199	.0239	.0279	.0319	.0359
0.1	.0398	.0438	.0478	.0517	.0557	.0596	.0636	.0675	.0714	.0753
0.2	.0793	.0832	.0871	.0910	.0948	.0987	.1026	.1064	.1103	.1141
0.3	.1179	.1217	.1255	.1293	.1331	.1368	.1406	.1443	.1480	.1517
0.4	.1554	.1591	.1628	.1664	.1700	.1736	.1772	.1808	.1844	.1879
0.5	.1915	.1950	.1985	.2019	.2054	.2088	.2123	.2157	.2190	.2224
0.6	.2257	.2291	.2324	.2357	.2389	.2422	.2454	.2486	.2517	.2549
0.7	.2580	.2611	.2642	.2673	.2704	.2734	.2764	.2794	.2823	.2852
0.8	.2881	.2910	.2939	.2967	.2995	.3023	.3051	.3078	.3106	.3133
0.9	.3159	.3186	.3212	.3238	.3264	.3289	.3315	.3340	.3365	.3389
1.0	.3413	.3438	.3461	.3485	.3508	.3531	.3554	.3577	.3599	.3621
1.1	.3643	.3665	.3686	.3708	.3729	.3749	.3770	.3790	.3810	.3830
1.2	.3849	.3869	.3888	.3907	.3925	.3944	.3962	.3980	.3997	.4015
1.3	.4032	.4049	.4066	.4082	.4099	.4115	.4131	.4147	.4162	.4177
1.4	.4192	.4207	.4222	.4236	.4251	.4265	.4279	.4292	.4306	.4319
1.5	.4332	.4345	.4357	.4370	.4382	.4394	.4406	.4418	.4429	.4441
1.6	.4452	.4463	.4474	.4484	.4495	.4505	.4515	.4525	.4535	.4545
1.7	.4554	.4564	.4573	.4582	.4591	.4599	.4608	.4616	.4625	.4633
1.8	.4641	.4649	.4656	.4664	.4671	.4678	.4686	.4693	.4699	.4706
1.9	.4713	.4719	.4726	.4732	.4738	.4744	.4750	.4756	.4761	.4767
2.0	.4772	.4778	.4783	.4788	.4793	.4798	.4803	.4808	.4812	.4817
2.1	.4821	.4826	.4830	.4834	.4838	.4842	.4846	.4850	.4854	.4857
2.2	.4861	.4864	.4868	.4871	.4875	.4878	.4881	.4884	.4887	.4890
2.3	.4893	.4896	.4898	.4901	.4904	.4906	.4909	.4911	.4913	.4916
2.4	.4918	.4920	.4922	.4925	.4927	.4929	.4931	.4932	.4934	.4936
2.5	.4938	.4940	.4941	.4943	.4945	.4946	.4948	.4949	.4951	.4952
2.6	.4953	.4955	.4956	.4957	.4959	.4960	.4961	.4962	.4963	.4964
2.7	.4965	.4966	.4967	.4968	.4969	.4970	.4971	.4972	.4973	.4974
2.8	.4974	.4975	.4976	.4977	.4977	.4978	.4979	.4979	.4980	.4981
2.9	.4981	.4982	.4982	.4983	.4984	.4984	.4985	.4985	.4986	.4986
3.0	.4987	.4987	.4987	.4988	.4988	.4989	.4989	.4989	.4990	.4990
3.1	.4990									
3.2	.4993									
3.3	.4995									
3.4	.4997									
3.5	.4998									
3.6	.4998									
3.7	.4999									
3.8	.4999									
3.9	.5000									
4.0	.5000									

To use this table: First, find the Z-value you are interested in by selecting a row representing the units and tenths values and select a column representing the hundreths value. The cell represents the proportional section of the area from the mean to your particular Z-value.

Source: From Fisher and Yates: *Statistical Tables for Biological, Agricultural & Medical Research*, London: The Longman Group UK Ltd. Reprinted by permission of the publisher.

Table A.2   Critical Values of the Chi-Square Statistic

df	x^2 .90	x^2 .95	x^2 .99	x^2 .999
1	2.7	3.8	6.6	10.8
2	4.6	6.0	9.2	13.8
3	6.3	7.8	11.3	16.3
4	7.8	9.5	13.3	18.5
5	9.2	11.1	15.1	20.5
6	10.6	12.6	16.8	22.5
7	12.0	14.1	18.5	24.3
8	13.4	15.5	20.1	26.1
9	14.7	16.9	21.7	27.9
10	16.0	18.3	23.2	29.6
11	17.3	19.7	24.7	31.3
12	18.5	21.0	26.2	32.9
13	19.8	22.4	27.7	34.5
14	21.1	23.7	29.1	36.1
15	22.3	25.0	30.6	37.7
16	23.5	26.3	32.0	39.3
17	24.8	27.6	33.4	40.8
18	26.0	28.9	34.8	42.3
19	27.2	30.1	36.2	43.8
20	28.4	31.4	37.6	45.3
21	29.6	32.7	38.9	46.8
22	30.8	33.9	40.3	48.3
23	32.0	35.2	41.6	49.7
24	33.2	36.4	43.0	51.2
25	34.4	37.7	44.3	52.6
26	35.6	38.9	45.6	54.0
27	36.7	40.1	47.0	55.5
28	37.9	41.3	48.3	56.9
29	39.1	42.6	49.6	58.3
30	40.3	43.8	50.9	59.7

To use this table: First, find the row listing the appropriate degrees of freedom for your estimate. Then critical values of X^2 are listed in each of the four columns. Each column is headed by the level of statistical significance for which the X^2-value represents.

Source: From Fisher and Yates: *Statistical Tables for Biological, Agricultural & Medical Research,* London: The Longman Group UK Ltd. Reprinted by permission of the publisher.

Table A.3   Critical Values of the t Statistic

	Level of significance for nondirectional (two-tailed) tests			
df	.90	.95	.98	.99
1	6.314	12.706	31.821	63.657
2	2.920	4.303	6.965	9.925
2	2.353	3.182	4.541	5.841
4	2.132	2.776	3.747	4.604
5	2.015	2.571	3.365	4.032
6	1.943	2.447	3.143	3.707
7	1.895	2.365	2.998	3.499
8	1.860	2.306	2.896	3.355
9	1.833	2.262	2.821	3.250
10	1.812	2.228	2.764	3.169
11	1.796	2.201	2.718	3.106
12	1.782	2.179	2.681	3.055
13	1.771	2.160	2.650	3.012
14	1.761	2.145	2.624	2.977
15	1.753	2.131	2.602	2.947
16	1.746	2.120	2.583	2.921
17	1.740	2.110	2.567	2.898
18	1.734	2.101	2.552	2.878
19	1.729	2.093	2.539	2.861
20	1.725	2.086	2.528	2.845
21	1.721	2.080	2.518	2.831
22	1.717	2.074	2.508	2.819
23	1.714	2.069	2.500	2.807
24	1.711	2.064	2.492	2.797
25	1.708	2.060	2.485	2.787
26	1.706	2.056	2.479	2.779
27	1.703	2.052	2.473	2.771
28	1.701	2.048	2.467	2.763
29	1.699	2.045	2.462	2.756
30	1.697	2.042	2.457	2.750
40	1.684	2.021	2.423	2.704
60	1.671	2.000	2.390	2.660
120	1.658	1.980	2.358	2.617
∞	1.645	1.960	2.326	2.576

To use this table: First, find the row listing the appropriate degrees of freedom for your estimate. Then critical values of t are listed in each of the four columns. Each column is headed by the level of statistical significance for which the t-value represents.

Source: From Fisher and Yates: *Statistical Tables for Biological, Agricultural & Medical Research,* London: The Longman Group UK Ltd. Reprinted by permission of the publisher.

Sample Questionnaire (some items have been removed to make analytical examples conform to our page format)

Your Satisfaction with our Products and Service

1. How would you rate XYZ in terms of our products and services? Please tell us how satisfied you are with XYZ on each of the areas described below. For each area check one response from "Extremely Satisfied" to "Extremely Dissatisfied" in Column 1A below. If you've had inadequate opportunity to judge XYZ on a particular area, you may check the "Cannot Rate" box.

Then please tell us in Column 1B how you think XYZ compares with other medical equipment manufacturers in each area, by checking "Better," "Same," or "Poorer" for each area.

	Column 1A						Column 1B		
	How do you rate XYZ?						How Does XYZ Compare With Other Manufacturers?		
	Extremely Satisfied	Somewhat Satisfied	Neither Satisfied nor Dissatisfied	Somewhat Dissatisfied	Extremely Dissatisfied	Cannot Rate	Better	Same	Poorer
Purchase Power									
Our Salespeople									
professionalism	☐	☐	☐	☐	☐	☐	☐	☐	☐
follow-up support/responsiveness	☐	☐	☐	☐	☐	☐	☐	☐	☐
Order Process									
accuracy in invoicing	☐	☐	☐	☐	☐	☐	☐	☐	☐
Products									
ease of operation	☐	☐	☐	☐	☐	☐	☐	☐	☐
features (alarms, displays, etc.)	☐	☐	☐	☐	☐	☐	☐	☐	☐
reliability (dependable, works consistently)	☐	☐	☐	☐	☐	☐	☐	☐	☐
durability (withstands abuse)	☐	☐	☐	☐	☐	☐	☐	☐	☐

459

	Column 1A							Column 1B		
	How do you rate XYZ?							How does XYZ compare with other manufacturers?		
	Extremely Satisfied	Somewhat Satisfied	Neither Satisfied nor Dissatisfied	Somewhat Dissatisfied	Extremely Dissatisfied	Cannot Rate		Better	Same	Poorer
Educational Support										
inservice	☐	☐	☐	☐	☐	☐		☐	☐	☐
training materials (wall charts, videos, etc.)	☐	☐	☐	☐	☐	☐		☐	☐	☐
Our Clinical Education Consultants										
clinical/technical competence	☐	☐	☐	☐	☐	☐		☐	☐	☐
professionalism	☐	☐	☐	☐	☐	☐		☐	☐	☐
Biomedical Engineering Support										
quality of biomedical training	☐	☐	☐	☐	☐	☐		☐	☐	☐
availability of spare parts	☐	☐	☐	☐	☐	☐		☐	☐	☐
Technical Support										
competence of technical phone support staff	☐	☐	☐	☐	☐	☐		☐	☐	☐
quality of factory service repairs	☐	☐	☐	☐	☐	☐		☐	☐	☐
Overall										
Your overall satisfaction with XYZ	☐	☐	☐	☐	☐	☐		☐	☐	☐

2. In your opinion, what aspects of XYZ's products or services would you suggest be changed or improved?

3. Would you recommend the purchase of XYZ equipment and supplies in the future?

Definitely Would	Probably Would	Undecided	Probably Not	Definitely Not
☐	☐	☐	☐	☐

Why? _____

_____

_____

4. Now, considering the six overall areas from our scales on page 1, please tell us how important you consider each to be by dividing 100 points between them. The more important an area, the more points you would assign it. You may assign as many or as few points to each as you like.

purchase process   _____

order process   _____

products   _____

educational support   _____

biomedical engineering support   _____

technical support   _____

                  total 100

5a. Please describe how much influence you personally have in your facility's selection of type and manufacture of medical equipment.

very influential   ☐

somewhat influential   ☐

minimal influence   ☐

not at all influential   ☐

5b. How many years of experience do you have in your field?

less than 2 years   ☐

2–5 years   ☐

5–10 years   ☐

more than 10 years   ☐

Table A.4   The Medical Equipment Data

Medical Data   Page 1   05/25/97

ID	c1	c2	c3	c4	c5	c6	c7	c8	c9	c10	c11	c12	c13	c14	c15	c16	c17	c18	c19	c20	c21	c22	c23	c24	c25	c26	c27	c28	Region
2643	1	1	1	1	1	1	1	1	1	1	1	1	1	1	1	1	1	20	20	20	10	10	20	2	4	1	1	1	North
2230	1	2	1	1	1	2	2	2	2	2	1	2	2	2	2	1	1	20	15	40	10	10	5	3	4	1	1	1	Central
2658	2	1	2	1	2	1	1	1	1	1	1	2	2	2	2	1	1	5	5	60	10	10	10	3	4	3	3	1	South
2359	1	1	1	1	1	1	1	1	1	1	1	2	2	2	1	1	1	10	10	5	50	20	5	3	4	1	1	1	West
3010	2	2	1	1	1	1	2	1	2	1	2	2	1	1	1	1	1	10	10	50	10	10	10	3	4	3	3	1	Central
2744	1	1	2	1	1	1	2	1	2	2	2	2	1	2	1	1	1	10	10	20	20	20	20	2	4	1	1	1	North
2482	1	1	1	1	1	1	3	1	1	2	1	2	2	1	1	1	1	25	25	20	10	10	10	3	4	1	1	1	North
2409	1	1	1	1	1	1	1	2	2	2	1	2	2	2	1	1	1	10	10	50	10	10	10	2	4	3	3	1	North
2971	1	2	1	2	2	2	2	1	1	2	2	2	1	1	2	1	1	10	10	30	20	15	15	3	4	1	1	1	North
3281	1	1	1	2	1	1	2	2	1	1	2	1	1	1	1	1	1	15	15	40	10	10	10	2	4	1	1	1	South
2429	1	1	1	1	1	1	1	1	1	1	2	1	1	1	1	1	1	2	2	75	10	5	6	3	4	3	3	1	West
3419	1	1	2	1	1	1	1	1	2	1	1	2	2	2	2	1	1	20	15	7	10	19	19	3	4	3	2	1	North
3452	2	2	2	2	2	1	1	1	1	1	1	2	1	1	2	1	1	20	15	20	15	15	15	2	4	3	1	1	North
3182	1	1	2	1	1	1	1	1	1	1	2	4	1	1	1	1	1	5	5	50	15	10	15	3	4	3	3	1	North
3274	1	1	2	2	2	3	3	2	2	2	2	1	2	1	1	1	1	15	15	30	20	10	10	3	4	1	1	1	North
2802	1	1	1	1	1	1	1	1	1	1	1	2	2	1	2	1	2	20	20	20	20	1	20	3	4	1	1	1	North
2617	2	1	1	1	1	2	2	1	1	1	1	5	5	1	5	1	1	10	10	20	20	20	20	3	4	1	1	1	West
2850	1	1	1	1	1	2	2	1	1	1	1	2	1	1	2	1	1	15	20	20	20	15	10	3	4	1	1	1	West
2585	1	1	2	1	1	1	1	2	2	1	2	1	1	2	1	1	1	10	10	30	10	10	30	3	3	1	1	1	Central
3417	1	1	1	2	2	1	1	1	1	1	2	1	1	1	1	1	1	5	5	70	10	5	5	3	4	3	3	1	Central
2608	1	1	1	1	1	1	1	1	1	1	1	1	1	1	1	1	1	5	5	40	15	15	20	3	4	3	1	1	West
2640	1	2	1	1	1	1	1	1	1	1	1	1	1	1	1	1	1	7	7	50	7	7	20	2	4	3	3	1	West
2839	2	2	1	1	2	1	1	2	2	2	2	2	2	1	1	1	2	5	10	10	15	30	30	3	3	2	2	1	South
2914	1	1	1	1	1	1	1	1	2	2	2	2	1	1	1	1	1	5	5	50	15	10	15	1	4	3	3	1	Central
2808	1	1	1	1	1	1	1	1	2	2	1	2	2	1	1	1	2	10	10	50	10	10	10	1	4	3	3	1	North
3256	1	1	1	1	1	1	1	1	1	1	1	1	1	1	1	1	1	1	1	95	1	1	1	1	4	3	3	1	North
2430	1	1	1	1	1	1	1	2	2	2	2	2	2	2	1	1	1	13	12	50	5	10	10	1	4	3	3	1	North
2880	1	1	2	2	1	1	1	1	1	1	1	2	2	1	1	1	1	1	1	95	1	1	1	1	4	3	3	1	North
2631	2	2	2	1	1	1	1	1	1	1	1	2	2	1	1	1	1	5	5	50	25	5	10	1	4	3	3	1	West
145	1	1	1	1	1	1	1	1	1	1	1	1	1	1	1	1	1	5	5	10	20	20	40	3	4	3	2	1	West
83	1	1	1	1	1	1	1	2	2	2	2	2	2	1	1	1	2	20	20	10	20	10	20	3	3	1	1	1	West
528	3	3	2	1	1	1	2	2	2	2	2	2	3	2	2	1	1	20	1	30	30	10	10	3	4	1	1	1	South
1774	1	1	2	1	1	1	1	1	1	1	1	1	1	2	1	1	1	5	5	50	20	10	10	1	4	3	3	1	West
2158	1	1	1	1	1	1	1	1	2	2	1	2	2	2	2	1	1	10	10	50	10	10	10	1	4	3	3	1	Central
1734	2	2	2	1	1	1	1	3	2	2	2	1	1	2	2	1	1	5	5	70	5	10	5	1	4	3	3	1	South
2099	2	2	2	1	1	1	1	2	2	2	2	3	2	2	2	1	1	5	5	50	10	15	15	1	4	3	3	1	Central
324	2	2	2	1	1	1	1	2	2	1	2	2	2	1	1	1	1	5	5	75	5	5	5	1	4	3	3	1	North
923	2	2	2	1	1	1	1	2	2	1	1	4	1	2	2	1	1	5	5	50	10	10	20	1	4	3	3	1	North
535	2	2	2	1	1	1	1	2	2	2	1	2	1	1	1	1	1	20	10	40	10	10	10	2	3	3	1	1	North
1076	2	2	2	1	3	1	1	1	1	1	1	1	2	1	1	1	1	1	5	40	15	20	20	1	4	3	1	1	North
372	2	2	2	2	2	1	2	2	2	2	2	1	1	2	2	1	1	10	15	5	5	25	40	2	4	3	2	1	North
809	1	2	2	1	1	1	2	2	2	2	2	2	2	2	2	1	1	10	10	30	10	20	20	1	4	3	1	1	West
95	2	2	2	3	3	1	1	2	2	2	2	2	2	2	2	1	1	10	15	20	20	5	30	1	4	3	1	1	South
797	1	1	1	1	1	1	2	2	2	2	2	1	1	1	1	1	2	20	20	10	10	10	30	1	2	3	2	1	Central
759	1	1	1	1	1	1	1	1	1	1	1	1	1	1	1	1	1	10	10	40	10	20	10	3	3	1	1	1	North
2977	1	1	1	2	2	2	2	2	2	2	2	2	1	2	1	2	1	10	10	60	5	5	10	1	4	3	3	1	North
3000	2	2	2	2	2	1	1	1	1	1	1	2	2	2	1	1	1	10	10	50	10	10	10	1	4	3	3	1	North
466	2	2	2	2	2	1	1	2	2	2	2	2	2	2	2	1	1	5	5	75	5	5	5	1	4	3	3	1	North
3093	1	2	1	1	1	1	1	1	1	1	1	3	3	2	3	1	1	5	5	70	5	10	5	1	4	3	3	1	North

Table A.4—*Continued*

Medical Data   Page 2   05/25/97

ID	Symptom codes	Percentages	Codes	X	Region
1332	2 2 2 1 1 1 1 2 2 2 2 1 2 2 1 1	20 15 25 15 5 20	3 4 1 1	1	West
2999	2 2 2 2 2 2 2 2 1 1 2 2 2 2 2 2	10 20 40 10 10 10	3 4 1 1		Central
1307	2 2 2 2 2 2 2 2 1 1 4 3 2 3 2 1	3 15 30 7 25 20	3 4 1 1		Central
2711	2 2 2 2 2 1 1 2 2 2 2 2 2 2 2 2	5 5 50 10 20 10	2 4 1 3		Central
3103	2 3 2 3 3 4 4 1 2 1 1 3 3 3 3 2	3 1 1 90 5 2	1 2 4 2	3	West
3377	2 2 2 1 2 2 2 2 2 2 2 2 2 2 2 3	10 20 40 5 10 15	2 4 2 1		North
3356	2 3 2 1 1 1 1 3 2 2 2 2 3 2 2	10 10 40 15 15 10	1 3 2 1		North
2400	1 2 1 1 1 1 1 2 2 1 2 2 2 2 2 1	5 5 50 10 20 10	1 4 2 3		North
2505	2 2 2 2 2 3 2 2 2 2 2 2 2 2 2 3	10 10 30 10 20 20	1 4 2 1		North
2957	2 2 2 1 2 2 2 2 2 2 2 2 2 2 2 3	10 10 50 10 10 10	2 4 2 3		North
3280	1 1 2 1 4 1 2 1 1 1 1 2 1 3 2 2	17 18 5 20 20 20	1 4 2 2		West
2761	2 3 3 2 2 3 4 3 3 2 2 2 3 3 2 2	15 15 25 15 15 15	3 4 2 1		West
2569	2 3 3 2 3 2 2 2 2 2 2 2 2 2 2	5 5 50 10 20 10	1 4 2 3		Central
2275	2 2 2 1 1 1 1 1 2 2 3 3 2 2 2 1	5 5 5 10 5 70	1 3 2 2		South
1440	2 3 2 2 2 1 2 2 2 2 2 2 2 2 2 2	50 10 10 20 5 5	2 3 2 1		West
1823	1 1 3 2 1 1 1 1 1 1 3 3 3 3 2 1	20 20 20 20 20 20	1 4 2 1		West
977	3 3 2 3 3 3 4 2 2 2 3 3 3 3 2 2	20 20 45 5 5 5	2 3 2 3		Central
1039	3 3 2 2 2 3 3 2 3 2 2 3 2 2 2	2 2 90 2 2 2	2 4 2 3		Central
309	2 2 2 2 2 2 3 3 2 2 3 3 2 2 2 2	15 15 15 15 20 20	3 4 2 1		South
17	2 3 2 2 1 1 4 2 2 2 4 2 1 2 2 2	3 3 3 10 40 40	2 4 1 2		Central
578	2 2 2 1 1 1 1 2 2 2 2 1 1 2 2 1	20 15 15 10 20 20	2 3 1 1		West
742	2 3 1 2 2 1 1 2 2 2 3 3 2 2 2	5 5 70 5 10 5	1 4 1 3		West
459	2 2 2 1 1 2 2 2 2 2 2 2 1 1 2 1	2 3 75 10 5 5	1 2 1 3		West
285	1 2 2 2 2 4 5 3 3 2 2 1 1 1 1 2 2	10 10 30 10 20 20	3 4 1 1		South
893	2 2 2 2 1 2 2 2 2 2 2 2 2 2 2 2	20 20 20 10 10 10	3 4 1 1		South
491	3 2 3 2 2 2 2 3 3 3 2 3 3 2 2 2	25 5 25 10 25 10	1 2 1 1		Central
756	2 2 2 2 2 2 3 2 2 2 2 4 2 2 2 2	5 5 30 10 40 10	2 4 1 1		Central
492	1 3 2 2 3 2 1 2 2 2 3 2 2 1 2 2 2	5 5 50 10 30 5	1 2 1 3		South
007	3 3 3 1 2 1 2 3 3 2 3 4 3 3 3 2 2	5 5 40 10 20 20	2 4 1 1		West
668	1 2 2 2 2 3 4 2 2 2 2 4 2 1 3 2 2	10 5 50 20 5 10	2 4 1 3		West
979	2 2 2 1 2 2 3 2 2 2 2 2 2 2 2 2	5 5 75 5 5 5	1 3 1 3		Central
31	2 2 3 2 1 2 3 2 2 2 2 3 2 2 2 2	5 5 50 20 10 10	1 4 1 3		West
740	2 2 2 1 2 2 2 2 2 2 2 2 2 2 2 3	10 10 20 30 15 15	3 4 1 1		Central
912	2 2 2 2 2 2 2 2 1 1 1 2 2 2 2 1	5 5 20 5 30 35	2 4 1 2		West
3085	2 2 2 1 1 1 1 2 2 2 2 2 2 2 2 1	5 5 50 10 15 15	3 4 1 3		West
165	2 2 2 1 2 1 2 2 2 2 3 2 2 1 2 1	5 10 30 5 30 20	2 2 1 1		South
3081	3 2 2 3 2 2 4 3 4 4 3 2 2 3 2 3 3	5 5 50 5 20 15	2 4 1 3	0	South
1917	2 2 3 2 2 1 1 2 2 2 2 2 2 2 3 3	10 5 10 25 30 20	2 4 1 2	0	West
1644	2 2 3 1 2 2 2 2 2 2 2 2 2 3 2	5 5 10 25 30 25	2 4 1 2	0	West
3174	3 4 3 1 2 2 2 1 1 2 1 2 2 2 3 3	5 10 5 20 30 30	2 4 1 2	0	West
2334	2 3 3 2 2 4 4 2 2 2 2 2 3 2 3 3	10 10 10 20 20 30	2 3 1 2	0	South
3411	3 3 3 4 3 4 4 3 3 2 2 2 2 2 3 2	5 5 50 10 10 20	2 4 3 3	0	West
2858	3 3 3 2 2 3 2 5 3 3 2 2 3 2 3 3	16 16 16 16 16 16	2 4 3 1	0	West
3143	2 2 2 2 4 4 2 2 2 2 2 2 3 3	5 5 25 25 15 25	1 4 3 1	0	North
1226	3 4 4 1 2 2 3 3 3 3 2 2 2 3 2	10 10 50 10 10 10	1 3 3 3	0	Central
2307	2 3 2 2 4 2 2 4 4 2 3 2 3 3 3 3 2	5 5 65 10 5 10	2 4 1 3	0	South
1198	3 4 3 1 4 4 3 2 2 2 2 2 3 2 3 3	10 10 25 10 25 20	1 4 1 1	0	North
728	3 4 3 1 3 4 4 4 4 4 3 3 3 3 3 3	10 5 30 20 15 20	1 4 3 1	0	North
3021	4 4 4 2 2 2 4 2 2 2 3 5 2 4 3	10 10 50 10 10 10	1 4 3 3	0	North
2907	2 4 4 1 1 1 2 2 2 2 2 2 2 4 3	5 5 15 50 20 5	1 4 3 1	0	North
1416	2 2 1 2 2 2 2 2 1 2 2 2 2 2 4 3	10 10 50 20 5 15	2 4 2 3	0	North

A Bibliography
of Customer Satisfaction

BOOKS

Barsky, Jonathan D. *World-Class Customer Satisfaction.* Burr Ridge, IL: Irwin Professional Publishing, 1995.

Bates, Janet. *Steps to Improving Service Quality and Customer Satisfaction.* Washington, DC: American Bankers Association, 1990.

Bergman, Bo, and Bengt Klefsjo. *Quality: From Customer Needs to Customer Satisfaction.* New York: McGraw-Hill, 1994.

Bhote, Keki R. *Beyond Customer Satisfaction to Customer Loyalty: The Key to Greater Profitability.* AMA Management Briefing, 1996.

Bly, Robert W. *Keeping Clients Satisfied: Make Your Service Business More Successful and Profitable.* Englewood Cliffs, N.J.: Prentice-Hall, 1993.

Bruno, Albert V., and Alan S. Cleland. *The Market Value Process: Bridging Customer and Shareholder Value.* Jossey-Bass Business & Management Series, 1996.

Camp, R. C. *Benchmarking: The Search for Industry Best Practices That Lead to Superior Performance.* Milwaukee: ASQC Quality Press, 1989.

Carlzon, Jan. *Moments of Truth.* Cambridge, MA: Ballinger Publishing Co., 1987.

Crosby, Philip B. *Quality is Free.* Bergenfield, NJ: New American Library, 1979.

Davidow, William, and Bro Uttal. *Total Customer Service.* New York: Harper & Row, 1989.

Dutka, Alan. *AMA Handbook for Customer Satisfaction.* Lincolnwood, IL: NTC Business Books and the American Marketing Association, 1994.

Eastman Kodak Company. *Keeping the Customer Satisfied: A Guide to Field Service.* Milwaukee: ASQC Quality Press, 1989.

Eureka, W. E., and N. E. Ryan. *The Customer-Driven Company.* Dearborn, MI: ASI Press, 1988.

Green, George, and Roger Cartwright. *In Charge of Customer Satisfaction: A Competence Approach.* In press.

Grenier, R. *Customer Satisfaction Through Total Quality Assurance.* New York: Hitchcock, 1988.

Hanan, Mack and Peter Karp. *Customer Satisfaction: How to Maximize, Measure and Market Your Company's "Ultimate Product."* New York: AMACOM, 1988.

Hayes, Bob E. *Measuring Customer Satisfaction: Development and Use of Questionnaires.* Milwaukee: ASQC Quality Press, 1991.

Hill, Arthur V. *Field Service Management: An Integrated Approach to Increasing Customer Satisfaction.* Homewood, IL: Business One Irwin/Apics Library of Integrative Resource Management, 1992.

Hinton, Tom, and Wini Schaeffer. *Customer-Focused Quality.* Englewood Cliffs, N.J.: Prentice-Hall, 1994.

Horovitz, Jacques and Michele Jurens Panak. *Total Customer Satisfaction.* Burr Ridge, IL: Irwin Professional Publishing, 1994.

Karten, Naomi. *Managing Expectations: Working with People Who Want More, Better, Faster, Sooner, Now.* New York: Dorset House Publishing Co., 1994.

Kessler, Sheila. *Measuring and Managing Customer Satisfaction: Going for the Gold.* Milwaukee: ASQC Quality Press, 1996.

Leebov, Wendy, and Gail Scott. *Service Quality Improvement: The Customer Satisfaction Strategy for Health Care,*

Naumann, Earl, and Kathleen Giel. *Customer Satisfaction Measurement and Management: Using the Voice of the Customer.* New York: Van Nostrand Reinhold Publishing, 1995.

Nykiel, Ronald A. *Keeping The Customer in Good Times & Bad.* Stanford, CT: Longmeadow Press Publishing, 1992.

Oliver, Richard L. *Satisfaction: A Behavioral Perspective on the Consumer.* New York: The McGraw-Hill Companies, Inc., 1997.

Pardee, William J. *To Satisfy & Delight Your Customer: How to Manage for Customer Value,* New York: Dorset House Publishing Co., 1996.

Quinn, Feargal. *Crowning the Customer: How to Become Customer-Driven,* Dublin, Ireland: The O'Brien Press, 1990.

Rust, Roland T., and Richard L. Oliver. *Service Quality: New Directions in Theory and Practice,* Thousand Oaks, CA: Sage Publications, 1993.

Sasser, W. Earl. *The Service Profit Chain: Linking Profit and Growth to Loyalty, Satisfaction and Value. In press.*

Second Congress on Customer Satisfaction. Customer Satisfaction: Focus on the Customer. May 17–20, Disney Grand Floridian Resort, Lake Buena Vista, FL, 1992.

Shapiro, Benson P., and John J. Sviokla. *Keeping Customers,* Cambridge, MA: The Harvard Business Review Book, 1993.

Society for Consumer Affairs Professionals in Business, *Customer Satisfaction Survey Collection.* Edited by M. Lauren Bashem. Arlington, VA: SOCAP, 1996.

Teal, Thomas and Frederick F. Reichheld. *The Loyalty Effect: The Hidden Force Behind Growth, Profits, and Lasting Value,* Cambridge, MA: Harvard Business Press, 1996.

Unruch, James A. *Customers Mean Business.* Reading, MA: Addison-Wesley Publishing Company, 1996.

Vandermerwe, Sandra. *The Eleventh Commandment: Transforming to 'Own' Customers.* New York: John Wiley & Sons, 1996.

Wilson, Paul F., Larry D. Dell, and Gaylord F. Anderson. *Root Cause Analysis.* Milwaukee: ASQC Quality Press, 1993.

Woodruff, Robert B. and Sarah F. Gardial. *Know Your Customer: New Approaches to Understanding Customer Value and Satisfaction.* Cambridge, MA: Blackwell Publishers Inc., 1996.

Zeithaml, V. A., A. Parasuraman, and L. L. Berry. *Delivering Quality Service: Balancing Customer Perceptions and Expectations.* New York: The Free Press, 1990.

Books from Related Fields

Churchill, Gilbert A. *Marketing Research: Methodological Foundations.* Fifth Edition, Chicago: The Dryden Press, 1991.

Fowler, Floyd J., Jr. *Improving Survey Questions.* Thousand Oaks, CA: Sage Publications, 1995.

————. *Survey Research Methods.* Thousand Oaks, CA: Sage
  Publications, 1993.

Krueger, Richard A. *Focus Groups: A Guide for Applied Research.* Beverly
  Hills, CA: Sage Publications, 1988.

Lavrakas, Paul J. *Telephone Survey Methods: Sampling, Selection, and
  Supervision.* Thousand Oaks, CA: Sage Publications, 1987.

Lehman, Donald R. *Market Research and Analysis.* Burr Ridge, IL:
  Irwin, 1989.

Payne, Stanley L. *The Art of Asking Questions.* Princeton, N.J.: Princeton
  University Press, 1951.

Schuman, Howard and Stanley Presser. *Questions and Answers in Attitude
  Surveys.* Thousand Oaks, CA: Sage Publications, 1996.

Settle, Robert B. and Pamela L. Alrick. *Survey Research Handbook.* 2d ed.
  Burr Ridge, IL: Irwin, 1995.

Sharma, Subhash. *Applied Multivariate Techniques.* New York: John
  Wiley & Sons, 1996.

Yin, Robert K. *Case Study Research.* 2d ed. Thousand Oaks, CA: Sage
  Publications, 1994.

NEWSLETTERS

The Customer Communicator. Customer Service Institute, 1010 Wayne
  Avenue, Silver Spring, MD 20910. (301) 585–0730.

Customer Profit Report. Customer Service Institute, 1010 Wayne Avenue,
  Silver Spring, MD 20910. (301) 585–0730.

Customer Service Bulletin. Arthur D. Little, Acorn Park, Cambridge, MA
  02140. (617) 864–5770.

Customer Service Management Bulletin. Bureau of Business Practice,
  Rope Ferry Road, Waterford, CT 06386. (203) 442–4365.

Customer Service Newsletter. Customer Service Institute, 1010 Wayne
  Avenue, Silver Spring, MD 20910. (301) 585–0730.

Executive Report on Customer Satisfaction. The Customer Service Group,
  215 Park Avenue South, Suite 1301, New York, NY 10003.
  (212) 228-0246.

Positive Impact. Resort Impressions, Ltd., P.O. Box 4018, Evergreen,
  CO. (303) 670–1001.

The Service Edge. Lakewood Publications, 50 South Ninth Street,
  Minneapolis, MN 55402. (800) 328–4329.

PERTINENT ARTICLES

Anderson, E. "Cross-Category Variation in Customer Satisfaction and Retention." *Marketing Letters* 5 (1994):1.

———. "The Antecedents and Consequences of Customer Satisfaction for Firms." *Marketing Science* (Spring 1993).

———. "Customer Satisfaction, Market Share, and Profitability: Findings from Sweden." *Journal of Marketing* (July 1994): 53–66.

Anderson, Rolph E. "Consumer Satisfaction: The Effect of Disconfirmed Expectancy on Perceived Product Performance." *Journal of Marketing Research* 10 (1973):38–44.

Andreason, Alan R. "A Taxonomy of Consumer Satisfaction/Dissatisfaction Measures," in *Conceptualization and Measurement of Consumer Satisfaction and Dissatisfaction.* H. Keith Hunt, ed. Cambridge, Massachusetts: Marketing Science Institute, 1977.

Anonymous. "Logistics' Mandate: Customer Satisfaction." *Transportation & Distribution.* 34, no. 12 (December 1993): 28–33.

Band, William A. "The Art of Listening to Customers." *Sales & Marketing Management in Canada.* 36 (October 1987):15–16.

———. "Defining Customer Satisfaction." *Sales & Marketing Management in Canada.* (January 1990):14–15.

———. "How to Gain Competitive Advantage Through Customer Satisfaction." *Sales & Marketing Management in Canada.* 29, no. 4 (May 1988):30–32.

———. "How to Conduct a Customer Satisfaction Audit." *Sales & Marketing Management in Canada* (Canada) (October 1988):24–25.

Bartram, Peter. "Satisfied or Satiated? How The Appetite For Customer Satisfaction Research Can Be Sustained." *Marketing and Research Today.* (September 1993).

Bearden, William D., and Jesse E. Teel. "Selected Determinants of Consumer Satisfaction and Complaint Reports." *Journal for Marketing Research.* (February 1983):21–28.

Bearden, William D., and Richard L. Oliver. "The Role of Public and Private Complaining in Satisfaction with Problem Resolution." *The Journal of Consumer Affairs.* 19, no. 2 (1985):222–38.

Bechtell, Michele L. "Listen to the Voice of the Customer." *Best's Review* (Life/Health). (December 1989):40–44.

Bennet, Rex. "Gaining a Competitive Advantage Through Customer Satisfaction." *Bank Marketing.* 24, no. 12 (December 1992):24–26.

———. "Marketing and Competitive Advantage: How to Satisfy the Customer, Profitability." *Bank Marketing.* 24, no. 1 (January 1992):36–37.

Bleuel, Bill. "Customer Dissatisfaction and the Zone of Uncertainty." *Journal of Services Marketing.* (Winter 1990):49–52.

Bolfing, Claire P. "How Do Customers Express Dissatisfaction and What Can Service Marketers Do About It?" *Journal of Services Marketing.* (Spring 1989):5–23.

Caba, Susan. "Angry Customers Who Go Quietly May Not Return." *Shopping Centers Today.* (October 1988):81–86.

Cadotte, Ernest R., and Larry M. Robinson. "Measurement of Consumer Satisfaction: An Innovation." *Journal of Marketing.* (July 1978):8–58.

———. Robert B. Woodruff, and Roger L. Jenkins. "Expectations and Norms in Models of Consumer Satisfaction." *Journal of Marketing Research.* 24 (August 1987):305–14.

"The Challenges of Measuring Consumer Satisfaction (Marketing Review Panel Addresses the Topic)." *Marketing Review.* (November 1990):17–28.

Chandler, C. H. "Beyond Customer Satisfaction". *Quality Progress.* 22, no. 2 (1989):30–32.

Churchill, Gilbert A., Jr., and Carol Surprenant. "An Investigation Into the Determinants of Customer Satisfaction." *Journal of Marketing Research.* 19 (November 1982):491–504.

Cina, Craig. "Creating an Effective Customer Satisfaction Program." *Journal of Consumer Marketing.* (Fall 1989):31–40.

Clow, Kenneth. "Building a Competitive Advantage for Service Firms: Measurement of Consumer Expectations of Service Quality." *Journal of Services Marketing.* 7, no. 1 (1993).

Cooke, Ernest F. "Post-Shipment Services: Turning Customer Complaints Into Assets." *Journal of Business and Industrial Marketing.* (Summer 1987):17–22.

Cosenza, Robert M., and Jerry W. Wilson. "Managing Consumer Dissatisfaction: The Effective Use of the Corporate Written Response to Complaints." *Public Relations Quarterly.* (Spring 1982):17–19.

Cox, Edwin, and John Lasley. "Customer Attitudes, Behavior, and Satisfaction: Implications for Financial Institutions." *Journal of Retail Banking.* 6, no. 4 (1984):1–7.

Crosby, Lawrence. "Toward a Common Verbal Scale of Perceived Quality," in Marketing in the New Europe (45th ESOMAR Congress, Joint Session on the Race Against Expectations), Madrid, Spain: The European Society of Marketing Research, 1992.

Day, Ralph L., and E. Laird Landon, Jr. Toward a Process Model of Consumer Satisfaction," in *Conceptualization and Measurement of Consumer Satisfaction and Dissatisfaction.* Edited by H. Keith Hunt. Cambridge, MA: Marketing Science Institute, 1977.

———, and E. Laird Landon, Jr. "Collecting Comprehensive Consumer Complaint Data by Survey Research" in *Advances in Consumer Research.* Cincinnati: Association for Consumer Research. III (1975):263–68.

Doherty, Edward. "How to Steal a Satisfied Customer." *Sales & Marketing Management.* (March 1990):40–45.

Edwards, A. L., and K. C. Kenney. "A Comparison Of The Thurstone And Likert Techniques Of Attitude Scale Construction." *Journal Of Applied Psychology.* 30 (1946):72–83.

Elbeck, Matt. "An Approach to Client Satisfaction Measurement as an Attribute of Health Service Quality." *Healthcare Management Review.* 12, no. 3 (1987): 47–52.

Ettlie, John. "Product Development Benchmarking Versus Customer Focus in Applications of quality Function Deployment." *Marketing Letters.* 5, no. 2 (1994).

Flanagan, J. C. "The Critical Incident Technique." *Psychological Bulletin.* 51:327–58.

Finkelman, Dan. "McKinsey's Secrets of Satisfying Customers." *Boardroom Reports.* (July 1, 1990):1–6.

———, and Tony Goland. "The Case of the Complaining Customer." *Harvard Business Review.* 68 (May/June 1990):16.

Fonvielle, William H. "Customers Are Key to Measuring Service Quality." *The Quality Executive.* (September 1989):8.

Fornell, C. "A National Customer Satisfaction Barometer: The Swedish Experience." *Journal of Marketing.* 56 (January 1992).

Fornell, Claes, and Robert A. Westbrook. "The Vicious Circle of Consumer Complaints." *Journal of Marketing.* 48 (Summer 1984):68–78.

Fried, Lisa I. "Trying to Keep Customers Satisfied." *Management Review.* (May 1989):46–52.

Gale, Bradley T. "Customer Satisfaction—Relative to Competitors—Is Where It's At." *Marketing & Research Today.* 22, no 1 (February 1994):39–53.

Goodman, J. 1989. "The Nature Of Customer Satisfaction". *Quality Progress* 22(2):37–40.

Hanna, Nessim, and John S. Wagle. "Who Is Your Satisfied Customer?" *Journal of Consumer Marketing.* (Winter 1989):53–61.

Hausknecht, Douglas, "Measurement Scales in Consumer Satisfaction/Dissatisfaction," *Journal of Consumer Satisfaction/ Dissatisfaction and Complaining Behavior,* Vol. 3, 1990.

Levine, Joshua. " 'How'm I Doin'?' " *Forbes.* (December 24, 1990):106–09.

Jacoby, Jacob, and James J. Jaccard. "The Sources, Meaning, and Validity of Consumer Complaints: A Psychological Analysis." *Journal of Retailing.* 57, no. 3, (1981):4–24.

Johnson, M. "A Framework For Comparing Customer Satisfaction Across Individuals And Product Categories." *Journal of Economic Psychology.* 12 (1991).

Kearns, Robert. "Is Everybody Happy?" *Business Marketing.* (December 1989):30–31, 34–36.

Kohnke, Luane. "Designing A Customer Satisfaction Measurement Program." *Bank Marketing.* (July 1990):28–30.

LaBarbera, Priscilla A., and David Mazursky. "A Longitudinal Assessment of Consumer Satisfaction/Dissatisfaction: The Dynamic Aspect of the Cognitive Process." *Journal of Marketing Research.* 20 (November 1983):393–404.

LaTour, Stephen A. and Nancy C. Peat. "Conceptual and Methodological Issues in Customer Satisfaction Research" in *Advances in Consumer Research.* Edited by William F. Wilke. Ann Arbor, MI: Association for Consumer Research. 6 (1979):34–37.

Lele, Milind M., and Jagdish N. Sheth. "The Four Fundamentals of Customer Satisfaction." *Business Marketing.* (June 1988):80–94.

Leslie, Floyd R. "Where Customer Satisfaction Begins." *Quality.* 30, no. 10 (October 1991):46–47.

Likert, R. A. "Technique For The Measurement Of Attitudes." *Archives Of Psychology.* 140 (1932).

Lissitz, R. W. and Green, S. B. "Effect Of The Number Of Scale Points On Reliability: A Monte Carlo Approach." *Journal Of Applied Psychology.* 60, (1975):10–13.

McGahan, A. M. "Competition To Retain Customers." *Marketing Science.* 13, no. 2 (Spring 1994).

Oliver, Richard L. "Cognitive Model of the Antecedents and Consequences of Satisfaction Decisions." *Journal of Marketing Research.* 17 (November 1980):460–69.

———. "Measurement and Evaluation of Satisfaction Processes in Retail Settings." *Journal of Retailing.* 57 (Fall 1981):25–48.

———, and William D. Bearden. "Disconfirmation Processes and Consumer Evaluations in Product Usage." *Journal of Business Research.* 13 (1985): 235–46.

———, and Wayne S. DeSarbo. "Response Determinants in Satisfaction Judgments." *Journal of Consumer Research.* 14 (March 1988):495–507.

Olson, Jerry C. and Philip Dover. "Disconfirmation of Consumer Expectation Through Product Trial." *Journal of Applied Psychology.* 64 (April 1979):179–89.

Peck, Bobbi. "Tools For Teams Addressing Total Customer Satisfaction." *Industrial Engineering.* 27, no. 1 (January 1995):30–34.

Pfaff, Anita B. "An Index of Consumer Satisfaction: Measurement of Consumer Satisfaction and Dissatisfaction." H. Keith Hunt. in *Conceptualization and Measurement of Consumer Satisfaction and Dissatisfaction.* Cambridge, MA: Marketing Science Institute, (1974):36–71.

Reichheld, Frederick, and W. Earl Sasser. "Zero Defections: Quality Comes To Services." *Harvard Business Review.* 68 (Sept–Oct. 1990): 105–111.

Resnik, Alan. "Consumer Complaints And Managerial Response: A Holistic Approach." *Journal Of Marketing Research.* 19 (November 1982).

Rust, Roland T., and Anthony J. Zahorik. "Customer Satisfaction, Customer Retention, and Market Share." *Journal of Retailing.* 59, no. 2 (Summer 1993):193–215.

Sarazen, Stephen J. "Customer Satisfaction is Not Enough." *Quality Progress.* (December 1987):31.

Schlossberg, Howard. "Satisfying Customers Is a Minimum; You Really have to 'Delight' Them." *Marketing News.* (May 28, 1990):10–11.

Schroeder, Gary A. "Using an Attitude Survey to Increase Sales Effectiveness." *Personnel.* (February 1989):51–55.

Schul, Y. "Measuring Satisfaction with Organizations." *Public Opinion Quarterly.* 57 (1993).

Shields, John J. "Corporate Commitment to Customer Satisfaction." *Executive Excellence.* (November 1988):14–15.

Singh, Jagdip. "A Typology of Consumer Dissatisfaction Response Styles." *Journal of Retailing.* (Spring 1990):57–99.

Smith, Ivan Campbell. "Auditing Customer Satisfaction." *Management Review.* (May 1989):52–54.

Stershic, Sybil F. "The Flip Side of Customer Satisfaction Research (You Know How Your Customers Feel, But Have You Talked to Your Employees Lately?)." *Marketing Research.* (December 1990): 45–50.

Swan, John E., and I. Frederick Trawick. "Disconfirmation of Expectations and Satisfaction with a Retail Service." *Journal of Retailing.* 57 (1981):49–67.

Thurstone, L. L. "Theory Of Attitude Measurement." *Psychological Bulletin.* 36 (1929):224–41.

Tornow, Walter W. "Service Quality And Management Practices: A Look At Employee Attitudes, Customer Satisfaction, And Bottom-Line Consequences." *Human Resource Planning.* 14, no. 2 (1991):105–15.

Tse, David K., and Peter C. Wilton. "Models of Consumer Satisfaction Formation: An Extension." *Journal of Marketing Research.* (May 1988):204–12.

Van Gorder, Barbara E. "Satisfying the Customer of the '90s." *Credit.* (March/April 1990):10–15.

Watner, John A. and Benjamin Schneider. "Legal Regulation and the Constraint of Constituent Satisfaction." *Journal of Management Studies.* 24, no. 2 (1987): 189–200.

Westbrook, Robert A. "A Rating Scale for Measuring Products/Service Satisfaction." *Journal of Marketing.* (Fall 1980):68–72.

―――. "Sources of Consumer Satisfaction with Retail Outlets." *Journal of Retailing.* 57 (1981):52–55.

————, Joseph W. Newman, and James R. Taylor. "Satisfaction/Dissatisfaction in the Purchase Decision Process." *Journal of Marketing.* (October 1978):54–60.

Wiley, Jack W. "Customer Satisfaction: A Supportive Work Environment and Its Financial Cost." *Human Resource Planning.* 14, no. 2 (1991):117–27.

Woodruff, Robert H., Ernest R. Cadotte, and Roger L. Jenkins. "Modeling Consumer Satisfaction Processes Using Experience-Based Norms." *Journal of Marketing Research.* 20 (August 1983):296–305.

NEWSPAPERS

Band, William, "Customer Satisfaction Research Can Improve Decision Making," *Marketing News,* February 5, 1990, pp. 13–17.

Band, William A. "Performance Metrics Keep Customer Satisfaction Programs on Track" *Marketing News,* May 28, 1990, p. 12.

————. "Customer-Satisfaction Studies Changing Marketing Strategies," *Marketing News,* September 12, 1988, p. 14.

————. "The Three I's of Customer Satisfaction Need Your Vision," *Marketing News,* October 23, 1989, p. 17.

Dixon, George, "Keep 'Em Satisfied: Competitive Heat Is On to Learn What the Customer Really Wants," *Marketing News,* January 2, 1989, pp. 1–14.

Gulledge, Larry, "Measure Satisfaction, Performance to Meet Customers' Expectations," *Marketing News,* March 14, 1988, pp. 34–35.

Gulledge, Larry, "Simplify Complexity of Satisfying Customers," *Marketing News,* January 8, 1990, pp. 6–7.

Harley, Dale R., "Customer Satisfaction Tracking Improves Sales, Productivity, Morale of Retail Chains." *Marketing News,* June 22, 1984, p. 15.

Klopp, Charlotte and John Sterlicchi, "Customer Satisfaction Just Catching On in Europe," *Marketing News,* May 28, 1990, p. 5.

Moore, James S., "Proper Training Ensures that Employees Learn Dynamics of Customer Satisfaction," *Marketing News,* December 19, 1988, pp. 13–14.

Pollack, Andrew, "A Novel Idea: Customer Satisfaction," *New York Times,* May 27, 1990, sec. 3, pp. 1–6.

"Satisfying Customers Is Easier Said Than Done—But Do It," *Marketing News,* May 8, 1989, p. 22.

"Survey Shows Consumer Dissatisfaction with Service," *Services Marketing Newsletter,* Summer 1989, p. 5.

Uller, Frank, "Follow-Up Surveys Assess Customer Satisfaction," *Marketing News,* January 2, 1989, p. 14.

Willis, Lindsay, "Apply Trial and Repeat Measures to Customer Satisfaction Research," *Marketing News,* May 28, 1990, p. 16.

Wulfsberg, Rolf and David Pulaski, "It Takes More Than A Simple Survey To Measure Customer Satisfaction," *Marketing News,* 24, no. 11, May 28, 1990, pp. 14, 19.

"Well-Trained Employees Are Key to Customer Satisfaction Research," *Marketing News,* January 2, 1989, p. 14.

CONFERENCES AND SEMINARS

Congress on Customer Satisfaction and Beyond, American Marketing Association, 250 South Wacker Drive, Chicago, IL 60606–5819, (312) 648–0536.

Creating a Customer-Centered Culture, ASQC Professional and Technical Development, 310 West Wisconsin Avenue, Milwaukee, WI 53203–2213, (414) 272–8575.

Customer Satisfaction & Quality Measurement Conference, American Marketing Association and American Society for Quality Control. AMA: 250 South Wacker Drive, Chicago, IL 60606–5819, (312) 648–0536; ASQC: 310 West Wisconsin Avenue, Milwaukee, WI 53203–2213, (414) 272–8575.

Designing and Implementing Performance Measurements for Customer Satisfaction, International Quality & Productivity Center, 150 Clove Road, Little Falls, NJ 07424–0401, (800) 303–9160.

Designing and Implementing Customer Satisfaction Surveys, The Institute for International Research, 708 Third Avenue, 4th Floor, New York, NY 10017–4103, (212) 661–3500.

Measuring & Improving Customer Satisfaction, Institute for International Research, 708 Third Avenue, 2nd Floor, New York, NY 10017–4103, (212) 661–8740.

INDEX